More praise for

Hell Hath No Fury

"A great new genre has been born: the kiss-off letter. The fury of these missives could power rockets to far-off galaxies!"
—ERICA JONG
Author of *Fear of Flying*

"It may sound mad, but this book is a turn-on. I want to fall in love with all the writers in here—they are funny, brilliant, tenderhearted, enraged, loony, and sexy. I guess it's that old theory proved true: Love burns brightest just as it's dying, and lovers are never more desirable than when they say goodbye. This collection, like the song of a chorus of Furies, is a sustained, heartbreaking, and searing read."
—JONATHAN AMES
Author of *My Less Than Secret Life*

"This compendium, sometimes hilarious, sometimes heartrending, includes letters from the famous, the infamous, and the nonfamous, circa 10 B.C. up to 2002."
—*The Star-Ledger* (Newark, NJ)

"Literary romantics will have fun thumbing through this unique assemblage of send-off notes."
—*Publishers Weekly*

"This collection is both involving and amusing, perfect either for a long read, or for 'dipping in' as the reader chooses."
—*Booklist*

Hell Hath
No Fury

WOMEN'S LETTERS FROM THE END OF THE AFFAIR

Hell Hath No Fury

Women's Letters from the End of the Affair

Edited by Anna Holmes

Foreword by Francine Prose

BALLANTINE BOOKS · NEW YORK

For all the men I've loved before . . .
No, scratch that. For my sister.

Foreword

by Francine Prose

How strangely long it's taken us to realize what was so obvious all along—namely, that the break-up letter constitutes a separate genre. Certainly, it's a subspecies of the epistolary form, with its own rules, its own language, its own poetry, its own rhetoric. And as *Hell Hath No Fury* so convincingly demonstrates, the genre has its own distinguished and venerable tradition.

Unlike, say, the chatty Christmas letter, the kiss-off cuts directly to the chase without newsy circumlocution. Unlike the gossipy note, these letters, though they may touch on the lives of subsidiary characters, on the perfidies of "other women" and "other men," have essentially two major players in the drama they are describing—and completing. They're driven by what Chekov called "the engine of he and she." Unlike the casual letters that friends, family members, and colleagues exchange, the good-bye letter conveys a profound sense of urgency, a determination to be clear, a desire to get things right, a definite need for compression; for those reasons, this anthology shares something with collections of "famous last words." And in fact these are last words, the last gasps, the final utterances of dying romance. Indeed, in their intensity, their passion, their absorption, their reckless disregard for convention and euphemism, they most closely resemble the love letter. And in fact they are love letters. Of a particular sort.

Anyone—male or female—who has ever suffered a broken heart will be delighted and comforted to find him- or herself in such brilliant, extraordinary, or merely famous company. Here is the future Lady Emma Hamilton expressing her justified outrage on finding that her lover has, in essence, become her pimp. Here is Madame de Stael forgoing her usual delicacy of expression as she begs for the friendship of a man who has rejected her, while elsewhere Rebecca West retains her wit and charm and intelligence even as she is (half) ironically threatening suicide and telling H. G. Wells that "You want a world of people falling all over each other like puppies, people to quarrel and play with, people who rage and ache instead of people who burn." Here is Princess Margaret breaking off, for reasons of duty and obligation, a relationship with a man she truly loves: "Not many people are lucky enough to have known any love like this. I feel so happy that it has happened to me . . . I will try and come back to you one day."

The age of the writers ranges from the sixteen-year-old Anne Sexton to the forty-six-year-old Edith Wharton addressing the man who first introduced her, late in life, to physical passion to a sixty-three-year-old North Carolina woman trying to get at the "absolute truth" of what happened and what went wrong with a man she met through the Internet. The letter-writers' backgrounds vary even more widely; these authors come from the French nobility and from the ranks of ordinary women who are no less articulate in telling their lovers why they will miss them. "No one makes mac and cheese quite like I do or makes chocolate milk better," writes one young woman, in an inadvertent echo of what George Sand told her faithless lover: "No other soul than mine will understand you, nor have for your greatness this immense love that stretches even to your misery, even to your defects, seeing them, kissing them in tears, holding them to its blood-stained breast, wishing to absorb them so they might hide from the light of day."

They catalogue their ex-lovers' character flaws, they list the wrongs they have suffered, and they gleefully tell the truth about all the things about which—until now—they have politely kept quiet ("Your guitar playing never turned me on"). As parting shots, these letters offer fashion advice ("Wide-legged jeans should never, I repeat, NEVER, be worn with those sandals") and darts of pure invective, graceful turns of phrase ("Lest you mismap my motives, recall that you have never known me"), and incisive analyses of the lover's psyche. "I have studied you," writes Lady Mary Wortley Montagu* "and studied you so well that Sir Isaac Newton did not dissect the rays of the sun with more exactness than I have deciphered the sentiments of your soul." And Lady Christina Falkland tells Lord Byron that "You delight in being wretched yourself, and . . . you like to have partakers in your self-inflicted misery."

They ask their lovers why they don't write, they defend themselves, they dissect the dead or moribund relationships, they feint and thrust and try to absorb and recover from the wounds they have received. And, like Zelda Fitzgerald, they give voice to their pain and grief with an astonishing purity and directness: "Now that there isn't any more happiness and home is gone and there isn't even any past and no emotions but those that were yours when there could be any comfort—it is a shame that we should have me in harshness and coldness where there was once so much tenderness and so many dreams."

On every page they remind us that women—when they pick up a pen or tap away at the keyboard—are capable not only of hellish fury but of near-divine humor, intelligence, vision, eloquence, and great beauty.

Contents

The Autopsy

The "Just Friends?"

The Other Woman/Other Man
(Real and Virtual)

The Divorce Letter

The "Dear John"

The Marriage Refusal

The Classic

The Prescriptive Letter

The Fictional Letter

The Unsent Letter

The Goodbye Letter

Introduction

Heaven has no rage like love to hatred turned,
Nor hell a fury like a woman scorned.
                                    —William Congreve, *The Mourning Bride*

This book was born out of anger, humiliation, disbelief, and disgust.

It was the fall of 2000 and I been dating a younger guy—let's call him Arthur—for a number of months. Arthur was a tall, smart, aspiring fiction writer in his mid-twenties. He was cute (think Edward Norton), liked baseball as much as I did, and seemed to get along with my friends. We E-mailed each other from work all day long—he at his hospital job, me at my gig at a women's magazine—and talked on the phone into the wee hours of the night. He came over a lot, or met me when I was already out, and he liked to put his arm around me, and kiss, and tell me he was crazy about me. He didn't have much money, and was involved in a curious living situation with a strange, middle-aged man, but what did I care? The man had potential, I had my own place, and he was obviously not gay. *Ka-ching!*

Well, not quite.

Two months into the relationship, in the span of one week Arthur twice—not once, but *twice*—stood me up. The first time I was upset and told him so, but he explained himself and apologized, and I forgave him (the cute little-boy voice didn't hurt either). He said he wanted to "make it up" to me, and so he made plans to come over a few nights later; I would make dinner, he'd bring dessert. Those few nights later, I made dinner. He never showed. And neither did dessert.

Perhaps it was the influence of working among a group of smart women who knew how to speak their minds. Maybe it was the fact that I was getting older and had found that stuffing my feelings when it came to men (or otherwise) just wasn't working for me, that I had let men come and go in my life without telling them how they affected me, whether negatively or positively. Or maybe it was just the effect of intense disgust, rage, and humiliation working its charms. (When I'd called him the next day demanding an explanation, he had mumbled something about "being asleep" and "calling me later.")

Whatever the reason, I sat down to write Arthur a breakup letter.

The first draft was quite nasty, with cruel comments about the possibility that Arthur's mother had not loved him enough and allusions to his past difficulty with substance abuse. I also believe I told him he would never get published and that I was certain the reason he'd been mugged the week before was retribution for his bad behavior. After some minor soul-searching, I cut out the comments about his mom, the drugs, his chances of getting published, and the karmic justice of his mugging and decided to stick to the facts at hand, which were (1) numerous and (2) irrefutable.

It wasn't exactly my first time writing such a letter, but the ones that came before Arthur's were more like long, colorful, essay-drawings interspersed with doodles, contained in journals and sketchbooks, and stored away in dusty file folders and drawers for my eyes only. This letter was different: there were no drawings of glistening tears or shredded hearts, and the text was written not with Prismacolor rainbow markers but on a keyboard. Most importantly, it was a letter written in a medium with storage options that did not include closets and dented file cabinets but the following: SAVE, SEND, & DELETE.

I chose SEND.

Then, I reopened the E-mail, changed the subject line to "MY BREAKUP LETTER," addressed it to ten of my closest friends, and hit SEND again.

From: Anna
Sent: Wednesday, October 04, 2000 11:00 AM
To: Arthur
Subject: Re: re: how bout them yankees

arthur, i don't want to talk about the dream, let's just say it
repeated itself all night long, was brought on by the fact
that you didn't show up last night, was bad and caused me
to get very little sleep and wake up in tears. anyway, enough
of that. yes i am angry, and i'm more than angry, i'm
REALLY FUCKING PISSED OFF. i'm not into this, i'm
not into being ignored, i'm not into being disrespected, and
i'm most certainly not into giving my time and energy to
someone who proves himself untrustworthy. last week,
after all that drama, i told you how i felt and gave you and
your bad behavior the benefit of the doubt, simply because
i believe i am a good person and i'd like to think that others
(i.e. you) are as well. i also realize people make mistakes,
and as such, i was willing to try to trust you again. and then
you pull this disappearing bullshit on me AGAIN, only a
WEEK AFTER the last time? uh uh, i don't think so. i
thought you were going to attempt to REGAIN my trust,
not push it away further. i can smell a pattern.

and by the way, last night was NOT informal! i mean,
what went through your head? "i'm supposed to hang out
with the girl i'm dating but i'm busy doing something else
and i'm JUST NOT GONNA CALL HER AT ALL"????
was there anything there? and you didn't even have the
decency to talk to me this morning, mumbling silliness
about getting caught up with friends and not even apolo-
gizing to me. puhleeze.

i—every woman, actually—need a guy i can count on,
regardless of whether it is serious or not, informal or
formal. i told you a while ago that the most important
thing i ask for is honest communication. i'm being honest

with you now and i was honest with you before. i outlined my needs upfront. i was also willing to overlook your "colorful" history and a few other things, as long as you were honest with ME.

listen, your being self-destructive is NOT an excuse for your behavior. it is a reality and not something to just throw out there, like, "aw, shucks, i guess i'm just self-destructive". as you said yourself, you ARE better at destruction than construction. BUT THAT'S FUCKED UP. what does it feel like to have someone come into your life able to give you her tenderness and affection, and to sabotage it and push her away? really, i'm curious: how does that feel? i can't imagine what it's like to go through life alienating the people around you.

on the one hand you keep your promises and show me affection and concern protesting and saying things like don't i know you're "crazy about" me. i love laughing with you, and cuddling with you, arthur. but i can get that elsewhere. and so here's the news: whether you're "crazy about" me or not, this situation is too toxic for me and as of today i am hereby removing myself from it.

I never heard back from Arthur. But I didn't want to. I had designed the letter not only to cut him loose, but to do it in such a way that he'd have been a fool or an emotional masochist to respond. Others' reactions, however, were swift and overwhelming. Coworkers came over to congratulate me and recite their favorite lines. Flowers arrived from another coworker in the afternoon with a note that read something along the lines of "You Go, Girl!". One friend asked me, only half-jokingly, if I'd be available to write a letter for her the next time she got dumped.

The triumph of my tell-off lasted only a day or so—the hurt and anger resurfaced and stayed for weeks afterwards—but it did spawn a number of ideas. I toyed with the notion of a breakup letter–writing business. Women could come to me with complaints, and

I'd translate them into mordant wit, stinging sarcasm, and unequivocal condemnation. I soon realized, however, that not only did I not have the emotional energy to take on such a task, but that the breakup-letter–writing girl was a concept better suited to a television or film character than a real career. I considered putting together a book of sample breakup letters, but was quickly informed by an astute features editor that such a book was already in the works and scheduled to come out later that year (see p. 282).

The inspiration I was most taken with was the idea of an anthology of the best and most famous breakup letters in history. Certainly, if my peers reacted so strongly to my own hastily scribbled scorn, they would find others' letters—particularly those of notable women—even more fascinating. But I was skeptical, too, not about the potential of the idea—I was sure it was good—but with the very high probability that someone had thought of such a book long before I had. I went straight to amazon.com. Nothing. Then I looked in the library and in used bookstores. Still nothing. A query went out to those friends more literate than I. Nothing again. The only thing that came close to what I was envisioning was a column of famous "poison pen" letters compiled by Thomas Vinciguerra for Valentine's Day, 2000, and published in the "Week in Review" section of the *New York Times*. Breakup letters had certainly been published—even commented on—before, but in the sorts of anthologies that focused more on love than loss. Lucky for me, too, for what intrigued me personally about these letters was not pleasure, but pain: Misery, as they say, loves company.

———

What I like about letters are their immediacy, the sense they impart that you are right there along with the letter-writer . . . even if she or he lived many centuries ago. As Janet Gurkin Altman put it in her book *Epistolarity: Approaches to a Form*, whereas the reader of a memoir is transported to the world of the past, in the letter narrative, the past is an interloper, serving to shed light on what is happening in the present. There is something intimate, startling, and infinitely more satisfying in reading someone's actual words regarding a life event than hearing it described after it has taken place (which is why the actual letters in this book are far more fascinating than their setups). With handwritten letters, the emotion expressed is even more profound: the author's handwriting, deletions, stains, and misspellings all serve to communicate even more of his or her social and mental state. (They also sometimes are very difficult to read, which is why all the letters in this book were transcribed and typeset instead of reproduced.)

I have been especially taken with the letters written by women who had in some way been hurt, neglected, abandoned, or otherwise injured by the men in their lives. When it comes to love, I try not to get hurt, neglected, abandoned, or otherwise injured but it has happened, as it has happened to all of us. And it's nice to know that we're not alone in it. But what impresses me the most about the letters in this book was not what happened to the women who wrote them but how they reacted to what happened, and the range of possibilities those reactions open up for all of us. In my experience, at least, the "end of the affair" usually elicits a disturbingly familiar pattern of self-pitying pronouncements along the lines of "I'll never love again", no matter what (or who) precipitated the breakup. But why play that same old song when I can summon the spunk of Harriette Wilson or the self-possession of Fanny Burney; why follow my own script when I can live by others' examples?

———

Although the Sorbonne recently added a course of study in professional letter-writing, the future for letters does not exactly look bright: in an age of the fax, the T1 line and the bullet train, we don't exactly write as many letters as our parents and grandparents did. This fact was underscored for me each time I added a new letter to the manuscript of this book and my word-processing program, confronted with the phrase "Dear", would inevitably ask me if I needed "help" writing the letter, as if the concept of the personal address had gone the way of the dodo. The case for letter-writing has been undermined even further by the emerging threats to our many infrastructures, most notably the postal service, which was used last fall as a means to deliver biological agents. Suddenly the personal handwritten letter seemed not so much a gift as a threat; I remember thinking ruefully that the term "poison pen" letter had in fact become a reality.

Where letters will remain an attractive outlet of communication, I think, is in their difference from, not competition with, technology. Writing a letter is an almost meditative and selfishly solitary exercise that allows a sort of unencumbered thought, lack of interruption, and escape from immediate response. It's hard to tell a story, to determine feelings, to reiterate a sequence of events, or to simply express emotions when every point or opinion can be refuted, analyzed, or otherwise called into question. In fact, these sorts of letters are written as much for the writer as for the intended recipient because the act of writing a letter is a sort of rebellion both against our own and others' experiences or perceptions. Through letter writing we can literally change, shape or rewrite a narrative or a history: the wallflower can summon strength she never knew existed; the tyrant can unearth emotions he thought he wasn't supposed to feel.

That said, it's important to remember that some of the women whose letters appear in this book knew that they would eventually be read by others, and may have not only recognized their significance to history but modified their words because of it. It is also important to keep in mind that a letter is one of the most effective ways to control and shape a history, and that opinions, allegations, and even facts that are presented in these letters probably looked very different from the perspective of the men they were written to. In the case of letters written by notable women or historical figures, I made every attempt to balance the background of the letter as much as possible. However, the letters written and contributed by ordinary women were taken as is, with no attempt to verify—either with the recipient or otherwise—the validity of the opinions, allegations, or facts presented.

There was no historical precedent for me to follow in terms of ordering or defining the types or subgenres of women's breakup letters, and so I ordered the letters in this book by theme, circumstance, and tone. What I quickly discovered in the process of arranging these letters was that many of them—if not most—straddled subgenres and defied easy categorization. A letter that seemed perfect for inclusion in The Tell-Off chapter could have resulted from an infidelity, and therefore might also work well in The Other Woman/Other Man. Or vice versa. In fact, so many subgenres reared their ugly heads during the course of my research that by the time the original manuscript was turned in on Valentine's Day, 2002, it ran 1,468 pages and was made up of over twenty chapters. (Some chapters that were considered but eventually, ahem, dumped: The After the Brush-off; The Call the Police; The I'm Confused; The Drama Queen; The He Left Me; The He Married Someone Else; The He Was Gay/She Was Gay; The I'm Leaving; The E-mails; The Mad Mothers; The Poets and Poetry; The Song Lyric; The Teenage Tome; The Last Word; The Slow Fade; The String-Along; The Third-Party letter; The Unrequited; The You've Changed.) Over the next few months, my editor and I would whittle down the book to a more manageable size. Most of the thirteen categories I kept for inclusion are fairly straightforward and require little or no explanation: How hard is it to discern the meaning behind a chapter titled "The Marriage Refusal" or "The Divorce Letter"? However, there were a few categories that needed—or merited—further explanation, and those explanations can be found at the beginning notes to each chapter.

———

I trust that this book will be a source of curiosity, inspiration and humor to the women—and, I hope, men—who read it, and I also hope that the stories presented herein will engender interest in many of the women and writers whose work is presented . . . that a woman who picks up the book because her first love left her will put it down a few hours later with an interest in the work of Trollope or Kathy Acker. Not only do I want women to buy and borrow this book as needed, I have the (albeit far-fetched) fantasy that some of these same women will use the book in lieu of a breakup letter. (Just drop the book on his doorstep with your favorite and most appropriate letter bookmarked.) I strongly doubt this will actually happen, but I do hope that *Hell Hath No Fury* will be a book that is read aloud, and used, again and again.

A final note: About a month before I turned in the first draft of *Hell Hath No Fury,* in the quiet, cold dead of winter that marks the days immediately following the Christmas holidays, I took the train to a major East Coast university to post some flyers requesting research assistance. I taped about three of them on a wall in the Women's Studies corridor and then made my way across campus to the university's English Department. It was a bright, sunny day, but the students and professors were still on winter break, and so the streets and pathways were populated only by support staff and a few chittering squirrels. When I reached the English office, I was unsure where to post my flyers and so I approached a young man sitting partially turned away from me, his gaze directed at a book in his lap. He didn't sense my presence, so I cleared my throat or ruffled my papers—can't remember which—and he quickly turned toward me. He was cute. He also looked familiar—really familiar—and he was looking at me funny and then I realized that this cute young man was in fact my ex. As in Arthur. We stared at each other for what seemed like forever (real time: probably 2 seconds) before he straightened up and asked me in his most official, departmental voice if he could . . . eh, help me with anything. I thought about it for a second, and about him, and about my book, and about the ridiculousness of the situation, or the meaning of it, and how in the scheme of seemingly random yet meaningful events that define my life and make it worth living, I should have expected something like this. Then I smiled at him, cocked my head, and said that, no, he couldn't help me, but that I appreciated him asking, and that I hoped he had a nice day. And I really did hope he had a nice day. My story had come full circle. I realized I wasn't mad anymore, or sad, but that maybe I felt sorry for him, and that maybe—just maybe—this seemingly random event was a sign that I was doing something right. I just wished I'd been dressed better and put on a

little lipstick and mascara, but one can't plan for unexpected meet-
ings with exes in university English departments, and I felt so good
about myself at that moment that I probably looked just fine and
didn't need makeup anyway.

Anna Holmes
New York City
May 2002

Editor's Note

Chronology:

The letters in each chapter are arranged chronologically except for cases in which I am presenting a series of letters; a letter in a series may actually be dated later than a letter that follows it in the chapter.

Dates:

Dates that appeared on the actual letters are indicated; if the letter itself was not dated but the envelope it came in was postmarked, this is indicated. Dates supplied or guessed at by editors of publications that previously published the material are noted in brackets. If no date is known, I have noted the letter undated in brackets.

Names:

Names marked with an asterisk (*) have been changed.

Style:

When the author of a letter underlined a word, I have used italics. When the author of a letter used all caps, I have done the same.

Spelling, Grammar, and Punctuation:

In most cases I have corrected spelling, unless misspellings were frequent and/or conveyed something about the voice or personality of the letter-writer. In such a case, a misspelled word will be noted as such with the requisite [*sic*]. If a writer neglected to include a word or mark of punctuation, I have indicated the missing word or punctuation mark in brackets. However, if a missing word or punctuation mark indicated something interesting about the personality or emotional state of the writer, I did not correct the text.

Clarity:

Although a person's handwriting often says a lot about his or her emotional state of mind, handwriting is frequently difficult to read. In cases in which a word was completely illegible, I have indicated so with the word "illegible" in brackets. If the word was somewhat but not definitively clear, I have put the word in brackets with a question mark following it.

Editing and ellipses:

Except for the letters listed below, in which ellipsis points are used to denote where a letter has been edited or where material was missing, the ellipsis in letters in this book appeared in the originals and were used by the letter-writer for stylistic reasons.

Letters in which ellipsis points indicate editing:

> Tanya to Ryan
> Jean Gelatt to Jack
> Dorothy Thompson to Josef Bard
> Catherine Texier to Joel Rose in Breakup: The End of a Love Story
> Maggie Kim to Michael
> C.T. to G.L. in Li Ang's A Love Letter Never Sent

Letter in which ellipsis points indicate missing sections of a letter:

> Mollie Bidwell to Josè Maria Eça de Queiroz

Background Information:

In some letters, a word in brackets is used to (1) illuminate a word or phrase and put it into context, (2) translate a foreign word or phrase into English or (3) supply an interesting bit of trivia about the letter or the people, places, and things that appear in it.

Hell Hath No Fury

WOMEN'S LETTERS FROM THE END OF THE AFFAIR

The
Tell-Off

Tell off (tĕl ôf): —*phrasal verb*. Informal. To rebuke severely; reprimand.

The Tell-Off *n.* A breakup letter in which the writer rants and raves at a loved one who has wronged or angered her. A succinct and defiant appraisal of another's failings and injustices, often involving withering critique of that person's social, physical, or sexual weaknesses.

From Emma Hart (1765–1815, later Lady Hamilton) to Charles Gre-
ville (1749–1809), with whom she had been involved for five years.
This letter was written after Greville, the second son of the Earl of War-
wick, wrote Hart, his mistress, to say he felt she should turn her atten-
tions to his uncle William Hamilton, who had been courting her.
Greville and Hamilton had cooked up a scheme to help Hamilton secure
Hart's affections: Greville would neglect her, and Hamilton would
swoop in to take his place and would settle Greville's many debts in
return. But Hart was obsessively devoted to Greville, and badly hurt
after he betrayed her. According to Colin Simpson's biography Emma,
The Life of Lady Hamilton *(Bodley Head, 1983), the letter below*
"begins with Emma's writing that she misses the lips that had sealed the
envelope, and then suddenly she explodes . . . she had by now read the
letter right through, for tucked into the final paragraph is Greville's sug-
gestion that the sooner she climbs into Sir William's bed the better it will
be for all concerned." Hart married Hamilton in 1791. She is better
known as the mistress of Admiral Horatio Nelson and mother of his
daughter Horatia.

Naples

1st of August 1786.

I have received your letter, my dearest Greville, at last, and you dont
know how happy I am at hearing from you, however I may like
some parts of your letter, but I wont complain, it is enough I have
paper that Greville wrote on, he as foldet up, he wet the wafer—
happy wafer, how I envy thee to take the place of Emmas lips, that
she would give worlds had she them, to kiss those lips, but if I go
on in this whay I shall be incapable of writing. I onely wish that a
wafer was my onely rival, but I submit to what God & Greville
pleases. I allways knew, I have ever had a forebodeing, since I first
begun to love you, that I was not destined to be happy, for there is
not a King or prince on hearth [earth] that could make me happy
without you; so onely consider when I offer to live with you on the

hundred [pounds] a year Sir Wm. will give, what can you desire, and
this from a girl that a King etc, etc, etc, is sighing for. As to what
you write to me to oblidge Sir. Wm. I will not answer you for Oh if
you knew what pain I feil in reading those lines whare you advise
me to W . . . nothing can express my rage, I am all madness, Greville, to advise me, you that used to envy my smiles, now with cooll
indifferance to advise me to go to bed to him, Sr. Wm. Oh, thats
worst of all, but I will not, no I will not rage for if I was with you,
I would murder you & myself boath. I will leave of[f] & try to get
more strength for I am now very ill with a cold.

I wont look back to what I wrote. I onely say I have had 2 letters
in 6 months nor nothing shall ever do for me but going home to
you. If that is not to be, I will except [accept] of nothing, I will go
to London, their [there] go in to every exess of vice, tell [till] I dye
a miserable broken hearted wretch & leave my fate as a warning to
young whomin [women] never to be two [too] good, for, now you
have made me love you, made me good, you have abbandoned me
& some violent end shall finish our connexion if it is to finish, but,
Oh Greville, you cannot, you must not give me up, you have not
the heart to do it, you love me I am sure & I am willing to do everything in my power that you shall require of me & what will you
have more and I onely say this the last time, I will either beg or pray,
do as you like.

I am sorry Lord Brook is dead and I am sinecerly [sic] sorry for
Sr James & Lady Peachey, but the W——k family wont mind it
much. We have been 7 weeks in doupt [doubt] wether he was dead
or not for Sr. Wm. had a letter from Lord Warwick & he said Lord
B. was better, so I suppose he must have had a relapse. Poor little
boy, how I envy him his happiness. We have a deal of rain hear
[here] & violent winds, the oldest people hear never remember such
a sumer, but it is luckey for us. The Queen is very poorly with a cold
caught in the Villa Reale & mine is pretty much like it. We dont
dine at Passylipo today on the account of my cold. We are closely
besieged by the K. in a round a bout maner, he comes every Sunday
to P——po but we keep the good will of the other party mentioned

abbove & never gives him any encouragement. Prince Draydrixton's our constant freind, he allways enquiries after you, he desires his compliments to you; he speaks English, he says I am a dymond of the first watter & the finest creature on the hearth [earth], he attends me to the Bath, to the walk etc. etc. etc. I have such a head ake [headache] today with my cold I dont know what to do. I shall write next post by Sr. Wm, onely I cant lett a week go without telling you how happy I am at hearing from you. Pray write as often as you can & come as soon as you can & if you come we shall all go home to England in 2 years & go throug[h] Spain & you will like that. Pray write to me & dont write in the stile of a freind but a lover, but I wont hear a word of freind, it shall be all love & no freindship. Sr. Wm. is our freind, but we are lovers. I am glad you have sent me a Blue Hat & gloves; my hat is universaly admired through Naples. God bless you, my dear Greville prays your ever truly and affectionate

Emma Hart

P.S. Pray write for nothing will make me so angry & it is not to your interest to disoblidge me, for you dont know the power I have hear [here], onely I never will be his mistress. If you affront me, I will make him marry me. God bless you for ever.

————

From French/Swiss novelist (Corinne, see p. 287), Germaine de Staël (1766–1817) to the printer and writer Chevalier François de Pange, with whom she was in love, after he wrote that he was too ill to see her. De Staël—then married for nine years to the Swedish ambassador Baron de Staël-Holstein—had known de Pange since 1786, and in 1795, in her late twenties, her friendly affection turned to passion. But de Pange, in love with another woman—his younger cousin Madame de Serilly—resisted her attempts to turn the friendship into a romance. Following the publication of de Staël's political pamphlet Reflections on

Hell Hath No Fury

Domestic Peace *in August 1795, de Staël was accused of protecting émigré aristocrats, among other things, and was forced into exile, leaving for Switzerland that October. The following January, de Pange married Serilly, who had been widowed when her husband was guillotined during the Great Terror. De Pange died of tuberculosis soon after his marriage.*

Midnight, 11 September 1795

I am so upset by your letter that I don't know how to express or how to contain a feeling which is capable of producing on you an effect so contrary to the desires of my soul. What expressions you are using! 'Breaking off a friendship—avoiding a commitment— not knowing when you will be able to come—believing me happy where I am.' Ah, Monsieur de Pange, has love taught you nothing except its injustice, its forgetfulness, its inconstancy? . . . You have no right to torture me. Remember what you said to me about friendship. What life there is left me depends on that friendship; for the past four months I owe everything to it and, what is worse, I need everything still. I have no intention of intruding on your independence . . . But if to need you means to disturb you, then you have a right to be afraid of me . . . You know as well as I do what is missing from my happiness here, but you cannot know as well as I know that you are perfection itself in the eyes of those who know you, that you are, to me, something even more desirable than perfection, and that I should find in your friendship all the happiness there is for me in this world, if only you removed that sword that hangs over my head.

I beg you on my knees to come here or to meet me in Paris or at Passy for just one hour . . . I refuse to give up what I have won; this friendship is to me a necessity—I do not care if it is not one for you. Give me what you can spare, and it will fill my life. . . .

The following letter was sent from British novelist Rebecca West (1892–1983), author of <u>Black Lamb and Grey Falcon</u> (1941) to the then-married author H. G. Wells (1866–1946), when West was only twenty-one years old. The two met after West published a scathing review of Wells's <u>Marriage</u> in 1912, and became lovers in early 1913. At the time this letter was written, Wells had broken off the relationship, then only a few months old. The couple got back together soon afterward, had a son, Anthony, in 1914, and continued their volatile relationship until West, fed up with what she characterized as Wells's "increasingly demanding behavior", left him in 1923 and moved with Anthony to America. The original letter was unsigned and incomplete and probably a draft, according to Bonnie Kime Scott, editor of <u>The Selected Letters of Rebecca West</u> (Yale University Press, 2000). This letter was edited by Kime Scott and appeared in the above book; as she formatted the letter, words that appear in <angle brackets> were words crossed out by West and words in {curly brackets} were words West inserted above the line.

[circa March 1913]

Dear H. G.,

During the next few days I shall either put a bullet through my head or commit something more shattering to myself than death. At any rate I shall be quite a different person. I refuse to be cheated out of my deathbed scene.

I don't understand why you wanted me three months ago and don't want me now. I wish I knew why that were so. It's something I can't understand, something I despise. And the worst of it is that if I despise you I rage because you stand between me and peace. Of course you're quite right. I haven't anything to give you. You have only a passion for excitement and for comfort. You don't want any more excitement and I do not give people comfort. I never nurse them except when they're very ill. I carry this to excess. On reflection I can imagine that the occasion on which my mother found me most helpful to live with was when I helped her out of a burning house.

Hell Hath No Fury

I always knew that you would hurt me to death some day, but I hoped to choose the time and place. You've always been unconsciously hostile to me and I have tried to conciliate you by hacking away at my love for you, cutting it down to the little thing that was the most you wanted. I am always at a loss when I meet hostility, because I can love and I can do practically nothing else. I was the wrong sort of person for you to have to do with. You want a world of people falling over each other like puppies, people to quarrel and play with, people who rage and ache instead of people who burn. You can't conceive a person resenting the humiliation of an emotional failure so much that they twice tried to kill themselves: that seems silly to you. I can't conceive of a person who runs about lighting bonfires and yet nourishes a dislike of flame: that seems silly to me.

You've literally ruined me. I'm burned down to my foundations. I may build myself again or I may not. You say obsessions are curable. <But they're not not for> {They are.} But people like me <who> swing themselves from one passion to another, and if they miss smash down somewhere where there aren't any passions at all but only bare boards and sawdust. You have done for me utterly. You know it. That's why you are trying to persuade yourself that I am a coarse, sprawling, boneless creature, and so it doesn't matter. When you said, "You've been talking unwisely, Rebecca," you said it with a certain brightness: you felt that you had really caught me at it. I don't think you're right about this. But I know you will derive immense satisfaction from thinking of me as an unbalanced young female who flopped about in your drawing-room in an unnecessary heart-attack.

That is a subtle flattery. But I hate you when you try to cheapen <me to myself> {the things I did honestly and cleanly}. You did it once before when you wrote to me of "your—much more precious than you imagine it to be—self." That suggests that I projected a weekend at the Brighton Metropole with Horatio Bottomley. Whereas I had written to say that I loved you. You did it again on Friday when you said that what I wanted was some decent fun and that my mind had been, not exactly corrupted, but excited, by people who talked in an ugly way about things that are really beautiful. That was a vile thing to say. You once found my willingness to love you a beautiful and courageous thing. I still think it was. Your spinsterishness makes you feel that a woman desperately and hopelessly in love with a man is an indecent. . . .

———

From Violet Veitch Coward (1863–1954), the mother of playwright (Blithe Spirit, Hay Fever) Noël Coward (1899–1973), to her husband Arthur, a piano salesman. The two were married in 1890 after a courtship that took place at church services and amateur theatrical productions, and the following year, she bore their first son, Russell, who died of spinal meningitis in 1898, at age six and a half. Noël, her second child, was born a year later, and his brother Eric, in 1905. According to Philip Hoare's work, Noël Coward: A Biography (Sinclair-Stevenson, 1995), Violet wrote this letter in 1930 after becoming overwhelmed with anger at Arthur's unwillingness to work, his flirtations with local women, and his alcoholism. (As Hoare notes, Coward's 1932 musical, Words and Music, features the character of a mother who sings, "Then I married your father/Gay and handsome and frank/But it shattered me rather/When I found he drank.") Although Violet demanded that the two reside in separate rooms, they remained together until Arthur's death seven years later, in 1937.

[1930]

Dear Arthur,

This letter will probably come as a shock to you. I have made friends so often and it has taken me a long time to kill my affection for you, but you have at last succeeded in doing so. . . . As long as I can remember, not once have you ever stood up for me or the boys when we have been in any little trouble, you have always taken the opposite side and been against us. I remember so many times when you have failed me: and this has been the last straw. How dare you behave as you have been doing lately. I have never been so miserable in my life since I came from Ceylon, and who are you to dare to make my life so unhappy. What have you ever done for me or for either of your fine boys to help them on in life. You have never done anything to help anybody, and everything has been done for you. And yet you are so far from being ashamed of yourself that you plump yourself down on us, full of conceit, selfishness and self appreciation and spoil our lives for us. No one with any pretensions to being a gentleman could ever bully a woman as you bully my sister. It is *shameful* in front of those children too. She has as great a right to be here as you have. Noël chose to give her a home before he gave you one, and why are you not earning your living? You are strong and healthy and will not doubt live to be 100, a burden on Noël, not to speak of putting your wife on him too. Now I have come to a decision. I am going to add still more to poor Noël's burden and ask him to provide you with another home. If he agrees I will find you a cottage somewhere, with a little less grandeur than you have here which will do you good. Noël has always understood your character and what I have been through, and will do anything he can to make me happy again. For the present things must remain as they are and I must put up with you, but in a different way. I shall never stand up for you again as I have always done, and I tell you definitely, everything is over between you and me. The last scrap of my affection for you has gone and it is entirely your own fault.

Violet

———

A series of letters from <u>Delta of Venus</u> *(1977) writer Anaïs Nin (1903–1977) to society man and sometime poet C. L. (Lanny) Baldwin. According to Noël Riley Fitch's* <u>Anaïs: The Erotic Life of Anaïs Nin</u> *(Little Brown, 1993), the two became involved in 1944, after the married Baldwin invited Nin to dinner following a meeting* *in Manhattan's Gotham Book Mart. Later that year, Nin published a book of Baldwin's poetry, <u>Quinquivara</u>, to which she wrote the introduction and her husband contributed six engravings. (At the time of their affair, Nin was married to Hugo Guiler, a filmmaker, engraver, and illustrator known professionally as Ian Hugo.) The two parted romantically in August 1945, when Baldwin, torn with ambivalence over their relationship, returned to his wife and children. Baldwin responded to this letter, saying that he felt that Nin was "a kind of dog in the manger with men. You want them all to sit at your feet and be yours, all yours and only yours." His response to the second letter was to say "Is there to be no way of settling things without going to blows and insults? Can you kick me off your planet? Can I pull a switch and consign you to the proper section of hell?"*

They resumed contact a few months later, mostly in regards to business matters and monies owed to Baldwin from her publishing imprint.

[postmarked August 25, 1945]

My poor Lanny, how blind you are! A woman is jealous only when she has nothing, but I who am the most loved of all women, what can I be jealous of? I gave you *up long ago,* as you well know, also I refused you the night you wept—I only extended the friendship *as I told you then until you found what you wanted*—When you did I withdrew it merely because I have no time for dead relationships. The day I discovered your deadness—*long ago*—my illusion about you died and I knew you could never enter my world, which you wanted so much. Because my world *is* based on passion, and because you know that it is only with passion that one creates, and you know that my world which you now deride because you couldn't enter it, made Henry [Miller] a great writer, because you know the other young men you are so jealous of enter a whole world by love and are writing books, producing movies, poems, paintings, composing music.

I am in no need of "insisting" upon being loved. I'm immersed and flooded in this. That is why I am happy and full of power and find friendship pale by comparison.

But in the middle of this fiery and marvellous give and take, going out with you was like going out with a priest. The contrast in temperature was too great. So I waited for my first chance to break—not wanting to leave you alone.

You ought to know my value better than to think I can be jealous of the poor American woman who has lost her man to me continually since I am here—

Anaïs

[postmarked August 26, 1945]

I would like to point out a few injustices in your letter and then put an end to the letters as well as the futile talks, to prove to you there is *no* understanding between us of any kind.

About the harem: I didn't have one when you first met me—I was writing and printing quietly, and therefore the picture you draw of me as wanting absolutely to add you to my harem is rather comical. About the dog in the manger: I was the one to encourage you to love, to seek a woman etc. so you see I had no possessiveness whatever.

About wanting you "not free and *all* for myself." If it were so I would not have fallen in love with Bill. I fell in love with Bill because you killed completely the illusion I had about you—and so I was free of you.

About enslaving men etc. That is a [joke?] too, because men have come to me to be *freed,* to be made strong and free and creative and alive. I have a letter of Henry's recently saying: "no woman ever made me feel free as I feel with you," and regretting his marriage of today.

That is what I call your destructiveness—You, in all the time I knew you, never admired or constructed, but only *criticized* and pulled down. I don't know why you should try to make all this ugly now. You were the one who courted me, who harmed me, who failed, I didn't harm you. Why are you so full of criticalness now? Doesn't it sound like sour grapes? I never said that I wanted anything from you—I merely tried to discard a dead relationship to give my time to the alive ones—that is no crime.

I'm afraid your male vanity is leading you astray.

As to a woman who "feels gently"—have you asked yourself how *you* feel about woman? Do you feel gently? You recognized yourself in the portrait of my father as the one who takes from woman and cannot give anything—

There is "dirty work" to do in the world, but I don't think you will be the one to do it. You are much too busy criticizing—

I at least am asserting the strength and power of whole love, that is total passion—in a world that is full of men like you talking about gentleness while full of hatred and criticalness, and full of what Rilke called "impure emotions" because they are not whole, not big enough.

If you still don't believe that I don't love you and feel only compassion for the women you deal with, then I'll have to read you from my diary to convince you when and where and how and why I rejected you, and that out of vanity you took my compassion for your weeping that night for something else and showed your wanton destructiveness for the second time at the party—

Oh, Lanny, what a shabby role you played. Because you were [impotent?] to take something you wanted but didn't dare you had to harm this person who didn't harm you, whose only crime was to turn away from impotency to fulfilled men, and from a friendship built upon the tomb of an abortion—the tomb of a feeling killed by you!

American poet Anne Sexton (1928–1974) was known as a heartbreaker as a teenager, but, according to <u>Anne Sexton: A Portrait in Letters</u> (Houghton, Miflin, 1997) the poet did not take well to boys who were "as ruthless in affairs of the heart as she was." The following letter was written when she was sixteen, and addressed to a young man she met at a dude ranch that summer.

Hell Hath No Fury

[undated—probably 1945]

Dear Torgie,

I promised you last that I would write you just what I was thinking. I had not intended to do this; however, I felt so sorry for you that decided you better have the truth. [several words missing here] not love me in the slightest; however, upon thinking it over, I wouldn't marry you even if you had $100,000,000.

Undoubtedly, Torgie, your dislike for me has now reached great heights. I have proved so little and yet a great deal in this so-called play. I started it in order to prove my abilities as an actress. Perhaps at the same time I have proved to you that someone with mercenary intentions will invariably receive the same treatment. I hope that in the future you will change your philosophy, expressed by "No one or nothing stands in the way of the mighty Torginson and what he wants." You think you are a gentleman with your effect of polished clothes and mannerisms, but a true gentleman is one that has a kind and humble heart. You may wonder at my saying this for my actions have not displayed me in a very flattering light. But you do not know me, Torgie, except to realize I have a perverse enough character to be able to show your true inferiority—in retrospect to sincere people. It is too bad, Torgie, that you know the price of everything and the value of nothing. At any rate, there have been a lot of laughs and it has been great fun co-starring with you in our little play, "There are all Kinds of People"—What you are you will find.

Chalk it off to experience, Torgie
Anne S. Harvey

From Jessica, to her ex-boyfriend, Scott after she discovered he was married following a yearlong affair. Jessica, now twenty and a college student in California, met Scott in 1997 when she was sixteen years old and he twenty-six; he was the manager of a restaurant at which she waitressed.*

[Summer 1998]

Dear Scott,

I hope you realize that you lost the best thing that you ever had—me—and no matter how many apologies you give me, or flowers you send you'll never win me back. You'll never get to listen to my voice or see my face ever again. You have lost that priveledge [*sic*] for forever. Granted you'll probabally [*sic*] come begging me for a job in the future when kharma comes and bites you in the ass and you can be the fella who scrapes gum off the carpet because I am gonna be the bigger person. In fact, out of the two of us you make me seem god-like—you are like four steps below me on the food chain. I still don't understand why I allowed you into my life in the first place. You were like a fucking nubbin the entire time and I should've grabbed the nailclippers and just pried you off, it would've been a lot quicker and less painful . . . then [*sic*] what you have put me through the last few months. You are in some serious need of help! I am done being your doctor, your mom, your psychologist and I am through being your friend. You put me through hell and back and no matter if I grant you "forgiveness" I will never forget what you did to me. You have left a permanent stain in my life, and I am going to try to foster nice thoughts about you, but you leave me no choice but to hit the "eject" button from our relationship. Miss me yet? You should. You will. Id [*sic*] put money on it. No one makes Mac and Cheese quite like I do or makes chocolate milk better. No one would listen to you yap about nothing like I did and no one will ever tickle that spot right behind your knee that makes you laugh for hours like I used to. No one will be a more loyal friend or trustworthy [*sic*] friend—like I was. You know that. That's why you cried. That's why you called. You called twenty seven times in two days. What part of "its [*sic*] over" don't you understand? Good luck trying to replace me—I know that I can replace you. In fact—not only will I replace you, but [I'll] actually fill the gap with a person worthy of my time, someone, nothing like you. A man, not a boy. An understanding, trusting person, not a blabbering, jealous fool.

Grrrrrr. Just thinking of you makes me mad!! I don't even know why I am bothering writing this. I don't care about you. I don't miss you. I don't care where you are right now or who you are with. I don't care anymore I don't have the energy anymore—and it's just not worth it. When it finally sinks into your thick skull that you blew it you don't need to call, or write, or show up at my front door!! Respect me. Respect my space and respect the fact that I would rather have my eyebrows singed than ever see you again. So . . . take care and fuck off.

Jessica

From Kylie, 28, a resident of Queensland, Australia, to her ex-fiancé, Jamie*, in January 1999. Kylie sent Jamie this letter through his lawyer who, she says, found it "quite amusing." "I didn't have the heart to delete it and every time I feel depressed I open it and read it again," says Kylie. "It always makes me feel better and reminds me that even though things are tough, they used to be a lot worse." After receiving it, she says, Jamie "apparently swore quite profusely, then tore it up and threw it at the woman who gave it to him."

[January 1999]

Dear Jamie,

I missed you today, I missed you yesterday and with any luck I won't see you tomorrow either. I am writing this letter for two reasons. I am writing it because I want to thank you and I am writing it because I never want to speak to you ever again.

I want to thank you for being so selfish, otherwise I would never have known what I was going without.

I want to thank you for being so rude, otherwise I would never have learned to appreciate the good manners and politeness my parents instilled in me.

I want to thank you for spending all our money on crap, otherwise I would never have been able to justify the hire cost of a trailer to transport it all to the rubbish tip [garbage dump].

I want to thank you for running our phone bill up so high, otherwise I would never have learned to appreciate the visits of my friends (as they can't phone me, they visit instead. Or is that just because you're no longer here?).

I want to thank you for leaving me in so much debt the car has now been repossessed, otherwise I would never have lost so much weight by walking everywhere.

I want to thank you for telling all your friends that I was such an evil person, basically because I don't like any of them any more than I like you and I no longer have to deal with them either.

I want to thank you for telling me that our daughter was 'the biggest mistake you ever made', otherwise I would wonder how to explain to her why you're no longer here.

I want to thank you for leaving me with the kids while you went for a holiday overseas to meet the woman you hooked up with in a chat room, otherwise I would never have realised how well I could do without you and would probably still be putting up with your crap now.

Mostly, I just want to thank you for getting the hell out of our lives. We're so much happier now and the house is filled with the sound of the kids' laughter instead of the sound of you yelling at them to shut up.

In closing, all I can say is that after all these years you finally did something right and I hope your new girlfriend appreciates it as much as I do.

Kylie.

PS: You know that burning sensation you thought was an STD and you were too afraid to tell me about it? I put Tiger Balm in your jocks!

Hell Hath No Fury

This letter was written by Lola Fondue,* twenty-four, a New York City writer, to Ira,* her twenty-three-year-old musician boyfriend. A few days before this letter was written, Ira had E-mailed Lola a list of all the things that were wrong with her and why she wouldn't ever have a healthy relationship. The following is her response, one she initially planned on sending via E-mail but ended up reading to him over the phone.

[October 2000]

Dear Ira,

1. You have B.O. even after a shower.
2. You hinted on our very first date that you're [*sic*] penis was small.
3. You're [*sic*] penis is ridiculously tiny.
4. You're [*sic*] college nickname was Mushroom Dick and no one has ever told you that.
5. Three separate friends of mine commented on how midget-like your hands are.
6. You told my best friend's sister that you like to masturbate when you drive.
7. Your father scolded you after he found out you had made over 30 calls to 1-900 numbers.
8. Your mother laughed and thought it was cute.
9. You grunt like a pig during sex
10. You get food on your mouth at every friggin' meal.
11. You don't shut up EVER.
12. When you're on stage singing, you really look like you have Down's Syndrome.
13. You love therapy more than you like pizza.
14. You love telling me that you spent 2 months of therapy sessions talking about me.
15. You find it informative to let me know what your therapist thinks about me.
16. You tell your friends I'm "crazy" and you tell them that I have a heroin problem.

18

17. You don't tell your friends how I've not only never done heroin but that the only time I've ever seen ANYone do heroin EVER was when I was 19 in the bathroom at the Limelight.
18. You had a wart on your dick when you were 20 and told your mom.
19. You want to have sex with your mom.
20. You never stop talking about your mother, who, [*sic*] is a therapist.
21. You were way too excited to show me the videotape of your high school graduation.
22. You looked really fat and ugly.
23. You are better looking now but still fatter and uglier than the average guy.
24. You actually thought I was listening to all of your sorry stories.
25. You never knew that when we had sex, I had to shut my eyes tightly and fantasize about other guys.
26. I fantasized about your friends.
27. Two of your friends hit on me.
28. I kissed one of them in your bedroom. Yes, that was the night you left your own party because you had a cold.
29. Your sheets smell like vomit because you don't wash them, ever.
30. Your guitar playing never turned me on.
31. You've memorized too many literary passages and continuously quote them out of context.
32. Your SAT score was 970.
33. You call menstruation the "bloody bitch from hell."
34. You slobber when you kiss.
35. The sex was absolutely horrid.
36. I dated you because I really liked your group of friends.
37. I liked to see them wonder why a girl like me would date a guy like you.
38. I wondered myself.
39. I wanted to see how it would feel to date a really ugly guy.

40. At first I felt sorry for you. Then I realized that ugly guys are assholes too.

41. Your lyrics sound like kindergarten limericks and that's why your band won't play them.

42. You told me you kissed a few of your male friends at a New Year's party.

43. When I brought it up among your male friends, they didn't remember sharing that experience.

44. Your response was, "It did happen but they were just too drunk to remember."

45. Why would a guy make that up?

46. You love making fun of my CD collection.

47. You made me a really awful mix tape with a photo of yourself taped to the outside cover.

48. You were so mad when I told you that I had ruined the tape because it got caught in my tape player. You referred to me that evening as an "uncaring" feline.
A) it was an accident. B) I'm not your cat. C) It was an act of God that ruined the tape and not me being a cunning mean bitch. D) divine intervention.

49. There were 3 Neil Diamond songs on the tape.

50. You spent 60 minutes explaining why Neil Diamond is your musical god.

51. You liked talking about my past relationships almost as much as you liked having sex.

———•———

The following "Cruelest Breakup Letter Ever" was found on the internet at the URL http://www.everything2.com/index.pl?node-id=823193&lastnode_id=117106. It was written by a young woman to her ex-boyfriend, in October 2000, and posted on November 5, 2000. After many attempts, Tanya,* the author of the letter, now twenty, was finally located. According to Tanya, she wrote the letter to her ex-boyfriend Ryan* about two weeks before actually breaking up *with him—at times on a laptop in his presence—and frequently showed it to friends, who made suggestions "on how much worse I could make it." The two first met in high school and dated for two weeks before Ryan broke it off. A few years later, they ran into one another and started anew; this time the relationship lasted for four months, at which time Tanya became pregnant and Ryan "acted like an ass." Tanya works in a methadone clinic in Baltimore, Maryland.*

My cruelest breakup letter ever
(thing) by Tanya

Sun Nov 5 2000 at 02:31

DISCLAIMER—
The cruelest breakup letter ever

Allow me to clear a few things up real quick . . . to give some explanation as to why something this extreme was necessary:

1) When I told him that I was pregnant, his response was something along the lines of, "How could you do this to me . . . you're trying to destroy my life . . . you're getting rid of it, that's the end of it, you have no choice . . . you're trying to destroy my fucking life . . ."

2) Soon after this, he wandered off to confide in [*sic*] an undisclosed source that he was going to do his damnedest to make me get an abortion and that as soon as it was done (read: the day of the procedure, probably when he got me home) that he was going to break up with me

3) I was getting really emotional a couple of weeks later, to which he responded, "It's okay . . . it's not a big deal . . . it's nothing . . . just a clump of cells. . . ." When I said nothing, he got really pissed and came up with, "I was trying to cheer you up, you psychotic bitch!"

4) I went in for an ultrasound (normal procedure when pregnant) and again, got really emotional. He asked if I had scheduled the procedure and I said no, and that I didn't think I would be able

to. He got very angry and said, "If you don't get this done, don't ever fucking talk to me again!"

Is any more explanation really necessary? Have fun reading . . . (I must admit, it's probably not as funny if you don't know the guy, but just know that he deserved every last bit of it)

Dear Ryan,

I heard that you wanted to break up with me today, after, of course, you forced me into doing something that I don't want to do, and am going to hate you for the rest of my life. But I'd just like to say a couple of things before you do that, and hopefully, I will make your day as miserable as you were going to make mine had I still even remotely liked you. Fortunately, I've hated you for quite awhile now, so that's not a problem.

First of all, I'm breaking up with you first, because you're an asshole, and you deserve it. I hope if you ever manage to be in this situation again, you will have a much better diplomacy about you. Obviously you could see that I wasn't having an easy time with this, and what did you do? You made it ten times fucking worse!

You were such a prick, and there is no fucking excuse for your behavior. You are a selfish fucking idiot. Why did you want me to get an abortion? Because you didn't want me to ruin "your" life. Did you care in one way or another about my life? No. Did you ultimately let me make this decision? No. Even by backing off at the end (Took you fucking long enough, dick), you were still, in a way, pressuring me into it. What would you have done if I had told you that I didn't want to go through with having an abortion? Killed me? I wouldn't have put it past you. You might want to put a check on that damn temper of yours, since I honestly thought you were going to hit me during that one argument in your backyard. But honestly, maybe it is best that I get this done, because the thought of something of yours growing inside me makes me want to get out the knitting needles, and just fucking do it myself. Not to mention, you're pretty ugly, I wouldn't WANT to procreate with you. Screw diapers, your kids are gonna need tire swings and bananas, Monkey Boy.

By the way, I'd like to let you in on a little secret here. We dated for, what, about four months? Honestly, I think I got sick of you about two and a half—three months ago. All those times I said I love you? You think I meant it? But you were all about letting me know that if you were single, you'd either become a Christian or blow your head off, so I didn't feel right just saying, "Yeah, well, I'm not really in love with you, go shove your finger up your ass, since you seem to like that sort of stuff". Honestly, I've been waiting for a good moment to break up with you for a very long time now, and as sick as this is, the whole pregnancy thing presented a good reason, since you did a warp drive into Asshole-of-the-Month. Yeah, you always tried to play the good boyfriend, but can I just tell you how much you ended up getting on my fucking nerves? You're boring, you're predictable, and good god, you're a fucking dork. You'd think I would've learned, but NOOO. . . . And I gotta tell you, for as much as you acted all fucking superior about your writing, Mr. Ooooo Look-at-me-I'm-a-stupid-english-major-dork-boy-who-thinks-he's-god's-gift-to writing, your stories fucking suck. No wonder every major magazine in the country rejected that one story of yours. My unborn child can write better than you can, idiot. As for criticizing me for getting emotional and writing about my mother, well, look, you unsympathetic bastard, maybe I kinda, gee, I don't know, MISS her. Hey, it beat writing about what a fucking loser you are. Oh, and also—I don't know why you think that you are so great at dancing, but I've got to be honest and tell you that you look like you're having a fucking seizure or something. I mean, who the hell taught you? An epileptic on crack? You know why it seems that no one else can "dance as good as you"? Because everyone else actually knows what the hell they're doing! Thank god I never went to a club with you . . . I think I would have been embarrassed to death. Which brings me to my next point. You seem to think that you have such a wonderful sense of fashion . . . good god in heaven, WHY??? You look like a fucking retard! As someone I know put it, you look like you're trying to be a beat poet/mime/train wreck. Billy*? Knows how to dress. Stuart*? Knows how to dress. You? Should be run over for some of the things you wear out in public. Let me point out—wide-legged jeans should never, I repeat, NEVER be worn with those sandals. Also—those stupid shiny shirts that you always wear? A) they give me a headache just looking at them, b) they are not "pimp", as you so annoyingly keep referring to them as, (by the way, no one else I know uses that phrase . . . probably because it's only used by idiot dorks who think they are cool, but really aren't) and c) God, I just don't have anything else to say. You just suck, and you annoy the fuck out of me. You laugh WAY too loud, especially at things that aren't even that god-damn funny, you're too much of a goody-two-shoes (again, with the boring thing), your poetry sucks pretty bad, and news flash! I don't give a goddamn fuck about that bonus you got, so stop fucking rubbing it in my face. I don't know if you specifically did that on purpose, but let me tell you, that pissed me off to no end when that was every other goddamn thing out of your mouth. If I CARED, I would have told you I cared! Did I act interested? Noooo. So therefore, did I give a shit? Noooo. Go fuck yourself, monkey boy. Not to mention—how the fuck did you get so hairy? You might want to, like, shave your back or something, because I gotta tell you, every time you took your shirt off, I almost threw up. Haven't you ever heard of a razor? NAIR?? ANYTHING, for chrissakes?? You're lucky I never puked on you. That's just disgusting, but it seriously does further my ape theory here.

Oh, sweetie, you think this is bad? You poor thing. . . . I haven't even gotten to the half of it yet. Let me tell you a little story here— About three or four days after I started dating you, I went up to see Stuart (who, by the way, is NOT hairy, and NOT fat). And boy, does he get my libido going. So needless to say, I fucked him that day, and many, many other days after that. In fact, I've fucked him for the entire length of our relationship. Did you ever notice how I'd randomly disappear for an evening, and then give you some lame excuse like "Oh, I was at Claudia's* reading and I lost track of time", or "I was hanging out with Melanie*, one of my friends from high school"? No, I was up in Baltimore, getting my brains fucked out by someone who turns me on in ways you never could. Do you remember that day we watched "Life is Beautiful"? Fucked him that night. The day I went up there to "just give him his birthday present"? Yup, fucked him then, too. When I went up there to have him help me on my laptop? Yeah, you guessed it. I'd say that this has been a regular occurrence of about once, every week or so. Let's see . . . when was the last time I had sex with him? Hmmm. . . . That would have been on Thursday night (the 19th) . . . would you like to hear all about it?? I know you do. In excruciating detail, here goes:

[section deleted]

> . . . we slide apart, sweaty, breathless.
> God, he was good.

And you're definitely not. Just to let you know—the reason I got off all the time with you, and the reason I liked it when we did it doggy-style—Because as long as I didn't have to look at your face, I could just imagine you as Stuart instead, and that made it a whole hell of a lot easier to come. I'm wondering . . . did you ever notice that certain nights, I tasted a little . . . funny? Well, it just so happens— those were nights that I went up to see Stuart, and you may not have realized it, but that funny taste was you licking another man's cum out of me. Brutal, huh? Oh well, guess that's just too bad for you. So, uh . . . I guess you thought that you were gonna be the asshole, and break my heart as soon as we set foot outside the clinic, huh? Well, sweetie, looks like I got the last laugh. Happy fucking birthday, prick.

Tanya

P.S.—You know, I would have been a lot more diplomatic about this whole thing had you not reacted the way you did. I would have just left it at "we should be friends", and kept the dirty details to myself. But unlucky for you, you pissed me off. Guess you'll think twice about that in the future, huh?

Let the downvotes begin . . .

Hell Hath No Fury

[added posting]
12/06/01—Oh . . . um, I think I forgot to mention that I gave this to him all wrapped up in a pretty envelope as his birthday present . . .

———

From Natasha Carrie Cohen, twenty-three, to her ex-boyfriend Peter* after he broke up with her in late summer 2001. The two met during their freshman year at Syracuse University, but did not officially date until their senior year, when she punched him in front of a whole party of people. "We had had sex the previous week for the first official time, and when I saw him all over some skanky freshman, I became infuriated, even more so when I found out he had brought the girl home despite my having punched him," says Cohen.

A few days later the two sat down and discussed the situation at length and, she says, "after a lot of crying (on my part) and begging for forgiveness (on his part) we became an item and spent the remainder of my senior year together."

After Cohen's graduation in May 2001 and her move to New York City, she suggested they try "the long-distance thing." It didn't work. "He basically decided he couldn't handle it and broke up with me," she says. "It's still really hard because so many of my memories of college are tied to him. But I'm starting graduate school at Columbia this fall and I guess, despite everything—the horrible pain—I pulled through."

[August 2001]

Guess what? You didnt need to block me. I had no intentions of ever IMing you again. Amy* said youre sorry Im taking it "so hard" cause oh it was really only like 5 months. Oh gee thats nothing, nothing at all. I was only your first real girlfriend, your first real lover. The one who was patient and gave you like 25 chances before you were decent at sex. Im so glad you can go on w/ yr life w/o me w/o a backwards glance. I thought you had feelings only to learn how callous and selfish you really are. I TRUSTED you. Something

26

I swore I would never do again after James.* I trusted you because we had YEARS of friendship behind us. I never thought you of all people would turn out to be as big a jerk if not the worst of them all. Because you became my best friend. I let my guard down. I trusted you. I was an idiot. I know that now. I never never never should have given you another chance after you brought that freshman home. I should have gone w/ my gut feeling then.

And as for us being friends somday [sic], that will be a cold day in hell because you are not only a horrible boyfriend, you are a horrible friend. You are selfish and self-centered. You never even asked me once when we had sex if I had come. It was always about you. Im glad I meant so little to you. Its done wonders for my self-esteem. Thank you so very much for everything you never did for me you fucking bastard.

Thank you so much for leading me on. Thank you for letting me spend $110 on a plane ticket to be with you because I thought you loved me. Thanks to you I dont know if I will ever trust another man again as long as I live. Wait did I say man? I meant little boy. Youre not a man. Youre the most immature guy I have ever known. You run away from things instead of facing them. You are a scared little coward and thinking you were anything more than that was probably the biggest delusion of my life.

Umm yes you did block my IM name and youve always prided yourself on not being a liar but I know u lied because I was signed on and Amanda said she was talking to u and u did not come up on my buddy list. This leads me to believe u blocked me. And what do u care if i have an apartment or not? I learned a lot this summer—like not to trust anyone, even if ive known them since i was 18, even if ive known since i was 8, like miri. id like to throw out a big warm thank u to all the people who turned on me and left me out in the cold.

As for our breakup, i was willing to put in whatever effort necessary to make things work. You were the one who shut me out and pushed me away. So you remember that. This is completely yr fault. And this is unusual for me because in the past I have known when ive fucked up but i honestly always had yr best interest at heart and tried my best to make u happy. It didnt seem to matter. everything i said or did became wrong in yr eyes. youve made me insecure in myself. i second and third guess everything i say or do. i think its going to be forever before i get involved w/ some one else because i dont trust your gender at all. I mean how can i when all i ever do is get hurt? I feel ugly, i feel unattractive and i feel incredibly depressed. Thank you so much for taking something so incredibly special and tossing it away, me away, like a bag of trash.

The
Silent
Treatment

Si•lent treat•ment (sī´lənt trēt´mənt) n. Informal. Maintenance of aloof silence toward another as an expression of one's anger or disapproval.

The Silent Treatment n. A breakup letter or letters written after a relationship has apparently ended, albeit with no such confirmation on the part of the recipient; a letter increasing in frustration and desperation in response to being ignored or disregarded by a loved one.

From Sophia Dorothea of Celle, Electress of Hanover (1666–1726) to her lover, the Swedish Count Philipp Christoph von Königsmarck (1665-1694). The German-born Sophia, wife of Prince George Louis (later King George I of England), embarked on her affair with von Königsmarck in her early twenties; the relationship lasted from 1689 until 1694, when the affair was discovered and von Königsmarck was murdered upon leaving her bedroom. Prince George, although he too had been unfaithful, promptly divorced Sophia and imprisoned her in a castle for life. In this letter she berates von Königsmarck for not having contacted her.

Hanover, August 5 [1693]

This is the sixth day since you left, and I have not had a word from you. What neglect and what disdain! In what way have I deserved such treatment? Is it for loving you to adoration, for having sacrificed everything? But of what use to remind you of this? My suspense is worse than death; nothing can equal the torments this cruel anxiety makes me suffer. What an ill fate is mine, good God! What shame to love without being loved! I was born to love you, and I shall love you as long as I live. If it be true that you have changed, and I have no end of reasons for fearing so, I wish you no punishment save that of never finding, wherever you may be, a love and fidelity equal to mine. I wish, despite the pleasure of fresh conquests, you may never cease to regret the love and tenderness that I have shown you. You will never find in the whole world anyone so loving and so sincere. I love you more than woman has ever loved man. But I tell you the same things too often; you must be tired of them. Do not count it ill, I implore you, nor grudge me the sad consolation of complaining of your harshness. I am very anxious for fear they have detained the letter you were to have written to me from Zell. I have not received a word; everything conspires to crush me. Perhaps in addition to the fact that you no longer love me, I am on the eve of being utterly lost. It is too much all at once; I shall break down under it. I must end this tomorrow; I shall go to Communion. Farewell. I forgive you all you make me suffer.

———

From protofeminist writer Lady Mary Wortley Montagu (1689–1762), to Italian Francesco Algarotti (1712–1764), later an art critic and scholar, with whom Montagu fell in love in 1736, while nearing her fifties. The two had known each other (though they were very seldom in physical proximity) for about three years when Montagu arranged for a secret rendezvous with Algarotti and left England in July 1739, hoping to live with him in Venice. He never arrived there. Instead, he left for Prussia on the accession of Frederick the Great, to be chamberlain at the (largely homosexual) court assembling in Berlin. For the first five years that they knew one another, a frustrating, but familiar dynamic reigned supreme: that of the lovelorn woman and the indifferent man— (Algarotti, like most of the court, was gay)—who declined to respond to repeated letters. According to Robert Halsband's The Life of Lady Mary Wortley Montagu *(Oxford University Press, 1960), Montagu sent this letter after she had "forced herself to recognize that her romantic scheme had been an impossible self-induced, perhaps self-indulgent, vision." Montagu and Algarotti reconciled—as friends—in 1756.*

[Spring 1739 or May 1741]

Yes, I will spend the morning writing to you even if it makes you furious. I have begun to scorn your scorn, and on this subject I will no longer restrain myself. In the time (of foolish memory) when I had a frantic passion for you, the desire to please you (although I understood its entire impossibility) and the fear of boring you almost stifled my voice when I spoke to you, and all the more didn't stop my hand five hundred times a day when I took up my pen to write to you. It's not that way any more. I have studied you, and studied so well, that Sir [Isaac] Newton did not dissect the rays of the sun with more exactness than I have deciphered the sentiments of your soul. Your eyes served me as a Prism to discern the Ideas of your mind. I watched it with such great Intensity that I almost went blind (for these prisms are very dazzling). I saw that your soul is filled with a thousand beautiful fancies but all together makes up only indifference. It is true that separately—divide that Indifference (for example) into seven parts, on certain objects at certain distances—one would see the most lively taste, the most refined sentiments, the most delicate imagination etc. Each one of these qualities is really yours. About manuscripts, statues, Pictures, poetry, wine, conversation, you always show taste, Delicacy, and vivacity. Why then do I find only churlishness and indifference? Because I am so opaque as to strike out nothing better, and I see so clearly the nature of your soul that I Despair of touching it just as Sir [Isaac] Newton despaired of enlarging his discoveries by means of Telescopes, which by their own Powers dissipate and change the Light rays.

———

From an Italian housewife and mother, Girolama "Moma" Piccolomini (ca.1728–1792) to her lover, the Scottish biographer James Boswell (1740–1795). The two met in August 1765 in Siena, Italy during Boswell's tour of Italy, Corsica, and France. According to Frank Brady and Frederick A. Pottle, editors, Boswell on the Grand Tour (McGraw-Hill, 1955), Boswell initially pursued "Moma" to induce jealousy and acquiescence in another Italian conquest, Porzia Sansedoni, and "intended no more than a brief and essentially unsentimental interlude according to the ground rules of gallantry, but he discovered that Moma played for keeps."

Boswell, then in his mid twenties, could be described as being somewhat of a ladies' man (he contracted gonorrhea countless times) and was enamored of the idea of himself as a gallant; during his travels he wrote to his acquaintance and idol, the author Jean-Jacques Rousseau (see p. 247), of his many female conquests (single, married, and for hire), saying that the women of Siena in particular made love "as their inclinations suggested," that he yielded to this custom and "allowed myself to become all sensation and immediate feeling. I did not wish to extend my mind to encompass a series of prudent considerations." He also added, quite happily, that in Italy, "no longer does one have to fear the stiletto of a jealous

husband" (the thirty-something Moma was married to Orazio Piccolo-
mini, the mayor of Siena, and was the mother of four children).

Although he did develop tender feelings for Moma, Boswell left Siena
five weeks after their meeting to continue on to Corsica and then to
Scotland. According to Peter Martin's A Life of James Boswell *(Weiden-*
feld & Nicolson, 1999), "when he failed to return to Siena, or to write
as she thought a man in love should, Moma showered him with com-
plaining letters and continued to do so for two years . . ." The letter was
the first of her letters to bear a signature, a strange formality that may
convey her disappointment in him.

Siena, 20 March 1767

Sir,—You are the man who swore to me in person and by letters that
you would never stop writing to me, and that *twenty years from now*
I would still be receiving letters from you filled with the same expres-
sions. Those are your own words. I keep the written record of them,
not for my own sake, for I remember in minute detail all you ever
said, but to have documentation for my saying and reflecting on the
fact that one can count little on a man's friendship, even though he
is credited with a good character and a good heart. When the object
of love is gone from his eyes, all fades away. And in truth these
thoughts are not new, but I am sorry to say that sad experience con-
firms their truth in regard to you.

I received a single letter on your arrival in Scotland, which I did
not fail to answer immediately, addressing it according to your
instructions, as I shall do with this one; but I am afraid they have
not reached you with that address, and I do not understand why
you do not give me your address in your own country.

I am well so far as health is concerned, and except for some
minor illnesses I always have been well. My councilors are always
the same. The only new thing this season has been a German gentleman who has called on me. The *turno grosso* (as you called it) is
over, and everyone has gone back home. The country is not very
gay, because of the sufferings of the poor and the deaths of many

people, but in May our Sovereigns will come, and then there will be great celebrations and many people.

Now, give me news of yourself in detail. What are your love affairs? Do you ever think of me? Do you understand Italian? Are you as inconstant as ever with women? Do you still keep up your friendship with Rousseau and with Signor de Paoli? I beg you to answer all these questions. You may be sure that a letter from you will give me great pleasure, the more so because I have despaired of hearing from you. You promised me your portrait, and I do not intend to release you from your promise. Therefore you must keep it, or I shall appeal to your friend Rousseau; I am sure he will take my side, because of the justice of my claim and because the thing you promised is so valuable.

If I can serve you, I expect you to command me. Be assured that neither time nor space will alter my feelings. You will be ashamed to know so faithful a lady without being able to imitate her example, and without being able to say to yourself, "I have no reservations"— which *I* can say, and which I now set my name to, taking my leave of you with this letter. Who knows whether it will come to your hands, and if it does, who knows whether you will be able to read it? But sometimes one must take risks, just as I am now doing.

Your most devoted and most obliged friend,
Girolama Nini Piccolomini

———

From Lady (Christina) Falkland (ca.1779 -?), the daughter of a West India merchant, to the poet George Gordon, Lord Byron (1788–1824). During the early 1800s Byron had become friendly with Lady Falkland's husband Lord Falkland, a naval officer and prodigious drinker. In 1809 Lord Falkland died from the injuries incurred in a duel and Byron, upon hearing that his friend had left Lady Falkland and their four children without a penny, sent her what the anthology To Lord Byron feminine profiles based upon unpublished letters, 1807–1824

(J. Murray, 1939) calls "a substantial sum of money." In early 1812, Lady Falkland began complaining to Byron that he had not responded to her previous letters, and that she wished him to meet her children and to thank him personally for his generosity. Byron responded by saying that any sort of correspondence with Lady Falkland might give rise to gossip.

Things grew worse in March of that same year, after Lady Falkland read Byron's recently published <u>Childe Harold</u> *and began to believe that not only were women mentioned in it representations of herself but that the Byron was, in fact, in love with her. She wrote to him that June, saying that she would most "joyfully accept" his hand in marriage but that "I must be loved exclusively—your heart must be all my own . . . I could not, my beloved Byron, brook a second time to be slighted by my husband." She also enclosed a lock of hair. There was no reply, but Lady Falkland was not discouraged; in fact, she wrote him that July to say that she understood that his silence was part of his generosity and nobility of soul. It was only in February 1813 that she was notified through the grapevine that Lord Byron would neither read her letters nor respond to them. After writing one more letter to him that month, in which she proclaims she "cannot any longer endure this dreadful agony of mind," and asking what she had done to forfeit his affection, she seemed to get the point, which she elaborates on in the following letter. A year after she sent this letter, she wrote again, asking Byron to lend her £200. He refused.*

[1813]

For the last time, Byron, I address you. Human nature can bear much, which has been exemplified by me, but there are boundaries at which it stops, which you have certainly not attended to. After what has passed I will not enter into further explanation than to say our ideas are so perfectly dissimilar (though the minds may be congenial and the hearts certainly allied) that we could never be happy. I therefore entreat that you will forget everything that has passed. Don't write to me. I will not open any letters from you—nor will I see you if you call.

I had heard that you had behaved very ill to the young lady you were going to marry some years ago. I fear that tale was true, and, believe me, no woman possessing one article of sense or reflection would submit to be treated as I have been—like a *puppet*. I trust it will be a lesson to you in future not to pursue the romantic course you have now taken, *but it appears to me you delight in being wretched yourself, and that you like to have partakers in your self-inflicted misery,* . . . God bless you—rest assured I will ever feel the warmest affection for you.

———

The following letter was written by French novelist George Sand (1804–1876) to Louis-Chrysostome Michel (1797–1853). Sand met the young lawyer and militant, who was known as Michel de Bourges, soon after her relationship with Alfred de Musset ended. De Bourges immediately set off on a voluminous correspondence; Sand said that his letters "follow with a rapidity without time for replies. This ardent soul has resolved to take hold of mine." In late 1835 Sand asked de Bourges to assist her in separating from Casimir Dudevant, her husband of sixteen years from whom she was estranged (they were legally separated in July of the next year). Although the Sand-de Bourges relationship was a passionate one, Sand found herself involved with a man who was two-timing another woman, yet flew into a rage when she herself sought sexual pleasure elsewhere. The relationship deteriorated as de Bourges pulled away, and the two parted for good a few months after this letter was sent.

[Nohant, January 28, 1837]

Michel, why haven't you written me? What new crisis is this? Are you sick, my God? Are you sulking on me again? Are you in love with someone else? Alas! I believe it, and the conviction hasn't left me for a minute since I last saw you. Your face wasn't like it used to be, and even in your renewed tenderness, you had trouble hiding your boredom and your impatience to leave me. If such is the case, why humiliate me with your patience? Why doubt my courage and my honor? Why not confide your withdrawal in me, or, if it's impossible to admit to, why not dare tell me that you don't love me like you used to? Do you think I'd stop loving you? No! That would be impossible. Do what you will: I know I'll be able to show the required dignity, I'll even be able to keep quiet if my affection bothers you, but I'll also be able to keep the faith that I swore to you before God, a faith I can no longer break. Give me back your friendship, at least. Forbid me for ever from calling on your love; I have utter control over myself: what demons haven't I conquered? But my soul needs yours! No other soul than mine will understand you, nor have for your greatness this immense love that stretches even to your misery, even to your defects, seeing them, following them, kissing them in tears, holding them to its blood-stained breast, wishing to absorb them so they might hide from the light of day. Yes, I can pardon you for everything, even the crime I suspect you of; I can hide it in the depths of my soul and cry over it and not speak of it, as though it were my own, as though I shared its remorse or shame.

Alas! how unhappy I am! My son carries in him, perhaps, the germs of coming death. Two nights ago, I felt little hope: today he is doing better, and I think about the absence of your letters. I'm horrified: I dream you are dying, too, and I cannot escape one anguish except by falling prey to another. Oh! no, you do not love me anymore, because you wouldn't be able to see me in such despair without speaking a word of consolation. But I don't want to complain; if you don't love me anymore, it is as much my fault as yours. I couldn't bend to your whims. I couldn't win your confidence. But, if I was unable to keep your senses from succumbing to other temptations, I am still the faithful companion who took care of you with such devotion and happiness, the comrade who would have gone to the scaffold with you and whom you may one day find there by your side; for events are in the hands of fate, and there is nothing certain, nothing unbending other than that I love you and will follow you wherever you may need a strong and patient servant, a stoic friend, an attentive and submissive disciple. What did you ever have to reproach me, while I was in your sight? My only wrong, my only sorrow, is not being permanently there.

Now, at the present moment, what do you reproach me with? Are you looking for an excuse to leave me? Unfortunate man! Do you need an excuse, with me? So then you think you're dealing with a servile creature who'll drag herself at your feet, accusing you of cowardice, or who'll take her revenge by slandering you? I hope you don't feel contempt for me, Michel; be honest, in God's name; if you have something to reproach me for, tell me, because if it's true that you still love me, if you weren't mistaken in feeling a momentarily renewed tenderness, if you weren't lying to yourself in writing to me—not even eight days ago—that I should know that you love me even if you say the opposite, then I want—I must—I can feel justified. But, if you don't love me, what's the use? If you gave me a few caresses out of some remnant of love which has already vanished again, I have nothing to say. I accept all the wrongs it pleases your unreasonable pride to heap on woman, in order to take the load from your shoulders. Once again, I would request and invoke the confidence and esteem due me as a friend—the *only* friend you have—admit it. And as for you, are you not my friend? How many times have you said, and sworn, that no one would love me like you? Ah! if you love me, if you have loved me, at least, how can you play with me as a tiger its prey? How I have suffered, these past six months! My soul is broken, it has undergone a terrible struggle against itself. Love conquered pride in me, and pain is left as my reward, forever. But I've withstood so much weariness and anguish for the past three months, at my child's bedside, I am so tired that it seems I'll break, one of these mornings, with the frail existence I'm supporting and which only breathes through me. Alas! And if my son died tomorrow, I would not even have a word of tenderness from the only being I love as much as him, from the only one whose voice I can hear at this supreme moment! What, then, is love? Less than the very last of all friendships, since an impulse of worried selfishness or an irresistible need for infidelity closes against all pity a heart on which one was counting exclusively. And in your souls, oh creatures born of clay, does nothing of your ephemeral passions remain? When desire ends, has your wearied heart no concern, nor tears, nor devotion? O Spirit of wisdom! o Solitude, o Death, how you draw me toward you with iron chains on my arms, hacking out the way with an ax! How you chop down, so that I may walk more quickly, all the flowers and the fruits that could tempt me! How you destroy my joys, my illusions, my hopes! How you push me on this arid slope, toward the abyss at the bottom of which lies the unknown, the void perhaps, opening its arms to me! So be it! God's justice, whim or truth, I believed in you, but I didn't want to be happy on this earth without love, the only true belonging You let men glimpse.

———

From actress Sarah Bernhardt (1844–1923) to poet and playwright Jean Richepin (1849–1926). The two were lovers from early 1883 to 1884, when Bernhardt's husband, Jacques Damala, was away in North Africa and ailing from an addiction to morphine. Bernhardt had a difficult time with loyalty, not only to her husband, but to her lovers. This letter was written after Richepin disappeared in anger after one of her many infidelities. According to the biography The Divine Sarah *(Knopf, 1991), Bernhardt believed for years that Richepin would forgive her and return to her. He never did.*

[Summer, 1884]

Jean,

My despondent letters have been sent everywhere I thought you might be. No doubt not one of them has reached you. Will this one have the same fate? I do not know. I shall write all the same, and your friend Ponchon has taken it upon himself to bring it to you. I beg you on bended knee . . . to send me a word.

I am mad with grief. I cannot live in the deadly silence around me. I am suffering, Jean, suffering. Where are you going, what are you doing, and if you are hurt, and if—My God, I have done nothing to deserve such torture. Yes, yes, I was bad the other day. Oh, how I weep for that badness in me. How I regret having spoken evil words that you think of now that you are alone. Oh, my adored lover, my beloved idol, my seigneur, think only of the sweet, tender words I've said to you, my prince, of my absolute passion, my adoration, my devotion. I no longer have any pride. I am tamed! I am at your feet, submissive and repentant. Never, never again will I be bad; my wild love lives only to love you, to listen to you. My God, Jean, what have I done to deserve such treatment?

But then, you cannot know the anguish I feel since your departure. When I received your note, I collapsed, and I haven't left my bed since. Ponchon will tell you that only he can calm me . . . for with him I can speak of you . . .

Listen! Since you know so well how to hide, and since no one knows where you are, would you like me to join you? Nothing is important to me, not the theatre, not Maurice, nothing but you. I want you. I shall never look back. I shall be cowardly. I shall be despicable, but I shall be at your feet. Or tell me to kill myself, that you have had enough of me, that you no longer love me, that my love is a burden to you.

Seriously now, did you think that I could wait in silence? Have you never looked at me, never understood me when I made love to you? I weep, that's all. I weep and weeping makes me ugly. If you wanted to destroy my pride, subdue my will, force me to see that you are clearly the master, it is done . . . I fully realize that your will is stronger than mine since it allows you to make me suffer so . . . I no longer take pride in anything except loving you. Make me your slave, your possession, but keep your love for me. What dreadful nights I spend! I look for you, I pound your pillow, then I kiss it and beg it to confide in me, to tell me your last thoughts, the ones that carried you so far from me. How enormous the space is that separates us! The pillow does not answer, and I weep alone.

Pity! Have pity, my master. I beg you for mercy. I cannot go on. Everything has crumbled around me and those with me, stupefied

and desolate, watch me dying of love for you. None of that matters
. . . But what if you no longer love me. Tell me that you permit me
to come and look at you. I shall say nothing to you, nothing. I shall
kiss your lips, and, in a spasm of love, I shall gently kill myself with
your ivory knife. And you will throw your mistress's body into the
street. And no one will know, and then you will show them this
letter, and you will say, "You see, she was mad." And Ponchon, when
he shows them the insane things I've written to him, will also say,
"She was mad."

You see, Jean, that would be for the best, since I cannot go on
suffering. It is too much! I am suffocating. Perhaps to live is not all-
important, when I should have died in order to soften your heart.
Oh, my lover, let yourself be touched. You have tortured me so
much that you cannot do more. I beg you, take pity on your slave,
your mistress. I do not dare to kiss your lips if you do not wish it.

I love you.

———————

*The following letter was sent from American author Edith Wharton
(1862–1937) to the American journalist W. Morton Fullerton
(1866–1952). The two met in the spring of 1907 at the house of a
mutual friend in Paris, and Fullerton offered to help Wharton with the
publication of the French translation of The House of Mirth. They soon
were engaged in a full-blown courtship, although Wharton made every
effort to conceal the romance from her servants and peers. The two
exchanged letters after Wharton returned to America from France in
May 1908, but Fullerton's correspondences declined in frequency and
finally he stopped writing completely.*

*They did see one another in January of 1909; Wharton discovered
that there was at least one other woman in his life, and things seemed
to patch themselves up. As R. W. B. and Nancy Lewis say in The Letters of Edith Wharton (Collier, 1988): "The relationship with
Fullerton . . . passed recurringly through several distinct phases" and*

that "early in 1910 she starts to press for an end to the sexual part of their relationship." By the time this letter was written, say the Lewises, Wharton's involvement with Fullerton was marked by "diminishing conviction and dwindling passion. By 1911, they had become 'companions' . . . and were acting as one another's literary adviser."

[Mid-April 1910]

Don't think I am "fâchee," as you said yesterday; but I am sad & bewildered beyond words, & with all my other cares & bewilderments, I can't go on like this!

When I went away I thought I shd perhaps hear once from you. But you wrote me every day-you wrote me as you used to *three years ago!* And you provoked me to answer in the same way, because I could not see for what other purpose you were writing. I thought you wanted me to write what was in my heart!

Then I come back, & not a word, not a sign. You know that here it is impossible to exchange two words, & you come here, & come without even letting me know, so that it was a mere accident that I was at home. You go away, & again dead silence. I have been back three days, & I seem not to exist for you. I don't understand.

If I could lean on *some feeling* in you—a good & loyal friendship, if there's nothing else!—then I could go on, bear things, write, & arrange my life . . .

Now, ballottée [tossed] perpetually between one illusion & another by your strange confused conduct of the last six months, I can't any longer find a point de repère [landmark]. I don't know what you want, or what I am! You write to me like a lover, you treat me like a casual acquaintance!

Which are you—what am I?

Casual acquaintance, no; but a friend, yes. I've always told you I foresaw that solution, & accepted it in advance. But a certain consistency of affection is a fundamental part of friendship. One must know à quoi s'en tenir [what to hold on to]. And just as I think we have reached that stage, you revert abruptly to the other relation, &

assume that I have noticed no change in you, & that I have not suffered or wondered at it, but have carried on my life in serene insensibility until you chose to enter again suddenly into it.

I have borne all these inconsistencies & incoherences as long as I could, because I love you so much, & because I am so sorry for things in your life that are difficult & wearing—but I have never been capricious or exacting, I have never, I think, added to those difficulties, but have tried to lighten them for you by a frank & faithful friendship. Only now a sense of my worth, & a sense also that I can bear no more, makes me write this to you. Write me no more such letters as you sent me in England.

It is a cruel & capricious amusement.—It was not necessary to hurt me thus! I understand something of life, I judged you long ago, & I accepted you as you are, admiring all your gifts & your great charm, & seeking only to give you the kind of affection that should help you most, & lay the least claim on you in return. But one cannot have all one's passionate tenderness demanded one day, & ignored the next, without reason or explanation, as it has pleased you to do since your *enigmatic change in December*. I have had a difficult year—but the pain within my pain, the last turn of the screw, has been the impossibility of knowing what you wanted of me, & what you felt for me—at a time when it seemed natural that, if you had any sincere feeling for me, you should see my need of an equable friendship—I don't say love because that is not made to order!—but the kind of tried tenderness that old friends seek in each other in difficult moments of life. My life was better before I knew you. That is, for me, the sad conclusion of this sad year. And it is a bitter thing to say to the one being one has ever loved d'amour.

The following letters were written by writer Aline Bernstein (1881–1955) to novelist Thomas Wolfe (1900–1938), author of Look Homeward, Angel (1989) and Of Time and the River (1935), after their romance had ended. The married Bernstein met Wolfe when she

*was forty-four, he twenty-four. Five years later, in 1930, finding Bern-
stein's possessiveness and demands too much to bear, Wolfe stopped
responding to her letters. (He was then living in Europe.) Not until the
following year did he confess that his feelings toward her had changed.*

Armonk, N.Y. [July 1930]

My dear—

Rita Vail came up here for dinner last night and told me she had
seen you in Paris, in fact you had taken her out for a day somewhere. I also had a cable from Emily saying she did not know your
whereabouts but you are working hard. If she doesn't know where
you are how does she know you are working? At any rate it was kind
of her to answer. Thank God you are alright. Suddenly and for no
reason that I know, you have cut off all communication with me.
The effect on me is terrible, possibly I am crazy, for it is not sane for
one human being to be so sensitive to another. A course so wantonly
cruel is not sane, either. I can't do anything, I can do nothing but
think about you. I dread to wake up in the morning, the day is just
a horrid pain to be got through.—Have you no imagination, don't
you know by this time what you are doing, or do you know and is
that what you want.

I have never done you any harm. My love and my entire will have
always been directed to what was best for you, within my knowledge. I ask you to write to me and let me know what this is about.
This is the way things were when you left. You told me you no
longer loved me in anything but friendship and you demanded the
same of me. Of course I can't change my feeling on your demand,
but I had hoped that we would be those two loving friends. I can't
help loving you with all the intensity of my soul.

I believe that you are doing something in your behavior to me
that you don't understand. I think that you have no conception of
what it means, otherwise how could you eat your food or sleep or
work when you know what you are causing these thousands of miles
away. Fortunately I am by myself all day long. I have wild dreams of

coming to find you. I telephoned to two of my friends yesterday and was promised enough money.—Possibly you do not read my letters. Anything is possible. Possibly some miracle will happen. Aline

Armonk, N.Y. [August 1930]

My dear,

It is a week since your cable. I have waited hoping to have some letter from you. I am relieved that you are well, but wicked enough to have had some secret hope that it was not your intention to treat me so but some circumstance—I fear that you do not even read my letters now.

I stayed by you through your hard days, years, and now when I am down and you are secure, and I beg you for a little comfort, you won't even write me a word.—You must never revile people again, when your own performance is so base. How can you ever escape the evil of your own action to me, your best friend. In your last letter you sent me all your love. I want to believe it, I want still to think you are good. This is a tragedy you are making, and you or I or both of us will go down with it. I have had to refuse work because my mind can't do it and God knows I need the money, I am stony broke. You are now even with whatever ill you think life has done you. You have done so much to this life of mine. Just because you take this ruthless way. And you know that I love you too dearly to harm you. But some day your friend Mr. Perkins when he suffers at your hand the way I do now, will find you out. If you can hurt a dear friend once, you will do it again. Tom all I ask of you is to be my dear friend as you said you would. Surely that can't interfere with writing this new book of yours.

I am bound to you heart and soul forever[.] Aline

Armonk, N.Y./Westchester Co. [Late September 1930]

My dear—

I hope that wherever you may be this note will reach you on your birthday or before it. I send it off in good season. My head is filled with wishes for your success, and my heart is filled to overflowing with love for you. Aline

This is a drop of blood from the middle finger of my right hand. I opened it with a needle.

[New York, August 1931]

[no salutation]

I cannot sleep, this is what I think, there is nothing in life that cannot be made beautiful. Years ago I bought a jar on Allen street, because it had a good shape. I paid 65 cents for it. I scraped and polished it, and found it was made of copper with circles worked all round the bowl. It comes from somewhere in the east. I had it made into a lamp and every night when I put on the lights, its surface gives me back fires. It gives me this because I knew and recognized its beauty under the grime of its wandering. Last Saturday when it was so ghastly hot I went to market early, to White Plains. The roads here about are all being repaired. It was so hot the men worked with only pants, no shirts at all. One big man breaking stones [was] nearly as big as you are. I did not see his face, his back might almost have been yours, but nothing on God's earth would make me touch man's flesh that is not you. I thought if I put my hand upon a back, the tissue skin muscle is the same as yours, but nothing but you is you. So I am convinced that we are not nature's fools. We have soul, I review my life for you, and find I have come to a time so like the sadness of my childhood. I know now what I only feared then. If I show you this it is only so much stuff for you to use. You can't look into my heart. You have not the proper light to see. Time is not a dream, time has brought you to touch upon my life and now is moving you past in a widening arc. But what of time and me, I stay fixed in my circle like the planets.

Any plausible female will do for you, to spend the night or day, or to lie with. Only Tom will do for me. Since you left me I passed through fire and hell, maybe before I am through even jealousy will be burned from me. Only loving pity will be left for you who do not see. You said I am maudlin, if that is what I am, you will live to see the day when you will stand ashamed at your use of such a word. It is true I am maudlin, only because of the strength of a love that confuses my mind. You would put upon my love the ugliness of your desertion and a fidelity, but that does not change my undying fire- Your book will be so great that possibly the sum of my entire life will be nothing compared to it. So something beautiful may come of this constant misery I live.

[no signature]

The
Autopsy

au•top•sy (ô´tŏp´sē): *n.*, A critical assessment or examination after the fact.

The Autopsy *n.*, A breakup letter in which the writer recounts a relationship and attempts to explain exactly what went wrong; a breakup letter that employs critical techniques—including armchair psychoanalysis and the word "remember"—to create a detailed portrait of a romance and its failings.

From novelist Kate Field (1838–1896) to American artist Albert Baldwin (?–1896), whom she met in Florence, Italy and contemplated marrying. In a letter to her friend Cordelia Riddle Sanford in January 1861, Field said that Baldwin "will never be an artist, but he is a noble character and very well-educated" and that "his father is very wealthy." It is unclear exactly what happened between the two, but in <u>Kate Field: A Record</u> *(Little, Brown, 1899), author Lilian Whiting wrote that Baldwin had sought Field's hand in marriage numerous times, described the artist as "slow, hesitating, uncertain," and explained— somewhat cryptically—that their relationship, which lasted for seven or eight years, "persisted through a variety of stages." Field wrote a some- what-autobiographical poem about her love affair with Baldwin, titled "Drawing Room Drama," which was published in* <u>Appleton's Journal</u> *in 1877. In the poem, a woman tries to comfort her young cousin, whose heart has been broken by her lover, much as Field's was by Baldwin.*

Baldwin did not respond to this letter for five months, and when he did, on December 4th, 1868, he said that he was "inconstant" to her "because I could no longer shut my eyes to the fact that there was great incompatibility in our natures; that we had many traits of character, habits of thought, tastes, whims, or prejudices—whichever may be the proper term—that were too antagonistic to blend or to harmonize by contrast." Three years later, Field recorded in her diary that "this man has made a long journey to ask my forgiveness and declare his love, and I have refused him."

May 31, 1868

[108 W. 27th St.]
New York

It is five months since I received your last letter, and you undoubt-edly imagine that my silence has been owing to disgust or indigna-tion. Neither. I was at first disgusted, naturally, and therefore put your letter aside until I should be perfectly cool. The coolness came much before leisure. I have been so engrossed in business, people, and things—Dickens, especially, about whom I have written a series of photographs in book form—that I have never seen the moment until now that I could sit down and tell you my opinion of you and your letter.

First let me tell you that I renewed our correspondence after a year's cessation because I heard you were very ill, and because I at that time could write to you, having no other feeling toward you than that of a friend. I supposed you would understand this from the fact of my writing at all. It seemed to me consequently that your letters were anything but friendly, even brutal at times, but I so believed in your honesty and principle that I gave you the benefit of the doubt and laid all the shortcomings to bad health. We are the slaves of our nerves.

The letter you wrote last December ought to have been written in 1862. You were a moral coward not to have written it then. Now you know you were; therefore I shall say nothing further because I don't care. That episode has passed out of my life, and is as dead to me as if it were buried six feet under the ground. The friendship I entertained for you is very sensibly diminished by knowing more of your real character, but I have, at the same time, a certain respect for a man who even at the eleventh hour will voluntarily enter the confessional and show himself in his true colors.

By not writing that letter you made me fancy that I had allowed myself to be much more interested in you than you were in me. This is what made me so indignant *with myself* that ever since I have been trying to make the *amende honorable* by showing you that I was, after all, nothing more than a friend, that I had recovered from the delusion, after considerable mortification. Now I know that I was no such fool, that you were deeply interested in me, as I had reason to suppose at the time. I was young then and inexperienced, but not so inexperienced as to fancy myself admired without any foundation. This has always been the mystery to me,—that I, who never imagine I am making impressions, who give men the widest possible margin and rarely believe a word they say—when it comes to sentiment—should have made such an idiot of myself.

Your tardy letter assures me that I was not this idiot, and my regard for my own common sense is much greater that it has been for six years. I thank God that you did not remain longer in Florence and that I did not tarry in Paris, for had you offered me your hand, I should have accepted it, believing you to be other than you are,—and been cured. When my eyes open they open very wide. I am not one to submit tamely to wrong, and separation if not divorce would have been the inevitable consequence of such an ill-assorted union. You do well to say that you will never marry. No woman should be subjected to such a miserable fate. As a single man, infidelity hurts no one but yourself, provided you have honor enough to confine your flirtations to those who are educated in the art. I have no sympathy with flirtation. It must be a very cold nature that can play with fire. Neither do I admire fickleness. But your nature in no way concerns me, and pray don't imagine that I am lecturing. I am simply giving my opinion of you and your letter. It is unavoidable, and is given for the very last time.

I am not the Deity and having no claims to perfection do not intend to visit anathemas upon your head. You undoubtedly have many admirable qualities, and so long as you live I shall have hope of you. I believe that the time will come when you will be tired of your present order of exercises, and will care for more earnest friends. If you desire to retain me as an earnest friend, you can. I shall never flirt with you, never entertain you flippantly, *never go down to your lower nature.* You must come to me with the best there is in you. I will never tolerate any more cruel, unkind letters. Now we understand each other. If you choose to accept my terms, you can. If you do not care to do so, why, we will part. If ever I meet you it will be in the kindliest manner, for I shall always wish for you health, happiness, and ultimate regeneration. There is something of divinity in you, and the sooner it develops the better for you. You may laugh, but if you have a heart it will be more inclined to weep that a beautiful dream has vanished into such thin air.

Yours earnestly,
The Once Mistaken

———•———

These two letters were written by British mystery writer Dorothy L. Sayers (1893–1957) to John Cournos (1881–1966), a fellow author of thrillers with whom she had a brief affair. The two met in 1921 and Sayers fell immediately in love, but Cournos refused to marry her, saying he did not believe in marriage and did not desire children. Sayers ended the romance in mid-1922. Despite his pronouncements regarding marriage and children, that October Cournos returned to the United States and married detective novelist Helen Kestner Satterthwaite (who wrote under the pseudonym Sybil Norton) and supported her two children from a previous relationship. Sayers depicted the relationship in her novel Strong Poison *(1930), in which Cournos appeared as Philip Boyes, the victim of murder by arsenic poisoning.*

24 Great James St
W.C. I

22 August 1924

I say—wasn't I clever. Nobody knew—and don't tell anybody, please. Didn't even have to chuck my job!

Dear John,

I've heard you're married—I hope you are very very happy, with someone you can really love.

I went over the rocks. As you know, I was going there rapidly, but I preferred it shouldn't be with you, but with somebody I didn't really care twopence for. I couldn't have stood a catastrophe with you. It was a worse catastrophe than I intended, because I went and had a young son (thank God, it wasn't a daughter!) and the man's affection couldn't stand that strain and he chucked me and went off with someone else! I don't quite know what I'm going to do with the infant, but he's a very nice one!

Both of us did what we swore we'd never do, you see—I do hope your experiment turned out better than mine. You needn't bother about answering this unless you like, but somehow I've always felt I should like you to know. I hope you're ever so happy—

Dorothy

24 Great James St
W.C. I

[27 October 1924]

My dear John—
Have I really succeeded in astonishing you! And you who used to boast that you knew me better than I knew myself!—But if you really didn't know to what a desperate limit of endurance I had been pushed, you should never put a woman into your books again, for very lack of understanding! 'But why not me?' (He said with true masculine vanity.) Because (she replied) the one thing worse than bearing the child of a man you hate would be being condemned to be childless by the man you loved. So now you can sit down and apportion the praise and the blame and the motives and consequences for your next plot.—God bless you, man, I didn't want *his* son—that I've got one only goes to show that Nature refuses to be driven out, even with pitchforks—or other implements. However, since I suppose it is something to come out of such a hell with one's reason, one's health and one's job intact, I will accept your congratulations.

I tried to answer your letter before, but the result would not have made pleasant reading. To be frank, I'm badly disappointed. I wrote because I understood from somebody (who said they'd seen it in the papers), that you had really been generous to somebody after all, and I was sorry I'd misjudged you. But now you say that is an error—and when I ask if you are happy, you reply with shallow brutality about babies. Look here, John—when I see men callously and cheerfully denying women the full use of their bodies, while insisting with sobs and howls on the satisfaction of their own, I simply can't find it heroic, or kind, or anything but pretty rotten and feeble. Of course I know no woman wants to have bastard children—but that's why it's so jolly mean to take advantage of it. You see, I *know* now, what I only was sure of before, that the difference between the fruitful and the barren body is just that between conscious health and unconscious—what shall I call it?— uneasiness, discomfort, something that isn't quite health. Please take this from me—I have bought the right to say it to you. The fact is, I'm afraid that I'm the person you are always talking about and don't like when you meet her—a really rather primitive woman. I mean, I really do feel (not think, certainly, but feel) it disgraceful to be barren, or to give birth to girls (all girls, I mean—obviously there must be some)—and I'm disgustingly robust and happy-go-lucky about the actual process. And coarse and greedy like the women in the comic mediaeval stories. And really quite shameless. If I could have found a man to my measure, I could have put a torch to the world. Would you like to find me one, even now?

Now why in the world should you want to meet me? Last time we met, you told me with brutal frankness that you had no use for my conversation. Do you think my misfortunes will have added new lustre to my wit? Or am I to provide you with material for a new chapter of John Gombarov's philosophy? If I saw you, I should probably only cry—and I've been crying for about 3 years now and am heartily weary of the exercise. Or do you just want to know 'How *did* I do it?'—I can tell you that, without wallowing in sentimental misery in an atmosphere of toasted tea-cake. To carry it through one needs two things: a) guts, b) iron health. I was away from my job exactly 8 weeks. The day I met you in Southampton

Row was the day I left London 'on account of illness'. When I came back, I was congratulated on looking so much fatter than when I left. You can put that in a book if you like; no one will believe it.

These trifling vicissitudes have, as you may guess, somewhat delayed my new book. There are limits to even my creative energy. However, the original *Lord Peter* behaved like a trump in the way of paying doctors' bills, which was as well, since the individual who has the honour of being my son's father is penniless—and, indeed, somewhat indebted to me. Meanwhile, the younger generation displays a physical strength and general precocity which are quite alarming. I don't know what I shall do if he turns out an infant prodigy of any kind. It is very irritating to have no one to whom I can boast about him, but I'm afraid you don't sound as though you would be a very sympathetic listener. It's a 'ard world—peopled by savage women and tame men, isn't it, my civilised friend?—Don't grudge me that gibe—you can laugh at me if you like—the world's great lover—out of a job!

Dorothy

From author (<u>Save Me the Waltz,</u> 1932) Zelda Sayre Fitzgerald (1900–1948) to her husband, F. Scott Fitzgerald (1896–1940), author of <u>The Great Gatsby</u> (1925), while Zelda was in the psychiatric ward of a Maryland hospital. The couple, who met at a summertime dance following Zelda's graduation from high school in 1918, married in 1920; their daughter Frances Scott (Scottie), was born in 1921. By their own account, the marriage was a happy one in the beginning, but it was soon troubled by problems both internal and artistic: Zelda suffered her first nervous breakdown—she was later diagnosed as a schizophrenic—in 1930, and struggled to be taken seriously as a writer. (Her husband didn't help: he once called her a "third rate writer" and claimed that the story of their lives was his "material.") F. Scott, for his part, wasn't exactly devoid of difficulties: not only was he dealing with *a mentally ill wife, but struggling with severe alcoholism, mounting debts, and frustration with his writing. In 1933, after an awful and insulting three-way conversation with Zelda's psychiatrist, F. Scott consulted a lawyer about divorcing her, but, according to Nancy Milford's biography <u>Zelda</u> (Harper & Row, 1970), "He chose not to. They continued living together under . . . conditions of strain and distrust." In this letter, Zelda seems to be acknowledging an end of sorts and looks back on their early years with fondness and regret. F. Scott died of a heart attack five years after this letter was written, at the age of forty-four; Zelda died in a hospital fire in North Carolina in 1948.*

[Sheppard and Enoch Pratt Hospital
Towson, Maryland]

[June 1935]

Dearest and always
Dearest Scott:

I am sorry too that there should be nothing to greet you but an empty shell. The thought of the effort you have made over me, the suffering this *nothing* has cost would be unendurable to any save a completely vacuous mechanism. Had I any feelings they would all be bent in gratitude to you and in sorrow that of all my life there should not even be the smallest relic of the love and beauty that we started with to offer you at the end.

You have been so good to me—and all I can say is that there was always that deeper current running through my heart: my life—you.

You remember the roses in Kinneys yard—you were so gracious and I thought "he is the sweetest person in the world" and you said "darling." You still are. The wall was damp and mossy when we crossed the street and said we loved the south. I thought of the south and a happy past I'd never had and I thought I was part of the south. You said you loved this lovely land. The wistaria along the fence was green and the shade was cool and life was old.

—I wish I had thought something else—but it was a confederate, a romantic and nostalgic thought. My hair was damp when I took off my hat and I was safe and home and you were glad that I felt that way and you were reverent. We were gold and happy all the way home.

Now that there isn't any more happiness and home is gone and there isn't even any past and no emotions but those that were yours where there could be any comfort—it is a shame that we should have met in harshness and coldness where there was once so much tenderness and so many dreams. Your song.

I wish you had a little house with hollyhocks and a sycamore tree and the afternoon sun imbedding itself in a silver tea-pot. Scottie would be running about somewhere in white, in Renoir, and you will be writing books in dozens of volumes. And there will be honey still for tea, though the house should not be in Granchester—

I want you to be happy-if there were justice you would be happy—maybe you will be anyway—

Oh, Do-Do

Do-Do—

Zelda.

I love you anyway—even if there isn't any me or any love or even any life—

I love you.

———

From novelist Kate Christensen, author of <u>In the Drink</u> (Doubleday, 1999) and <u>Jeremy Throne</u> (Broadway, 2001). This letter was written when Christensen was twenty-six, and sent to John,* a thirty-year-old man she "was deeply in love with, had strong, passionate feelings for, but whom I didn't understand and who didn't understand me. We'd only been together a few months when I wrote this, but they felt like years. When I wrote this, I had just bought a one-way ticket to New York and was planning to move there and leave him, but after I left, the affair *went on for another few months (at least for me it did)—but for me, at the time, this letter was good-bye. I don't actually know whether I sent or showed or gave this to him. The point was to write it, I guess, to clarify things to myself. I might have sounded self-possessed and true to myself in the letter, but I certainly didn't act that way, or really feel that way, I was psyching myself up—it's always easier for me to be true to myself in writing than in real life. In the actual relationship, I was a mess . . ."*

[1987]

Dear John,

This whole incident bores and frustrates me so much I almost don't ever want to think or write or talk about it again. I left you that note yesterday in a hurry, asking you to come and see me last night—I had no time to say more, to apologize for the other day, and it didn't say what I was really feeling, which was sadness that I'm leaving. I dashed it off and thought no more about it, trusting that you would read it the way I'd intended it. And then you poked me awake at 1:30 in the morning, drunk in that mad way you get, and told me you thought it was a hostile note, and demanded some sort of explanation, apology, atonement . . . I don't really know what the fuck you wanted. During the next hour, while we were arguing about it, I had the feeling that nothing I could say or do could ever get through that impenetrable thickness of you, that no matter how hard I try I can't explain what I mean or why I am the way I am or who I am, even.

So you went away and I lay awake for hours, and I thought about why I'm leaving, because I don't think I've ever fully articulated it to either of us: I'm so tired of constantly feeling so wrong and in the wrong, wronging you constantly, when all I want to do is to express love for you, which I can do only in the ways I know how, which are never the right ones for you. You say over and over that I don't understand you, challenge you, "get" you, take you seriously enough, or myself. You think I'm a "case," you think I have "problems with men," when in fact I have problems with you, men aside.

And maybe it's not me. Maybe it's that I'm light and you're heavy, it's like oil and water, clouds and stones, it's temperamental, bio-chemical. There are great things between us, you're charming, hand-some, sexy, brilliant, and sometimes a lot of fun, generous, warm. But all along we've run smack against come fundamental incom-patibility that feels almost as if it's at a cellular or molecular level, or as if we're different subspecies, as if there's something too deeply dif-ferent about us to ever work through.

What makes it hard for me to be angry back at you is that I remember feeling this way from the minute we got together. Instead of listening to my gut, I started trying to take on ballast, to seem grounded and serious and responsive to your sadness and rage in hopes of connecting with you—I tried to adapt myself and change and be who you wanted instead of moving on . . . I sort of gave myself willful amnesia, hoping things would just "work out," thinking, I suppose, that I could "do this." I've felt all along that being with you is like some grueling physical challenge, like climbing Everest without oxygen, saying my macho diehard mantras and gritting my teeth . . . It also makes me loathe the way I am and question everything about myself. I've been trying to make myself known and understood in the face of what feels to me like your hard, unyielding, single-minded literalness: that's the challenge.

But my feeling after you left last night was: NO. I don't ever want to be poked awake again for leaving a silly, fond note that suddenly becomes a symbol in someone's mind for who I am, how I live my life and my "problems with men." All along, I've refrained from accusing you of having problems with women. I still will, it's irrele-vant how you were with anyone else—I'll stick to what's going on with me. Repeatedly, you leap to conclusions about me that infu-riate you and cause you to lash out at me about my perceived defects instead of asking me (calmly, rationally, open-mindedly, with real curiosity) to clarify or explain, and then listening to what I tell you—right away, before I've even finished, you leap at my throat and tell me I'm bogus, or full of shit, or elitist, or a nut case, or juvenile, or gutless, or in need of therapy (which I am, I know, but that isn't something to hurl at someone else accusingly).

And some dark, bottomless-pit part of me believes you and almost yearns to hear those things, even though they fill me with self-loathing and hopelessness and utter frustration, even though I know this relationship is, at bottom, destructive and bad for me and I shouldn't be in it, I shouldn't have to fight to be heard. I wasn't this way when we got together. I seem to recall feeling articulate, and knowing exactly what I thought—I was like a completely different person: confident, intelligent, ambitious, loving, kind and easy-going. I demanded to be listened to with the same respect I afforded others. I didn't take this kind of shit from anyone. Now I feel like I'm in a cult of two, not to get overly dramatic here, like I've been worn down and made to behave in ways that are anathema to who I really am. I fully admit my own culpability, my own part in this— no one held a gun to my head here.

You told me once that you have to make a conscious effort not to vent all the mean, nasty, cruel things you think about me. This rang alarm bells in my head (even though another part of me believed you, and agreed with you that it's all my fault, that those things are real)—and this keeps coming back to me in my saner moments. Why should I make someone feel such mean things? Is it really me? It strikes me that you take everything I say and do and am so per-sonally—as if at bottom I represent someone, something else, and you don't see me at all, it's not me you're reacting to. Meanwhile I'm reacting to my own phantoms, I grew up watching my father beat and abuse my mother and now I'm feeding into your treatment and your ideas of me so easily, effortlessly—that part of our relationship is what feels most natural to me, the core of our being together. And that's so fucked up, because I never thought I would let my father and my experience with him victimize me in this way, I never thought this could happen to me. Well, now I see that it can, and I have a horrible feeling it could get worse, a lot worse—physical abuse, total loss of self—before I'd end it. I'm afraid of being alone or left more than I'm afraid of being treated badly.

I see all this and have somehow seen it all along, and yet, astonishingly, I've continued to be involved with you. When things are good between us, I conveniently forget, I start to hope that these things are gone, an aberration. But lying awake last night I took a long honest look at our history, the things I've written about you in my journal, some of which I'm writing now in this letter—they're real and they'll never go away. I have to go away. I have to go back to integrity and self-love and what I truly believe in, to lightness, warmth, taking responsibility for yourself. I have to stop trying to win your approval because I know I never, ever will—you're identified with some sick, destructive kind of romance I can have no part of for very long, maybe because I'm not made that way. Your attachment to your own tragedy bores me, your heavy self-seriousness makes me itch to burst out laughing, to misbehave in school. I want to be with someone who loves me because I'm light and not in spite of it, someone who doesn't try to turn me into someone else, someone buoyant and glass-half-full who can laugh at himself and the world and human folly without minimizing any of the real darkness and sadness we all live with.

There's so much more to say but I can't say any more. Writing this letter about ending this with you is just another way to keep it all going, when what I need to do is sign off, and get out.

K.

———

From Danielle, twenty-one, to her ex-boyfriend Adam, whom she met the first week of college at the University of Hartford in September 1999. "Imagine: I was a freshman girl . . . with a junior boyfriend who was in the best fraternity. I was absolutely obsessed with him." Adam graduated in May 2001 and the two broke up that November, due to the pressures of maintaining a relationship between a student and a graduate. Danielle wrote the letter a few weeks after they parted, feeling that Adam did not understand that she did not want to be with him* *any longer, and that "he should see in plain text that this wasn't what I wanted anymore."*

[Fall 2001]

Dear Adam

It's so hard to deal with fights and drama with you every day and it makes me want to walk away from this relationship all together. I still want be able to talk to you on the phone and I want to stay talking to you for a long time and maybe one day in the future something could become of us. who knows what the future holds. Please don't be so negative when we talk. I am trying to be good with this whole thing and I can't get over the fact that you told me to get off my Gucci Prada Jappy ass and that you think I am shallow. Well honestly it takes a shallow person to know one. I don't even know you anymore and how dare you ever say to me that you think that I have problems and that I am nothing but problems. You have serious issues. I understand why you get upset with me but I want to be honest and open with you and make it so we can stay friends but if we are going to fight every second of everyday I just can't do this anymore. I can't stay involved with you. We shouldn't fight anymore and try to be civil. You were once the love of my life for so long and it will take a while for things to sink in but I feel it would be easier to have space permanently. Let me know how you feel without yelling at me. I can't handle when we fight. I don't want it to be like that. Please be honest with me about things. Write me back call me do whatever but you should really try talk to me without your snobby attitude.

Danielle

———

This letter was written by Jean Gelatt,* sixty-three, a museum administrative assistant in North Carolina, to Jack,* sixty-three, her *ex-boyfriend of a year. The two met in September 2000, through an internet personal ad, and dated until January 2001, when Jack announced that he was not ready for a romantic relationship. After a hiatus of a few months, Jack contacted Gelatt on Memorial Day of that year, writing her a "long and intense letter because the holiday had caused him to have some intense feelings," she says. She responded, and the two reconnected emotionally. In late October 2001, he "did another one of his flip-flops and decided that, even after he made declarations of deep love, that he hadn't really meant it," explains Gellat. "What he really wanted was to be able to call me up at any hour, drunk or sober, and pour his angst out . . . have a shoulder to cry on and someone to feed his ego without the investment of anything else." She wrote the letter the day after Jack called her "drunk and whiny." She never heard from him again.*

[November 17, 2001]

This is the way that I see it.

Between Thursday night, October 25th and October 27th, I sent you six emails in which I expressed a lot of thoughts and feelings. I have no way of knowing whether or not you got any of them because they were sent at a time when you were having a lot of trouble with your computer. Judging by last night's conversation, you either never read them or never got them or chose to not deal with any of that for whatever reason. So, I am going to cover some of that same material here as well as what I have learned since that time that serves to bring me to the place I find myself in today.

I once again last night told you what I thought you wanted to hear because each time I try to say what I am really feeling and thinking, that seems to upset you. (I set you free with a lie about how I truly felt once. You came back to me that time.) Each time I do that, I realize the error in that because what I am really feeling and thinking is my truth and it is my job to take care of me and to protect myself. It is not my job to make any of this easy for you. After I got off the phone last night, I spent some sleepless time trying to figure out why

I always elect to do that and I figured out that it is because I really do love you and I have for a long time. If that makes you uncomfortable in any way, how you handle that discomfort is your issue and not mine. This time I am going to set you free with the absolute truth as I see it . . .

When we met, I was recovering from my relationship with Don. That wasn't terribly healthy for either he or I because we had both been rebounding and acted far too hastily but I had done the grieving part of getting over that and was really ready to get on with my new life here in North Carolina. I was probably the healthiest I had been emotionally and mentally in a very long time. Although I found you very attractive, I was a bit hesitant to take things too terribly fast considering that unwise. You were nice looking, charming, smart, funny, and a great conversationalist. What was not to like? Over time I fell in love with you. I sensed that somewhere you were beginning to care a lot for me. Then you backed off and we drifted apart. Although that hurt me I was beginning to get over it and then you came back into my life and we resumed the "mating dance." (Live with it. It is my metaphor.)

In giving my heart and my love totally to you, I gave you the present of myself. View that as my having given you an Erector Set with a motor and control panels with pushbuttons and all the wonderful parts you could ever imagine. I handed the present to you and you happily opened it up. You declared that you loved it. Together, we began to build something really awesome with that Erector Set. From the moment that you declared yourself to be in love with this gift (me) and all of it's [sic]many and complex parts, and told me of all of the reasons that you have avoided letting yourself fall in love with other people's gifts to you in whatever form, something changed. It seem now as if you were so frightened by the prospect of what was growing between us that you made yourself physically sick and emotionally distant as a means of dealing with the anxiety that caused. You actually told me that I scared you to death and when I asked you how I scared you, you told me it was that you were beginning to care for me more than you could handle at the time.

The Autopsy

While we were in the process of building this wonderful construction with the Erector Set, you said a lot of marvelous things to me. You needn't have said any of them to get me into your bed because I got there on my own. You didn't need to say any of them to make me fall in love with you because I did that by myself as well. Since those appear to be the typical reasons men seem to use those words and since you were well aware of where I was, I took them to be real statements of your true feelings for me. At the time, it seemed to be a pretty obvious conclusion. (Later you would own up to "I probably meant that at the time. Probably? And that doesn't sound like something a jerk would say? Puh-lee-ee-ezz!) If you truly, as you stated, don't really know what love is and don't seem to think that you can feel those emotions, then how do you know when they are there and when they are missing?

When you got out of your comfort zone with all of this, rather than discuss any of this with me, you opted to begin to dismantle what we had been building and you did that in secret. At some point here, I began to recognize that some of the pieces that had been part of that creation had disappeared and when I looked for them, they were back, where you had put them, in the box with the unused parts. I tried in a lot of ways to get you to address this issue but you put up a lot of blocks to that happening. At some level I am sure that you had to recognize what you would risk losing by allowing that kind of a conversation.

Finally, after you had completely dismantled the thing that we had been building (keeping me at a physical distance with various maladies and other excuses) I finally was able to get you to at last declare your true feelings. Or at least the version you were able to deal with. It was not lost on me that you expected and welcomed hugs from Ron* and Phoebe* or your children but that you were avoiding as much physical contact with me as possible. You told me that touch made you anxious and that it was unwelcome. What you neglected to tell me was that it was only my touch that did that to you. Is it possible that was because it made it harder for you to remember that you were not in love with me? . . .

What I was trying to get across to you last night that seemed to get you so upset is that it is simply not fair for you to expect things to be business as usual between the two of us now that you have decided that you can't handle the whole package. You want the benefits that come with the level of communication and intimacy (mental and verbal) that came with your relationship with me. At the same time you are rejecting the parts of the gift I offered to you and you enjoyed playing with for awhile that you can't handle. From your point of view, that seems to be perfectly normal. From my point of view it is anything but normal. I am not "one of the guys." I am not, by your declaration, just another of your legion of female friends. I was/am in love with you. You declared yourself to be in love with me. You still insist that our relationship was different than any other for you. I really don't handle rejection well. If the situations were reversed, would you? A Leo? A pleaser? Hardly likely. . . .

You tell me that you experienced a level of intimacy (I'm not talking physically . . . well, there was one time when we both went somewhere physically, together, we had never been . . .) with me that you had never done with any woman in your lifetime. I know that is also true for me. There was not anything that I could not talk to you about. There was no direction in which I was not willing to go with you. There was nothing you could not ask me to do, either in or out of bed, that I would not have done. Did it ever occur to you that in order for that to happen, you just might have had to be in love with me? That is the way it works for me. Even having said all of that, I have to admit that there was something so awesomely different that I experienced with you that I never experienced with any other man I have ever known. But then you already know that. That's what empowers you. I willingly gave you that power. For me to regain all of my power is a process I must go through. (Part of the feeling I told you about having yesterday morning was that I once again owned my own power and that being able to say that out loud and know that it was true made me feel really great. It is apparent now that I still have some work to do on that issue.) It is part of what I have to do to move away from you since that is what you obviously want. It is not what I want but the choice is no longer mine. Therefore, I must act to handle that in the best way that I can find and that is my only option here.

So you have three glasses of wine and read something funny that I sent on to you and then you call me and for nearly an hour of that conversation we dissect our relationship and the aftermath of the disassembly of that creation and the return of that gift. In that hour, you declare as you have before in conversation in October with me, that you are not in love with me. That you tried very hard to fall in love with me but it just didn't happen. Since I am aware of your position on this issue from that previous conversation, whom are you trying to convince of the truth of that, you or me? I'm not the one you need to convince. I don't need to hear again that our relationship is the only one that ever inspired you to maintain contact with the woman you pushed away. That kind of special to you I don't need to be. Or at the very least, I don't need to be reminded of that again. How many times do you think that you have to repeat that litany to me? I got the message some time ago, first in the realization that you were pushing me away and then in finally making you say what was on your mind. I'm pretty intelligent, remember? How many times can I listen to those same words when each time I hear them, I realize just how much I do love you and how much I miss what we had constructed together that you lacked the courage to deal with? Why do you think that you need to imply that maybe I really am not in love with you to give credence to the idea that you are not in love with me? Give me a break here. I need time to heal. I had made much progress toward that goal and now here I am, back at square one. Spare me the lecture about how I will recover and get past all of this because I could teach the Ph.D. course in how to get on with one's life after a relationship dies. I have had some really good instructors lately.

The problem facing you, and it IS your problem and not mine, is that you are going to have to be willing to let go of all of me. You are going to have to take the risk that this one is just not going to go your way, now or ever. You are going to have to understand that, if life really is a crapshoot, then you have to roll the dice and know that they may come up snake eyes. You cannot eat your cake and have it too. It's time to stand up and act like a man and not a petulant little boy who has been told that he can't ride his bike for a week. You are not allowed to keep a part of what we had and send me packing to figure out what to do with the rest of the package. You cannot expect to call me up, either drunk or sober, and lay out your troubles with your neighbors or your family or whatever issue you are dealing with and let me be the one who provides the insight you seem to need from me to deal with those issues. In order for me to do that for you, I have to go to the place in me that loves you deeply. (The place that we began to build together on that memorable weekend in early June when we pretty much bared our souls to one another without a thought of baring our bodies even being involved. The same time when I realized how very special you were to me and exactly how much I loved you.) When you are content with what you have taken from my words and thoughts and go blissfully and numbly away, I am left to deal with the chaos in my heart that stirs up. You are not allowed to abuse me in that way. I no longer allow anyone to abuse me. If you cannot grasp that or if that causes you some angst or pisses you off, so be it. I am sorry to have caused that but I am responsible only for me. . . .

This letter is the biggest risk I have taken in this journey with you. I run the risk of losing touch with you completely because I have done something I always say that I will not do in a relationship and that is define rules. I firmly believe that although we all need boundaries and space, if we need rules within the framework of a relationship, we don't have much of a relationship. Or at least not a wholesome one. What I mean by that is, at this point, we either have a relationship or we don't. Apparently we don't. We all know that the transition from friendship to love is always easier than the one in the other direction. You appear to have made that one already. I have some work to do on it. I am not really sure who is the biggest loser here. It is probably about even.

Everything in my being right now is screaming, "Don't burn any bridges!" At heart that is not my intent. My intent is only to relate to you how I see the situation, how I feel about the situation, and how I know that I must deal with the part of the situation that is mine to deal with. I fully understand that neither my words nor my actions can take you where you decide you do not want to go. You must understand that if I am put in a position where I must open myself up to the kind of pain I am experiencing now, I may not always take this long and be so careful to choose the words that I think will best convey my feelings and my intent. And that would certainly burn bridges.

The thought of never seeing you again, of never hearing your voice again, of not having you in my life for the rest of my life as my friend, lover, companion, champion causes me pain to a depth that you can't even be aware of. The concept of having only part of that with you causes even more pain. The thought that I will someday recover from the pain gives me no comfort right now. A part of that concept last night appeared to be causing you some pain, also. Why? Because you need to feel that you can still get only what you want and need from me without giving back to me what I want and need? And you want to do that without feeling guilty?

And so with these words and thoughts, I set you free. As the Japanese say, if you come back to me it is because that will be your choice. Know that I do this with all my love and the truest wishes that you come to find true peace and serenity and happiness some-where on your journey. Know also that as you fly in whichever direction you feel guided toward, if you turn to look back at me, you will always be able to see me there, arm outstretched, palm up and open, a safe haven if you choose to return.

Love, Jean

The "Just Friends?"

just (jŭst) *adv.* Precisely; exactly. simply; certainly; perhaps; possibly; merely; only.

friend (frĕnd) *n.* A person whom one knows, likes, and trusts.

The Just Friends? *n.* a breakup letter written in which the writer attempts to ease a failed romance into a friendship, prevents an already-existing friendship from becoming romantic, or questions whether a friendship has romantic potential; exposition on the age-old issue as to whether men and women can simply be friends.

From 17th-century French courtesan Anne (Ninon) de L'Enclos (1616–1706) to the Marquis (Charles) de Sévigné (ca.1649–?), the son of the Marquis (Henri) de Sévigné (ca.1623-1651) and the celebrated letter-writer Madame (Marie) de Sévigné (1626–1696). Although Antonia Fraser's book <u>Love Letters: An Anthology</u> (Weidenfeld & Nicolson, 1976) asserts that the recipient of the following letter was the elder Marquis de Sévigné (Henri), with whom Ninon did have an affair when Charles was a young child, details and facts published in biographies of both Ninon and Madame de Sévigné (see Bibliography) indicate that Charles—not Henri—was the recipient.

The exact nature of the relationship between Ninon and Charles, however, remains unclear. According to <u>The Illustrated Life and Adventures of Ninon de L'Enclos</u> (T. B. Peterson and Brothers, 1849), Ninon began a correspondence with Charles after he asked her to school him on such topics as love, courtship, and gallantry. At some point the relationship became more than just epistolary: according to the biography <u>Madame de Sévigné: A Seventeenth-Century Life</u> (Berg, 1990), Ninon and the unmarried Charles did have some sort of romantic or sexual relationship but she soon broke it off. (She once said that Charles had "the simplicity of a dove, a soul of a panado [boiled, sweetened bread], a body of wet paper, and a heart of orange gourd, soused in snow.") What <u>is</u> clear is that the two did correspond, and that in the following letter Ninon is rebuffing him emotionally.

Ninon was celebrated for her numerous and high-profile lovers, including the Bourbon prince Louis de Condé, Gaspard de Coligny, and the writers Charles Saint-Evremond and François, duc de La Rochefoucauld. In 1671, after breaking off with Charles, Ninon retired and became a patron of the arts and hostess of a well-regarded salon. Of love, she said, "I have always sworn to my lovers to love them eternally, but for me eternity is a quarter of an hour."

Hell Hath No Fury

[ca.1670]

Letter LIII

I declare, that I shall at once break off all manner of commerce with you, for the future, if you continue to accost me in the way you have lately done. What evil spirit has put into your head to attempt rivalling the absent? Was any creature ever so teased and rallied as I was yesterday evening? However, you entered into your part with such address, that whatever mind I had to be angry with you, I could not find it in my heart to be so. What kind of issue this may take, I cannot say; but this one thing is certain, that you spend your time very idly; for, be assured, that I have not the least symptom of passion for you at present; and, what is more, I can answer for it that I never shall. Yes, Sir, never. But, 'tis merry enough, to persuade persons they are afflicted, that they want consolation, and, in short, to take upon you to judge of others' feelings better than they can themselves! This is like the impertinence of the shoemaker, who pretended to tell his customers where the shoe pinched them.

But to speak of this matter a little more seriously. Prithee, reflect for a moment on the folly of your attempt. Would it be generous, would it be decent in me, think you, to supplant my friend? For a woman, who has assumed the character of a Mentor, who has acted the part of a pare to you, to dwindle, after all, into that of a mistress? Rambling libertine, as you are, if youth and beauty could not hold you, what bands should such an old maid as I pretend to tie you with? Perhaps your sole view in my conquest, may be merely to know whether love is the same with me in practice as it is in speculation. But I will save you the expense of so much time and trouble, and shall satisfy your curiosity gratis.

You must know then, that women, one and all, rarely act conformably to their sentiments. This is what you would have the fullest instance of in a commerce of gallantry with me. All that I have said on love and women, would not instruct you in what manner I should conduct myself on such an occasion. There is a vast difference between thinking and feeling, between acting for ourselves and reasoning for others. You would then discover in me a number of singularities, that would soon make you weary of your engagements. I have quite a different cast of mind from most women. You may know them all without knowing Ninon. And believe me, that all you might discover new or extraordinary in me would not repay half the expense of investigation. You set my price too high, I tell you beforehand: you expect too much in expectation, more than I am responsible for. I should never quit cost, believe me. Dispose of yourself in a more brilliant list. The court affords you groups of young and fair, with whom you will run no hazard of tiring yourself with exertions of wit and philosophy.

I confess, however, that I should have been pleased if you had called on me today; for I was most of the afternoon plagued with a dispute about the ancients and moderns. It perplexes me so much still, that I am very near accepting your compliments seriously, that I am not yet far enough on the decline to occupy myself entirely with the study of science, or to bury myself alive with musty ancients. If you would behave a little rationally, and drop the humor of making speeches, I really think I should prefer your company to any other, to interrupt and enliven, now and then, to serious occupations. But you are so ungovernable, and such a profligate, that I dare hardly invite you to sup with me to-morrow; for it is now near two o'clock in the morning, and I consider that my letter cannot reach you till noon: so take notice, that it is this very evening I expect you.

Will you complain of me now? Is not this an assignation in form? But let this careless freedom convince you, that I am not much afraid of you, and that I shall attend to your amorous views no farther than will just amuse me. You ought to know that I am not a person to be easily imposed upon that way. I have you all by heart. Adieu.

From Dorothy Osborne (1627–1695), to Sir William Temple (1628–1699), in which Osborne attempts to talk Temple out of continuing *their relationship. Osborne, the daughter of a supporter of King Charles I, met Temple in 1647 as he crossed the English Channel into France and, according to <u>The Letters from Dorothy Osborne to William Temple</u> (Dulton, 1914), "Temple soon became, in the phrase of that time, her servant, and she returned his regard." But their families did not approve of the union—Dorothy's older brother happily took it upon himself to champion a series of far wealthier suitors for her—and the two corresponded in secret, their servants transporting their letters back and forth. Although this letter suggests that they abandon hopes of legitimizing their love and remain friends, the two did marry in 1655. Temple later became the Archbishop of Canterbury.*

[Thurs. –Sat. 8–10 Dec. 1653]

Sr

Having tired myself with thinking, I mean to weary you with reading, and revenge myself that way for all the unquiet thoughts you have given me. But I intended this a sober letter, and therefore, *sans raillery* [without jesting], let me tell you, I have seriously considered all our misfortunes, and can see no end to them but by submitting to that which we cannot avoid, and, by yielding to it, break the force of a blow which if resisted, brings a certain ruin. I think I need not tell you how dear you have been to me, nor that in your kindness I placed all the satisfaction of my life; 'twas the only happiness I proposed to myself, and had set my heart so much upon it that it was therefore made my punishment, to let me see that, how innocent soever I thought my affection, it was guilty in being greater than is allowable for things of this world.

'Tis not a melancholy humour gives me these apprehensions and inclinations, nor the persuasions of others; 'tis the result of a long strife with myself, before my reason could overcome my passion, or bring me to a perfect resignation to whatsoever is allotted for me. 'Tis now done, I hope, and I have nothing left but to persuade you to that, which I assure myself your own judgment will approve in the end, and your reason has often prevailed with you to offer; that which you would have done then out of kindness to me and point of honour, I would have you do now out of wisdom and kindness to yourself. Not that I would disclaim my part in it or lessen my obligation to you, no, I am your friend as much as ever I was in my life. I think more, and am sure I shall never be less. I have known you long enough to discern that you have all the qualities that make an excellent friend, and I shall endeavour to deserve that you may be so to me; but I would have you do this upon the justest grounds, and such as may conduce most to your quiet and future satisfaction. When we have tried all ways of happiness, there is no such thing to be found but in a mind conformed to one's condition, whatsoever it be, and in not aiming at anything that is either impossible or improbable; all the rest is but vanity and vexation of spirit, and I durst pronounce it so from that little knowledge I have had of the world, though I had not Scripture for my warrant. The shepherd that bragged to the traveler, who asked him, "What weather it was like to be?" that it should be what weather pleased him, and made it good by saying it should be what weather pleased God, and what pleased God should please him, said an excellent thing in rude language, and knew enough to make him the happiest person in the world if he made a right use on't. There can be no pleasure in a struggling life, and that folly which we condemn in an ambitious man, that's ever labouring for that which is hardly got and more uncertainly kept, is seen in all according to their several humours; in some 'tis covetousness, in others pride, in some a stubbornness of nature that chooses to go always against the tide, and in others an unfortunate fancy to things that are in themselves innocent till we make them otherwise by desiring them too much.

Of this sort I think you, and I, are; we have lived hitherto upon hopes so airy that I have often wondered how they could support the weight of our misfortunes; but passion gives a strength above nature, we see it in most people; and not to flatter ourselves, ours is but a refined degree of madness. What can it be, to be lost to all things in the world but the single object that takes up one's fancy, to lose all the quiet and repose of one's life in hunting after it, when there is so little likelihood of ever gaining it, and so many more probable accidents that will infallibly make us miss of it? And, which is more than all, 'tis being mastered by that which reason and religion teaches us to govern, and in that only gives us a pre-eminence above beasts. This, soberly consider'd, is enough to let us see our error, and consequently to persuade us to redeem it. To another person, I should justify myself that 'tis not a lightness in my nature, nor any interest that is not common to us both, that has wrought this change in me. To you that know my heart, and from whom I shall never hide it, to whom a thousand testimonies of my kindness can witness the reality of it, and whose friendship is not built upon common grounds, I have no more to say but that I impose not my opinions upon you, and that I had rather you took them up as your own choice than upon my entreaty. But if, as we have not differed in anything else, we could agree in this too, and resolve upon a friendship that will be much the perfecter for having nothing of passion in it, how happy might we be without so much as a fear of the change that any accident could bring! We might defy all that fortune would do, and putting off all disguise and constraint, with that which only made it necessary, make our lives as easy to us as the condition of this world will permit. I may own you as a person that I extremely value and esteem, and for whom I have a particular friendship, and you may consider me as one that will always be

Your faithful
Dorothy Osborne . . . [postscript omitted]

———

From actress Sarah Bernhardt (1844–1923) to the actor Jean Mounet-Sully (1841–1916), whose roles included Oedipus and Hamlet. The two became intimate in 1872, when Mounet-Sully was rehearsing the part of Oreste in Racine's tragedy <u>Andromaque,</u> and Bernhardt approached him, commenting on his good looks and inviting him to see her later that night. The two were soon in the throes of a torrid, volatile affair marked *by Mounet-Sully's outrage and frustration over Bernhardt's refusal to commit and her characteristic flightiness. She wrote this letter after another of Mounet-Sully's outbursts with regard to the direction their relationship was taking.*

[January 1874]

As far as I know I have done nothing to justify such behavior, I've told you distinctly that I do not love you any longer. I shook your hand and asked you to accept friendship in place of love. Why do you reproach me? Surely not for lack of frankness. I have been loyal: I have never deceived you; I have been yours completely. It is your fault that you have not known how to hold on to what is yours.

Besides, dear Jean, you must realize that I am not made for happiness. It is not my fault that I am constantly in search of new sensations, new emotions. That is how I shall be until my life is worn away. I am just as unsatisfied the morning after, as I am the night before. My heart demands more excitement than anyone can give it. My frail body is exhausted by the act of love. Never is it the love I dream of.

At this moment I am in a state of complete prostration. My life seems to have stopped. I feel neither joy nor sorrow. I wish you could forget me. What can I do? You must not be angry with me. I'm an incomplete person but a good one at heart. If I could prevent your suffering I would do so!!! But you *demand* my love, and it is you who have killed it!

I beg you, Jean, let us be friends.

From Stella Bowen (1893–1947), Australian artist, to writer Ford Madox Ford (1873–1939) (<u>The Good Soldier,</u> 1915, and <u>Parade's End,</u> a quartet of novels published posthumously in 1950), at the conclusion of their eleven-year affair. The two met in London in spring 1918 at a group dinner of writers and artists hosted by Ezra Pound. Though they never married—(Ford's wife Elsie refused to grant a

divorce)—Bowen and Ford lived together from 1919 to 1928 and pro-
duced a daughter, Julia, born in 1920. In 1928 they separated, in part
because of Ford's attachments to other women and Bowen's increasing
inability to deal with Ford's demanding personality. As Bowen put it,
"The obvious and banal business of remaining in love with someone
who has fallen for someone else is anybody's experience and no one will
deny that it hurts." But she was not so much bitter as contemplative
about the rupture: "Falling out of love is a delicate and important busi-
ness, and as necessary to the attainment of wisdom as the reverse expe-
rience," she said. The following letter was written during a trip Bowen
took to the south of France to think things over.

[n.p.]

18 April 1928

My dear.

I feel I ought to write something definite to you just as soon as possible, so that you may make your own plans and be relieved of the strain of uncertainty.

I am sure that there must be an absolute and public break between us. You yourself dismissed the idea of a 'half and half' separation and indeed I have come to think that it would not be feasible. And the complete camouflage would be impossible to me.

I shall therefore tell people, when I get back to Paris, that my absence until after your departure was because we had mutually agreed to separate for good. I cannot make up any tale of having 'chucked you out' nor will I use the word 'divorce' except when driven to it as for instance with Julie and the servants and strangers. My reason for avoiding the word 'divorce' is not because I want to make difficulties for you and R., [Rene Wright, his new lover] but because it seems to me undignified and ridiculous, when everyone knows the truth, and when Violet [Hunt, a former lover of Ford's] has so exhausted the topic of her marriage or non-marriage to you.

I cannot remain always in a false position and I can't face the world unless I may tell people something like the truth or be silent. But you know I am *very* good at being silent! If pushed, I might say that your interests seem to have shifted so much to New York, that in any case you do not propose being much in Paris, and that I have asked for my freedom, rather than to continue on the terms you offer. On your side you might represent me as having become impossibly independent, or anything you like.

I want *not* to be the one to begin any scandal about you and R., and in any case I will not say ill of either of you. We have had too good a time together for me to want to malign you now. And I should like you to remember that you said I might always tell people that we remain good friends in spite of it all, and that we keep in touch and will meet from time to time. It will be *much* better for Julie that this should be so and will do much for my happiness if it may be a real fact. You said R. might object to your remaining friendly with me except for the sake of keeping up appearances to protect your reputation. That protection of course you will lose, but I think public opinion—for what it is worth—would be softened if we announce that our relations remain cordial, and if I might continue to know what you are writing, etc., and be able to give people some news of your career. I think R. might be asked to be a sport about his. I am making everything else as easy as I can for her!

Don't let me become a 'bogie' for you both. I should hate that!

If it ever becomes known that we separated on account of R. I should like it also to be known that you wanted not to break with me outwardly, and that it was I who wished to end it all.

Of course I quite realize that by asking for a definite separation I give up all right to dictate on your acts and movements. I only ask that you should consider the disagreeableness to me of your taking R. to the houses of our friends in Paris, or living with her very publicly near to me and Julie.

My dear, I really decided all this before leaving Paris, but I thought it would hurt us both so much to discuss it again. But ever since I *did* decide it, all my bitter feelings have gone and I feel so much more sympathetic towards you and so much more anxious that you should be happy. It was the revolt against a false position that made me feel savage. So do try to think nicely of me, I have been so proud of my connection with you, and I have got my darling Julie out of it, not to mention a wonderful education in life! Our separation will make me all the more devoted to Julie—and she will be so happy when you come back to your little flat, and she can be with you.

My dear, there is little enough I can do for you now, except to wish you luck, and hope that this decision will bring you as much peace of mind as it has brought me. Please don't ask to see me again to discuss it. I shall pass through Paris early next week without seeing anybody, and will fix up the business at the mairie [mayor's office]. I hope the plans for the baptism go forward. I shall tell Julie I am going through on a non-stop train with a friend.

Any other material details will do for another letter. I will send you my Bandol address as soon as I have it. Goodbye my dear. Do remember sometimes, as I always shall, that we were very happy together and do let us stay friends. God bless you always—

Stella

———

A letter from writer/artist Elizabeth Waugh (1894–1944) to author Edmund Wilson (1895–1972). Waugh was married to Coulton Waugh, an artist and textile designer, and she became friends with Wilson in Provincetown, Massachusetts in the early 1930s. Wilson soon became romantically and sexually interested in Waugh, but she rebuffed him for some time, as is seen here. After this long flirtation, they consummated their passion in February 1937. The affair ended later that year after Wilson became involved with and later married author Mary McCarthy. The Princess with the Golden Hair (Fairleigh Dickinson University Press, 2000), a collection of Waugh's letters to Wilson, takes its title from the story of Imogen Loomis in Wilson's Memoirs of Hecate County (1946); the novella's main character was closely modeled after Elizabeth Waugh.

[January 23, 1937]

[From NYC]
Dear Bunny:

I've been thinking about you. It appears that I have thought only of you for four years. Also I've been thinking of murder. I feel as if I had committed one. It's horrible. You are right about my imagination's [being] too realistic. It has been as if we had had an affair. As if we had quarreled bitterly because I could not give you more time; as if our friends with malicious eyes had seen us; as if Coulton had found out (as he heard me call you up so mysteriously last summer). I see many details it would be too provocative to mention.

Let me go! No good will come of it. You can see the tragedy under my eyes. I mean back of my eyes. Did you ever have an electric light bulb burst and almost blind you? That's what would happen to me with too much emotion—. I'm not like other people. My life has not been like other lives. Men on the street, all kinds, look at me and don't take their eyes away. Yet I'm not young any more. I think it's because I seem strange to them.

It will be just as hard for you as it will for me. I know that you need me. I need you too, but it would be terrible for you too, because you love me and you would regret your part as you have never regretted any thing before.

I am prepared to do anything to really get away, but I don't want to be driven to these measures. I want you to help in this. You ought to help.

Elizabeth

Saturday

I'm able to paint now. Perhaps I shall be brought to bed of my talents.

Hell Hath No Fury

From The Second Sex *(1949, tr. 1953) author Simone de Beauvoir (1908–1986) to Nelson Algren (1909–1981), author of* The Man with the Golden Arm, *with whom she began a love affair in early 1947, while she was visiting Chicago. Although de Beauvoir, in a letter to her long-time companion Jean-Paul Sartre, described Algren as " . . . a typical American with a wooden face and an inexpressive body . . . ," she was in love. In May of that year, de Beauvoir returned to Paris and the couple—now separated by the Atlantic Ocean—kept up their romance with numerous letters and trips back and forth. In July 1950, de Beauvoir went to visit Algren in Chicago, only to find him emotionally detached, unable to make love, and claiming that he was incapable of ever loving a woman again. The frequent separations had finally had an effect on him: he wanted someone permanent in his life, and he was going to remarry his ex-wife Amanda Kontowicz. (They remarried in 1953 and divorced again two years later.) The letter below was written that September, as de Beauvoir was on her way back to Paris. As she recounted in her autobiography* Force of Circumstance *(1963, tr. 1965), before she left Chicago, she told Algren that she had had a very nice time and was glad that they still had a real friendship. "It's not friendship," he replied. "I can never offer you less than love." Despite this statement, the two kept in touch until 1964, when Algren cut off all contact with de Beauvoir after the American publication of* Force of Circumstance.

Hotel Lincoln, New York 30 Septembre 1950

Nelson, my dearest sweetest one,

You had just left when a man came smiling and gave me this beautiful crazy flower, with the two little birds and the love from Nelson. That nearly spoilt my fine behaviour: it was hard to "weep no more." Yet, I am better at dry sadness than at cold anger, for I remained dry eyed until now, as dry as smoked fish, but my heart is a kind of dirty soft custard inside. I waited for an hour and a half at the airport, because of the weather; the plane from Los Angeles had not been able to land in this fog. It was right that you went away; this last waiting is always too long, but it was good that you had come. Thanks for the flower and for coming, not to speak of the other things. So I waited with the purple flower on my breast, pretending to read the MacDonald mystery, and then we took off. The trip was very easy—no tossing at all. I did not sleep but pretended to read the mystery to the end, and kept fondling you in my dirty, silly heart.

New York was a beauty: hot, sunny, and grey at the same time. What a glamorous city! I did not want to break my heart by going to the Brittany. I picked the Lincoln where I had landed three years ago, when I knew nobody in this whole continent and did not suspect I should be so strangely trapped in Chicago. I got exactly the same room I had, a little nearer the sky, but identical. How queer to find myself in this faraway past again! As I did three years ago, I went to Lincoln beauty shop: no trouble either, the hotel seems empty, the beauty shop empty. Then I bought the pen for Olga, which was fourteen, so I am glad you gave me so much dollars; I'll just make it. And I walked and walked in the town, along this Third Avenue, which we walked thoroughly down the last night, two years ago, all around the Brittany, too, and once more I found you everywhere and reminded everything. I wandered in Washington [Square] park where they have a kind of flea-market and bad painting sale; I went up the Fifth Avenue bus and saw the night come down on New York.

Now it is nine, I just had a little sandwich since the plane, no sleep since Wabansia; I am awfully tired. I came to my room to write to you and drink scotch. But I don't think I can go to bed now. I feel New York around me, behind me our summer. I'll go to bed now. I'll go down and walk and dream around, until I am utterly exhausted.

I am not sad. Rather stunned, very far away from myself, not really believing you are now so far, so far, you so near. I want to tell you only two things before leaving, and then I'll not speak about it any more, I promise. First, I hope so much, I want and need so much to see you again, some day. But, *remember, please,* I shall never more *ask* to see you—not from any pride since I have none with you, as you know, but our meeting will mean something only when you wish it. So, I'll wait. When you'll wish it, just tell. I shall not assume that you love me anew, not even that you have to sleep with me, and we have not to stay together such a long time—just as you feel, and when you feel. But know that I'll always long for your asking me. No, I cannot think that I shall not see you again. I have lost your love and it was (it is) painful, but shall not lose *you*. Anyhow, you gave me so much, Nelson, what you gave me meant so much, that you could never take it back. And then your tenderness and friendship were so precious to me that I can still feel warm and happy and harshly grateful when I look at you inside me. I do hope this tenderness and friendship will never, never desert me. As for me, it is baffling to say so and I feel ashamed, but it is the only true truth: I just love as much as I did when I landed into your disappointed arms, that means with my whole self and all my dirty heart; I cannot do less. But that will not bother you, honey, and don't make writing letters any kind of a duty, just write when you feel like it, knowing every time it will make me very happy.

Well, all words seem silly. You seem so near, so near, let me come near to you, too. And let me, as in the past times, let me be in my own heart forever.

Your own Simone

———

From traveler, explorer, spy, author and Middle Eastern expert Dame Freya Stark (1893–1993) to her husband Stewart Perowne (1901–1989). Stark married Perowne, a gay British colonial official and writer, in 1947, when she was fifty-four years old and he was forty-six. But within six months, Stark was complaining to friends that the marriage was not going well: Perowne sulked if she became too lively and snubbed her often. In 1948 he confessed to her that he was gay. In the spring of 1952, after the mandatory five years of marriage had passed, they divorced.

Asolo, 19 March 1951

My darling,

Things are so sad and superficial between us that I have long been feeling that they cannot go on as they were and have only waited to write or speak because I could not bear you to think that any trivial cause, or want of affection, made me do it; and also because I hoped that you yourself might feel this thing so near your heart as to make you speak before I left.

I don't know whose the fault, anyway it doesn't matter. If it were just that the thing has failed, it would be simple. We are both independent, and we could separate and go back to where we were. I do care for you, but I have tried to take myself out of this account and to think of the whole thing without any bias as far as I can; one of these days I believe you will discover that you do care.

Let it be friendship meanwhile, and not just acquaintance. Half a dozen people around us tell me their hearts more intimately than you do. Better just to come and go as friends and that I will always be. There is nothing but true affection in my heart.

I have kept this for a day before sending, feeling perhaps that I might not send it at all, but there *must* be a truth between us, and it is the truth. Let it not make any difference to what we are to each other, such dear friends, and with true and safe affection, let it only take away what there was of pretence. I long for you to come here and you know it is your true home.

Love,
Freya

From American poet Sylvia Plath (1932–1963) to her childhood friend, Wellesley, Massachusetts neighbor, tennis partner, and brief lover Philip McCurdy. The two met in 1946 when Plath was in the ninth grade, and became close friends, confiding in one another about everything from sex *to their hopes for the future. In 1952 Plath wrote in her journal that she and McCurdy had brushed hands accidentally while both were leaning down to pet his dog, and wondered if there was more than just friendship afoot. According to Paul Alexander's biography <u>Rough Magic</u> (Viking, 1991), Plath lost her virginity to McCurdy two years later, in early 1954, when the two became intimate while sitting in McCurdy's car outside of her house. (A competing biography says that her high school boyfriend Dick Norton was her first lover.) They made love again a second time soon afterwards, but Plath—only months past her first suicide attempt—decided that it was better that they remain friends and wrote him this letter. McCurdy inspired the hero of Plath's first published story, <u>And Summer Will Not Come Again,</u> which was published in the August 1950 issue of <u>Seventeen</u> magazine, and concerns a young girl who falls for her tennis instructor. Plath killed herself on February 11, 1963.*

[Mr. Philip McCurdy]
[Adams House B-15]
[STREET & SMITH PUBLICATIONS]
[INTER OFFICE MEMORANDUM]

TO: Phil
FROM: Syl
SUBJECT: Life in general
DATE: Feb. 4 1954

Hello . . .

I am being very naughty and un–Emily Postish by using up my favorite tag ends of interoffice paper for stationery . . . but I did enjoy employing them this summer, and I trust that you know me well enough not to mind my little idiosyncrasies . . . and my penchant for typing personal missives. Which this is.

You should, by the way, feel a bit honored, since this is The First letter I am writing to anyone from my new and most agreeable abode, in spite of the fact that I have a list of unanswered letters about as long as the road from here to Harvard. I hope you don't hate yellow paper. But I like writing on unique things . . . like birch bark, for instance.

Your most excellent and quite delightful letter arrived in the mail this morning, and for some reason . . . or reasons, made me rather happy. You said everything so well, and I very much was pleased with the gist of your statements . . . Even the letter paper you used made me realize how close we are in so many of our tastes, . . . the small material ones as well as the larger philosophical ones. Because I like gray paper with red letterheads (have some myself), and I always use black ink. Minor observation perhaps, but of interest nevertheless.

Before plunging into the more basic personal and philosophical topics, just a few words about what has happened since we last saw each other. I don't know if I told you over the phone Saturday that last Sunday I spent the afternoon at the Crockett's [*sic*] home. The whole affair was delightful; a ruddy fire was leaping and crackling in the fireplace, Mrs. Crockett served tea and homemade raspberry tarts, Mr. C. was at his intellectual best, and Little Deborah was a dear—we got along well immediately, and evidently she was crushed that I couldn't stay to eat supper with her. We all discussed Eliot's play, which we'd seen, and then listened to an excellent collection of Robert Frost records. The poet's voice is so appropriate to his poems—as rough and textured as granite or the bark of wood; it's just as if he were leaning over a split-rail fence and chatting in a neighborly fashion about country life. All in all, I had a fine time.

Warren drove me up to Smith through snow and sleet after I talked with you, and we almost had a rather drastic accident which left me pale and rather shaky for about half-an-hour afterwards. Coming into Northampton we drove into a thick dark blizzard, and as we began to descend the steep unplowed hill by Paradise (ironic name!) Pond, the car turned into a skid the likes of which I've never seen before and hope never to see again. We sped down the hill sideways, tilting dangerously and completely out of control. Ahead there were three possibilities, all equally unpleasant: We could smash through the glass windows of the green house on the left, crash into the car in front of it, or roll down the steep incline into Paradise Pond. I just remember saying in a repititious [*sic*] conversational way: oh god god god god god god . . . as we spun around and ended up facing up the hill from whence we had come. All's well that ends well, as the cat said as he devoured the last of the canary.

Anyhow, I'm here, in my old room (now a single) in my dear old cooperative house, with two bookcases full of my books. and the sun streaming in the three big windows. I'm passionately in love with all my courses: early American Lit. (Hawthorne, Melville and Henry James), Modern American Lit. with the well-known critic R. G. Davis (the one who went to Washington for the Communist trials last year), European Intellectual History of the Nineteenth Century with a magnificent and powerful German woman, Russian Lit. (Tolstoy and Dostoevsky) and Medieval Art History.

Honestly, I wish you could some day come up just to audit some of my courses with me . . . I know you'd enjoy them immensely. I've spent most of my free afternoons (all my classes are in the morning) shopping for books and necessities to make my room look like home, plus having appointment with the powers that be in College Hall . . . all of whom have welcomed me back with open arms, so to speak, the lovely people.

Litza Olmstead (or however you spell it) is in my house . . . a very attractive girl, I must say. In fact the underclassmen are all most intelligent and friendly.

Enough of this external commentary. If you are the way I am about such things, you have been impatiently skimming through all this and wanting me to begin on the more abstract and internal issues. So I will.

As far as seeing you again is concerned, you have no need to wonder at all about that. I'd really like very much to continue to see you often in the future, because you are, and most probably will always be, one of my favorite people. So if you ever feel like coming up for a day or so some weekend, just let me know ahead of time, and I'll plan to be free for some good long walks and talks and so on. I don't know if I'll have the chance to come home for a weekend before spring vacation begins on March 24, but I certainly hope I will be able to, and if so, I'll let you know, and perhaps we can get together. It's all up to you about convenient times, etc.

As to our rather unique evening—any departure from conduct and "ritual" which has been agreed upon tacitly involves complexities in that it demands a reassessment of the situation, a consideration of former intentions in the light of an altered context. And for that reason our evening may have given rise to problems which, although complicated, may be resolved.

Our contact in the past has been what one may call "platonic" . . . and, I think, quite satisfying on an idealistic and intellectual plane, while involving walks, tennis, biking, and so forth. And our platonic relationship, as such, I think is capable of continuing without any emotional and physical involvement: in other words, it can continue to burn like a fire to which new kindling (of an evolving mental sort) is always being added. As long as we continue to grow individually, I think we will be close friends. . . .

But the recent addition of a new quantity to our relationship, while intrinsically pleasant, may confuse the issue, perhaps even unwisely so. Both of us Phil, I am pretty sure, know a good deal about physical attractions to the opposite sex (to be pedantic, and perhaps euphemistic) and have no doubt even accepted physical relationships of a temporary and unsubstantial sort just for the ephemeral transient pleasure of it . . . but while a kiss, let's say, can be just a simple physical act performed out of mere biological hedonism, it can also be symbolic of a great depth of mental and philosophical rapport and appreciation. The difficulty is in distinguishing between the two aspects of the same act, and the effort can sometimes prove confusing. You expressed essentially the same thing when you talked about the difficulty of endowing the same words with new and sincere meaning. It's a difficult job, I think.

And while we can satisfy ourselves physically with a great range of other males and females, an intellectual and spiritual (damn it, the words sound so trite) relationship such as we have had is rather at a premium, and therefore is much more important to retain than anything else. And since a physical relationship can add such complications to a companionship (which we hope to maintain far in the future,) it might be wiser to return to what we had before and leave it at that; I don't know. But I don't ever want to run the risk of spoiling the continued knowing of you, Phil . . . and somehow after a close physical relationship becomes impractical or impossible (for any number of reasons,) it is relatively unusual to continue the comradeship that gave rise to it originally. And I don't want anything like this to happen. So it might be safer to just keep on seeing each other—for lectures, plays or dances or just talks and tennis—and let the rest of alone as far as each of us is concerned. I'm not sure just how you feel about it, but perhaps we can talk about this at length the next time we see each other . . . sometimes it's easier to talk face to face, you know . . .

Anyhow, I hope my attempt to explain a little of how I feel about the situation had been at least partially coherent . . .

I will enjoy hearing from you, Phil, and hope that we can get together again soon—-and in the meantime, my very fond love. . . .

as ever
Syl

From Princess Margaret, younger sister of Queen Elizabeth II, to Robin Douglas-Home, the nephew of Alec Douglas-Home, British Prime Minister from 1963 to 1964. Margaret, who had long suspected her husband Anthony Armstrong-Jones (the Earl of Snowdon) of engaging in extramarital affairs, had carried on a brief but passionate relationship with Douglas-Home. But her husband, furious over her infidelity, confronted her and in this letter she breaks off the relationship (she was reported to have taken up with comedian Peter Sellers soon afterwards). On October 15, 1968, Douglas-Home committed suicide by overdosing on pills in the bed he had slept in with Margaret. Two weeks before his suicide, he told Noel Botham, author of Margaret: The Untold Story

(Blake, 1995): "Margaret said she was putting duty before happiness. That's what she's always said to get out of a romance." Margaret and Snowdon divorced in 1978, the first divorce in the royal family since Henry VIII parted from Anne of Cleves (see p. 143). Margaret died on February 9, 2002, at the age of seventy-one.

25 March 1967

Darling,

I have never had a letter like it. I don't suppose one has even been written. The beauty in it and the poetry lifted my heart again . . . I think all the time of you . . . and I would do anything as you know to make you happy and not hurt you . . . And know always that I want you . . . Trust me and trust you and love me as I love you. Our love has the passionate scent of new mown grass and lilies about it—Not many people are lucky enough to have known any love like this. I feel so happy that it has happened to me . . . I will try and come back to you one day. I [daren't] at the moment . . . you are good and loyal, think that I am too whatever I may seem to do or say. All my love my darling,

M.

———

From poet Anne Sexton (1928–1974) to Philip Legler (1928–1992), a poet (<u>The Intruder and Other Poems,</u> 1972) and professor of English. The two met in April 1966, at a reading of Sexton's work at Sweet Briar College. At a party afterwards, Sexton, who had taken some "pills" and become disoriented, had to be carried by Legler to her motel. Immediately infatuated, (and seemingly unhinged), Legler wrote her a love letter later that night, and the next day checked himself into a psychiatric hospital in Richmond. Over the next few years the two kept in touch and, in early 1973, Legler, having heard news of Sexton's impending divorce from her husband Alfred ("Kayo") Sexton, invited

*her to give a reading at Northern Michigan University where he was
then teaching. That July, Sexton spent a week with Legler in Michigan
and fell deeply in love with him; they carried on an affair until Legler
broke it off in late September. Sexton divorced Kayo—which Kayo con-
tested, afraid that she was not in her right mind—in late 1973 and
committed suicide a year after the divorce, in October 1974.*

[14 Black Oak Road]

May 19th, 1970

Dear Phil Baby,

I will have to burn your letter as incriminating evidence . . . but
that's not the point. Your letter is full of love and I wish I could keep
it. I do know you love me more than most people do. Perhaps my
husband more because he had to live with me. Sometimes I think he
deserves an award for putting up with me. Other times I think he's
pretty lucky. Lucky because I'm quite naturally a loving, affectionate
person. But then, even that can get to be a bore.

I'm sorry I put your hand in a tin box. God, I'm sorry. I didn't
mean to really. You know I've never slept with anyone on a reading
. . . never a one-night stand . . . never something so casual or light-
hearted. I'm just not the type. I'm a pretty faithful type when you
come right down to it. Sleeping with someone is almost like marrying them. It takes time and thought. If you lived in Boston or I
lived where the lovely fog horns are . . . but even then I'm not sure.
Just that it wasn't possible that time. I've got to be true to myself as
well as to you. Further, I think I'm so busy fighting the suicide
demons that I have little time for love. You saw how I go to sleep—
not sleep at all. You said it[:] "death touched me." I hope to hell my
present shrink can help me work this out before it's too late.

I zapped into your life and I'm so glad I did. I'll never really zap
out. Put me there, friend, friend, forever.

. . . next day . . .

I've been out killing dandelions. It's a lovely spring day. I think

I'll go out into [it] again. The manager (Bob) of "Her Kind" (my rock group) is coming over for lunch, or rather bringing the lunch. I will sit in the shade (thorazine makes me allergic to the sun) and he will sit in the sun. How I miss that!

I finished that fairy tale ("The Maiden Without Hands") last week and am thinking about doing Hansel and Gretel. My transformations of the Brothers Grimm are full of food images but what could be more directly food than cooking the kids and finally the wicked lady. Smack in the oven like a roast lamb.

Readings are accumulating for next year. I'll do a few of them I hope. Enough to pull in some dough to help out but not enough to drain me too much. I find them very hard to do . . . particularly those informal classes where (as they say) I can do anything I want . . . Mostly I don't want. That's the trouble. But you, Phil, make it easy on me and helped in every way. I thank you. That's still the nicest Holiday Inn I ever stayed in. And I can remember those ghost-like fog horns. I remember too you tucking me in bed and patting my head so gently. I don't forget! Love to you, my dear,

Annie Babe

The following letter was found on a street in downtown Manhattan in the spring of 2001. Efforts were made to find the author, based on the name of an independent film that is mentioned in the letter, but they proved futile.

Dear Guile,*

I'm writing this for me. I've been silenced for too long, and since we might have to see each other through work, I'd rather be straight about my feelings. I've been overly considerate of yours and it's time for me to consider mine. I sometimes forget relating is a two-way street, in my efforts to understand others.

I thought you were a kindred spirit amidst all the noise of [name

97

of independent film]. A gentle soul who understood that "pushing your way through life" pushes away the beauty of human experience.

I walked a fine line between you and Samantha.* She telling me things about you, you would never tell me, things I didn't want to know, things that explained your sad smile, your shadow of loneliness. But it was too personal for me to ever reveal. So I choose to remain silent and try to make you laugh instead. What amazed me was with all that she knows, she still seemed not to know you. Maybe that's why you trust her so much? She hears and sees but doesn't perceive?

I guess that's why I feel so hurt by your indifference, your need to contain me. To be put away in a box, like some favorite toy you've outgrown. I kept your secrets without you asking and yet you treat me like I've tried to stormtroop my way into your life. As if you have the right to respond to me when you feel like it and I'm supposed to reciprocate. But I don't have the right to respond to you. Some examples:

You were very aggressive in asking me personal questions about my life and family regardless of who was present. "Are your parents divorced?" "Why do you always quote your mother?" "Were you out with your boyfriend?" etc. etc. Yet when I asked you a few questions you said I was consuming you. As if I was being rude and how dare I ask questions.

Your public flirting made me very uncomfortable, knowing that I was in no position to respond to you because of Samantha. You'd nuzzle my nose and feet, say things of a suggestive nature. Were you doing this for Samantha? To play games? To prove you were your own man? Well you forgot about me in the middle. She's not over you. I saw how jealous she became at your screening when any woman came near you. Perhaps your male ego "gets off" on this?

When I tried to reciprocate, but privately, through my card or dinner invitation, you completely ignored them. Again showing you believe in your right to play and get a response. But not mine.

The final straw was my call to you early this month. You were quick to put me in my place, making me feel like I'm imposing on your precious time.

I guess this shows I'm a sucker, and actions speak louder than words. In the end, I'm the one who doesn't perceive, not Samantha. For I saw things that were obviously not there.

Louise*

From <u>Sex and the City</u> writer/executive producer Cindy Chupack, thirty-seven, to her friend Rick,* for whom she had feelings, but whose intentions she was unable to read. "I felt like I knew the answer—that he just wanted to be friends—yet I wanted him to have to say it, because we'd been out several times and it didn't feel like we were just heading for a friendship," says Chupack. "I was at a point in my dating life where I just wanted everybody to be clear. I can take rejection, but it's the grey areas that kill me."

At the time this letter was written, Chupack had been inviting Rick to be her date to parties in the Hamptons; one night, after heading back to her motel room together, she discovered that she'd lost her room key and asked him, "What would happen if we kissed?"

He replied, "Maybe we should just take care of the matter at hand."

"It was pretty awful," says Chupack, "because I had to put on my helmet and sit behind him on his motorcycle right afterwards so he could take me back to the party where we might find someone who could help me get into my room." Eventually, Rick confessed to Chupack that soon after meeting her he had started seeing someone he really liked, "someone in her twenties who worked in a gallery and who, I imagine, wouldn't lose her room key because she wouldn't have her own room. You know the type."

[Summer 2001]

Hey Rick,

I just got back from the Hamptons tonight and I felt like writing you to clarify something, but I'm not sure I should write, and I know you're not regularly checking your e-mail, so it's almost like not writing. How's that for logic?

I'm getting some slightly confusing signals from you, but I'm pretty sure you just want to be friends because A) you haven't kissed me yet and in fact, you seem downright averse to it, B) you talk about other women to me a lot, and C) you keep mentioning the fact that you want to surround yourself with these radiant friends who are doing great things and "cresting." (I'm not sure you've used any of those exact words, but that's the impression I'm left with, and I'm also left with the impression that I am one of these people who is meant to inspire you, or develop with you, or crest with you, or write with you, but not anything beyond that.)

So . . . if you do just want to be friends, let's just be friends and not do date-like stuff, because then I end up wanting to kiss you, and then you don't, and then I just feel stupid, which is not helping me "crest" or meet other people who might actually want to kiss me and date me, which is something I rather enjoy.

In any case, I thoroughly loved having you as my date for the parties this weekend right up until the moment I discovered I had lost my room key and asked what would happen if we kissed and was politely but decisively shut down. In fact, when I put on your spare motorcycle helmet so you could drive me back to the party, I briefly considered keeping it on indefinitely, because you're much more likely to crash and burn on a date (or what you think is a date), and yet there's no safety gear for that.

Cindy

The
Other Woman/
Other Man
(Real and Virtual)

Oth•er (ŭth´ər) *adj*. different from that or those implied or specified; additional; extra; alternate; second.

wo•man (wo͞om´ən) *n*. An adult female human being. Feminine quality or aspect; womanliness. *Informal*. A wife. A lover or sweetheart.

man (măn) *n*. An adult male human being. *Informal*. A husband. A lover or sweetheart. *Slang*. A person or group felt to be in a position of power or authority. *Interj*. Used as an expletive to indicate intense feeling.

re•al (rē´əl´, rēl) *adj*. Being or occurring in fact or actuality; having verifiable existence. Genuine and authentic. Not to be taken lightly; serious.

vir•tu•al (vûr´cho͞o-əl) *adj*. Existing or resulting in essence or effect though not in actual fact, form, or name. Existing in the mind, especially as a product of the imagination.

The Other Woman/Other Man (Real and Virtual) *n*. A breakup letter resulting from an infidelity on the part of the writer or recipient, whether the infidelity actually occured, or was a figment of someone's colorful imagination.

The Other Woman/Other Man (Real and Virtual)

From Anne Boleyn (ca. 1507–1536), second wife of Henry VIII and mother of Queen Elizabeth I. Boleyn had long been unpopular among her subjects, who blamed her for unfavorable tax policies and political troubles, but it was after her second miscarriage that Henry VIII began to suspect that God was denying him a son and that Boleyn had bewitched him into marriage. After news of a romantic spat with a Sir Henry Norris and rumors that she was planning to bring about the king's death in order to marry Norris, Boleyn was put on trial, imprisoned in the Tower, and eventually beheaded. This letter was supposedly the last she wrote before her execution, but its authenticity has long been in doubt.

[6 May 1536]

Your grace's displeasure and my imprisonment are things so strange to me, that what to write, or what to excuse, I am altogether ignorant. Whereas you send to me (willing me to confess a truth and so obtain your favour), by such a one, whom you know to be mine ancient professed enemy, I no sooner received this message by him, than I rightly conceived your meaning; and if, as you say, confessing a truth indeed may procure my safety, I shall with all willingness and duty, perform your command. But let not your grace ever imagine that your poor wife will be brought to acknowledge a fault, where not so much as a thought ever proceeded. And to speak a truth, never a prince had wife more loyal in all duty, and in all true affection, than you have ever found in Anne Bulen—with which name and place I could willingly have contented myself, if God and your grace's pleasure had so been pleased. Neither did I at any time so far forget myself in my exaltation or received queenship, but that I always looked for such alteration as I now find; for the ground of my preferment being on no surer foundation than your grace's fancy, the least alteration was fit and sufficient (I knew) to draw that fancy to some other subject.

You have chosen me from low estate to be your queen and

companion, far beyond my desert or desire; if, then, you found me worthy of such honour, good your grace, let not any light fancy or bad counsel of my enemies withdraw your princely favour from me; neither let that stain—that unworthy stain—of a disloyal heart towards your good grace ever cast so foul a blot on me, and on the infant princess your daughter.

Try me, good king, but let me have a lawful trial, and let not my sworn enemies sit as my accusers and as my judges; yea, let me receive an open trial, for my truth shall fear no open shames. Then you shall see either my innocency cleared, your suspicions and conscience satisfied, the ignominy and slander of the world stopped, or my guilt openly declared. So that, whatever God and you may determine of, your grace may be freed from an open censure; and my offence being so lawfully proved, your grace may be at liberty, both before God and man, not only to execute worthy punishment on me as an unfaithful wife but to follow your affection already settled on that party [Jane Seymour] for whose sake I am now as I am, whose name I could some while since have pointed unto—your grace being not ignorant of my suspicion therein. But if you have already determined of me, and that not only my death, but an infamous slander must bring you the joying of your desired happiness, then I desire of God that he will pardon your great sin herein, and likewise my enemies, the instruments thereof; and that he will not call you to a strait account for your unprincely and cruel useage of me at his general judgement-seat, where both you and myself must shortly appear; and in whose just judgement, I doubt not (whatsoever the world may think of me), mine innocency shall be openly known and sufficiently cleared.

My last and only request shall be, that myself only bear the burden of your grace's displeasure, and that it may not touch the innocent souls of those poor gentlemen, whom, as I understand, are likewise in strait imprisonment for my sake. If ever I have found favour in your sight—if ever the name of Anne Bulen have been pleasing to your ears—then let me obtain this request; and so I will leave to trouble your grace any further, with mine earnest prayer to the

Trinity to have your grace in his good keeping, and to direct you in all your actions.

From my doleful prison in the Tower, the 6th of May.

———

From Harriette Wilson (1786–1846), a well-known nineteenth-century courtesan and author of <u>Harriette Wilson's Memoirs of Herself and Others</u> (1825) to her lover Lord Craven (1770—1825), when she was seventeen years old. Craven, a neighbor who took Wilson as his mistress when she was fifteen, sent her a letter accusing her of an intimacy with a man named Frederick Lamb, writing, "Let me add, Harriette, that you might have done anything with me, with only a little more conduct." This is Wilson's response. Years later, Wilson fell in love with the poet and rake, George Gordon, Lord Byron. (See also p. 35.)

[1803]

My Lord,

Had I ever wished to deceive you, I have the wit to have done it successfully; but you are old enough to be a better judge of human nature than to have suspected me of guile or deception. In the plentitude of your condescension, you are pleased to add, that I 'might have done anything with you, with only a little more conduct', now I say, and from my heart, the Lord defend me from ever doing any thing with you again! Adieu.

Harriette

———

From writer and translator Sarah Austin (1783–1867), to Prince Hermann von Pückler-Muskau (1785–1871), with whom she was conducting an epistolary affair. Austin, wife of the legal scholar John

Austin (1790–1859), began to correspond with Pückler-Muskau, a married German prince, in the early 1830s, while working on a translation of one of his books into English. The two corresponded in secret, using German embassy couriers to transport their letters. Although Austin wrote at length about her unhappy marriage and her passion and love for Pückeler-Muskau, she was adamant about not hurting another woman in the process of the affair: "You know I told you that if any other woman had claims upon you, I could not accept what was stolen from her . . . remember that disloyalty to women—above all to a loving woman—is a crime in my eyes of atrocious cruelty and of despicable baseness," she wrote in 1832.

Austin was also suspicious of Pückler-Muskau, who had a reputation for being a womanizer and was rumored to have threatened to publish the letters of a married woman with whom he had had an affair. Becoming increasingly concerned that the relationship would be found out by her husband, Austin finally demanded that Hermann stop writing her. The two corresponded until the early 1840s, although the tenor of the relationship had changed. They met for the first time in 1842.

[Dec. 26 1836]

Listen now and accept the perfect sincerity of what I tell you. Not only do I not want to receive, but it is a real pain for me to receive your letters if you persist in writing to me in the tone you adopt. My friend, I have no choice—I dare not, *cannot* because without doubt he will see some letter, and do you think he would want others? He has found and with reason that I have too much correspondence, that this occupies too much time and spirits and costs me too much money. You have no idea how much I have renounced entirely. If you care for me, you will hear with pleasure that our [my husband's and my] relationship is very much changed—that we get along better, and each of us having talked together with perfect frankness we [now] live in perfect accord—which is made possible by the fact that there is, dare I say it, recognition of a fund of qualities on both sides, that some faults would never alienate us from one another. If only he would be well, I now do not despair of spending the rest of our lives very tranquilly and very affectionately together, and I am resolved to cut out anything that could trouble that precious peace . . . if this has no appeal to you, I have to renounce the great pleasure of receiving news of you. Whatever be your decision, I will always have interest and admiration for your talents and zeal for your reputation and happiness . . . which I have so often expressed to you and now express once more.

———

From Etta May White to George H. White after less than a year of marriage. The divorce complaint, dated March 17, 1906 and stored in the Sacramento Archives & Museum Collection Center in Sacramento, California, says Etta had committed adultery with a "certain man, other than [George White] . . . particularly on or about the ___ day of November, 1905, at a room known as Number 18 in a certain lodging house known as No. 1026 8th Street" and that Etta "has been and she is now guilty of habitual intemperance, from the use of intoxicating drinks, to that extent which disqualified her during a great portion of said time, from properly attending to business or her ordinary domestic affairs." Etta moved from Sacramento, where she lived with George, to Trail, British Columbia, soon after leaving him.

Trail, B.C.

Dec 1905

Dear Husband,

I received a letter from you yesterday asking when I am coming home.

Know my dear I might as well tell you the truth, I am never coming home again. I can not live with you and love another.

Hell Hath No Fury

When I married you the tenth day of Feb. I thought I could forget my past affection for another but I find out I never can. Although we can never be to one another as we have been, for that is the thing of the past, and there is no use for us to live together any longer for I do not love. Many a lonesome day I have put in at 716–8 St.

I had [Janice?] come down to see if that would make me more contented but it did not I have done everything to content myself but I have failed. Now in regard to the things [illegible] them. Except the sofa pillows and scarf and things on the mantel bedding silver ware things on the piano and also mandolins. If you can get two hundred for my piano let it go if not store it and send me the receipt for it ship the things to me I speak of, I do not think I will stay in Trail B.C. long but send those things here also my pictures. And if you will send me what you think is right after selling the furniture everything will be all right. [Campbell?] will consent to you selling remember the least said about me not returning the better it will be for us bouth [sic]. no my dear there is no use for me to return knowing my feelings for it would only be a matter of time before I would leave again. There will be no use for you to ask me to return or even come where I am for I have told you the truth. You know I have told you time and again when I was tired of you I would tell you and we would quit and you consented and said when that time came we would part good friends. Now my dear that time has come so keep your *word*. And keep your own [counsel?] and tell no one about your trubbels [sic] for they only *laugh*. When you don't get a letter from me you talk to a certain *party* I get it second handed that *party* talks about you all the time. He is not a friend to no one so take my tip, well my dear you know my feelings so I guess I will close for this time. hope to receive an early reply soon stating if you will send those things to me or not.

Take good care of your-self for you will meet the right party yet; I have done every thing to make it pleasant for you but I can not deceive you any longer. so don't blame any one for me going away for it is my own doings. Hope your finger is well by this time. It is snowing to [beat?] the band this morning well I will close and mail this answer soon.

Yours
Etta Box 286

P.S. I shall never get a divorce if you want one get it. For my part I am through with *all men sex*

———

From dancer/choreographer Isadora Duncan (1878–1927) to the millionaire Paris Singer (1868–1932), her lover and one of twenty-four children of Isaac M. Singer, the founder of the Singer sewing machine company. The two met in February 1909, when Singer showed up at Duncan's dressing room door in Paris, and were soon in the midst of a tempestuous love affair, replete with breakups and infidelities. (Of her relationship with Singer, Duncan said, "We loved each other, and I think we hated each other by turns.") In 1910 Duncan gave birth to a son, Patrick, but the next year, Singer caught Duncan in her bedroom with another man and soon left for Egypt with a female companion. The two did not talk for over a year until April 19, 1913, when Singer invited her and the children to lunch.

Later that day, tragedy struck when Deirdre, six (Duncan's first child from her relationship with Gordon Craig), and Patrick, three, drowned after the car they were riding in fell into the Seine. According to Singer's obituary in the June 25, 1932 New York Times, Singer was married throughout the course of his relationship with Duncan. In 1912, the same year this letter was written, he celebrated the twenty-fifth anniversary of his marriage to an Australian woman; she divorced him in 1918.

[1912 undated]

Please if I really bore you as you say, if you are tired of me, or if there is anyone else . . . please dear tell me *now*—I am far too proud to care to stay with you if you do not want me—I love and adore you and I love little Patrick [their son]—the same, perhaps even more, when he cries as when he is amusing. Please tell me the *truth* if you do not care for me any longer—if there is anyone else—it would be much *kinder* to say so—I find it too humiliating to take everything from you and have you say that in return I only annoy you. If I am no longer any pleasure to you, tell me now. . . . The idea that you may continue to see me from a sense of duty and not from love makes me quite sick & desperate. You know I never accepted anything from anyone before I met you—and I cannot *bear* the idea of taking things from you unless you love me. Answer me the *truth*—

Isadora.

———

From New York stage actress Beatrice Forbes-Robertson (1883–1967) to her husband, lawyer and poet Swinburne Hale (1884–1937) to whom she had been married for eight years. Hale had been unfaithful during their marriage and, although Forbes-Robertson found it in her to be somewhat gentle and optimistic with regard to his infidelities, the couple eventually divorced in 1920. After moving to England with their three daughters, Forbes-Robertson became an advocate for women's suffrage and an author (<u>What Women Want,</u>* 1914) and lecturer; Hale remarried in 1921 and served as a Captain of the Intelligence Division to the General Staff of the U.S. Army.*

5749 Kimbark Ave.

Mon: Dec: 9th, '18

Dear Bob,

There seem to be one or two things I ought to add to what I said yesterday.

First, your missing letter has not come; so if there was anything else of importance in it (besides the amount of your check to my bank) you had better write me.

Second,—as far as I now know, I shall be recalled to Washington about January 1st. This would probably mean two or three days in the flat with you before you left, or I went on another tour. For this I should not be sorry, since apparently it will be the last time we shall ever be together again. There will be many practical details to discuss, such as the legal machinery, the disposal of our joint belongings, & so forth. Also, I want you (if he is still there) to introduce me to your British I.O. [Intelligence Officer] I fear the Grants will have left, & I must have one or two special introductions on the British side, in view of my trip to England. I will let you know in good time, of course, when to expect me. I should be sorry not to see you in "joint" surroundings, once again.

About ourselves Bob, I confess I never really believed it would come to this. My words about divorce were dictated by the state of frozen disgust to which your recent "affair" had reduced me. But I think you ought to know that I should never have taken the actual step. I felt we must separate & go our different ways for a time. But I had hoped that after a year or two of absence you would come to feel that sex was not the only thing, that my companionship & the children's love would mean more, in the long run. If you had been willing to be a little patient, I had hoped to be able to make you a home in which to pursue your writing, though of course it would not have been on the $7,500 scale. Nor have I ever been conscious of that "difficult friction" between us, of which you write, *except* as growing out of the sexual difficulty, which I thought would lessen as you grew older.

I write this, not to interfere with your decision, but because I feel honesty demands you should know where I really stand. I had felt much more cheerful the last few days, surrounded here by your family; for these seemed to be the real things, which would count in the end. Of course, I never expected, or could have accepted, any more sexual life between us; but I did hope for the loving comradeship of last year at Scituate, after a solitary period of separation & freedom from emotional strain.

But I see that it is now too late.—We shall never ever be able to write "Johnny Starfish" together.

It is difficult for me to understand how you can feel so sure of your love, with less than two weeks' knowledge of the lady. I am sure she is all that you say of her; but I think I too was always "kind" to you till you tried me, these last weeks, past bearing; and I think I, too, have always loved and appreciated your art. The one test (it seems to me) is not whether she is kind or well-to-do or distinguished, (several of us, including myself, are the last)—but whether you feel for her such a deep & all-consuming love that life without her would be unthinkable. That is the only test—after my experience of life—which I would dare trust to, myself.

You write of your happiness my dear. I trust you may find it. For my part it is unthinkable that happiness of the lasting kind can be obtained through the brunt-sacrifice of all those nearest to me by blood, who love me best; & by the evasion of one's parental responsibilities. The loss of their father by the children will be irreparable, and your parents will never recover from this blow. Of myself I cannot speak, since I had already given my verbal allegiance to the possibility of divorce. I have always hoped, with you, that if I left you perfectly *free* to act—with no feeling of dragging demands from me—you would chose the finer way! In this I have proved *myself* wrong more than once; yet I *could* not have tried coercion. I thought last month "If Bob knows he is free, to get a divorce, he will come to realize he does not want me."—Circumstances were too strong for me, however. Miss Evelyn seems to have arrived at the phsychological [*sic*] moment.

I am willing to admit that in the end a clean break will be better for my happiness; though not for the other five people involved. Your parents also think your way will be best for me, in the long run.

But meantime, of course, the knowledge that all one's giving & loving & serving & suffering for 8 1/2 years is as *nothing* beside a new [illegible] of a financial crisis, is terribly bitter, & I shall carry the scars of it as long as I live.—Don't make any more people unhappy in your life Bob, let this holocaust be the last.—I don't want to refer to any of this when we meet, dear; which is why I feel bound to write it now, I get it off my chest. I want my last memory of you to be a pleasant & peaceful one, lighted with a sort of after-glow from the past. I want a day or two in Washington with the old original Toodie,—to hear his plans, wish him well, & perhaps darn his socks! So only can I go out—of his life without bitterness.

For you will never see me again dear; I always told you that would be impossible for me, if you once subjected me to the final humiliation of thrusting me and mine out of your life, to make way for someone else. I wish I could feel differently in this; God knows I don't want to lose you out of my life—the one person for when I have lived all these years. But I am so sure of it that to say anything else would be insincere. Don't let us discuss these things any more by letter—all has now been said, & it is too painful.

Beatrice

P.S. You have taken from me bit by bit *everything* I had except the children—love, comradeship, pride, home, leisure. Such losses are almost insupportable—yet must be supported!

———

From writer/journalist Dorothy Thompson (1893–1961) to her first husband, Joseph Bard (1892–1975) a Hungarian writer whom she met while she was a European correspondent for a number of publications, including the <u>Christian Science Monitor</u> and the <u>Philadelphia Public Ledger</u>. Thompson and Bard met in the lobby of the Ritz Hotel in Budapest in 1921, sparks flew, and the two were married in 1923. Writer Rebecca West said of Bard, "[He was] not an unkindly soul, but the equivalent of a hairdresser, with a naïve passion for fancy vests."

After Thompson moved to Berlin to become bureau chief for the Curtis-Martin newspapers, Bard fell in love with English painter Eileen Agar, and the marriage became increasingly strained. Bard also committed a number of infidelities with some of Thompson's closest friends. (Apparently this was nothing new; according to Peter Kurth's biography of Thompson, American Cassandra (Little, Brown, 1990) Bard even seduced another woman on his and Thompson's honeymoon.)

In 1927 Bard told Thompson that "under no conditions and in no form" did he "wish to resume matrimonial relations"; she filed for divorce soon after, although she asked him repeatedly to reconsider. The divorce became final on July 9, 1927—her birthday—which was also the day she began a romance with writer Sinclair Lewis (see p. 158), whom she married the following year.

It is interesting to note that in the following letters, which were written at the end of 1926 and the beginning of 1927, Thompson spells her husband's first name with an "f," even though Bard preferred the English spelling; Kurth says that Thompson "persisted in addressing her letters to a Magyar, 'Josef,'" because she was "dreamy with some notion of the Hungarian soul. . . ." It is not clear if she actually sent all of these letters, but, according to Kurth, the letter dated January 25, 1927, was at one time in the possession of Agar, which implies that it was, in fact, sent to Bard.

[December 29, 1926]

Between us, Josef, you have piled such mountains of insecurities and lies that I see no way of ever bridging them into that friendship which you pretend to want from me. That is why I have not written—why I have not sent the scores of letters which I have written—because I find, in the end, I have nothing to say. My life, my emotions, myself, have become somehow entangled in a web not of my spinning, whose beginnings and whose ends I do not know. There is myself as you see me when we are face to face alone, and myself as you picture me to Eileen, and myself as you paint me to [Viennese Expressionist painter Oskar] Kokoschka, and myself [implicit?] and degraded in your letters to Dorothy Burlingham. And there is yourself in relation to all these and countless other people; and never yourself alone but always me with you, somehow. So that what you have done to me, Josef, is not at its worst that you have made me mentally and spiritually ill, but that you have disintegrated my whole personality. I no longer exist, and not existing have nothing to offer you—neither joy of life, nor trust, nor courage, nor straightforwardness. Nothing that you say to me means anything, and I think the reasons for that is that nothing you have ever said or thought in any human relationship has had any firm relation to the reality of conduct. When you say that you love me, as you repeatedly say, even now, you only express the appreciation that I am lovable, or a temporary emotional state which is never born into any deed or sacrifice or loyalty. When you say that you want my affection you express a vague yearning to be admired, accepting no responsibility that you will not exploit that affection to the point where not only you, but I, too, will be degraded by it. When you ask for friendship, you ask for loyalty, but only the loyal know to *use* loyalty, and to *be* loyal is more than to *wish* to be.

When I look back upon the last two years I see that I have been unconsciously in hell. I see that what I have been striving for is not another man, but another you. To keep an illusion in the hope that it would become real I wanted so desperately, so passionately that you should be someone of whom I could be proud, in my own heart. I have never in my whole life, wanted anything so passionately. I thought I saw this same yearning reflected in you, in your striving toward the west, in your longing to get away from Budapest where everything is so futile and *verlogen* [dishonest; false]. I never saw you otherwise than as two black eyes, and a clear forehead looking strainingly ahead, and not long ago I so described you to Stefan Grossman: "A young man seeking his way." With what passion I desired to help you build that way. But now I know that the west toward which you strive is not outside, but within . . .

[January 25, 1927]

. . . it is amazing how you misunderstand me. This constant casting off: this "insistence" on a divorce; this fear to come back to Vienna

lest I hold you. Josef, in heaven's name! You humiliate me horribly!
Did I not, myself, send you to Paris? Did I not come back from
England determined to leave you! Did you not yourself beg for a
respite "to find yourself." What kind of a woman do you think I am?
"Straight forward, stubborn, courageous." Also, Josef, with sensibility. A great deal of sensibility. I found out in Vienna what I did
not find out in Berlin, from you, that for two years you have not
been *unfaithful* to me but *faithless*. For two years you have tried to
get away from me, you have told other people so, and for a year, at
least, all near? Relations with me have been painful to you. Nevertheless you have kept me "on a string." You have taken my love, my
work, my affection, and my trust. Above all my ambition for you,
and used them to make a search for another woman who could help
you to get free from me. Josef, my indignation against you, is not
that you have left me now, but that you hadn't the guts to leave me
earlier. That, knowing yourself as you did, you ever married me.
Josef, in Munich you asked me, "If I have a friend with whom I can
work, and talk, who suits my peculiar temperament—would you
mind? You always said you didn't care so long as you don't know
about it." And I replied with absolute clearness—I see the scene,
vividly, with myself throwing things into a suitcase and you lying on
the couch with that *verlogen* look which sometimes used to freeze my
heart—"Josef, I don't particularly mind little affairs, if they are discreet, spontaneous, and don't influence your feeling toward me, but
if you find the woman you describe, then go to her, because she is
the friend/woman/wife you want." And I said, "I have the courage
to break if you have not." And on top of that you planned to go on
leading a double life, using my love, trust and work, using my
youth, frustrating me in every way, as a woman. You wrote me from
Paris a monstrous letter, saying that only economic considerations
would keep you with me. Monstrous, first of all because it presumed
I would try and help you. I wanted you to come to Vienna in order
to arrange immediately for a divorce, but I couldn't bring myself to
write you, believing as I have always believed, in a sensibility which
you do not possess. Saying to Genia "Josef and I must part, but we

have been too much to each other to part in this way. We must part with every consideration possible for each other, as two civilized human beings." And on top of that your telegram—not to me, to Genia—your letters "in no form and under no circumstances could nor do I wish to resume matrimonial relations with you;" and then your diaries—I read them, quite shamelessly—once in my life I must see the truth—with nasty little digs at me (better to say it openly, Josef) and all the passages underlined in Don Juan which justified your hatred of me . . .

. . . I have also my complexes, of course. They are quite clear to me. But these talks with Dr. [Theodor] Reik showed me that they aren't nearly so serious as you persuaded me to believe. I was a rather abnormally "normal" American woman, who loved you once absolutely as a woman, but who simply undertook more than she could do. If I turned into being a mother to you it was because that was *precisely* what you wanted from me—everything else you took elsewhere without question. It might have been different if I had stayed in Budapest & let you support me, but you see, I always thought that pull toward the west the noblest thing in you; if it was the thing I loved most in you, and being a woman, my greatest need was to help you. A real woman can be two things to a man: metaphysically speaking: a [illegible] or a [Mary?]: Heavenly or Earthly Love. I should have preferred to be [Mary?]. There is more beauty in me, more rest, more *quiet* strength, more poise, than you have ever known. But when we met, Josef, you needed energy, and pull, far more than you needed anything else. And you never let me be anything else, or helped me to be.

When you say "So on with the life you have built up," you again show that curious lack of imagination this life was centered on my house. I have told you time and again that I hate doing journalism. It tears at my nerves: it kills the best things in me. But you never listened. I was a success at it and this success was, as a bridge, useful to you. I am sure you haven't an idea what this last year has been to me. What a torture. Bills, work, moving, always trying to suit you. Never knowing just what you wanted. Trying to find a place where you would have quiet and rest—knowing in my heart it would not go—compensating for a lack of love by every form of distraction—always getting uglier, over-eating, over-drinking—trying to play an open card game with a partner who had some extra cards up his sleeves. And who preferred to confide to others. If it had gone on I should have gone to the devil. And then I might have given you syphilis, as you so [cruelly?] said. And everything in me is really passionate and clean. This I know.

I've got to tell you these things, because—because if I don't they will eat in me and destroy me. I've got to tell you them because they destroy my faith in and love for you Don't be afraid of the word love. Platonic enough—I am proud—but only people who love you, Josef, will ever be your friends. Because one requires that illumination of the imagination which love gives, in order to believe in you. And I've got, somehow to have faith in you, because this faith hangs together with my faith in life . . .

[January 27, 1927]

I want to tell you, Josef, how I loved you.

I loved you as I love beauty.

That is the determinant thing in my life: not "energy" or "the will to life"; these were the things you saw: but what drove me out of my village and across the ocean and into your life, was my longing for beauty.

Beautiful work: beautiful thoughts—like stars, clean and free. Conduct can be beautiful too. [Illegible] is not the least of life. To be honorable and clean.

To serve beauty and help create it.

As a child, I wanted to be a painter; as a girl a poet-writer. Something came in between—People flashed across my imagination and I had to serve them. My little sister . . . you. That was then what I could do. Make beautiful people. Beautiful lives for beautiful people.

Journalism was only a means to an end. At the [illegible] a home.

I would take money from the world and use it to make a home and to open a way for a creator of beauty. Not a career, but a life. With love at the center of it. Not sex. Or perhaps sex lifted into something more. Something imaginative, [illegible], kind, strong, passionate, clean-cutting, wall-holding: enduring. Creative companionship, inner loyalty.

But we had so little time together the work piled up, piled up. And in free moments, staleness. Why? I used to come to you, thinking you would say "we will go to the country for a weekend." Thinking you would make the plans. Never any. The work pulled me away and when I was here you went away.

But I thought it will pass. Josef will make a success. Then I will do other work. We shall be more secure. More quiet. Then will come his great, creative companionship.

But you drifted like sand through my fingers . . . I am thirty-three years old, and childless. I who was born to be a mother. And you, where are you, Josef? Do you really think you are going on, forward? Do you really think you will accomplish more alone, than with an arm around your shoulders, and a friend at your side who would fight the world for you? Were all those affairs which finally killed your love for me worth the sacrifice of that dream of a creative marriage? Is even your love for Eileen worth it? It is curious how I do not think you love Eileen. She is a relief for you . . . a rest . . . beauty. But you loved *me* Josef. Because I am better than Eileen. Better as a river is better than a pond or the sea than a lake, or a mountain than a hill. Better because my shade is like the shadow of a great rock in a weary land. I know I am better than Eileen. I know it because I have read one letter and seen one picture. What Eileen does for you she does because she is in love with you. What I did I did because I was in love with life and beauty. I painted a far better picture of you than Eileen & Kokoschka. I demanded far more of you than she will ever demand. I loved you well enough to kill your love for me, by being uncomfortably truthful . . .

. . . Six years of my life have gone by. The best six years . . . as a woman. The year when I should have laid the foundation for a life, kept and developed beauty, born my children—other opportunities for love have gone by. Because when they were offered I was arrogant and loyal. So loyal that when I seemed driven to test again whether I was wholly uncharming as a woman I took a wayfarer— used him—and let him go.

But because I loved you, because I love you—not you, skulking in London—but you as I created you. Ah, well, I will always have you, and out of that love I will yet make something as beautiful as flame, as beautiful as the flame which was in my heart, passionate and purging. I will make that flame burn me to the cleanest thing God ever made.

The following letter was written by Agnes Boulton (1893–1968), a writer of short stories and novels (The Road Is Before Us, 1944) to her then-husband, the playwright Eugene O'Neill (1888–1953). The two met in a Greenwich Village bar in the fall of 1917 and were married in April 1918. They had two children: a son, Shane, and a daughter, Oona, who became somewhat of a wild-child New York City socialite and later the wife of Charlie Chaplin. By 1926 O'Neill had become involved with the actress Carlotta Monterey, who starred in his 1922 play, The Hairy Ape; Boulton attempted to save the marriage, but O'Neill began to divide his time between New York (where Monterey was living) and Bermuda (where Boulton was living); he made the decision to stay with Monterey in 1928. Boulton and O'Neill were divorced on July 2, 1929, and O'Neill married Monterey twenty days later, in Paris.

[September 13?, 1927]

Dearest Gene—

Your letter—all but the post script—was so encouraging to me— made me happy—then the fatal addition, in which you seemed again so blue & so hopeless. I am looking forward very anxiously to a letter from you on [the] next boat. It has been hot here, & I have felt rather low this week. Also rather discouraged about getting anything ever done here.

Shane is writing you a letter. He loved yours. He has had a slight bilious attack, and had to stay in bed for a couple of days.

How did things turn out about Ridgefield? I sent you a cable, saying "telephone W.V. Elliot, Wilton, Conn. Has prospect $37,000" as I thought you would want to investigate that before selling to the other man for $35,000.

I am dying to see the birthday present—you have me very excited. I hope it comes on today's boat.

Just got your two letters, and am sending this off on supplementary mail. I feel pretty damn hopeless—you being so *continually* miserable—the way the luck is breaking—everything. To anyone with any practical or common sense, the thing I did, of staying here, is the thing that should have been done—however, it merely gives you an excuse to say that I must have a lover,—you, who know as well as I do that such an idea, from any angle, is absurd. Who, pray? God damn it, if you knew how damned bored & lonely I was here—never mind, I think I'll pack up & arrive in N.Y. next boat, kids & all—then we'll see how that will work. I see through—of course you intended me to—your remarks about taking to drink— or love. Well, do it. (Love, not drink.) Remember your conversation with me, in which you told me you wanted to divorce me— remember the days & days of silent dislike & hatred on your part— remember the things you've said & done—Do you think I can forget all that—You love me & need me now, yes, because you're bored and lonely but that love speedily deteriorates into an intense irritation as soon as we've been together two weeks. And even now, your letters betray a resentment at me for not doing an absurd thing—leaving here in August with two children & opening up a big place which was likely to be sold at any minute—Well, don't worry about Spithead. I've lost all interest in it. It's finished, as far as I am concerned—I really mean that, nothing has been done here, & I'm not interested in doing anything. I wonder how I could have been so interested in "chickens" "cow" "flowers" etc. I have sent the horse back today. I am spending very little money to live on, as I wrote you . . . you don't mention that in your letter. I've got my little pistol locked up in a drawer, & lost the key, otherwise I think I'd take out the punt & finish it, right now, tonight. Bermuda is so empty & lonely, and then, no top of that one hears again the old mistrust. Honestly, I almost wish there was an interesting man around somewhere. Don't you know that letters like yours are enough to make a woman go out into the "hedges or [illegible]" *looking for a lover?* Damn you anyhow 'Gene—something must be all wrong for you to say such things.

Goodby. I'm glad Carlotta's nerves are gone. Do you think she would be interested in taking charge of Spithead? If so, tell her I've given up the job. She is certainly much more beautiful than I am. Yours.

Agnes.

P.S. The present hasn't come yet!

———

From novelist Katherine Anne Porter (1890–1980) to writer and biographer Matthew Josephson (1899–1978), with whom she became involved in 1928. Josephson, then in his late twenties, was charming, successful, and handsome. (Hemingway once said of him, "If I looked like Matty, I wouldn't need to be a writer.") But he was also married, and this other relationship would haunt Porter for the three years that she was with him. Josephson encouraged Porter's writing, inspiring her as a muse and going to bat for her with interested publishers, but the affair ended when his wife, Hannah, learned of his philandering and insisted that he choose between the two of them. He chose Hannah, but continued to contact Porter, presenting her with gifts and letters that sounded startlingly seductive. Porter later used the painful affair as the basis for the relationship between Dr. Schumann and La Condesa in her novel, Ship of Fools (1962).

The Other Woman/Other Man (Real and Virtual)

[Ernesto Pugibet 78 Mexico, DF]

[January 7th, 1931]

Dear Matthew:

I keep getting glimpses of you in some continually novel and useful incarnation, not so much rebirth as a change of role. Now you are [a spectral?], furtive author, converted by Rousseau to Romanticism: when I first knew you, you were just emerging from the Zola period, when a literary man should engage in battles for the right and keep a mistress. . . . Later, remember, you were the man of action warring single handed against great cities. Later when you feared I might stubbornly keep on being in love with you when the occasion that called for me had passed, you wrote that "our emotional feats" were of no consequence compared to the realistic businesses of life such as running a household, begetting young and writing books. We were to be machines, I remember distinctly, functioning with hair's breadth precision. I wasn't convinced nor deceived then, dear Matthew, and still I'm not when you decide that we must all be romantic rather than decorous. One might be both if one's nature was such? I think it means merely that you have found some one or something new to play with, and this point of view may be for the moment useful to you? You are like a good golfer who chooses just the right club to hit the ball in a certain way. I suffered a good deal because you *would* model your relations with me on literature: first it was Gertrude Stein, and then Kenneth Burke, and I forget who else . . . and too often I was met with defensive quotation marks; I told you then I was all for a running fight in the open, and I could not deal with these ambushes from unexpected bushes and briar patches. . . . Myself, I do not change much, except to go farther on the road I began on; what I was when you knew me, I am now, as I had been for some time before, granting always the natural gatherings and discardings which ceaselessly alter the superficies [outer surfaces] of pattern. . . . I think you are, too, quite definitely a fixed center, but you fly off at tangents. . . . Once, you were lecturing me because I thought in a circle, I believe it was, whereas you had decided that one must think, if I recall properly, outward in something like the spokes of a wheel from the hub. . . . Or was it in a square? I swear I do not now remember. But I suspect sharply that we are both thinking pretty fairly in the shapes we have always thought in, whatever they may be. . . .

My feeling for you was, I regret to say, deplorably shapeless.

It is pleasant to know you are working as well. I seem to have come to some kind of pause, I work but very little is worth keeping, I could despair somewhat if despair were not so easy. For relief I have turned to the study of music, and sit at the piano several hours a day, working out problems that than God have an answer I need not challenge. Paul Higgins the painter was a musician first, and a better musician than painter. He gave me six weeks of lessons, hastily knocked the principles of harmony into my resistant hand, taught me my notes and to read, explained the system of balance and weight in getting tone, sat me firmly in the middle of third year music, and left me to my fate. He was going on to New York, I believe. I am staggering through my sixth Bach Prelude and Capriccio by Scarlatti. I am very happy about it. When Peggy and Malcolm gave you news of me, maybe they did not tell you about my little grand piano, made in 1820 in England, which I bought, a wreck, from the grand niece of the first owner, and had repaired. It tinkles a little, but in time I shall be able to have it completely restored. The study of music is the real news about me. For years I have meant to study, but now I am glad I did not, for I have it now, something very new and satisfying.

I never knew until you told me that you had written the "blurb," (I love that word like a hot baked stuffed potato full of butter) and maybe Mr. Harcourt didn't tell you I had objected to being classed with the younger generation, on the ground that I had belonged to the younger generation ten years ago and simply hadn't the time or energy to do it again. To say nothing of the wish. Youth was no career for me even when I had it, and so most certainly is not now.

I like the "feel" of living chronologically, of being what Gertrude Stein (aha! my revenge!) called "being a contemporary"—I think I may be a contemporary for my time. Maybe even after one is dead one might well belong with the younger generation! But I have no ambitions to speak of. I wish I might have.

I see that my vice of letter-writing has me firmly gripped. A violent wrench, and so, there! Its [*sic*] ended.

Yours, Katherine Anne

Except, of course, that you're to give my remembrance to those who ask. . . . New York seems very far away, it seems unreasonable to think I shall not see it again for long and long. . . . It baffles me that I have never been able to manage to live there, when I love the place so much.

I wish to make a bargain with you: will you exchange me the copy of "Flowering Judas" you have for the one I have inscribed for you, which has been wrapped and waiting for an address since October? In simple faith I shall send it on.

———

A letter sent in 1950 from Frances Boldereff (b. 1905), a typographic designer, scholar and author of books on James Joyce, and feminist manifestos, including A Primer of Morals for Medea, *(Russian Classic Nonfiction Library, 1949), to the poet Charles Olson (1910–1970). The relationship began in 1947 after Boldereff picked up a copy of a new book by Olson about* Moby-Dick, *titled* Call me Ishmael *(1947), and wrote to him in care of his publishers. The two entered into a correspondence and love affair that lasted for decades, although, at the beginning of the relationship, both were married and kept their affair secret. After Olson received the following letter, the two took a break from the relationship and did not correspond for two years.*

Hell Hath No Fury

Brooklyn to Washington

3 September 1950 [postmark]
Sunday morning

Charles dear—

A beautiful thing has happened to me and while it will cause you pain—it is part of the reality now between us that you also must share. There came to me straight out of God's hand a beautiful young Negro—he saw me—he sat beside (near) me in the subway—he rode to where I got off—he went his way I went mine—I hunted around for a bus station—in the station I saw him—smiled asked him if he knew where you buy a ticket for Freeport bus—he didn't—said—"If I had my car here I would drive you"—waited two 1/2 hours in the bus station for me to come back—I didn't—so he waited inside a subway station—watched all the cars—saw me—came in and sat down beside me—and rode home with me—

He has the purest most beautiful soul I think I have ever been in the presence of—and a body to match—and he wants me—I told him all about you—he wants me and I am drawn—I am going to meet him again—at least that is the plan—and I want you to know, Charles, that I am very seriously thinking of him—that we have already been together . . .

———

From writer Catherine Texier, to her ex-husband Joel Rose, as published in her book Breakup: The End of a Love Story (Doubleday, 1998), essentially one book-length letter to Rose, who began to pull away from her after taking up with his editor in 1996. These are the most notable excerpts, written by Texier between September 1996 and May 1997.

Another night. Twisting the stiletto sideways for maximum damage.
    But why? What happened?

I am so passive-aggressive, you say, I don't understand how you can take it. If I were you I would have booted me out already. I admire what you're doing. Don't think that I am oblivious to that. You're very brave.

I know, I say. It's because I love you.

I am like the welterweight in the ring taking the punishment taking it and taking it, but standing on her feet. They say about those kinds of boxers that they have heart. I have a lot of heart.

4 or 5 A.M., both of us lying naked on the bed, holding each other. The easy companionship of bodies that know how to make one another come and come and come. I believe in our relationship. I believe that we still have this thing. That, deep down, you still have it for me.

Maybe, you say, brutally honest, or maybe provocative, but I don't feel it.

You're still angry at me, right?

Maybe.

Don't you love this apartment, don't you love coming down for coffee in the morning with me, don't you love what we have?

Yes, you whisper.

But you want to give up the great sex, the great apartment, living with the kids, you want to give up all that?

In answer you get up sullenly and go downstairs to make coffee, and we drink it in silence at the yellow table . . .

You're taking your revenge. Your revenge cannot be satiated.

Revenge for what? What did I do?

I will never forgive you. I will never make love with you again. I do not love you anymore.

I will never forgive you. I will never make love with you again. I do not love you anymore.

Did you ever say to me: I will always love you? I can't remember. A little over a year ago, in the summer of 1995, you took me to a little bar on East Ninth Street and told me: you are the woman of my life. And I said: you are the man of my life. We kissed passionately, our knees entwined. And I still feel the same today, even if your love has suddenly dissolved . . .

Yesterday I held you in my arms and I said: I love you, I know you're going through a major crisis, and I accept it.

Yeah, you said, I'm going through a crisis. And you repeated, again, lest I might have forgotten: I'm only here because of the children. I am still leaning toward leaving rather than not.

Are you open to the possibility that you might change your mind? I asked you. And you said yes . . .

At night, in a half sleep, you took me in your arms, and when you fully woke up, turned your back to me.—

Sometimes I feel so rejected, like when you fell asleep on Juliet's bed because you so obviously didn't want to lie down and read next to me on our bed, that my stomach churns and I want to throw up. Throw up the pain.

Sometimes I think I should be the one who leaves. I am the one who doesn't belong, the wanderer, the foreigner. Go back to France, travel. Live in Paris again, or in Latin America. Roam the jungles of Vietnam or the Ivory Coast. There's something wrong in this picture, you leaving. I am the restless one, the one who can't stay still. I've been stable all these years because of you. Or was it the opposite: you were stable because of me. All I know is that we've been each other's anchor . . .

Something has changed between us. You've pulled the plug. Hold it, you said. I've had it. We were caught in some shit, some vicious taunting, cat and mouse game, and now the jig is up.

The hero moves on to another adventure, freed of his chains, leaving the heroine behind to crawl into a corner and die. Or to stand up as a martyr, cloaked in her haunting weakness. Maybe she has a nervous breakdown. Is committed to an insane asylum, nineteenth-century style, like Camille Claudel after her breakup with Rodin. He went on creating powerful sculptures and she never set foot again in her studio.

I wouldn't write a story like that, I would find it laughable, full of exhausted clichés. Passé. I wouldn't read it either. I refuse to live it.

This is the story I would tell: the hero needs to spread his wings, free himself, test himself, renew himself. The heroine freaks and puts the screws on him. The hero flees. End of first act. The heroine comes back on stage: okay, I hear you. You've been wounded, you need space, so do I. The story goes on. But it's now about something else. There's death and resurrection. The second act is only starting.

Your story leaves me no room at all, no other option than to accept the ritual killing of me—the wife—so that the liberated hero can fly off on his own.

Is my story better than yours? I don't know. All I know is that I am not going to play the part you've assigned me . . .

I don't want to romanticize it, you say.

Romanticize what? What are you talking about? Romanticize your desire to leave? I thought we were romantic.

You say: I want you to be fully yourself.

You say: I have very deep feelings toward you.

You say: we have this sexual chemistry between us that will always be there. But emotionally and intellectually I am shut down.

You also say: if you had pulled yourself together a year ago . . .

Why: "a year ago"? What happened a year ago?

Your words are sibylline.

A year ago I spent the month of August in France at my mother's house with Juliet and Lola. A year ago I met my father for the first time in my life in a little restaurant in Provence. A year ago you got laid off from your job. A year ago your behavior began to change: you took the habit of returning videotapes after dinner while I was putting Lola to bed and not coming home until 2 A.M.; you left for the supermarket on Sunday mornings and didn't come back until 4 or 5 P.M. When I asked you where you had been, you said: I went out for a drink, or I had to do some errands, or I went out to watch the ballgame. If I insisted, you said: don't cling to me. I don't have to answer to you.

A year ago, I began to lose you.

Maybe there's been a breakdown of trust, you say. And I don't really know what you mean, but I believe that maybe trust can be rebuilt . . .

The rage of being rejected. It's one thing to be with a guy and see that he's losing interest and maybe you are too, and quite another to have built a family and two literary careers and a house and eighteen years of shared companionship, the passion still going full swing in spite of the mounting tensions, and to feel the plug being pulled out overnight without warning.

Like being shot in the back by a cop.

I didn't know, you said, I didn't know I would find myself on the edge so fast. For a long time the edge seemed far away, then all of a sudden the edge was right here . . .

Three A.M. Friday morning, the day we are to fly to Florida to visit your parents, the weekend of Halloween, I wake up with the brutal, unshakable conviction that you are having an affair. You know these drawings one finds in kids' entertainment books, with an object cleverly hidden in the picture by a trick of the illustrator: in full view, yet invisible. You stare at the drawing again and again and it looks normal to you, a plain family scene: a father and mother waiting for a train on a crowded platform and two kids playing at their feet. And all of a sudden you blink and here it is, staring at you, unmistakable: the lady's profile tucked into the pleats of the father's overcoat. And once you've seen it you cannot unsee it again.

So I decide to finally face the truth. I get up and check around the house to see if I can find any evidence of your betrayal. And here it is, so easy to find: a bunch of receipts from the summer, including expensive hotels, and a page torn off your appointment book with these words: UPS/FEDERAL EXPRESS, deliver any packages to X.X. and Y.Y. (her name, your name) to Z. I stare at the paper as if it's written in code, hoping the words might mean something else than what they seem, but I don't have a clue how to decode them. There are other receipts in that folder where we keep all our receipts. Another weekend, another hotel, in New Jersey. You had told me you were camping out at night in your sleeping bag.

I put everything away and go back up to our bedroom and you wake up and ask me, angrily, in that tone you use with me right now: what's up?

I sit down on the bed next to you and ask you the classic question (we are back in the bad screenplay, uttering tired clichés): are you having an affair? And you say: what has it got to do with anything? So I ask again: are you having an affair? And you duck a second time. The third time you finally say yes, a wisp of a word, blowing through your clenched teeth. For how long? And you say: for fifteen months. Like you've been counting the days, or maybe you've told someone else before, and the answer hits me right in the gut.

Fifteen months. That was the summer before last, the whole time you were writing your novel, the summer we went to Porquerolles Island in the Mediterranean together, the fall when we were making love all the time, the New Year's Eve party when we flirted with each other all evening and I sat on your lap and we kissed at midnight and you were all over me. But it was also the time when you were coming back at 2 A.M., several times a week, refusing to answer my questions, accusing me of clinging to you, and I had convinced myself it was better not to pressure you.

Is it her, your editor?

Yes, you said. How did you know?

I could tell she wanted you. I could see it in her eyes, in her body. I didn't know she had you already.

Did somebody tell you?

I didn't want to tell you about the receipts, about the page torn off your book. It seemed cheap to me, another cliché, the wife rummaging through her husband's papers looking for evidence. I didn't want to admit that I had played the part.

No, I said. But every time I saw her she was always flirting with you. And one time she left a message on our machine, about your book, and it was so erotically charged it was unbearable, but I told myself it was just flirting, that it was the way she was with everybody. But I felt it the minute I first saw her, a couple of years ago, at that party on Gramercy Park. I dismissed her because I thought she came on so strong, she was a little too obvious. I didn't think you'd go for her, But I should've known better, because I am very seductive too, and you fell for me.

So that's why she bought your book, I said.

I meant it as a blow, and you felt it.

Thanks, you said, tersely.

There was a moment of silence.

When did you see her?

Whenever she could, whenever I could.

The tone you used to say those words sounded a little whiny, sorry for yourself and for her, as if you two were victims of society's conventions. My victims, so to speak, since I was standing in the way.

When you came back at 2 A.M.?

Yes, not always.

You said you were always roaming the streets to write your book. So in fact you were seeing her?

No, sometimes I was in the streets.

On Sunday, when you would disappear for hours, not coming back after grocery shopping until late in the afternoon?

Yes.

But you made love to me all the time. Did you make love to me after coming back from seeing her?

Yes, sometimes.

Did it turn you on?

No. Not really.

There's no word for this. Devastating is the word commonly used . . .

I thought I should lash out on you, unload my rage and my anger, at the very least throw some books against the wall. Make a scene. Destroy some furniture. But I didn't do anything. I told myself I didn't want to make a racket, I didn't want to wake up the girls. The truth is that I was dead inside. You had dropped a bomb. Right on the old wound: the fear of being abandoned, of not being loved, of being left behind.

My hurt turned to anger yesterday. You said, coming out of the bathroom, drying yourself: if I leave to sort my feelings out will you expect me to come back? You said: don't have any illusions. Things will never be the same between us.

Why are you repeating that all the time? Are you trying to convince yourself? Are you trying to provoke me into a fight? Do you think I don't hear you?

I hear you, but I don't believe you. Not entirely. Maybe that's why you have to repeat yourself so much. It's only when you leave that I will finally believe you.

HOW DARE YOU HOW DARE YOU HOW DARE YOU??? Dump me for another woman. Me plaquer pour une autre femme. In French the words sting worse, like the tip of a whiplash.

I am frozen in terror. I sit here and I let you hit me. I had put my life into your hands. I had made myself vulnerable to you. In your last novel you wrote about the narrator's first wife that she didn't fight back. I know you were talking about me. You think I don't know how to fight back. But maybe I can learn. Maybe I can finally let it out. You are very primal. For you it's all about the basic urges: sex, hunger, rage, hate. That's what I love in you. I didn't know you would turn them against me . . .

When I cannot resist torturing myself I imagine you telling her you love her, stretched on her bed, naked, your cock standing up. I imagine the two of you making love in Massachusetts by the ocean, or in that hotel in New Jersey where you checked in during the summer—that $273 receipt I found in the receipt folder. A weekend in August, crazy in love, your red motorcycle parked in front of the hotel. I love you, you tell her and she sits on your face and you suck her off, her red hair falling all over her face.

One day, last spring, you held me over you with your hands.

Your hips are so narrow, you said to me, as if you were surprised. Now I know why you told me that: her hips are wider than mine. You were comparing us . . .

Did you really fall out of love with me?

You never said: I'm unhappy with you. You were annoyed, angry, frustrated. You were running out of the house. Coming back late, going to bars, clubs, hanging out. Suddenly, overnight, you turned into another man. But you kept saying: I love you, I want you. You are the woman of my life. I've never been bored one minute with you. I love my life with you. You never stopped making love to me. You said you loved my breasts, you loved my cunt. You had your hand between my legs in public places. Why do you resist me now: are you afraid to betray her?

Our last year together has been contaminated. When I look back and remember moments, they have turned radioactive: when you fingered me in the car on our way to eat bouillabaisse in Saint-Tropez, you had already slept with her. When you gave me black lacy lingerie last Christmas and pulled my nipples out of the bra cups and told me how much you liked my tits, you were already falling in love with her. When you met her for a drink the day you sold your book and didn't come back until 2 A.M., you had fucked her. You always came back home between 2 A.M. and 2:30 A.M., like clockwork, you never came back later than that. I told myself you were hanging out with friends in a bar after business dinners, so many bars I tried to imagine; or maybe that there were women, but nothing serious, nothing that would threaten our relationship. You said you liked to hang out and roam the streets of New York late into the night, and I believed you; you said you used to do that in your twenties, that it was something you really liked to do.

When you made love to me at 2 A.M., had you even washed your dick, or did you dip it straight into my cunt? To be honest, a lot of the time during the spring you couldn't actually fuck me. I was concerned about that. Now I can see why. It was hard to service two women back-to-back, wasn't it? You wanted me to get you off while you kept your arm folded over your chest and closed your eyes, your forehead tense in concentration. Were you thinking of her? Were you thinking of me when you made love to her?

Is this journal an epitaph to our love affair? . . .

If you leave, I will take your head and smash it against our front door until your brain explodes and gray matter sticks all over the walls and ceiling. I want to hear the cracking of the bones, see the back of your skull splitting open and your face disfigured, pissing blood, teeth flying, your hair matted with the innards of your cortex, maybe you could make dreads easily with that sticky gooey matter.

Her, the concubine, I would take with a gun, a .38 aimed straight at her cunt, point-blank between the lips, one end of the barrel resting against the clit and emerging out of the pube like it was growing out of dark grass. She'd be lying on her back, her legs open, ready to take you in but it would be the cold barrel of the .38. Surprise, surprise, it would be me fucking her, in and out, in and out, getting her wet, baby, she likes that, doesn't she, doesn't she like a hard cold cock, is your cock as hard as the barrel of a .38? No way. I wouldn't use a snub-nose but a long barrel, as long as your cock, in and out, in and out, cocky, you know, very cocky, fucking macho, assertive, more macho than you could ever be, what man can compete with a fucking .38, until she starts moaning, her head lolling, her lips parted, you coming, baby, you coming, here you go, pull the trigger, BANG BANG BANG, straight up her cunt, up her cervix, up her uterus, up her fucking guts, little slut, and the walls of her stomach explode and all the guts pop out, the ovaries, spilling all over her glamorous clothes, Comme des Garcons or whatever Japanese designer du jour she's wearing, her stupid cunt reduced to red, runny porridge, gurgling female syrup.

I will not let you leave me or abandon me. I will not wait until you are ready to move on, as you say—whether it takes weeks or months until you have enough money or your guilt has abated or whatever it is that you are waiting for—and listen to you tell me: I am leaving, I am going to live with her. I will not let you say that to me. I will not hear those words. I will move faster than you, take you by surprise and tell you to leave: by the end of the day, or the week, or the month . . .

You are standing at the kitchen counter pouring fresh hot coffee into the thermos, about to go upstairs to your office to write, when I ask you if you are going to LA on your own or if she's going with you.

Your back is to me, the steaming mug of coffee in front of you.

You wait a beat.

I'm going with her.

The stiletto goes right in. It doesn't hurt as much now. The wound is numb. It's as if there are holes in my chest already open for your stabs.

You try to soften the blow: she's going for work, you say. I decided to go at the same time.

I didn't tell you how upset I was. To me it felt as if you were flaunting your affair in my face. I felt the rage come up, but I didn't know what to do with it.

I guess I could have said stupid words like: PACK UP YOUR BAGS AND GET THE FUCK OUT OF HERE, I NEVER WANT TO SEE YOUR FUCKING FACE AGAIN IN MY LIFE. I AM SORRY I EVER MET YOU AND HAD TWO CHILDREN WITH YOU. DROP DEAD, YOU AND YOUR LOWLIFE BITCH.

I don't say those words. They lie in my mouth like sick dogs. Instead I decide to spend the weekend out of town, and when I tell you about my plans in the evening, right before you are "going out," I can see you bristle with anger, maybe because that means you have to take care of the kids. For once. Instead of doing whatever the fuck you want to do. For once I am not going to be your fucking babysitter. Your maid. I don't care if you're angry. I don't care anymore . . .

I have used up all the matches I have found in the house from all the bars that you've been to in the last year (with or without her, I don't know, but certainly without me). I am quickly replacing them with matches culled from the clubs and bars I'm going to now with other men. Men who are not like you, maybe because they are younger and they belong to another generation. Or maybe because they are truly not like you. I don't know really. After nineteen years with one man, making love with another is a little like popping your cherry for the second time.

It's not you that I think of now when I go to sleep at night in the new sheets. I am falling out of love with you.

The Other Woman/Other Man (Real and Virtual)

From Helene Verin, forty-seven, a product designer in New York City, to Luke,* an architect in his early forties. Helene and Luke met and became friends in 1981 while they were both married; over a decade later, in 1995, the two had split up with their spouses and became involved. According to Helene, a year into the relationship, Luke told her that he wanted to "explore his homosexual fantasies." Helene says she "was totally devastated" and that it took her four years to get back on track.

[Summer 1997]

Dear Luke,

I should have known. Your good taste, swimming medals, love for Vanessa Daou, fridge full of caviar and champagne, thirst for details of my exes [*sic*], your devotion to gossip, and your GOD-DAMN looks, should have clued me into "I love you, I'm just not IN love with you." Well, fuck you and the last year of 8-hour fucking sessions. You say you're "bi" . . . I say "bye-bi."

Your parting words were, "I can't stand the thought of another man's penis in you."

DITTO!

———

From musician/writer Maggie Kim to Michael,* a man with whom she fell "in love at first sight" in late 2000 a week before his wedding. Kim, twenty-eight, wrote this letter during the week Michael was away on his honeymoon. "We'd met while my band was playing a television show that he was producing. The instant we shook hands and our eyes met, there was this weird, slo-mo kind of intense moment," says Kim. "I'd never felt like that before—and I was sure the feeling was mutual. I found out later that he was getting married and I was so disappointed: he was the perfect guy. I stopped myself from seriously flirting because he was engaged and he seemed to avoid me, too." But after the show finished taping, says Kim, Michael gave her his card and she *"conveniently" found an excuse to call him a few days later. "What started as a few business-related calls turned personal when he told me he was 'freaking out' about his impending wedding," says Kim. "I revealed my strong feelings for him and he wrote me back a poetic note that said he couldn't stop thinking about me since the moment we met and that he had to see me." The two met up in person and were soon in the midst of a passionate, albeit brief, affair, spending "melodramatic hours on the phone with each other up until the wedding."*

The day he left for his honeymoon, Kim received what she says was an "incredible love letter" along with a copy of Milan Kundera's The Unbearable Lightness of Being. She began writing the following letter that night and continued working on it for days afterwards, usually "after coming home, drunk and miserable, trying to forget that I'd lost the most perfect man I'd ever met who, more importantly, thought I was the perfect woman." She gave him the letter, at his urging, and says that sending it "was the point of no return when it came to our emotional entanglement."

November 17, 2000
Friday, 3:23 am

I am drunk. I think my mouth's not beautiful enough. In relation to my chin. I can't begin to know exactly what would make it more beautiful, but at right now, I think my mouth's not beautiful enough. I want to call you so badly without you knowing that I called. I just want to hear your voice on your outgoing message. To hear how differently you speak from everyone else I know. Oh god. I thought I was happier today. I was able to see the humor in this situation, but maybe there isn't any. I kissed another boy today. Experimented with someone else's tongue. And it was very nice because he was quite a nice kisser, but I was drunk and desperate and hoping he'd turn into you somehow, magically delicious. I fantasize about where you are, dulled senses that I am, my brain turgid and slow with alcohol. I wonder if you're having fun, if you're having sex. I'd imagine you are. That's what people do on their honeymoon, right? Oh, you fuck.

Can't you just be with me? Can't you just take that awful, frightening, risky chance and throw your dice in my direction? Lay all your bets on red. For passion and power and blood and Maggie. Me. You don't know what a sure bet I am. Winning lottery ticket and all that. Someone did recognize what they stumbled onto and that was you. But you let me go, barely grasping me and I'm hopelessly alone again. You really believe that I believe there's someone besides you out there for me? Maybe my vision's not strong enough yet. But at 26, at this age that's so even and round and adult I want to throw up, I can't imagine there's anyone else I want to spend my life with, share my genes with. I speak of you incessantly, thinking to conjure you up with my words, they're almost a spell or mantra. But I get no satisfactory answers, no solutions to you not with me.

From <u>Sex and the City</u> writer Elisa Zuritsky, thirty-two, to her ex Zach, twenty-eight. The two began dating in the fall of 1998 after meeting at a New York City club at which Zach's cousin was performing. Two months into the relationship, over drinks, Zach explained that he felt hesitant, claimed he "did not know" what he wanted, and that he was "too fucked up" for her. "I broke it off with him then, but only because he forced me to," says Zuritsky.*

In early 2002, Zach contacted Zuritsky again, seemingly wanting to make amends. "I wondered to friends: 'what does he want? Could I let down my guard again?'" she explains. "There were drinks, apologies, follow-up E-mails . . . even one night of smooching until 5 A.M. I was smitten all over again."

Sadly, Zach's elusiveness resurfaced: He E-mailed a few days later, saying, "Let's get together soon . . . this week is crazy . . . let's play it by ear," then dropped out of touch for a week and a half. "If that's not a blow-off, I don't know what is," says Zuritsky. But Zach had one more mixed message to send: Out of the blue, another email appeared, asking her out again. "My choices seemed to be: a) Go out with him, have fun, and be the play-it-by-ear girl; b) Go out with him and initiate a talk about feelings (ugh); c) Have the 'feelings' chat over E-mail," says Zuritsky. "After obsessing for a few hours about which road to take, I decided that none of them led anywhere good: Zach's interest had as much staying power as a splash of perfume."

Instead, she decided to tell Zach something she only wished were true—that she'd met someone else—and she wrote him a letter to this effect. "I felt better instantly, because as much as I prize the truth, this lie felt like the best way for me to quit without sounding bitter, vulnerable, or redundant," she says.

Zach's response, "in record turnaround time," described her, ahem, honesty as "refreshing and greatly appreciated." He went on to say how glad he was that she'd "gotten into something good" and invited her and her "beau" to a party later that month. "As hilarious as it was to be thanked for my faux-honesty, I couldn't turn away from the painful truth it elicited: Zach wasn't heartbroken or even bummed that I'd moved on. He was relieved," says Zuritsky. "So, moving on it is."

[April 2002]

Hey Zach,

On the personal front, there's also been some change since we spoke that affects upcoming plans. I met someone who I've been spending a fair amount of time with recently, and I think I should see where it all leads. Anyway, I hope this doesn't sound strange, but I'm glad you and I reconnected because it reminded me of why the last time around stung so much. You're special.

Love,
Elisa

The
Divorce
Letter

Di•vorce (dĭ-vôrs´, -vōrs´) ´*n*. the legal dissolution of a marriage. A complete or radical severance of closely connected things. Tr. To end marriage with (one's spouse) by way of legal divorce.

The Divorce Letter *n*. A breakup letter in which the writer asks for and justifies a divorce or responds to a request for a divorce or annulment.

From Anne of Cleves (1515–1557), to her husband Henry VIII (1491–1547) after being asked by him for an annulment of their marriage seven months after their wedding. The marriage was an arranged one, and Henry, upon seeing Anne for the first time, was displeased with his future queen's looks—he supposedly described her as a "Flanders Mare." He was also finding himself more and more involved with Catherine Howard, a young woman to whom he was attracted. Anne, King Henry VIII's fourth wife, did not protest the annulment (this being the man who had Anne Boleyn beheaded; see p. 103), and testified that the marriage had never been consummated. This letter is her response, acquiescing to his request.

11 July 1540

Pleaseth your most excellent majesty to understand that, whereas, at sundry times heretofore, I have been informed and perceived by certain lords and others of your grace's council, of the doubts and questions which have been moved and found in our marriage; and how hath petition thereupon been made to your highness by your nobles and commons, that the same might be examined and determined by the holy clergy of this realm; to testify to your highness by my writing, that which I have before promised by my word and will, that is to say, that the matter should be examined and determined by the said clergy; it may please your majesty to know that, though this case must needs be most hard and sorrowful unto me, for the great love which I bear to your most noble person, yet, having more regard to God and his truth than to any worldly affection, as it beseemed me, at the beginning, to submit me to such examination and determination of the said clergy, whom I have and do accept for judges competent in that behalf. So now being ascertained how the same clergy hath therein given their judgement and sentence, I acknowledge myself hereby to accept and approve the same, wholly and entirely putting myself, for my state and condition, to your highness' goodness and pleasure; most humbly beseeching your majesty that, though it be determined that the pretended matrimony between us is void and of none effect, whereby I neither can nor will repute myself for your grace's wife, considering this sentence (whereunto I stand) and your majesty's clean and pure living with me, yet it will please you to take me for one of your humble servants, and so determine of me, as I may sometimes have the fruition of your most noble presence; which as I shall esteem for a great benefit, so, my lords and others of your majesty's council, now being with me, have put me in comfort thereof; and that your highness will take me for your sister; for the which I most humbly thank you accordingly.

Thus, most gracious prince, I beseech our Lord God to send your majesty long life and good health, to God's glory, your own honour, and the wealth of this noble realm.

From Richmond, the 11th day of July, the 32nd year of your majesty's most noble reign.

Your majesty's most humble sister and servant, Anne the daughter of Cleves.

From Ellen Coile Graves, a young Pennsylvania woman, to her husband Henry Graves, after her desertion of him two years earlier. Ellen married Henry on November 16, 1841 and left him in September of the following year, according to divorce records kept in the Chester County Archives in West Chester, Pennsylvania. Merril D. Smith, author of Breaking the Bonds: Marital Discord in Pennsylvania, 1730–1830 *(New York University Press, 1991), asserts in her book that situations in which women abandoned husbands "became more numerous in the nineteenth century . . . some women married husbands whom they did not love, but who loved them" and "when the expected love did not materialize women such as Ellen Graves . . . felt trapped and unhappy —and sometimes guilty because they did not love their husbands."*

After leaving Henry behind in West Chester, Ellen dropped her married name and opened what Smith calls "a variety and trimmings store in Philadelphia." It was only two years after her departure, on

September 25, 1844, that Henry filed for a "libel in divorce" action,
which stated that on September 15, 1842 Ellen "hath willfully and
maliciously deserted and absented herself from the habitation of [Henry
Graves] without any just or reasonable cause and such desertion hath
persisted in for the term of two years and upwards and yet doth continue
to absent herself from [Graves]." In this letter, which was included with
the depositions submitted to the court, it is interesting to note that Coile
did not use punctuation but instead simply left spaces after the end of
sentences.

Philadelphia Oct. 13th, [18]44

Henry

I received your letter and in compliance with your request I send
you this answer stating my feelings towards yourself I thought that
you was fully acquainted with me to know that you had no cause to
imagine that I had for a moment entertained a thought of returning
to you it would be impossible for me to live *peaceable* [*sic*] together
after what has occured [*sic*] and in connection with my feeling,
towards yourself which is that of perfect boldness I do not and could
not love you I am not one of those lukewarm creatures who can
bestow their affection upon all alike where they please my affection
spring spontaneously I *cannot compel* myself to love where there is
no congeniality of feeling I did wrong very wrong in marrying you
without feeling a sincere attachment but I beleived [*sic*] you was
capable of attaching me to you by kind and affectionate treatment
you encouraged me in this beleif [*sic*] for you was not deceived in
this respect when I married you it was with the full determination
of loving you which I beleived [*sic*] to be An easy task I was mistaken I tried for three months as ardently as ever woman tried but
each day devolved something calculated to turn me from you rather
than win me to you I gave up the task for I found it impossible my
Punishment I think has paid for my indiscretion I am sorry that you
still love me and I trust that this letter will prove effectual in
removing your unfortunate attachment for beleive [*sic*] me that by

me it can never be returned and now let me remove every false hope by solemnly assuring you that you and I parted *forever* in this World it is better that I should speak thus plainly than that you should encourage hopes that will bring you only disappointment I wish you well sincerely [*sic*] from the bottom of my Heart I should be glad to hear that you was Happyly [*sic*] married and successful in your Business mother sends her Love to you and the Family give my love to them likewise and

Believe [*sic*] me I am your Freind [sic]
Ellen Coile

From Nina Eliza Pinchback Toomer (1868–1909), the daughter of Pinckney Benton Stewart Pinchback, the first U.S. governor (Louisiana) of African-American descent, to her husband Nathan Toomer (1841–?), after he had abandoned her and her infant son. Although Nina's father disapproved of the union on the grounds that Nathan was an unscrupulous businessman, the two were married soon after they met in early 1894. Nine months into their marriage, Nathan— a fifty-something Southerner who claimed to be the aristo- cratic heir of slave-owning North Carolina planters— and Nina had welcomed the birth of a son, Nathan Eugene, who would later become Jean Toomer (1894–1967), the novelist (Cane, 1923) and philosopher of the Harlem Renaissance.

But Nathan had a penchant for disappearing on unexplained trips, and in October 1895, after yet another of his disappearances, Nina took her infant son and returned to her father's home for support. In September 1898, a little over a year after this letter was written, Nina Toomer filed for divorce. She died of appendicitis in 1909, when Jean was only fourteen years old. Jean believed that Nina's struggles in life were the result of patriarchal oppression, and would later champion the cause of women's freedom in his works.

July 8th, 1897

Col. —

Your letter of June 27th was duly received and I have been trying to answer it. The extreme warm weather and the attention to baby have prevented me from doing so until this moment.

You ask me to point to a single thing that you have ever said or done. A single thing! Would to God it was only a single thing. A simple history of your conduct since our marriage is all that is required to show to the world that you have forfeited every claim upon my love and completely destroyed my confidence in you.

Three years ago last March I left a happy and comfortable home to marry you. I loved you devotedly and was willing to share your lot. When we commenced housekeeping I endeavored to do my whole duty as a wife. Often when without help I cooked our meals and did our own house work, something I had never been called upon to do before. It was very hard upon me but I did it cheerfully to show you how deep was my devotion to you, and if you had remained with me and done your part as a husband there was no sacrifice I would not have made for you.

It is true that I believed before we were married that you were able to furnish me a comfortable home and at least a fairly good living and you alone were responsible for this for you gave me assurances upon top of assurances upon this point and emphasized it by giving me before our marriage the money to purchase a home for myself and furnish the same.

In about six months after we went to housekeeping, the summer having passed, I asked you for money to carpet the house and after repeated promises you failed to furnish it. I then for the first time began to suspect that your financial condition was not such as you had represented it to be. Your failure to offer compensation to my father for the time we boarded with him and numerous other evidences of financial distress on your part which manifested themselves and which I do not care to enumerate here convinced me that you had misled me as to your financial condition. I confess this discovery alarmed me but it did not weaken my affection. I resolved to accept the situation and make the best of it.

Your frequent and long absences even in this early stage of our married life and your failure to provide sufficient means for the support of our home compelled me to come to the conclusion that we would not be able to live here. I therefore endeavored to overcome my dislike of a home in the South and wrote you that I had concluded to go with you to your southern home. For reasons best known to yourself you never made any reply to that proposition and it is disgusting in the face of this fact to have you charge me with a want of heart.

We married March 29th, '94. In June you went away and remained until the middle of August. In the latter part of September you again went away and returned December 23rd, three days before the birth of our son. Six weeks after the birth of the child you left me again. On your return you found me in bed sick. When you entered the room your greeting was, "In bed again? Through your carelessness I know." It is needless to comment on such a greeting at such a time. From that time things went from bad to worse.

Night after night you left me alone and sick with a young baby until a late hour and once you were out all night. During day time I seldom saw you after breakfast until six or seven o'clock in the evening and part of this time I had no help and was obliged to do my own work and look after the baby. Your conduct and the severe work I had to do taxed my nature beyond its endurance and one morning I became unconscious and fell in the bathroom. When I regained consciousness I was in bed and could hardly lift my hand. It was several days before I could leave the bed and stand upon my feet. As soon as I was strong enough I determined if possible to raise some money—you had given me none for some time—to go to some place where I could get sufficient nourishing food to give me a little strength. I would rather have died than seek aid from my father and let him know my distress, so I borrowed thirty dollars upon your diamond ring from Mr. McKinley. When I told you I was going away for a short time you asked, "Where did you get money?" I told you. I cannot recall your words but I shall never forget your base insinuation. It left a sting which time cannot remove. And well I remember how my indignant look caused you to blush for making such a remark. I took the baby to Harpers [*sic*] Ferry where we remained four or five weeks and returned home feeling some better but far from well. It was impossible for me to regain health and strength in my ill and weakened condition and constant worrying about your affairs which I knew were desperate as you failed to supply the means to defray the ordinary expenses of our home.

In October 1895 you again left me ill and burdened with our child and only five dollars for support. You directed me to call upon Mr. McKinley when the five dollars were expended and I obtained from him thirty dollars more. When these thirty-five dollars were exhausted Mr. McKinley declined to furnish me any more. I notified you of the fact and you sent me six dollars at one time, twenty-five at another, fifteen later, total $46.00 up to Nov. 14th, '95.

The peculiar manner in which these small sums of money were sent to me and your persistent refusal to let me know anything about your personal affairs created in me such a feeling of uncertainty that I concluded that it would be best to break up housekeeping, rent the house as soon as possible and take room and board at some suitable place where I would remain until your return. Accordingly in Nov. '95 I broke up housekeeping, stored the furniture at my father's—he was kind enough to let me place it there to save storage—and secured room and board at Mrs. Alberts. I did not secure a tenant for my house for six months.

You sent me $60.00 and then and there your remittance ceased. From the time you left me until you ceased to me assistance and stopped writing to me you sent in all $106.00 with which to feed clothe and pay the other necessary expenses of myself and baby. It was totally inadequate for the purpose and I found myself in a very embarrassing and humiliating condition. Added to all this you ceased to answer my letters and left me no alternative but to conclude that you had deliberately deserted me and your child. Still, hoping against hope for your return and desiring to have a place where you would be welcome on your return I kept the room at Mrs. Albert's until the first of August 1896, eight long sad and weary months. Could any wife show more loyal devotion to a husband?

Deserted by my husband, burdened with a young baby, wounded in my pride and sadly disappointed in the object of my affection. Ill and without the means of support, I was compelled to seek relief. There were but two ways open to me. Either encumber my house or appeal to my father. When I thought of the future of my child I could not do the former and so appealed to my father for shelter and support of myself and child. It was a bitter bitter thing for me to do but stern necessity compelled me to do it. With loving kindness he generously received me and my child where we have enjoyed a comfortable home ever since.

This in brief is the history of our married life. If you can find anything in it to warrant me in having any confidence in your professions of love now and desire and ability to care for me and baby in the future I would like to know where you can find it. It would be idiotic on my part to again abandon a comfortable home and subject myself to the misery and destitution you imposed upon me while depending upon you for support.

In reply to your notice that you are ready and willing to give me and our child the support that is due a wife and child it is only necessary for me to remind you that without cause and at a time when every dictate of sentiment and duty demanded your presence you left me and my child without the means of support and added insult to injury by refusing to write to me or answer my letters for such a long time that I accepted your action as a desertion and my self respect as well as my future welfare forbids my acceptance of any professions of affection or assurances of support for the future you may now make.

You cannot desert me and leave me to shift for myself when it suits your convenience and return to me at your pleasure even if I had a home to which you could come. It will soon be two years since you left me and when the two years expire I shall apply to [the] court for a divorce. I am sure my happiness lies in a life separate from yours. I do not detest you, as the father of my child I cannot; neither have I any passion against you or objection to your seeing our child. I will be glad to have any aid you may see fit to furnish for his support which is his lawful right but I shall not seek or expect it. I will endeavor as best I can to raise and educate our boy, if God spares our lives, in such a manner to make him a useful and honorable man. To do this will be a difficult task with the limited means at my command. But every dollar I have and all I may be able to earn, if need be, will be devoted to that purpose.

In our last conversation you assured me that if I desired a divorce you would make no opposition to it. I was glad to know it, as such a course on your part will be in some measure a reparation of the wrong you did me in taking me from a comfortable home and kind and loving parents when you knew you were unable or worse unwilling to give me decent support. Besides such a course will be better for both of us and our child. It will enable us to be friendly which doubtless would be beneficial to our son.

N.E.P.T.

———

From Clara Bewick Colby (1846–1916), suffragist, journalist, and newspaper editor. Clara married General Leonard Wright Colby (1846–1924), a lawyer, Nebraska senator, and veteran of the Civil War, in 1871. During the course of their marriage, the couple adopted two children, Clarence, and Marguerite Elizabeth, who was found at the age of four months next to her murdered Sioux mother. For many years before his separation from Clara, Leonard had been involved in an affair with his secretary Marie Moller, who bore him a son; according to biographer Kristin Mapel Bloomberg, "Clara tried to get Marie to relinquish the child to her to raise with Leonard as their own son. Marie, of course, didn't agree to that because her son was key to her future plans of marrying Leonard after his divorce from Clara." The

Colbys separated in 1894 and were divorced in 1906. In a diary entry dated August 11, Colby wrote . . .

> *"What do I owe to myself in the matter? I ought to have stood for my dignity as a wife ten years ago, but I was so much in the bondage of my love and of conventionality that I could not. I made myself believe and have up the illusion, that by my for-bearance I should win him back. How different my life would have been, how much more honorable and sincere if with one great wrench I had settled the matter then . . . Other women, alas how many women have been through with this and held their heads high, lived it down and been happy. But it has always seemed to me they were women who had not loved much and who could not, as I have done, forgive much."*

Mapel Bloomberg's biography of Clara Bewick Colby, published by University of Nebraska Press, is scheduled for release after the year 2004.

[Stationery: Federal Women's Equality Association]

August 22, '03 [1903]

My beloved husband: —

For such you are to me notwithstanding you say that the tie between us exists only in name. I think you have been so blinded with the transient and evanescent emotions of purely physical conditions that you have lost sight of the deeper relations between mind and soul. It was not without significance that we were born on the same day and brought together from far over land and sea.; that we chose each other when we each had a wide circle of friends of the opposite sex with whom we were acceptable; that we had the same intellectual ambitions, aesthetic tastes, and ethical ideals. All these made the foundation for a union of life interests, and with our solemn vows before God and our friends we expressed our realization of this and our deep sense of the fact that such a union holds over into the eternities. Can you remember your part of our solemn compact? I will recall one sentence from mine:—"And if God wills I shall but love thee better after death". A violation of such a union on the physical side would have to be persisted in with such wilful [sic] determination as to totally change the character and hence the basis of the intellectual and spiritual affinities, before one could truly say it destroyed the tie. Believing that we are eternally wedded in heart and soul, despite all your attempts to freeze me out of your life in order to deaden your conscience and make yourself comfortable in your chosen path, how can I do what you ask me? How can I ask man to put asunder what God hath joined together.

As a lawyer you have had many occasions to get divorces for people lightly and may have become so accustomed to the modern custom of fleeing to the divorce court instead of standing by duty, that you may not be able to even understand my point of view. It may help you to do so if you will remember that in my family, in all its numerous ramifications, there has never been a divorce or separation; and that such would be considered an irreparable disgrace. From any aspect of the case it is a confession of weakness, of failure, of cowardice, and of a desire to gratify a present whim at the expense of honor and duty. For more than twenty years we slept in each other's arms, with a restful stimulating exchange of magnetism from clean, wholesome, agreeable persons. This makes the true union on the physical plane. Our interests were identical and in all important matters we, to use your own expression, "stood by each other." We were a solid front to the world; our home the center of the best social life of the city, and often the best of the State and nation were welcomed there. We were prospered in business; honored by our community; loved by friends; a power in the state. Each successful individually, yet bringing the results of our experiences and our honors to the mutual altar of our home. Our absence from each other has changed many of these conditions, but things are not so bad but there is still a chance to right them in a measure, and to re-establish ourselves before God and the world as those who have learned wisdom and charity by their own sad experiences.

When you left Washington, you expressed the purpose of removing to Denver or Salt Lake, and making a home for us there. There was not, and never has been, a hint that you did not contemplate a future home together, and when I put the question to you the last time I saw you, you said you could not leave Beatrice until you had straightened out your property matters; giving me to understand that you still had it in mind. It goes without saying that I had to wait both until you should provide the home, and hold yourself ready to be loyal to it.

You know well at what agony to myself I helped you in your entanglement bravely and faithfully; and treated the erring woman with a mother's tenderness, anxious above all to save you the disgrace which you have since so recklessly invited, and seem now determined to bring upon yourself.

The story of that dreadful time never passed my lips even to my sister, and it is not my fault if the situation has been common talk in Beatrice and elsewhere. When I took my stand at first I believed your conduct was a lapse from honor which you deplored and would in future avoid I comforted myself with the assurance that this pertained to the weaker and the transitory physical while your love for me was a part of your very being. I have taken pains to speak of you so kindly and appreciatively that I have silenced any criticism, or questioning, that your absence would otherwise have elicited. I have confidently expected that you would make such arrangements for us to live together as would enable us to build up our lives again into honor, trust and peace. I have ever held myself ready to respond when you should call and you will find in earlier letters this hope many times expressed. It has been a great disappointment that by continuing the disastrous association, you have kept it impossible for me to take the initiative in restoring our home. Still I have kept my hope and faith, that as the years went by you would come to a truer estimate of values, a truer conception of what happiness depends on, and would want the comforts and the tender companionships of home and friends. You once wrote me that if I failed you—for you God, and Truth, and Beauty would die I have not failed you, and you must not slay the Trinity you believed in in your days of high ideals. Although apparently our paths have been so diverse, yet with me every day has been related to you; no night has passed without my prayer for your welfare, and that we might be restored to each other when the time should come that it would be for the truest spiritual development of both. I have striven for self-mastery; holding firm to physical improvement, to intellectual growth, to social friendships and opportunities, that I might bring a larger and better self to our new marriage that was to be.

I have this to offer in place of your dissolution of our difficulties.:— settle with the other once and for all on a money basis; and make a home with me in Beatrice or elsewhere— preferably the latter. United we could live everything down and dispel all clouds. Your letter convinces me you wish now to act openly and above board. This is the hour I have been waiting for when conscience should awaken. Your association with me covers the best years of our life and to it belong all the cherished memories of youth, of University friendships, of social and official honors.

I will not characterize what the other has been and what that covers, but I will ask you which can you best spare from your life? Which shall be the pattern for your remaining years. Judicially review the case.

If you should carry out your present desire could you endure the grief of your true friends; the cold shoulder of the community; the merciless taunts of your political ennemies [sic] who will save their darts to strike you if you develop any ambitions. There would be a ghost in your life which would never down. You are naturally too high-minded to be able to destroy your moral ideals with impunity. You will not give happiness, for you cannot confer the friendly countenance of society without which a woman is always, sooner or later, miserable; nor will you be able to inspire any confidence in new pledges when old ones have had no power to bind you. You will not be happy yourself, for when the stress of passion is past,—and at your time of life this cannot be far distant,—you will not be able to find satisfaction in purely physical ties, which is all this situation has to offer you. May God grant that you settle this matter in the only way that can round out our lives usefully, respectably, peacefully.

It is never imperative to take "matters as they are and not as you might hope or wish them to be". Let us make matters what they ought to be at any personal sacrifice. No new promise is binding that violates those you made to me which were ratified at the altar with prayer and benediction.

I do not know how to urge this with a tithe of the earnestness and persistence I feel. Naturally it is hard for a woman to open her heart fully under these circumstances. You must let my life as you have known it speak for me. You must answer it from your own best self.

How many times I have signed myself to you "Tua sempiturna", and "Semper eadem". I sign them now with my heart's blood.

Clara Bewick Colby

I must add to this letter a statement concerning the new divorce law of the District, of which you may be unaware. Divorce is now only granted for adultery, and the co-respondent must be named. Could you bear to be the accuser? Could you endure to be disgraced here where you have been so honored?

———

From Mabel Dodge Luhan (1879–1962), a wealthy left-wing patron of such radicals and artists as D. H. Lawrence, Willa Cather, and Georgia O'Keeffe, to her third husband, Maurice Sterne (1878–1957), a Postimpressionist painter. Luhan (then Mabel Dodge) met Sterne in 1915 at a New York performance of dancer Isadora Duncan (see p. 109) and married him in August 1917. After their divorce, Mabel married Tony Luhan, a Pueblo Indian whom she had met in Taos, New Mexico.

Taos, March 21 [1918?]

Dear Maurice,

I don't quite understand the tone of your letters. It is new from you. I cannot come east at present. If you decide after a little more thought that you want a divorce I can get one here. I think you exaggerate the talk people always chatter. They have been chattering about you too though I didn't write you of it. If people in New York know more about me than the people in Taos I am surprised to hear it. The whole town came to a party here two days ago— showing that their conclusions are different from the eastern ones. I have not forgotten [illegible] living in the west. I thank god for the west.

Of course if you want a divorce it will mean a cessation of the— maybe small— but any way partial income you have been getting. I am sorry for this for I hoped it would help to get you free to work. I do not consider myself to blame for your lapses in work. Nor do you. You always have lapses. If I were you I would keep working and stop paying attention to foolish chattering [tongues?]. However if you continue to want a divorce after some more thought, you shall have one. I have no fantasies at present. I am healthy [occupied?] and contented. If Dr. Brill saw me he would be satisfied.

As I said before I cannot come east now. Mrs. Austin is here— others are coming— [planting?] and so on are beginning. It I can get away later I will— but not because you threaten me [or for any?] such reason.

It is unfashionable for me to cut myself off from my real friends. If any are "cut off" they are not my friends and I don't miss them. Now as always my way of life is an honest endeavor to find out the essential meaning of life. In so far as I am able— I do not allow it to be self indulgent or wicked. We have both made each other unhappy— but happy too. There is no room for hate.

Mabel.

———

Hell Hath No Fury

From journalist Dorothy Thompson (1893–1961) to <u>Main Street</u> (1920) writer Sinclair Lewis (1885–1951) following Lewis' request for a divorce after eleven years of marriage. The two began a romance the day Thompson's divorce from her first husband, Joseph Bard, became final (see p. 113). Lewis proposed to her that night, and again numerous times over the course of the following months; she eventually accepted and married him in May 1928. Lewis—nicknamed "Red"— left Thompson at the end of 1937, with no explanation other than to say that Thompson's success had "ruined their marriage" and "robbed him of his creative powers." He asked for a divorce in the spring of 1939, but she delayed granting him one until November 1941, when she filed for divorce herself, charging "willful desertion." The divorce became final on January 2, 1942.

1938 [undated]

If you think it's wicked—go ahead and get a divorce. I won't oppose it. I also won't get it. For God's sake, let's be honest. You left me, I didn't leave you. You want it. I don't. You get it. On any ground your lawyers can fake up. Say I 'deserted' you. Make a case for mental cruelty. You can make a case. Go and get it.

What is 'incredible' about my not writing? What is 'incredible' is that I don't rush into the divorce court and soak you for desertion and 'mental cruelty.' I don't write because I don't know what to say to you. You have made it clear time on end that you dislike me, that you are bored with me, that you are bored with 'situations and conditions. And reactions.' You don't like my friends. You don't know my friends. You resent my friends. Shall I write you that I think Hamilton Armstrong has done a brilliant piece of journalism in his last book on the Munich conference? Or that Graham Hutton is in America and has a fascinating tale of Britain? Or that Peter Grimm has ideas on the Housing policy? Or that Gustav Stolper has introduced me to [Kurt] Riezler, who was the man who smuggled Lenin and Trotsky into Russia, and has just, at long last, left Germany? Are you interested in Alex Sachs' memo to Lehman Brothers on what

Mussolini plans in Tunisia? Or in Fodor's letters from Riga? Do you want to know what Raoul [de Sales] says about Bonnet? Or what Edgar [Mowrer] writes about Moro-Giafferi and Grynszpan?

You are happy. Happier, you write, than you have been in years. I congratulate you. I am glad that you are happy. I happen not to be. I am not happy. I am not happy, because I have no home, because I have an ill and difficult child without a father. Because I have loved a man who didn't exist. Because I am widowed of an illusion. Because I am tremblingly aware of the tragedy of the world we live in.

There are things in my heart that you do not dream of, things that are compounded of passion and fury and love and hate and pride and disgust and tenderness and contrition, things that are wild and fierce . . . and you ask me to write you conventional letters because you are in 'exile.' From what? From whom?

Give me Vermont. I want to watch the lilac hedge grow tall and the elm trees form, and the roses on the gray wall thicken, and the yellow apples hang on the young trees, and the sumac redden on the hills, and friends come, and your two children feel at home. Who knows? Maybe some time you might come home yourself. You might go a long way and do worse. As a matter of fact and prophecy—you will.

———

From Madeline, a subject in Christine Gallagher's book __The Woman's Book of Divorce__ (Citadel, 2001), to her ex-husband John.* As Gallagher says in her book, "Sometimes it helps to get things off your chest. Madeline found that the best method for her was to send her husband a Dear John letter. It went as follows:"

[1999]

Dear John:

I regret to inform you that you have been eliminated from the search for the position of Mr. Perfect. Please do not be discouraged in your efforts. The competition has been extremely strong and we have had to sift through many fine candidates.

There were however some specific reasons that came up during your trial run. Perhaps you might be interested in this feedback, which may be of use to you as you continue with your efforts.

1. Making love is not similar to going to the dentist in the sense that the sooner it's over, the better.

2. Occasionally women, even married ones, enjoy being taken out for dinner.

3. Leaving your dirty socks and underwear on the bedroom floor is not an attractive quality.

4. Likewise with the emission of bodily gasses—most unpleasant, especially if done under the bed covers.

5. When you rent a video on Friday night, it's polite to occasionally let your partner make the selection.

6. Next time you caress and cuddle and kiss that dog of yours, take a look in the mirror and ask yourself "What's wrong with this picture?" On the other hand, you and your pooch might make a lovely couple.

Good luck with your efforts in the future. Please pass on our condolences in advance to all your future partners. Last but not least, don't call us, wait for us to call you, which we probably won't.

Never yours,
Madeline

———

This letter was written by writer Kathy Fitzgerald Sherman (<u>A House-keeper Is Cheaper Than a Divorce: Why You CAN Afford to Hire Help and How to Get It,</u> Life Tools Press, 2000) to her husband of seventeen years. As Sherman puts it: "Although I (had) adored him, his lack of interest in meeting my needs—in fact, his total lack of interest in even understanding what they were—became a pain too great to bear. Divorce seemed to be the only option." After she sent it, something surprising hap-

pened. Her husband . . . changed. He responded within two days by writing "an impassioned and charming love letter," read it to her over dinner, and begged her to give him another chance. Two years later, the two are both in counseling, and, Sherman says, have grown enormously. "We still experience many bumps in the road, but we're learning how to deal with them together. Although I hope I never have to write another 'Dear John' letter again, I'm certain that the strength that I found within myself when writing it was the fuel that made possible my marriage's reconciliation and renewal." Words in brackets are the Sherman's.

October 4, 2000

Dear M—,

This is the hardest letter I've ever had to write, and probably the hardest one you'll ever have to read. I'm putting my thoughts and feelings on paper because I want you to hear me out fully before you react.

I have come to a decision that I believe serves the best interests of S—, L—[my children], and myself. I wouldn't presume to speak for you, but I predict that my decision will serve your best interests as well.

M—, I have decided to divorce you. The decision fills me with sadness—a deep, deep mourning for what might have been, but never was. I had so much hope for us in the beginning. But, as I look back on our history, I can see that that hope has been chiseled away, year after year, until now there is nothing left. For me, our marriage is empty. Yes, we are great intellectual partners, and we provide each other fantastic support in our entrepreneurial efforts. But that's not enough for a marriage. Large parts of myself have died (or, more accurately, are lying inside me, dormant, in a near-death state) and I'm no longer willing to live that way. I may not be living till the year 2100 like you [M—uses many strategies designed to improve his longevity], but at 43 I'm far too young to extinguish so many important parts of myself.

There are many things I appreciate about you, including your intellect and the fine financial support you've provided for all of us. Above all, you love S—and L—and they love you. You've had many wonderful moments with them and I know you'll have many more. But I believe that they are being harmed by the environment in which they're living. They witness the suppression of their mother's spirit on a daily basis and it hurts them. And they witness a continuous undercurrent of hostility between their parents which confuses and disorients them. I believe they need healthier relationship models. I'm hoping we can give them one in separation that we couldn't give them in marriage.

As I write this, I wonder how you'll be reacting. With anger? That's both my fear and my expectation. With sadness? I hope so, because I'm sad too. With at least a little relief? I believe that, if you're telling yourself the truth, the answer will be yes.

First, I want you to know that this decision was not encouraged or even influenced by R—[my therapist]. He supports me in the decision (and has been probing to discover any uncertainty, which doesn't exist) but I reached the decision on my own about two weeks ago.

Second, I want you to know that I have taken no legal steps yet. I felt that if I filed for divorce and had the papers served before speaking to you, it would set off an adversarial pattern that would benefit no one. As parents to our kids, we are a team and will be forever, married or not. I want to make sure we remain a team that works together rather than at cross-purposes.

My hope is that we can talk to each other in a civilized fashion and work out a dissolution that is fair, optimal, and, above all, protects the kids in every aspect of their lives. Ending our marriage will be further complicated by the fact that we each have a business that is located at [our address]. Neither of us can move our business on the spur of the moment and it's imperative, for our futures and our kids', that both enterprises continue to function throughout this process.

M—, let's not be vindictive with each other. I can hear your voice in my head saying, "I've always known you would divorce me."

Please believe me when I tell you that I didn't know it myself until two weeks ago. If you saw divorce on the horizon, then it's because you saw the pieces of me dying and knew that I would eventually call a halt to that process. I couldn't allow myself to see that process because if I had, I would have called it quits a lot sooner. I have been fully committed to our marriage (until my decision point) and have tried everything I know to make it work—est, therapy, sex therapy, more therapy, a housekeeper, religion (pastoral counseling), more therapy, even caving in and giving up all expectations. The fighting was hard, but the caving in became intolerable. Please don't allow yourself to believe that this is something I was plotting.

There is a lot more that needs to be said, but the rest has to be two-way, so I will stop writing now. Let's be a team, M—. There's too much at stake not to.

With deepest sadness and regret,
K—

The
"Dear John"

Dear (dîr) *adj.* Loved and cherished; highly esteemed or regarded. Used in directed address, especially in salutations.

John (jŏn) *n.* A common male name. The fourth book of the New Testament. A toilet. A man who is a prostitute's customer.

The Dear John *n.* A breakup letter sent by a woman to a man in the military, ending a relationship or confessing to a change in feeling.

"DEAR JOHN" has been used as a blanket term to describe any sort of "I'm leaving you" letter, but the origin of the phrase can be traced to the military, although exactly where and when is up for debate. The *American Heritage Dictionary of the English Language,* 4th edition (Houghton Mifflin, 2000), simply defines "Dear John" as "A letter, as to a serviceman, requesting a divorce or ending a personal relationship." In the *Random House Historical Dictionary of American Slang* (Random House, 1994), Jonathan Lighter cites a 1945 issue of the *Rochester Democrat & Chronicle* stating that the term came from "a current radio program made of letters addressed to 'Dear John.'" Gordon Angus Mackinlay, a veteran of the British and Australian armies, claims that the term came from a music-hall song popular just prior to World War I whose chorus went:

> Dear John I love you so
> Dear John you've got to go
> Dear John I love you so
> Dear John you must go

But no matter where the term originated, the letters themselves were painful and the men I spoke to used words like "cruel," "heartbreaking," "an ambush," and "crushing" to describe them. "I have vivid recollections of the first time someone shot at me directly, the first incoming mortar round, the first pool of blood and my Dear John," says Vietnam vet Kent Draper. A Korean War veteran, Jack Witter, remembers the day in 1951 that one of his dear friends was killed in action and was found carrying a "Dear John" from his girlfriend back home describing her first sexual experience with another man. Witter burned it before the soldier's belongings were sent home with his body. In *With the Old Breed* (Presidio Press, 1981), E. B. Sledge tells the story of a Marine in his unit during World War II who received a letter from his girlfriend in which she claimed to have taken a lover of another race;

the marine then stood up in the middle of a firefight with the Japanese the next day and allowed himself to be shot.

Some had a sense of humor about the Dear John. Novelist James Salter, stationed in the Philippines in 1946, remembers hearing a crudely done radio show (perhaps the same show mentioned by the *Rochester Democrat & Chronicle*) on AFN on which supposedly real Dear John letters were read aloud, much to the delight of listeners. "The show was immensely popular because the letters were allegedly absolutely real," says Salter. "They were a great hoot . . . everyone just laughed and laughed over these heartbreaking letters with this wonderful lugubrious violin music in the background." "Johnny Smack-O," the recipient of a Dear John letter sent in 1970 and tape-recorded by a friend (see p. 177), even giggles and laughs while reading it aloud, probably because he knows he deserves it, but perhaps also because he wants to preserve his macho image and so laughs not to cry.

As awful or funny as Dear Johns could be, the women behind such letters were often ostracized and tormented for sending them in the first place. Anne Gudis, whose 3-line Dear John letter to an American serviceman was published in *Yank* magazine in 1943, was besieged with angry mail after the recipient (Samuel Kramer, whom she eventually married), sent in the letter—which read "Go to Hell!" — to the magazine. Ray Merriam of Bennington, Vermont remembers hearing a story about a submariner who received a Dear John and retaliated by sending the woman a batch of pictures of strange women with a letter stating that he had forgotten which one she was, and would she please send the photos back, indicating which of the photos was of her.

Another veteran says that soon after the mail arrived onboard his Navy vessel, every Dear John letter would be circulated around the ship to other servicemen, who would then inundate the sender with "the most unprintable, hateful E-mails and letters imaginable." In the course of my research, I heard numerous variations on a story about a Dear John in the form of a photograph or videotape showing the soldier's girlfriend back home performing oral sex on her new boyfriend. As the story goes, the receiving soldier put the photo or tape right back in the mail and addressed it to her parents.

Even popular how-to books published in wartime encouraged women to keep Dear Johns out of the postal system and inside their heads, if only for the good of their country. "Commanders in all the services understand that nothing breaks morale faster than bad news from home," says Kevin Clark, an instructor in the history department at the United States Military Academy at West Point. "Dear John letters can best be compared to the Trojan Horse. Deployed soldiers are and were obsessed with mail and hearing from those back home . . . to eagerly open a letter only to get Dear Johned can be a crushing experience." G. A. Reeder's 1943 book, *Letter Writing in Wartime* (Books, inc.), included an entire section of *Dos and Don'ts For Sweethearts,* asserting that men in the military are "imagining that you are going out — every night in the week —with a succession of swains, each one ten times as handsome as he is and at least five times as brilliant." It goes on to instruct its female readers not to "write him anything that would confirm any of his fears" and makes a woman's change of heart seem almost unpatriotic: "Always reassure him of your love—even if at times you think you are going to change your mind before he comes back. (Do this for your *country,* if not for *him.*)" Mr. Reeder does warn, however, that women should mention men in their letters once in a while, "otherwise [the man] will know something is wrong. But let it be some friend of the family or some 50-year old uncle, or some other man he knows is perfectly harmless."

Stories of Dear John letters abound, but, for obvious reasons, the actual letters themselves are difficult to find. Michael Lee Lanning, an author and army veteran, says he remembers ceremonies in the service in which Dear Johns were burned or flushed down toilets. (Another veteran claims that Dear Johns were used as toilet paper.) Vietnam veteran Guy Hunter says that some of his fellow marines posted their Dear Johns on the walls in the platoon headquarters, where they remained to either fall apart or be ripped down and thrown away. As it was, I was lucky—or enterprising —enough to find several new, unpublished Dear John letters, and am happy to include them here for public viewing for the first time.

Hell Hath No Fury

From Agnes von Kurowsky (1892–1984) to writer Ernest Hemingway (1899–1961). The two met in July 1918, when Hemingway, then a nineteen-year-old ambulance driver for the American forces in World War I, was taken to the American Red Cross Hospital in Milan, Italy, after suffering shrapnel wounds to his right leg. Kurowsky, twenty-six, was working as a nurse on Hemingway's ward, and, after a month of increasingly flirtatious banter, the two became intimate. After a whirlwind courtship, and five months together, Hemingway returned to the United States to secure a home for the woman he thought would become his bride. Kurowsky, who in later years denied that she was ever in love with him, promptly fell in love with a Neapolitan millionaire and wrote Hemingway this letter about three months after his departure. According to James R. Mellow's biography of Hemingway, <u>Hemmingway: A Life Without Consequences</u> (Houghton Mifflin, 1992), Hemingway was so devastated by the letter that "he took to his bed, physically ill, for several days." But it was not a letter without reward: the text inspired Hemingway's short story, "A Very Short Story" (see p. 303), and the romance itself the basis for the relationship between Lieutenant Frederic Henry and Catherine Barkley in his novel <u>A Farewell to Arms</u> (1929).

[March 7, 1919]

Ernie, dear boy,

I am writing this late at night after a long think by myself, & I am afraid it is going to hurt you, but, I'm sure it won't harm you permanently.

For quite awhile before you left, I was trying to convince myself it was a real love-affair, because, we always seemed to disagree, & then arguments always wore me out so that I finally gave in to keep you from doing something desperate.

Now, after a couple of months away from you, I know that I am still very fond of you, but, it is more as a mother than as a sweetheart. It's alright to say I'm a Kid, but, I'm not, & I'm getting less & less so every day.

So, Kid (still Kid to me, & always will be) can you forgive me some day for unwittingly deceiving you? You know I'm not really bad, & don't mean to do wrong, & now I realize it was my fault in the beginning that you cared for me, & regret it from the bottom of my heart. But, I am now & always will be too old, & that's the truth, & I can't get away from the fact that you're just a boy—a kid.

I somehow feel that some day I'll have reason to be proud of you, but, dear boy, I can't wait for that day, & it is wrong to hurry a career.

I tried hard to make you understand a bit of what I was thinking on that trip from Padua to Milan, but, you acted like a spoiled child, & I couldn't keep on hurting you. Now, I only have the courage because I'm far away.

Then—& believe me when I say this is sudden for me, too—I expect to be married soon. And I hope & pray that after you have thought things out, you'll be able to forgive me & start a wonderful career & show what a man you really are.

Ever admiringly & fondly
Your friend
Aggie

———

From actress and Valley of the Dolls *(1966) author Jacqueline Susann (1921–1974) to her husband, television/film publicist and producer Irving Mansfield, in 1942, after three years of marriage (and at least one affair). According to Margie Hart, interviewed in* Lovely Me *(Seven Stories Press, 1996), Barbara Seaman's biography of the writer, Susann wrote Mansfield the following "Dear John" letter after he was drafted into the army in 1943. At the time, Susann was performing in the Broadway play* Cry Havoc, *and decided to read the letter aloud to the all-female cast. The couple reconciled in 1944.*

Irving, when we were at the Essex House and I had room service and I could buy all my Florence Lustig dresses, I found that I loved you very much, but now that you're in the army and getting fifty-six dollars a month, I feel that my love has waned.

———

From a young woman, Lois, to American serviceman Harry Leister, twenty, while he was stationed in England during World War II. Harry met Lois in July 1943 in a drugstore in Huntsville, Texas; she worked behind the counter "serving Cokes" and he lived nearby on the army base, where he was stationed for six months. After Harry left for England, Lois wrote him this Dear John letter, in which she confessed that she had married another man. In letters that followed, she announced that she had left her husband, would never let herself care for another man, and asked if Harry would help her financially. By then, Harry had married Winifred, (an English-woman to whom he is still married,) had returned to the United States, and was working for U.S. Rubber in Detroit, Michigan. He did not reply.

Friday 10/20/44

Dearest Harry,

Received your "why don't you write" card yesterday so here's a letter.

As you can see I'm not attending Sam Houston this year (not that I didn't want to) but it's my fault that I'm not. I work at Foley Brothers in the office now but can't say that I like it. Foley's is reputed as being the "largest store in the largest city in the largest state". How does that sound? I don't like to work and I'm lonesome all the time. My twin sister finally had her baby; it was born on August 31 and is a girl. She weighed 9lbs 4oz. at birth—which is a very large baby. Well I have two brothers and a brother-in-law across now so there's hardly anyone left. Sorry I didn't answer your cable gram but didn't feel it necessary to do so. It was so sweet of you to wire me. (over)

Honey if you ever intended to marry me I wished you could have done so before you left, although we had known each other such a short time. You see Harry darling I'm afraid it's too late now—as I am already married. I didn't mean to tell you while you were over there but I didn't want you to think that I had just stopped writing. Because you know Harry, I do still love you and guess I always shall. I know there'll never be another person like you, so decent, so sweet, and so kind and thoughtful. I mean it Harry—you're what every girl should want and you deserve the best, which I sincerely hope you get. Harry I turned out to be not the girl you would have wanted and it hurts like heck to tell you. I made a mistake and I'm sorry; I don't think there could be a more unhappy person on earth as I am. I'm thinking about getting a divorce but not sure yet. I shall always cherish the wonderful times you and I had together, as well as your beautiful ring—if I may keep it.

I don't have to work but I must do something to keep my mind occupied, to keep from going crazy.

Suppose this letter isn't much of a moral[e] build[er] to let you know the truth—although I didn't intend to tell you when I started writing.

Please lets [sic] be friends. I've told you how I felt about you and always will. I'll write you ever now and then and please Harry, let me hear from you.

I feel like a heel letting you down the way I have—can you ever forgive me?

As ever,
Lois

———

A recollection of a Dear John letter from Virginia K, then eighteen, to Leonard M. Owczarzak, then twenty, while Owczarzak was serving in the United States Army. The two met as teenagers through Owczarzak's next-door neighbor (Virginia's aunt) and started dating when Leonard was seventeen, and she was fifteen. Two years into their relationship, in 1943, the United States had entered the war and Owczarzek was drafted into the army and sent overseas to fight the Japanese in the

Pacific. He received the following letter while working as an antiaircraft machine gunner in the Solomon Islands. In January 1946, after Owczarzak returned home from the service, he received another letter from Virginia, inviting him to her infant son's birthday party, and adding suggestively that her husband was away on business. He met his future wife, Helen, in 1948; they have been married since 1949 and live in their home state of Michigan.

July 1944

Dear Len

Aunt Esther tells me that your mother told her that you might be going overseas soon.

I hope and pray that you will be careful and take care of yourself. I will be praying for you.

When you were home on leave we really did not become engaged or anything, only that we cared for each other since we were kids.

While the family was in Florida for the winter, I went to a dance and met a Marine. He was very nice to me, and after a few dates we thought we might get married after the war.

Please forgive me for not waiting for you. You know how much I cared for you.

All My Love
Virginia K

From Annette to Sylvan "Sol" Summers, then twenty-five, while he was serving aboard the USS Ajax, an auxiliary repair ship in the Pacific Ocean. After the war and his return to the United States, Summers met and married Rose Lee Nowack, to whom he is still married. This letter first appeared in War Letters: Extraordinary Correspondence from American Wars *(Scribner, 2001), edited by Andrew Carroll.*

March 25, 1945

Dear Sol,

I know its been quite some time since you last heard from me and no doubt you've been wondering why the long absence. This is by far the most difficult thing I've had to do and you must realize how much it pains me to do this.

I've always been honest with you Sol & I believe you deserve only the truth from me, for you yourself are so fine & wonderful a person. So I'll be perfectly honest with you. I've met someone I care for very much.

I realize too well how you must feel right now, but do you think it fair to give only part of my devotion to you? You deserve more than that, for you are too fine a person to receive anything half way about it. And it would never be fair to either of us.

Don't think for a moment that it was your fault Sol. I don't believe it was either of our faults. Neither of us wished to have things happen as they did. It just happened & we can't do anything about it. Guess they call it fate.

You've been wonderful to me all along & I think you are one of the grandest, sincerest people I've had the honor of meeting. I'm certain you'll meet someone in the very near future who will be able to give you what I can no longer give. For someone as fine and understanding as you Sol deserves only the best in life.

I'm returning your gifts & the ring to your mother, which I believe is the only fair thing to do. Thank her & your Dad for being so wonderful to me. If I could but spare you & them all this, believe me Sol, I would, but I see no way.

Please try to find some forgiveness in your heart, for I honestly didn't want it this way, but I guess it just had to be. I'd like very much to remain friends but that of course is entirely up to you.

Here's wishing you the very best in life, for all who know you, know full well, that you certainly deserve it. Good luck to you always & here's wishing you a happy voyage home & soon.

Annette.

———

From author Rosemarie Keller Skaine to Bob Trentz, a boy she was dating in 1954. The two, both from the same area of central Nebraska, began dating shortly after Trentz's then-fiancée broke their engagement in the early 1950s. Trentz, then nineteen or twenty, had entered the U.S. Navy and was stationed in San Diego when he wrote Skaine a letter to tell her that he missed her and that when he got home he wanted to marry her and make her his "life's ambition to love and cherrish[sic]." Skaine, at that time seventeen and a senior in high school, responded with the following Dear John letter a few days later. "Marriage to anyone was not something my mother had acculturated me to enter," she explains. "She wanted me to get educated first, and so, dating to me, was just that: dating."

Soon after Skaine sent off her Dear John, she received one in return, ostensibly from Trentz himself, but suspiciously sophisticated in content, grammar, and spelling. (In his earlier letter he had proudly announced to Skaine that he had learned how to use paragraphs in his writing.) "Trentz" said that her Dear John was "smug, rude, and completely conceited imaginary melodrama", a "horse-opera." Although the letter seemed to be written by someone else, its postscript was most likely written by Trentz himself: it asserted that he and his Navy buddies in the course of their enjoyment of her letter, had split a bottle of alcohol, and that it "was the best Champagne that money can by [sic]." Skaine married during college, and is now a writer and the author of books on women in Afghanistan, gender issues, and women's roles in the military during wartime.

[early 1954]

Dear Bob,
I wish it were as simple as Dear John, Sorry! Love Kate
Naturally it isn't. John will want an explanation and write Kate. To save this unwanted letter Kate should have given an explanation. Naturally the explanation will not suffice. Why? Because John,

although reason or reasons have been given, thinks, perhaps, Kate will change her mind. No one can blame John for trying and no one can blame John for loving Kate. Who then shall we blame? Kate? Let us see, how Kate actually feels inside. Is she really wearing her heart on her sleeve? Kate had been honest with John from their first date. She had agreed to date him because he had been dear "Johned" once before, only this incident included a diamond and sacred vows. Kate grew to like John very much and John grew to love Kate. Kate began to realize it would be a serious mistake to "lead" him on. She told him over and over. Heedless was he. Her like grew to dissatisfaction. Which brings us to our present Dear John letter. "What have I done?" asks John. "What haven't I done? Is there anything I can do to make up for what I have or haven't done?"

You have done nothing to offend me, Bob. I only want to be honest. I do not even have a "like" left for you in any way. Why? I can not explain, I really do not know my self. Age, I suppose, infatuation, complexes, and what have you. No one else, I assure you. Remember the time you asked me if I thought you were a man? My answer lies in your reaction to this letter, and how you attempt to comfort your emotions, by the bottle, prayer, tears, or laughter. I think I have made myself defiantly clear and therefore there is no need of pleading or answertive letters. If you are wondering—reread this letter. One request, whether it is granted or not is up to you. May I have my picture and I shall return yours upon the arrival of mine? A woman or man is as good as their word and I am my word.

Regretfully,
Rosie

———

From an unknown woman to an American soldier in the Vietnam War, known only as "Johnny Smack-O" (but perhaps named "Danny," according to a reference in the letter.) Dave Syster, who served in

Hell Hath No Fury

Vietnam in 1970–71, recorded Johnny Smack-O reading the following letter while Syster was stationed atop Monkey Mountain, Vietnam. The two spoke regularly over a military PRC-25 radio, and Syster tape-recorded Johnny Smack-O reading the letter aloud soon after it arrived. As Syster remembers it, "the letter was famous in the Da Nang area for months." A transcript of a radio conversation follows the actual text of the letter.

Johnny: A letter was written to me by my girl that I lived with for two and a half years, when I was in country [term for being in Vietnam] two weeks I wrote her a letter, a Dear Jane type and I received this one I think three months afterwards. It starts out: Hello . . . I'll substitute my real name for my call sign now, oh, Here we go . . .

"Hello Johnny,
   So today I got my head blown this night I found out just about everything I needed to know to put you out of my life forever. Tonight I received a phone call from a girl, I think you know her, she's been living up here since June, she said goodbye to you in Vista the night she came up here. Oh boy. Did we ever have a good time discussing the one and only Mister Stud. I just can't believe you and I ever existed. [he laughs] Oh Johnny how you lost, not only me, but Michelle, oh baby, you lost us both, trying your damndest to have the best of both worlds. I know so many rich foxy men, now just waiting for my OK and babe, when I do it, Michelle is going with me. There are too many for me to handle. Michelle can help me. I'm going to turn on to the foxiest and richest dude I know in this fucking city. When you come home, just try to turn us on oh Johnny. You just ate shit. For the first fuckin time, you, dear love, have bit the dust. Oh so clever you are, dear love, to make them believe in your great loyalty. You fucker. And to think I waited this long, I fucking wasted all this long time. So goodbye, my love, it is on this day, December 7th, 1970, I released my soul from your magic spell. Evil, evil man. My love for you is gone, never to return.

You wait, Johnny Smack-O, you're going to turn out just like that man you hate so deep down in your very guts. Your father. You go to hell, you're just like your father and you deserve the same fucked-up life."

And the next paragraph, there's a portion written about the guy she left to come and roll with me, you know, she was going with this dude at the time she met me and decided to leave him and here's what she says about it.

"[Name of her previous boyfriend], so beautiful, so at peace, this is god's man, god's child, why oh why did I give up such a beautiful man for such a two faced gutless swine? [Johnny giggles]. Michelle knows this as well as I, what a fool we've both been. To think a love letter sits on this very desk addressed to you, and a package also full of goodies and all my lasting love.

I don't want you now, or ever again, oh no, not for eternity. Oh oh my darlin, all those pictures of us. The beach, the old pools, the rocks, the Palace of Fine Arts, the swans, oh Danny, Danny . . . breakfast in bed, baths in an old bathtub, racing up Mason Street, motorcycle ridin' in the mountains, riding up and down the hills of San Francisco. Oh, balling, oh fuckin' and fuckin' till we both dropped, soaked in each other's sweat. For fuckin' what? For hell's sake, that's what for.

Oh Johnny, when I sit here at my desk, writing this letter, looking at all the walls and my desk covered with your picture and I feel an intimacy but, for some reason, it seems to be melting right before me, and I feel like throwing up. Why? Because I'm such a fool, such a fuckin' fool to have fallen for such a lowly bastard as you. Oh Johnny-Smack-O you're so, so fucked up, and to think I was still fuckin' waiting. What a fuckin' waste of not only my past three years but Michelle's. Three of hers. That makes six years for one fucked up fool. I think of all that love wrapped around my naked body. When I think of you feeling me, touching me, I just lay down and bawl my eyes out thinking about it. When someone else touches me, or kisses me, I close my eyes tight and pretend it's you. I cry inside, oh Johnny Johnny, touch me. I know how I suffered for the fucking last week. I thought I would die to think of someone else going inside of me, it tore me up so, so badly because I wanted so badly to keep it all for my Johnny. That man who loved me so much, so deeply. Oh I dream of you so often, think it was only you and me, me and you. Oh Johnny thank you for just one fuckin' thing: teaching me how to hate you. Oh I fuckin' love your fuckin' ass so much, I could just die right here. Johnny Smack-O, just fuck you, fuck you, fuck you, fuck you, fuck you, fuck you . . . love, forever, Susie Q."

[In the following conversation "Smokey" refers to Syster, "Johnny" to Johnny and "Tripper" to another man on the same frequency who heard the reading.]

Smokey: Johnny this is Smokey, well I'll tell you what, that letter, uh, it'll never lose its spark. It's got something in it, it'll never lose, but what can I say but . . . wow.

Johnny: Thanks a lot P [Slang for "good friend"]. What do you think of that chick, man?

Tripper: She's a pretty heavy chick, man. Uh, I don't know. I think that things will work out in the long run.

Johnny: Check it out, man. Everybody that's heard the letter, you know, about 95% of the people still agree that the chick's supposed to love me or something like that. I think I agree with it.

Tripper: Yeah, I think you should agree with it, I mean, the chick sounds like she's still hung up on you pretty bad, so I think things will work out for you okay.

Johnny: So. Check it out man. I don't want to go back and really get involved with the girl because she wants to get married, man, that's, uh, the big hang up that's, uh, hassling me so much.

Tripper: Well, I know what you mean, my chick's the same way but I just tell her, I just keep putting it off, I mean, I'll tell her, it's like this man, I says, you've got to run around for a while, you've got to check out the place and see what's going on, before you stop life, altogether.

Johnny: Yeah, it comes to a standstill. Hey um, alright Smokey, did you get a good recording that time, P?

Smokey: That's most affirmed, man, I'll tell you, it was just as clear as can be, and uh, wow, you know, I was just sitting here, more or less tripping on that letter. And uh, I thought, wow, you know, at the time she wrote that letter she must have had so much hate in her body. You know? She seems like, I mean I've talked to you before about her, about, uh, like you said she was such a perfectionist and everything, uh, she didn't really seem like the type of girl who could, uh, just come right down and call you a lonely, you know, uh, bastard and fuck you and fuck you and fuck you. She just doesn't seem like that type of girl. And uh, wow, she must've had so much hate in her body at the time that she wrote that letter that wow, I'll tell you . . . oh wow.

Johnny: Yeah, I really think she was really really pissed off. Because, uh, she gets mad every once in a while, but, uh, that's one of her really really mean trips, you know, she gets on . . . and, like uh, she sure did tell me to get fucked a lot. [giggles] and uh, she really, uh, oh I dunno. Just that when I get home she's gonna know where this letter has been, and who has heard it, and a good estimate on how many has heard it because, uh, I don't know if I told you before about this but uh, the letter itself, physically, has gone to a place called Belgium, in Europe, I'm sure you know, or have heard of Belgium before. And it's also gone to my cousin and he was in Japan and Korea during the time that he had this letter and plus that it's been read to many people over this Romeo [a radio] and to a lot of my friends, and uh, I really don't know what her reaction is going to be to, when I tell her this, but she will know someday.

Smokey: Yeah dig it, wow, you know, you'll have to tell her that you also have it on tape for a person to keep, like for a long time. Ha.

Johnny: Yeah, check it out. Oh shit, [inaudible] I don't know what she'll really respond to, violently or, you know, just take it in stride and laugh about it, because uh, I think the time that I tell her will be after I've just finished fuckin' her, and so, she really won't mind, I don't think.

Smokey: [laughs] Yeah, dig it. Yeah, she'll probably, uh, wow . . .

Yeah she won't have a bit of hate in her body then, I don't believe. I think it'll be all love then.

Johnny: Yeah, check it out man, because like uh, I do want to see her, because she promised me a motorcycle . . . she's good on things like that, if she says she's gonna get me something she will but, right now I think I gotta, ya know . . .

END OF TAPE

———

From a young American college student, Carol C., to Michael Hansen, then in the armed forces. The two began dating in May 1970, when she was eighteen years old and he was twenty; Hansen, who had enlisted in the U.S. Naval Reserve in August 1969, reported for duty in Florida, two months after they met, and left for Morocco in March 1971. During the course of their correspondence, the two discussed marriage, "jobs, school, apartments children and family relations."

Eight months later, Hansen received this "Dear John" from her. "I vividly recall the experience of receiving this letter," he says. "I was working a routine midwatch, 11pm to 7am, and one of my radios was tuned to Armed Forces Radio, Europe, as I drank coffee. Then the mailroom orderly entered our room and handed out the mail, and the instant I felt that letter between my thumb and index finger I knew. Carol always wrote her letters on 9"x 6" stationery, folded in thirds and mailed in a stationery envelope. This letter was in a plain white envelope and very thin. I was shaking as I opened it. The pink college-ruled three-hole notebook paper gave me a creepy feeling, and I read it over and over, trying to figure out what she meant by 'a man like you.'"

A few days later, he wrote her a letter back, expressing his disappointment. Eight years later, in 1979, he married Louise Ann Levengood of Racine, Wisconsin; they are still married and the parents of two children. Hansen works as a special-education teacher in Wisconsin and is a retired major in the U.S. Army Reserve.

November 27 [1971]

Dear Michael,

I'm sorry. I don't know what else to say but that I've changed and along with the change of myself changed my love for you.

I can't love you anymore. When I loved you I was someone else who loved you. But now I am different and I can't love someone like you.

I can't pinpoint everything except that in your absence I have grown apart from you instead of with you.

We don't have the same feelings & ideas anymore and it just wouldn't work out.

I'm sorry. I don't know what to say to make you feel better—but maybe to say nothing.

I'll pack all your pictures and things in a box and send them to your family to keep for you. I don't think it would be fair of us to keep the X-mas presents you have sent—so when you receive them, I'll send them to your house also.

You're a wonderful man and will make some woman happy in the future. But I'm not right for you or you for me. Please forgive me. I'm trying to be fair. It would be unfair to wait for you and tell you in June I don't love you anymore.

I'm sorry.

This was a very sudden thing. I haven't lied to you in any of my letters. The last letter you received from me was my feelings at that time. But it hit me one night when I was studying with a guy from one of my classes about two weeks ago—that I wasn't ready for marriage or engagement to you. And after thinking a lot the past two weeks, I realized that I would never be ready for you. I've changed. California, school, the people, my growing knowledge and experience and just living another year has changed me and my feelings. I have needs that must be fulfilled by a man in order for me to love him. You once filled those needs. But they have changed, and you no longer fulfill them. I'm sorry. But I wouldn't want you to change for me to fulfill my needs so that I would love you. I want you to be yourself. And someday, the right woman will come along and you will fulfill her needs. Then everything will be beautiful and right.

I'm sorry.
Carol

———

From Betsy,* to her sailor boyfriend Ben, a sailor stationed on the American amphibious transport ship USS Cleveland. Ben received the "Dear John" E-mail on Oct. 1, 2001.

Ben,

I fucked up Ben. I don't know any other way to put it but like that. I'm so sorry I've left you hanging for so long. Not knowing anything. And I'm so sorry I avoided your phone calls. I just didn't know what to say when I picked up. I don't even know how to start to explain. I do know that I owe you an explanation, though. This is so hard, even to write. I got scared. The more I thought of us getting a place together, the more scared I got, and I didn't know how to tell you. You always sounded so excited when you talked about it, and I was excited too at first. I started thinking about when I had that apartment in Tucson, and how much my roommate Melissa* had changed when we moved in together, and how everything got so screwed up. I started thinking about all of the responsibility, and how irresponsible I truly am. I guess I just freaked out. That isn't half of what I need to tell you, Ben. I was hanging out with Laz for the longest time, but then she got a boyfriend, and she didn't want to hang out with me anymore, she always wanted to be with her boyfriend, which I could understand because that's how we were. So I started hanging out with a couple guys in my class. Everything was cool at first, but then I started getting feelings for this one guy, and I didn't know what to think about it. I didn't know if it was real emotion, or if it was just because I was lonely. I remember calling my mom practically every day asking her what I should do. She told me that she thought it was just loneliness, too. I just missed being held, and being kissed, and most of all I missed you. This is so hard Ben. I'm trying to get to the point, but I know how much it will hurt you, and I don't want to do that, but I know I have to tell you. I can't go another day knowing that you're out there loving me with all your heart, and wondering if I'm OK, and not knowing that I did such a terrible thing to you. I did something that I never thought I was capable of doing to someone I love so deeply. I cheated on you Ben. I am so sorry. I don't know how I got so caught up. The worst part about the whole thing is that I don't regret what I did. I know that I still love you, and I always will, but I have feelings for him, too. I wish I could tell you that I didn't, but I can't lie to you. I do regret that I hurt you, and I do regret the fact that things will never be the same between us. And most of all I regret the fact that I left you in the dark for so long. I am not this perfect person that you think I am, and you have to know that. I thought that by finally writing this to you, I would feel relief, but I don't. I don't know how you will react when you read this, but I hope that you can write me back so I know how you feel about all of this I have told you. No matter how you feel, please write me back.

Betsy

The Marriage Refusal

Mar•riage (măr´ĭj) *n*. the legal union of a man and woman as husband and wife; wedlock.

Re•fus•al (rĭ-fyōō´zəl) *n*. the act or an instance of refusing.

The Marriage Refusal *n*. A breakup letter in which the writer (usually a woman) responds to a proposal for her hand in marriage with a definitive "no," often expressing the opinion that marriage is a relinquishing of personal freedom and creativity.

From Queen Elizabeth I (1533-1603), the daughter of Henry VIII (see pp. 103, 143) and Anne Boleyn (see p. 103) to Prince Erik (later King Erik XIV) of Sweden, three years after she acceded to the throne of England. The "Virgin Queen," as she was called, was finding herself besieged with offers from European royalty and nobility, and Elizabeth's advisers were eager for her to marry and "multiply," thereby guaranteeing the succession of the throne.

Elizabeth was hesitant to marry, unwilling to compromise her power or authority. However, Erik—who first proposed to her in 1554 before she became Queen—was not discouraged by the reports of her disinterest, and showered Elizabeth with love letters, presents, and visits for many years.

This letter was written after Erik had sent his brother, Duke John of Finland, to plead his case in person. In 1565, Erik attempted to capture Elizabeth's hand once more but failed yet again. Deposed in 1569, he died in 1577, poisoned at the hand of his brother, now King John.

[February 25 1560]

Most Serene Prince Our Very Dear Cousin,

A letter truly yours both in the writing and sentiment was given us on 30 December by your very dear brother, the Duke of Finland. And while we perceive therefrom that the zeal and love of your mind towards us is not diminished, yet in part we are grieved that we cannot gratify your Serene Highness with the same kind of affection. And that indeed does not happen because we doubt in any way of your love and honour, but, as often we have testified both in words and writing, that we have never yet conceived a feeling of that kind of affection towards anyone. We therefore beg your Serene Highness again and again that you be pleased to set a limit to your love, that it advance not beyond the laws of friendship for the present nor disregard them in the future. And we in our turn shall take care that whatever can be required for the holy preservation of friendship between Princes we will always perform towards your Serene Highness. It seems strange for your Serene Highness to write that you understand from your brother and your ambassadors that we have entirely determined not to marry an absent husband; and that we will give you no certain reply until we shall have seen your person.

We certainly think that if God ever direct our heart to consideration of marriage we shall never accept or choose any absent husband how powerful and wealthy a Prince soever. But that we are not to give you an answer until we have seen your person is so far from the thing itself that we never even considered such a thing. But I have always given both to your brother, who is certainly a most excellent prince and deservedly very dear to us, and also to your ambassador likewise the same answer with scarcely any variation of the words, that we do not conceive in our heart to take a husband, but highly commend this single life, and hope that your Serene Highness will no longer spend time waiting for us.

God keep your Serene Highness for many years in good health and safety. From our Palace at Westminster, 25 February.

Your Serene Highness' sister and cousin,
Elizabeth

———

A letter from actress and <u>Eveline</u> (1778) author Fanny Burney (1752–1840), then twenty-two, to a suitor, Thomas Barlow, twenty-four, who met her at a tea party given by a mutual friend in May 1775. Barlow, whom Burney described in her journal as "handsome" and "prodigiously civil," courted her doggedly, spurred on by the blessings of Burney's own family. She did not particularly like the idea of marriage, writing to a friend, "I had never made any vow against marriage, but I had LONG—LONG—been persuaded it was—for ME—a state of too much hazard and too little promise. . . . " In Burney's June 1775 diary, she recounts a hilarious story about Barlow—who was persistent to a fault—and includes her letter refusing his advances. At the age of forty-one, Burney did enter into marriage, to M. Alexandre D'Arblay, a Frenchman exiled during the revolution.

29 May [1775]

St. Martin's Street
Leicester Fields

Sir,

I am much concerned to find that my silence to the first Letter with which you honoured me, has not had the Effect it was meant to produce, of preventing your giving yourself any further trouble upon my Account.

The good opinion you are pleased to express of me, however extraordinary upon so short an Acquaintance, certainly claims my Acknowledgements; but as I have no intention of changing my present situation, I can only assure You of my good wishes for Your Health & Happiness, & request & desire that you will bestow no further Thoughts, Time, or Trouble upon,

Sir,
Your most humble servant,
F. Burney

———

From actress Fanny Kelly (1790–1882), to essayist Charles Lamb (1775–1834), after he wrote to her, proposing marriage. In 1817, after seeing a number of the actress's performances, Lamb became besotted with Kelly, brought her into his circle of friends, and fell in love. In July 1819 he wrote to her, proposing marriage, confessing that she had "for years been a principal object" in his mind, but that he would not "feel injured or aggrieved" by a rejection. This is her response, written the same day as his proposal. They remained friends.

July 20, 1819

An early and deep-rooted attachment has fixed my heart on one from whom no worldly prospect can well induce me to withdraw it but while I thus frankly and decidedly reject your proposal, believe me I am not insensible to the high honour which the preference of such a mind as yours confers upon me, let me however hope that all thought upon this subject will end with this letter, and that you will henceforth encourage no other sentiment towards me than esteem in my private character and a continuance of that approbation of my humble talents which you have already expressed so much and so often to my advantage and gratification. Believe me I feel proud to acknowledge myself your obliged friend,

F. M. Kelly

———

From Jane Eyre *author Charlotte Brontë (1816–1855) to Henry Nussey, a curate of Donnington, Sussex, who proposed to Brontë about a week earlier, on February 28, 1839. As she explained in a letter to his sister and her good friend Ellen Nussey on March 12, ". . . I asked myself two questions: Do I love him as much as a woman ought to love the man she marries? Am I the person best qualified to make him happy? Alas! Ellen, my conscience answered no to both these questions."*

[Haworth]

[5 March 1839]

My dear Sir

Before answering your letter, I might have spent a long time in consideration of its subject; but as from the first moment of its reception and perusal I determined on which course to pursue, it seemed to me that delay was wholly unnecessary.

You are aware that I have many reasons to feel grateful to your family, that I have peculiar reasons for affection towards one at least of your Sisters, and also that I highly esteem yourself do not therefore accuse me of wrong motives when I say that my answer to your proposal must be a *decided negative*. In forming this decision—I trust I have listened to the dictates of conscience more than to those [of] inclination; I have no personal repugnance to the idea of a union with you—but I feel convinced that mine is not the sort of disposition calculated to form the happiness of a man like you. It has always been my habit to study the characters of those amongst whom I chance to be thrown, and I think I know yours and can imagine what description of woman would suit you for a wife. Her character should not be too marked, ardent and original— her temper should be mild, her piety undoubted, her spirits even and cheerful, and her "personal attractions" sufficient to please your eye and gratify your just pride. As for me you do not know me, I am not the serious, grave, cool-headed individual you suppose— you would think me romantic and [ccccntric—you would] say I was satirical and [severe—however I scorn] deceit and I will never for the sake of attaining the distinction of matrimony and escaping the stigma of an old maid take a worthy man whom I am conscious I cannot render happy. Before I conclude let me thank you warmly for your other proposal regarding the school near Donnington. It is kind in you to take so much interest about me but the fact is I could not at present enter upon such a project because I have not the capital necessary to ensure success. It is a pleasure to me to hear that you are so comfortably settled and that your health is so much improved. I trust God will continue his kindness towards you—let me say also that I admire the good sense, and absence of flattery and cant which your letter displayed. Farewell—! I shall always be glad to hear from you as a *friend*—

[believe me Yours truly
C Brontë.]

Hell Hath No Fury

From pioneering suffragist Lucy Stone (1818–1893) to Henry Blackwell (1825–1909), her future husband, explaining why she did not want to accept his proposal of marriage. Despite the constant refusals and explanations, Stone eventually acquiesced and married Blackwell in 1855, but she did not enter the union lightly: On their wedding day, she and Blackwell read a protest against the then-conventional laws of marriage, in which they railed against such things as a husband's "custody of the wife's person . . . exclusive control and guardianship of their children . . . absolute right to the product of her industry." Stone was the first woman ever known to retain the use of her maiden name.

[Zanesville, Ohio, April 25, 1854]

Tuesday evening 10 o'clock PM

My last lecture is over, until the 10th of May. And I am so glad! I have dreaded these lectures, more than I can tell. But they are past, and very well too. Thank fortune! Now, Harry dear, I wish you were here, for an hour, I would tell you why, in *this* letter, I ask you to come east, and in the *last,* said I did not think it best. I said to myself, "it will cost Harry $50, to come east. It is not likely that he will get that value in return, for however much I love him, (and he is very dear to me,) the horror of being a legal wife, and the suffocating sense of the want of that absolute freedom which I now possess, together with the revulsions of feeling which continually recur, and the want of certainty that we are adapted, will never allow me to be his wife. And if he were sure that I would not be, he would not desire to come."

Now Harry, I have been all my life alone. I have planned and executed, without counsel, and without control. I have shared thought, and feeling, and life, with myself alone. I have made a path for my feet which I know is very useful; it brings me more intense & abundant happiness by far, than comes to the life of the majority of men. And it seems to me, I cannot risk it by any change. And when I ask, "*can* I *dare* to change," It rings an everlasting "*no*". And then I do not think it best, for you to spend time, and money, in vain. And so say, "don't come." I have lived alone, happily and well, and can still do it. I have always been superior to circumstances, and can continue so. My life has never seemed to me, a baffled one, only in hours that now and then come, when my love-life is consciously unshared. But such hours are only as the drop to the ocean. The great whole of my life is richly blest. Let it remain so. And then again, I say, "don't come." But when I know by your letters that you do not understand me, I long for *one more* talk in freedom, and blame me, for desiring it, at so much cost to you. If there were any way, to see you, without scandal, before I leave, but there is not. So do as you please. Come east, or not.

I sympathize most fully with you dear Harry, in your struggle, and desire to make your life wholly beautiful. What we earnestly strive after, we *can* attain. "All things are possible to him that *wills.*" We sometimes succeed in the *great* matters and fail in the lesser. "The *little* foxes spoil the vines." But I *expect,* that as you cultivate steadiness of purpose and deliberation, and love of & *trust in* the Truth, *without regard* to *consequences,* that you will find your life, most beautifully sphering itself about the Central life, finding *all* its *true* relations, and in each, blessing, and being blessed. Good night and may all the good which a noble life deserves, be abundantly yours . . .

With love to the household
Yours truly Lucy

From a young American woman, Mollie Bidwell, to José Maria Eça de Queiroz (1845–1900), Portuguese novelist (Os Maias, 1888) and former Portuguese consul general in Cuba. Bidwell, the daughter of the Pittsburgh industrialist J. C. Bidwell, met Eça in Havana during a trip with her father in early 1873; Eça came to visit her at her home in Pittsburgh in July of that year. The two corresponded for five months until this letter was sent. (It was found damaged and torn in 1995 by A. Campos Matos & Alice Lomath Ferreira, editors of a book of letters to Eça that was published in 1998.) After receiving this letter, Eça wrote to Bidwell again, against her wishes, and was greeted with a letter from Bidwell's father, who politely repeated that his daughter did not want to correspond further.

Mr. J.M. d'Eça de Queiroz

Grove Hill

Sept. 23, 1873

Mr. Queiroz

The time which has passed since your visit to Pittsburgh has been employed by me in carefully thinking over the question which concerns our future welfare.

After long thought I perceive that marriage between us is not possible; and I think . . . . . inform you . . . . delay.

. . . . decided this is not . . . . a hard struggle, but this decision neither time nor influence can change.

I shall consider it a great personal favor if you neither return to this city, nor write again to me.

Trusting that there may yet be much happiness in store for you.

I remain your friend always

Mollie E. Bidwell

From Russian actress Vera Fedorovna Komissarzhevskaia (1864–1910) to conservative diplomat and writer Sergei Tatischev (1846–1906), after he had written her, proposing marriage. Komissarzhevskaia met Tatischev in Vilnius in 1894, and he offered to help Komissarzhevskaia obtain a position in a St. Petersburg theater. The two corresponded for a few years, Tatischev alluding to his love for her and Komissarzhevskaia disuading him by insisting that her art was of supreme importance and the "first and foremost goal of my life." At the time this letter was written, Komissarzhevskaia was a rising star in the theater, and premiering the role of Nina Zarechnaia in Chekhov's drama The Seagull. *In 1909, while performing in Tashkent, she and the members of her company contracted smallpox. Except for Komissarzhevskaia, all survived.*

[23 January 1896]

I am writing you despite your request to send a telegram because I positively can not respond so briefly to the letter that I just received from you. To the question you proposed, I answer yet again—No. But I can not limit myself to this response, and don't consider it necessary to deny myself the need to say a few more words to you. Your letter didn't only distress me—it surprised me. It seemed that everything was clear when we last met, and that you, after you received my answer to the question you pose in today's letter, decided to remain my friend and give up the hope that you have nurtured even until now. But you were testing yourself and decided that this was not possible. So be it. It pains me so much to make you experience such difficult moments, as if this is my albeit involuntary reward for your sincere compassion and good will toward me, of which I have no doubt. Please don't be angry that I can not accept the favors—the sincerity of which I have never doubted and will never doubt—that you have so generously offered. You can't imagine how difficult it is for me to disappoint you and deprive myself of your friendship, but I have never been a hypocrite, and especially in the given situation I can only answer honestly and truthfully, at the risk of losing your kind attitude toward me. May God grant you all the best. I'm sorry.

Again, my deepest thanks.
—V. Komissarzhevskaia

Hell Hath No Fury

From Virginia Stephen (1882–1941, later Virginia Woolf) to her suitor Sydney Waterlow, after Waterlow had proposed marriage. Waterlow, a writer and employee of the British Foreign Office, had been a friend of Virginia's for many years, and was still married to his wife at the time she wrote this letter.

38 Brunswick Square, W.C.

Dec. 9th [1911]

Dear Sydney,

I mean to have answered your letter sooner. I'm very glad you don't reproach yourself, because I'm certain that there's nothing to reproach yourself for. All you say I think I understand, and it seems to me very reasonable.

But I feel that I must on my side make clear what I didn't make clear that night. I don't think I shall ever feel for you what I must feel for the man I marry. I am very anxious that you should know this, so that you may take it into account. I feel that you have it in your power to stop thinking of me as the person you want to marry. It would be unpardonable of me if I did not do everything to save you from what must—as far as I can tell—be a great waste.

Please write and say whatever you wish to me at any time, and behave exactly as you wish. I hope we shall go on being good friends anyhow.

Yours ever,
Virginia Stephen

———

The following letter was sent from Virginia Stephen to Leonard Woolf (1880–1969) in 1912. Woolf had proposed marriage to her, but uncertain, she refused. Three months after sending the letter, which outlines her reasons for not becoming his wife, they were married. She was thirty, he thirty-one. About a year later, on September 9, 1913, Virginia attempted suicide by taking a large dose of the sedative veronal. She survived, but succeeded in killing herself in 1941, when she drowned herself in the River Ouse, near her home in Sussex.

Asheham [Rodmell, Sussex]

May 1st, [1912]

Dearest Leonard,

To deal with the facts (my fingers are so cold I can hardly write) I shall be back about 7 tomorrow, so there will be time to discuss—but what does it mean? You can't take the leave, I suppose if you are going to resign certainly at the end of it. Anyhow, it shows what a career you're ruining!

Well then, as to all the rest. It seems to me that I am giving you a great deal of pain—some in the most casual way—and therefore I ought to be as plain with you as I can, because half the time I suspect, you're in a fog which I don't see at all. Of course I can't explain what I feel—these are some of the things that strike me. The obvious advantages of marriage stand in my way. I say to myself. Anyhow, you'll be quite happy with him; and he will give you companionship, children, and a busy life—then I say By God, I will not look upon marriage as a profession. The only people who know of it, all think it suitable; and that makes me scrutinise my own motives all the more. Then, of course, I feel angry sometimes at the strength of your desire. Possibly, your being a Jew comes in also at this point. You seem so foreign. And then I am fearfully unstable. I pass from hot to cold in an instant, without any reason; except that I believe sheer physical effort and exhaustion influence me. All I can say is that in spite of these feelings which go on chasing each other all day long when I am with you, there is some feeling which is permanent, and growing. You want to know of course whether it will ever make me marry you. How can I say? I think it will, because there seems no reason why it shouldn't—But I don't know what the future will bring. I'm half afraid of myself. I sometimes feel that no one ever has or ever can share something—It's the thing that makes you call me like a hill, or a rock. Again, I want everything—love, children, adventure, intimacy, work. (Can you make any sense out of this ramble? I am putting down one thing after another.) So I go from being half in love with you, and wanting you to be with me always, and know everything about me, to the extreme of wildness and aloofness. I sometimes think that if I married you, I could have everything—and then—it is the sexual side of it that comes between us? As I told you brutally the other day, I feel no physical attraction in you. There are moments—when you kissed me the other day was one—when I feel no more than a rock. And yet your caring for me as you do almost overwhelms me. It is so real, and so strange. Why should you? What am I really except a pleasant attractive creature? But its just because you care so much that I feel I've got to care before I marry you. I feel I must give you everything; and that if I can't, well, marriage would only be second-best for you as well as for me. If you can still go on, as before, letting me find my own way, as that is what would please me best; and then we must both take the risks. But you have made me very happy too. We both of us want a marriage that is a tremendous living thing, always alive, always hot, not dead and easy in parts as most marriages are. We ask a great deal of life, don't we? Perhaps we shall get it; then, how splendid!

One doesn't get much said in a letter [,] does one? I haven't touched upon the enormous variety of things that have been happening here—but they can wait.

D'you like this photograph?—rather too noble, I think. Here's another.

Yrs.
VS

The
Classic

Clas•sic (klăs´ĭk) *n*. an artist, author, or work generally considered to be of the highest rank or excellence, especially one of enduring significance. A typical or traditional example.

The Classic *n*. one of the earliest known and published examples of a breakup letter, usually appearing in epistolary novels, and written in France or England before the nineteenth century.

UNDOUBTEDLY, BREAKUPS ARE AS OLD as love itself and the breakup letter as old as the invention of the written word. As literature, however, most scholars trace these letters back to Ovid's *Heroides (Heroines)*, a series of letters from great ladies to their long-gone lovers, one of which is included here. Robert Adams Day, in his book *Told in Letters* (University of Michigan Press, 1966), even goes as far as to say that Ovid may be considered the father of epistolary, sentimental, and psychological fiction, and that the *Heroides* are some of the most important models for the emotional layer in the structure of modern fiction. Linda S. Kauffman uses the *Heroides* as the starting point of her book *Discourses of Desire: Gender, Genre, and Epistolary Fictions* (Cornell University Press, 1986), but also traces such "discourses of desire" back to the passionate monologues of fictional females like Homer's Penelope, Sophocles' Deianira, and Horace's Hypermnestra.

Regardless of who fathered—and it was *fathered*—the genre of women's letters as literature, the modern ascent of the letter-form as literature is easier to define and more populated with the voices of real women. The more modern trend in feminine love letters began in France the early 1600s and extended through the 1700s, and was most prominently featured in *The Love Letters of the Portuguese Nun* (1669) (see p. 226), but also included such works as *Letters from a Peruvian Woman* (1747) (see p. 238) and *Lettres of Mistriss Fanni Butlerd* (1757) (see p.245).

England, too, was enamored of the epistolary, as is evidenced by Catharine Trotter's 1693 work, *Olinda's Adventures* (see p. 232) and the anonymously written *The Female Critick* (1701) (see p. 234). Adams Day estimates that of a thousand works of fiction that appeared between the time of the Restoration and 1740 in England, one-fifth were works of letter-fiction. And this was well before Samuel Richardson swept onto the scene with his epistolary classics *Pamela* (1740) and *Clarissa* (1747) (see p. 241). As Ruth Perry explains in her book *Women, Letters and the Novel* (Ams Press, 1980), the letter-novel thrived in England for a number of reasons: it was accessible (the language used in letters was more casual than highbrow); it was relatable (the growing number of middle-class readers could identify with characters who used letters to tell stories of the agonies and ecstasies of love); and the public—women in particular—was becoming more literate.

Letters as literature provided not only reading material but career options to literate women, who saw few opportunities to earn their livings as professional, published writers. The epistolary style was one that required no formal education, and its success largely depended on a simple, personal voice . . . which had long been encouraged in women. Letters, says Perry, were the one sort of writing women were supposed to be able to do well. Of the seventeenth-century Dorothy Osborne (see p. 77), Virginia Woolf said: "Had she been born in 1827 . . . Osborne would have written novels; had she been born in 1527 she never would have written at all. But she was born in 1627, and at that date though writing books was 'ridiculous for a woman' there was nothing unseemly in writing a letter."

However "naturally suited" at letter writing women were thought to be, it is important to keep in mind that a substantial number of the letter-fiction during this period was actually written by men (as were some of the letters in this book). From the *Portuguese Nun* to the work of Jean-Jacques Rousseau and Richardson, men co-opted women's voices and experiences for their own creative and financial gain. Men saw women's writing as unselfconscious, naïve, emotional, and authentic; in his *Caractères* (1684), La Bruyère said that "the fair sex surpasses ours in this genre of writing." But, as Katharine Anne Jensen points out, women's talent at letter writing was in reference to it as a social art, while men flexed the muscles of the genre both socially and literarily. As Jensen asserts in her book *Writing Love: Letters, Women and the Novel in France, 1605–1776* (Southern Illinois University Press, 1995), the history of women's letters was complicated by the promotion of them by these male writers and editors, who not only launched the trend of women's letters through their own works—in which they impersonated female letter writers—but sustained it by presenting themselves as authorities on how women should write letters period, as is evidenced by the rise of the letter-writing manual (see p. 261).

The male domination over the letter-form as literature may also have created rigid boundaries that kept women confined to a specific and prescribed category of behavior and emotion. One of the culturally approved feminine personas in the seventeenth and eighteenth centuries, in fact, was what Jensen calls "Epistolary Woman," a woman "seduced, betrayed, and suffering [who] writes letter after letter of anguished and masochistic lament to the man who has left her behind." The popularity and acceptance of Epistolary Woman worked to women's sexual and literary detriment, Jensen says, because it represented woman's seduction, abandonment, and suffering and seemed to reinforce a male assertion of sexual privilege and supremacy.

† † †

From Publius Ovidius Naso (Ovid)'s <u>Heroides</u> (Heroines), a collection of letters in verse from the heroines of classic mythology to their absent husbands and lovers and published some time during the Roman literary figure's life (43 B.C.–A.D. 17). The first fifteen parts of <u>Heroides</u> are single letters from women to men; the last six are "double" letters, consisting of a letter written by the injurious man and the woman's reply. In this letter, one of the first fifteen, Phyllis, a princess, writes to her lover Demophoon, who has left on urgent business, promising to return, but never does. As Harold Isbell says in his edition of the <u>Heroides</u> (Penguin Classics, 1990):

> *In her narrative Phyllis has every opportunity for rage, not to mention threats of revenge. Yet throughout she forgoes this entirely predictable response to the great wrong to her by Demophoon . . . the fault is not, however, entirely that of Demophoon. His deceit has its counterpart in the eagerness of Phyllis to be deceived and finally to deceive herself.*

Phyllis sends her complaint to Demophoon:
>   you have not kept your promise to me.
I welcomed you to the shores of Rhodope
>   and when you left your pledge was precise:

205

Hell Hath No Fury

You would come when the moon's horns grew
    together.
      Since then the moon has grown full four times.
When will the tides bring a ship from Attica?
      Counting days is a lover's business:
if you counted out the days like I, you would
      see that my complaint comes none too soon.
I still have just a little hope left, for we
      believe slowly when belief brings pain.
I have deceived myself by defending you;
      I could not think you had injured me.
How often when the wind was good I have tried
      to see the sails of your ship coming;
I have cursed Theseus, because I thought that he
      kept you from your intended voyage;
there have been times when I thought your ship was
    wrecked
      and you were drowned in the raging waves.
With prayer and incense I have beseeched our gods
      that you might be hurried on to me.
When the wind blows and the sky is good, I think
      if he is well he is coming now.
You swore by the gods to come again to me
      but even they have not brought you back.
It is quite clear to me now, not even love
      will move your ship, you delay too long.
When you left this port you unfurled your white sails
      and the wind blew your promise away.
I have not seen your sails again since that day;
      the promise you made has not been kept.
Tell me what have I done? I loved unwisely,
      my crime was simple: I wanted you.
My fall becomes its own reward, I am left
      with nothing more than your faithlessness

You swore that we two were bound to each other
      but where now are those bonds that held us?
You put your right hand into mine and called on
      the living gods to witness your pledge
We stood betrothed and Hymen's bond was given
      by you to guarantee our marriage.
You swore fidelity by the raging sea
      over which you freely come and go,
By your grandfather [Neptune]—unless he too is one
      of your lies—who calms the sailor's way;
By Venus and those weapons that wound me now,
      the one the bow, the other the torch;
By Juno who guards the marriage bed and by
      the mystic rites of the torchbearer.
If these injured gods desired their just revenge
      even your life could not be enough.
Like a mad woman I believed your speeches,
      I took your word and rebuilt your ships;
I gave you beams and planks of seasoned timber
      and oars to rush you away from me.
My pain is caused by weapons that I gave you.
      I believed your many begging words;
At last your family's great names convinced me
      and I even believed in your tears.
But perhaps even tears can be taught to lie
      and flow whenever they are required.
I also trusted the gods by whom you swore;
      but why did you pledge so many times?
Any one of those pledges, even the least,
      would have been enough to trap my heart.
I have not regretted that I gave you aid;
      but my kindness should have ended there:
My welcome included myself and my bed,
      I pressed my body to yours; the night

Hell Hath No Fury

Before should have been the last night of my life.
    I should have been dead before you came.
But I hoped for better things, things I deserved:
    hope that rests in what is owed is just.
Remaining innocent, I would have received
    the proper reward for my goodness.
I was tricked by your words. Your glory is cheap,
    my trust deserved consideration,
I loved you as a woman loves. This will be
    the only thing remembered of you.
When men read the mighty deeds of the heroes
    they will read about Demophoon.
You might be a hero: let your statue stand
    with those of the sons of Aegeus.
Your father will be first with his great deeds carved
    in white marble, followed by Sciron,
Stern Procrustes, the mixed bull and man, Sinis,
    Thebes vanquished, the Centaurs defeated,
Pluto's kingdom assaulted—all will be there
    but last of all these, the inscription
Carved beneath your statue will tell your story:
    'By tricks he stole love from his hostess.'
Of all your father's great and wonderful deeds,
    you remember nothing more, it seems,
Than his abandonment of a bride from Crete.
    The only deed that causes him shame,
That is the one action you seem to admire;
    you have made yourself heir to his sin,
you take to yourself the shame of his deceit.
    Ariadne has a fine lord now,
without my envy, she drives a harnessed team
    of fine tigers before her high chariot;
but the men I rejected will not return
    because rumour has announced to all

the men of this country that I have preferred
    to take the offer of some stranger.
The opinion they hold is simple to state:
    'If her preference now is for the
Athenian wit, then let her go to Athens
    and let her seek the learning she wants;
another can be found easily enough
    to rule here in armed and warlike Thrace.
What has happened proves that she is more than wise.'
    Anyone who thinks the deed is wrong
because of its result ought to be condemned,
    for if your waters should foam beneath
the insistence of your mighty oars, then they
    will say I planned well and I will have
their undying loyalty for the wisdom
    that saved myself and my countrymen.
That is all impossible. You will never
    sleep in my bed or bathe in our surf.
It is my fate that I have been found unwise
    and without the counsel of wisdom.
I cannot lose sight of the day you sailed off.
    Your ships were waiting on the waters
of my harbour, ready to leave, and you closed
    your arms around me putting your lips
on mine mingling tears and lingering kisses;
    a whispered pledge of undying love,
you cursed the breeze that played in your sails. Your last
    words were even shouted in the wind:
'Phyllis, do not forget that I will return.'
    Is it your sails that keep you away?
Obviously, you had no plan to return.
    Do you think I will sit here and wait
even though your mind is already made up?
    But I cannot help waiting for you.

Though you are tardy, return to the woman
    who loves you more than anyone else.
Why should I beg? You have taken another
    by now, you have forgotten Phyllis;
hers now is the love that once you gave to me,
    by now, you have forgotten my name.
If you ever want to know about Phyllis,
    she, when you were nearly dead, rescued
you from the raging sea, she opened her port
    to you and your ships, she gave the wealth
of royal Thrace. She welcomed you and she gave
    freely and without the least regret
the priceless gift a maiden gives only once.
    The land of Lycurgus was too large,
she made it a part of her dowry; your hands
    deceitfully accepted all things given
that seemed of even the slightest worth.
    Finding you without riches I gave
a king's estate, from Rhodope to Haemus,
    through which the swift river Hebrus flows.
And my innocence also I gave as you
    undid the ties of my chastity.
This bridal was witnessed by Tisiphone
    shrieking her horrid hymns while a bird
that avoids the day's light sang her dismal song
    and throughout the ceremony small
serpents coiled around the neck of Allecto
    and the lights were torches from a tomb.
Though my soul is heavy I climb on the rocks
    and along the thickly grown shoreline
wherever the ocean spreads itself; whether
    the soil is loosened in the warm sun
or whether the cold constellations glisten,
    I survey the straits: whenever sails

appear from far away I pray that they be
      Gods bringing an answer to my prayers.
I run to the beach and stand there. As the sails
      come nearer, I grow weaker and soon
I fall backward fainting in my servant's arms.
      The bay is shaped like a bow pulled back,
its horns rising up out of the sea in cliffs.
      I want to drown myself in that place,
and I will if you are not faithful to me.
      The currents will carry me to you
and your eyes will see my unburied body.
      If you were hard as iron still you would
be driven to say, 'Not in this way, Phyllis,
      should you have followed me to this place.'
I long for poison; I wish that I could plunge
      a sword in my heart so that my blood
could be poured out and my life would be finished.
      Since you placed your arms about my neck
I should gladly tie a noose about it now.
      In choosing death, I will not delay.
You will be the cause of my dying; my tomb
      will have the following inscription:
'Demophoon killed Phyllis: a guest, he stole love
and by his theft caused the death that came from her
      hand.'

—

From _The Letters of Abelard and Heloise_ (first English publication, 1722). Peter Abelard (1079–1142) was a French philosopher and theologian who became involved in a forbidden relationship with his pupil Heloise (1101–1164), whose education and well-being were looked after by her uncle, Canon Fulbert. Heloise soon became pregnant and bore a child, Astrolabe. Abelard, believing that Fulbert's *wrath would be appeased by their marriage, pushed to wed Heloise. But Heloise opposed the marriage, thinking it would injure Abelard's eccliastical career. Nonetheless, the two married, although Abelard begged Fulbert to keep the marriage a secret. When word of their union leaked out, Abelard sent Heloise to stay at a convent for her own safety; but Fulbert, believing Abelard had rejected her, ordered his servants to enter Abelard's chambers one night and castrate him in revenge. Heloise remained at the abbey and Abelard, now a eunuch, became a monk.*

LETTER 3
To her only one after Christ, she who is his alone in Christ.

I am surprised, my only love, that contrary to custom in letter-writing and, indeed to the natural order, you have thought fit to put my name before yours in the greeting which heads your letter, so that we have woman before man, wife before husband, handmaid before master, nun before monk, deaconess before priest and abbess before abbot. Surely the right and proper order is for those who write to their superiors or equals to put their names before their own, but in letters to inferiors, precedence in order of address follows precedence in rank.

We were also greatly surprised when instead of bringing us the healing balm of comfort you increased our desolation and made the tears to flow which you should have dried. For which of us could remain dry-eyed on hearing the words you wrote towards the end of your letter: 'But if the Lord shall deliver me into the hands of my enemies so that they overcome and kill me . . .'? My dearest, how could you think such a thought? How could you give voice to it? Never may God be so forgetful of his humble handmaids as to let them outlive you; never may he grant us a life which would be harder to bear than any form of death. The proper course would be for you to perform our funeral rites, for you to commend our souls to God, and to send ahead of you those whom you assembled for God's service—so that you need no longer be troubled by worries for us, and follow after us the more gladly because freed from concern for our salvation. Spare us, I implore you, master, spare us words such as these which can only intensify our existing unhappiness; do not deny us, before death, the one thing by which we live. 'Each day has trouble enough of its own,' and that day, shrouded in bitterness, will bring with it distress enough to all it comes upon. 'Why is it necessary,' says Seneca, 'to summon evil' and to destroy before death comes?

You ask us, my love, if you chance to die when absent from us, to have your body brought to our burial-ground so that you may reap a fuller harvest from the prayers we shall offer in constant memory of you. But how could you suppose that our memory of you could ever fade? Besides, what time will there be then which will be fitting for prayer, when extreme distress will allow us no peace, when the soul will lose its power of reason and the tongue its use of speech? Or when the frantic mind, far from being resigned, may even (if I may say so) rage against God himself, and provoke him with complaints instead of placating him with prayers? In our misery then we shall have time only for tears and no power to pray; we shall be hurrying to follow, not to bury you, so that we may share your grave instead of laying you in it. If we lose our life in you, we shall not be able to go on living when you leave us. I would not even have us live to see that day, for if the mere mention of your death is death for us, what will the reality be if it finds us still alive? God grant we may never live on to perform this duty, to render you the service which we look for from you alone; in this may we go before, not after you!

And so, I beg you, spare us—spare her at least, who is yours alone, by refraining from words like these. They pierce our hearts with swords of death, so that what comes before is more painful than death itself. A heart which is exhausted with grief cannot find peace, nor can a mind preoccupied with anxieties genuinely devote itself to God. I beseech you not to hinder God's service to which you specially committed us. Whatever has come to us bringing with it total grief we must hope will come suddenly, without torturing us far in advance with useless apprehension which no foresight can relieve. This is what the poet has in mind when he prays to God:

> May it be sudden, whatever you plan for us; may man's mind
> Be blind to the future. Let him hope on his fears.

But if I lose you, what is left for me to hope for? What reason for continuing on life's pilgrimage, for which I have no support but you, and none in you save the knowledge that you are alive, now that I am forbidden all other pleasures in you and denied even the joy of your presence which from time to time could restore me to myself? O God—if I dare say it—cruel to me in everything! O merciless mercy! O Fortune who is only ill-fortune, who has already spent on me so many of the shafts she uses in her battle against mankind that she has none left with which to vent her anger on others. She has emptied a full quiver on me, so that henceforth no one else need fear her onslaughts, and if she still had a single arrow she could find no place in me to take a wound. Her only dread is that through my many wounds death may end my sufferings; and though she does not cease to destroy me, she still fears the destruction which she hurries on.

Of all wretched women I am the most wretched, and amongst the unhappy I am unhappiest. The higher I was exalted when you preferred me to all other women, the greater my suffering over my own fall and yours, when I was flung down; for the higher the ascent, the heavier the fall. Has Fortune ever set any great or noble woman above me or made her my equal, only to be similarly cast down and crushed with grief? What glory she gave me in you, what ruin she brought upon me through you! Violent in either extreme, she showed no moderation in good or evil. To make me the saddest of all women she first made me blessed above all, so that when I thought how much I had lost, my consuming grief would match my crushing loss, and my sorrow for what was taken from me would be the greater for the fuller joy of possession which had gone before; and so that the happiness of supreme ecstasy would end in the supreme bitterness of sorrow.

Moreover, to add to my indignation at the outrage you suffered, all the laws of equity in our case were reversed. For while we enjoyed the pleasures of an uneasy love and abandoned ourselves to fornication (if I may use an ugly but expressive word) we were spared God's severity. But when we amended our unlawful conduct by what was lawful, and atoned for the shame of fornication by an honourable marriage, then the Lord in his anger laid his hand heavily upon us, and would not permit a chaste union though he had long tolerated one which was unchaste. The punishment you suffered would have been proper vengeance for men caught in open adultery. But what others deserve for adultery came upon you through a marriage which you believed had made amends for all previous wrong doing; what adulterous women have brought upon their lovers, your own wife brought on you. Nor was this at the time when we abandoned ourselves to our former delights, but when we had already parted and were leading chaste lives, you presiding over the school in Paris and I at your command living with the nuns at Argenteuil. Thus we were separated, to give you more time to devote yourself to your pupils, and me more freedom for prayer and meditation on the Scriptures, both of us leading a life which was holy as well as chaste. It was then that you alone paid the penalty in your body for a sin we had both committed. You alone were punished though we were both to blame, and paid all, though you had deserved less, for you had made more than necessary reparation by humbling yourself on my account and had raised me and all my kind to your own level—so much less then, in the eyes of God and of your betrayers, should you have been thought deserving of such punishment.

What misery for me—born as I was to be the cause of such a crime! Is it the general lot of women to bring total ruin on great men? Hence the warning about women in Proverbs: 'But now, my son, listen to me, attend to what I say: do not let your heart entice you into your ways, do not stray down her paths; she has wounded and laid low so many, and the strongest have all been her victims. Her house is the way to hell, and leads down to the halls of death.'

And in Ecclesiastes: 'I put all to the test . . . I find woman more bitter than death; she is a snare, her heart a net, her arms are chains. He who is pleasing to God eludes her, but the sinner is her captive.'

It was the first woman in the beginning who lured man from Paradise, and she who had been created by the Lord as his helpmate became the instrument of his total downfall. And that mighty man of God, the Nazarite whose conception was announced by an angel, Delilah alone overcame; betrayed to his enemies and robbed of his sight, he was driven by his suffering to destroy himself along with his enemies. Only the woman he had slept with could reduce to folly Solomon, wisest of men; she drove him to such a pitch of madness that although he was the man whom the Lord had chosen to build the temple in preference to his father David, who was a righteous man, she plunged him into idolatry until the end of his life, so that he abandoned the worship of God which he had preached and taught in word and writing. Job, holiest of men, fought his last and hardest battle against his wife, who urged him to curse God. The cunning arch-tempter well knew from repeated experience that men are most easily brought to ruin through their wives, and so he directed his usual malice against us too, and attacked you by means of marriage when he could not destroy you through fornication. Denied the power to do evil through evil, he effected evil through good.

At least I can thank God for this: the tempter did not prevail on me to do wrong of my own consent, like the women I have mentioned, though in the outcome he made me the instrument of his malice. But even if my conscience is clear through innocence, and no consent of mine makes me guilty of this crime, too many earlier sins were committed to allow me to be wholly free from guilt. I yielded long before to the pleasures of carnal desires, and merited then what I weep for now. The sequel is a fitting punishment for my former sins, and an evil beginning must be expected to come to a bad end. For this offence, above all, may I have strength to do proper penance, so that at least by long contrition I can make some amends for your pain from the wound inflicted on you; and what you suffered in the body for a time, I may suffer, as is right, throughout my life in contrition of mind, and thus make reparation to you at least, if not to God.

For if I truthfully admit to the weakness of my unhappy soul, I can find no penitence whereby to appease God, whom I always accuse of the greatest cruelty in regard to this outrage. By rebelling against his ordinance, I offend him more by my indignation than I placate him by making amends through penitence. How can it be called repentance for sins, however great the mortification of the flesh, if the mind still retains the will to sin and is on fire with its old desires? It is easy enough for anyone to confess his sins, to accuse himself, or even to mortify his body in outward show of penance, but it is very difficult to tear the heart away from hankering after its dearest pleasures. Quite rightly then, when the saintly Job said 'I will speak out against myself,' that is, 'I will loose my tongue and open my mouth in confession to accuse myself of my sins,' he added at once 'I will speak out in bitterness of soul.' St Gregory comments on this: 'There are some who confess their faults aloud but in doing so do not know how to groan over them—they speak cheerfully of what should be lamented. And so whoever hates his faults and confesses them must still confess them in bitterness of spirit, so that this bitterness may punish him for what his tongue, at his mind's bidding, accuses him.' But this bitterness of true repentance is very rare, as St Ambrose observes, when he says: 'I have more easily found men who have preserved their innocence than men who have known repentance.'

In my case, the pleasures of lovers which we shared have been too sweet—they can never displease me, and can scarcely be banished from my thoughts. Wherever I turn they are always there before my eyes, bringing with them awakened longings and fantasies which will not even let me sleep. Even during the celebration of the Mass, when our prayers should be purer, lewd visions of those pleasures take such a hold upon my unhappy soul that my thoughts are on their wantonness instead of on prayers. I should be groaning over the sins I have committed, but I can only sigh for what I have lost. Everything we did and also the times and places are stamped on my heart along with your image, so that I live through it all again with you. Even in sleep I know no respite. Sometimes my thoughts are betrayed in a movement of my body, or they break out in an unguarded word. In my utter wretchedness, that cry from a suffering soul could well be mine: 'Miserable creature that I am, who is there to rescue me out of the body doomed to death?' Would that truth I could go on: 'The grace of God through Jesus Christ our Lord.' This grace, my dearest, came upon you unsought—as single wound of the body by freeing you from these torments has healed many wounds in your soul. Where God may seem to you an adversary he has in fact proved himself kind: like an honest doctor who does not shrink from giving pain if it will bring about a cure. But for me, youth and passion and experience of pleasures which were so delightful intensify the torments of the flesh and longings of desire, and the assault is the more overwhelming as the nature they attack is the weaker.

Men call me chaste; they do not know the hypocrite I am. They consider purity of the flesh a virtue, though virtue belongs not to the body but to the soul. I can win praise in the eyes of men but deserve none before God, who searches our hearts and loins and sees in our darkness. I am judged religious at a time when there is little in religion which is not hypocrisy, when whoever does not offend the opinions of men receives the highest praise. And yet perhaps there is some merit and it is somehow acceptable to God, if a person whatever his intention gives no offence to the Church in his outward behaviour, does not blaspheme the name of the Lord in hearing of unbelievers nor disgrace the Order of his profession amongst the worldly. And this too is a gift of God's grace and comes through his bounty—not only to do good but to abstain from evil—though the latter is vain if the former does not follow from it, as it is written: 'turn from evil and do good.' Both are vain if not done for love of God.

At every stage of my life up to now, as God knows, I have feared to offend you rather than God, and tried to please you more than him. It was your command, not love of God which made me take the veil. Look at the unhappy life I lead, pitiable beyond any other, if in this world I must endure so much in vain, with no hope of future reward. For a long time my pretence deceived you, as it did many, so that you mistook hypocrisy for piety; and therefore you commend yourself to my prayers and ask me for what I expect from you. I beg you, do not feel so sure that you cease to help me by your own prayers. Do not suppose me healthy and so withdraw the grace of your healing. Do not believe I want for nothing and delay helping me in my hour of need. Do not think me strong, lest I fall before you can sustain me. False praise has harmed many and taken from them the support they needed. The Lord cries out through Isaiah: 'O my people! Those who call you happy lead you astray and confuse the path you should take.' And through Ezekiel he says: "Woe upon you women who hunt men's lives by sewing magic bands upon the wrists and putting veils over the heads of persons of every age.' On the other hand, through Solomon it is said that 'The sayings of the wise are sharp as goads, like nails driven home.' That is to say, nails which cannot touch wounds gently, but only pierce through them.

Cease praising me, I beg you, lest you acquire the base stigma of being a flatterer or the charge of telling lies, or the breath of my vanity blows away any merit you saw in me to praise. No one with medical knowledge diagnoses an internal ailment by examining only outward appearance. What is common to the damned and the elect can win no favour in the eyes of God: of such a kind are the outward actions which are performed more eagerly by hypocrites than by saints. 'The heart of man is deceitful and inscrutable; who can fathom it?' And: 'A road may seem straightforward to a man, yet may end as the way to death.' It is rash for man to pass judgement on what is reserved for God's scrutiny, and so it is also written: 'Do not praise a man in his lifetime.' By this is meant, do not praise a man, while in doing so you can make him no longer praiseworthy.

To me your praise is the more dangerous because I welcome it.

The more anxious I am to please you in everything, the more I am won over and delighted by it. I beg you, be fearful for me always, instead of feeling confidence in me, so that I may always find help in your solicitude. Now particularly you should fear, now when I no longer have in you an outlet for my incontinence. I do not want you to exhort me to virtue and summon me to the fight, saying 'Power comes to its full strength in weakness' and 'He cannot win a crown unless he has kept the rules.' I do not seek a crown of victory; it is sufficient for me to avoid danger, and this is safer than engaging in war. In whatever corner of heaven God shall place me, I shall be satisfied. No one will envy another there, and what each one has will suffice. Let the weight of authority reinforce what I say—let us hear St Jerome: 'I confess my weakness, I do not wish to fight in hope of victory, lest the day comes when I lose the battle. What need is there to forsake what is certain and pursue uncertainty?'

———

From Les Angoysses (Invective Letters) *(1539) of writer Marguerite de Briet (pen name Helisenne de Crenne, ca.1510–?), a series of eighteen fictional letters, some from Helisenne to friends and relatives. The following letter was written to her husband in response to his accusations of unfaithfulness (de Briet married Philippe Fournel, an écuyer squire, around 1530 and was separated from him by 1539.) The* Invective Letters *are, as the English translation of them puts it, "a reconstruction of the main facts surrounding Helisenne's marriage, her ill-fated love, her publication of* Les Angoysses, *and her husband's hostility to the book's publication" and perhaps the first "progressive construction of a story through letters without the use of connective materials" in French literature. This model would be used again and again, in the works of Riccoboni (see p. 245), de Staël (see pp. 5, 287), Rousseau (see p. 247) and Laclos (see p. 255). What is unclear is the time frame of the letters in relation to the events of Helisenne's personal life. According to scholar Paul J. Archambault, who co-translated the English edition of* Helisenne's Personal and Invective Letters *(Syracuse University Press, 1985); "We don't know whether*

Helisenne is writing as a wife already living separately from her husband or is breaking off the relationship. We do know that Helisenne herself got an official separation and moved to Paris. An official divorce was not possible, although she could, of course, have had some sort of annulment based on consanguinity or something of that sort."

THIRD INVECTIVE LETTER

Helisenne to her husband. She accuses him of slander, the most damaging of vices because it incriminates all of womankind. Helisenne finds this intolerable and lists several arguments in refutation of her husband's opinion.

Every day your deadly hatred against me intensifies. I cannot hide the effect that your recent letter had on me. I must warn you that it helped me understand one thing: your condition is that of a madman who enjoys indulging in self-destruction while engaged in destroying someone else. You are so puffed up with your arrogance that when reason fails, you can only have recourse to slander, rage and insult. But I assure you that what you say is far less painful to me than what you force me to tell you. I should refrain from doing so had your malevolent words been addressed only to me; indeed you may be sure that my heart is so accustomed to suffering that it would have been easy for me to hide my pain. Besides, I know that insults hurt the attacker even more than the victim.

Seeing as how you loathe the whole feminine condition, however, it has seemed to me that your insult is particularly great because it is universal. I shall therefore be silent as to your accusations against me in particular and concentrate on refuting your incrimination of what you call our malevolent deeds. If my memory serves me right the first of your accusations is that women are unfaithful, inconsistent, fraudulent and deceptive—in short, if any one were to believe what you say, no one would ever get married.

I don't know what makes you despise that institution so, as it has been instituted by God and has been esteemed so highly that

Scripture has compared the state of the Church to the state of marriage, calling the Redeemer a bridegroom and the Church his bride. The state of marriage has been praised not only by Scripture but by the Natural Law and all of classical pagan literature. Everyone should endeavor to praise it as it deserves. What you say about Socrates, who suffered so greatly at the hands of his dreadful wife, does not amount to much. If you say that Socrates categorically railed against all women, you must remember that he himself belonged to the category of hen-pecked husbands. Therefore anything he saw bearing the same form, likeness or resemblance to that which caused him such annoyance, Socrates judged apt to produce a like evil. Because one woman was the cause of that philosopher's annoyance, Socrates thought that any woman coming within his sight was as malevolent as Xanthippe. His annoyance prevented him from seeing things clearly.

Notwithstanding this you might wish to pursue your diatribe, adding that Solomon and the Book of Wisdom despised the female sex and warned against Woman's deception, Woman's iniquity, and the mellifluous accent of a foreign woman. They have written many other things about bad women, but you must understand that this is a marvelous way of promoting good women. These, the aforenamed Solomon and the Book of Wisdom have praised, writing that in a woman of valor and strength the heart of a husband can find peace. They also state that Woman is Man's crown, the adornment of his home, his consolation and his joy. These are words of truth. What rejoinder could you possibly give?

Surely it is pointless for you to say that feminine beauty with its sumptuous dress is both vain and dangerous. To lend substance to your argument you remind us yet once more of the perils into which men have fallen in the post for having been fascinated by women's beauty. But if one reflects on this matter, it is not women who should be blamed, for if men are supposed to be wiser than women they should not deal with anything they know to be harmful or dangerous. Though men consider themselves rational they forsake reason for sensuality; then they blame women for making them succumb.

For the sake of sheer honesty, it seems to me, they should not proffer such lies. They should be ashamed to say that they have been deceived by women. What a shameful injustice it is for men to fault women for deception when in their heart of hearts men know that they are always the ones doing the deceiving. From the moment a man casts a lustful eye on the genuine beauty of a woman's face he is in constant pursuit of her and tries to conquer her no less persistently than if he were besieging a city with war machines. So loathsome is the malevolence of lustful men that the more virtuous the women, the more vulnerable they are to men's ways. We read in literature that it was not the beauty or even the gentleness of Lucretia, that flower of modesty, which stirred up the mad audacity of an incestuous Tarquin to rape her, but rather the lady's wholesome, pure and sincere life.

Nevertheless you spend your time blaming woman for their physical beauty: I can assure you it holds no danger for any man of integrity. If womanly beauty were as destructive as you say it is, the children of Israel would not have been allowed to select beautiful women from among their prisoners and captives, as found in Deuteronomy. We read of Abraham's servant that when he laid eyes on Rebecca he wondered whether this was the woman whom God had meant for Isaac. I also remember the example of Abigail, the wife of Nabal, a most evil man. She was no less wise than beautiful, which allowed her to preserve her husband's life and possessions in spite of David's ferocity; and thus was that iniquitous husband saved by his wife's beauty. For David said to her: "Go up in peace to thine house; see, I have harkened to thy voice and have accepted thy person." If you ponder this, surely, you will admit that you are wrong to hold in contempt what is held up for others to admire.

As to what you have said about women's willingness to experiment in rich and sumptuous clothes, Jerome has written that women and girls desire expensive clothes; and he knew several chaste women who did so, not in order to satisfy foolish men nor out of pride, but out of honest regard for the social state of their husbands or fathers. So affection too is a consideration. You might tell me that men are drawn into lasciviousness and lust by the way women dress, as the seventh book of Proverbs says. Women not bound by matrimony, who adorn themselves in order to please their lovers or any other man, offer an occasion to sin and incite to sin. If they do so they are guilty of serious sin; and if such is your opinion you are not far from the truth. But women who dress simply to satisfy a small need for glory or vanity and not to incite to sin often commit only venial sin; and since the things of the mind are concealed from us, we should not be too quick to judge the intentions of others.

Concerning what you have said about some women who powder and paint themselves and wear makeup in diverse colors, I cannot say what one should think of them. I remember that Suzanna, in the Old Testament, was molested by two perverse old men while she was washing at a fountain and awaiting the return of her servants whom she had sent to fetch her best and most perfumed lotions; she wished to both preserve her natural beauty and to please her husband. It is true that Saint Augustine has written that women who wear makeup offend God, for not being content to be as God has made them, they desire to correct nature. In keeping with that opinion, therefore, I should think that one shouldn't wear makeup, though I should think one might wear it with the right intention and not incur mortal sin. As Saint Thomas says (II,2, question 9): "They are not committing mortal sin if they are not doing it out of arrogance, lasciviousness, or contempt of God; for there are times when one does it not to show or pretend to show beauty but to hide one's viciousness; and even when the action proceeds from some extrinsic or chance cause, because the real reasons are hidden from us, we must always accept these things in their best light."

Therefore I beg you, don't be such a rash judge! I would suggest you begin to repent for having slandered those whom all good people endeavor to praise. For they realize that many women are deserving of eternal praise, among them Judith, of whom Saint Jerome said: "Take the woman Judith as an example of chastity and praise her with triumphal song and perpetual hymns and canticles.

For He who rewarded her chastity made her worthy to be imitated not only by women but by men; and He so favored her that He gave her the strength to gain victory over an enemy who had until that time been invincible."

O praiseworthy and excellent chastity, you have burned in many women's hearts like a constant flame! There are still a great many very noble ladies who kept the marriage bond with their gracious virtue, such as Arthemisia, the wife of Mansolus [Mausolus]; Argia, the wife of Polimetes; Cornelia, the wife of Gracchus; and Hippsicrates, the wife of Mithridates. Others there are, too numerous to count, who preferred virginity to any other way of life—Atalanta, the virgin from Calidonia, who for the preservation of her maidenhood spent her days in the woods, forests, mountains and plains; Camilia, the Queen of the Vulcans, who exercised military discipline with a manly courage. How many women have valued virginity: Iphigenia, Cassandra, and Chryseis in Greece, to whose number one might add the virgins of Sparta, Mylesia, and Thebes. These women honor and ennoble the Hebrew and Greek histories, which tell us how they faced violent death rather than lose their virginity.

Considering all this, I tend to think the plethora of your insults is unfounded. Many examples from history refute your inveterate ill-will; but that is not the only assistance I hope for. Many good men too will come to my aid, for reason will urge them to do so. I confess I am dumbfounded that you do not seem to fear the consequences that have befallen certain men who have spoken ill of women. Aren't you impressed by the punishment that Tiresias underwent for having said that the female sex was more lascivious than the male? This haughty and foolish opinion deprived him of his sight. Heavy too was the revenge which the goddess Ceres took on Erysichton for having despised her; if you remember correctly she reduced him to such an extreme state of hunger that he ended up eating himself. Ajax, the son of Aiolus, who had shown disrespect towards Minerva, also got what he deserved.

I could cite other examples, but I shall refrain from doing so as I fear that merely remonstrating with you would not be enough to root out your wretched opinions. I shall therefore give my tired pen a rest and pray God that He may liberate you from your obstinate opinions.

———

From <u>The Love Letters of a Portuguese Nun</u> by Gabriel Joseph de Lavergne, Vicomte de Guilleragues (1628–1685). When the letters were first published in 1669, they were believed to have been written by a nun named Mariana Alcoforado (1640–1723) to a French officer named M. Noel Bouton, later Marquis de Chamilly et St. Leger (1636–1715), who had seduced and then abandoned her. As the story goes, Bouton rode past the convent of Beja and was seen by Alcoforado; soon the two were involved in a full-fledged romance, but Bouton had to desert her after scandal became imminent.

LETTER FIVE

I write to you this last time, and hope to convey to you, in the revised terms and manner of this letter, that you have finally persuaded me that you no longer love me, and that therefore I am no longer to love you: I shall therefore take the first opportunity to return to you all I still possess of yours. Do not be anxious lest I write to you; I shall not even put your name on the package; I have left the arrangements all in the hands of Dona Brites, whom I had accustomed to confidences entirely remote from this one. I shall place greater reliance on her handiwork than I would on my own; she will take all the necessary precautions in order to be able to reassure me that you will have received the portrait and the bracelets you gave me. I want you to know, however, that for some days now I have felt ready to burn and tear up these tokens of your love, which I so treasured, but I have given you such a demonstration of weakness that you would never have believed me capable of going to such lengths. I mean therefore to exult in all the pain it has cost me to be parted from them, and afford you at least a little vexation.

I confess, to my shame and to yours, that I have found myself more attached to these baubles than I should like to say, and I felt the need once more to reflect fully in order to be able to part with each particular one, for all that I flattered myself that I felt no further attachment towards you; but one compasses whatever one wishes, on one pretext and another. I placed them resolutely in Dona Brites's hands, at what cost in tears! After any number of conflicting feelings and doubts of which you know nothing, and which of course I have no intention of imparting to you, I begged her never again to mention them to me, never to give them back to me, not even if I asked to see them one more time, and to send them back to you without telling me. I only became aware of the full strength of my love at the moment when I determined to make every effort to be cured of it, and I fear I should not have dared set hand to it had I been able to forsee such difficulties, such a wrench. I am sure I should have felt less of a horrible turmoil inside myself for loving you, thankless as you are, than in leaving you forever. What I felt was that I cared less for you than for my own passion, and I found it strangely painful to resist it after your offensive behaviour made me come to hate you.

The customary pride of my sex was of no help to me in hardening my resolve against you. I have, alas, endured your disdain, and I would have borne your hatred and all the jealousy occasioned in me by your attachment for another person; I should at least have had some passion to fight against. But it is your indifference that I cannot bear; your impertinent protestations of friendship and the ridiculous urbanity of your last letter showed me that you will have received all the letters I have written to you, but that they left your heart wholly unmoved, for all that you did read them. Thankless one, I am still foolish enough to be heartsick at the thought of not even being able to take comfort from the prospect that they never reached you, that they were not delivered to you. I detest your good faith: did I ever ask you to make a clean breast of things? You might have left my love intact! All you had to do was not to write. I was not looking for clarifications. Am I not wretched enough in having been unable to compel you to make some effort at deception, in being no longer in a position to find excuses for you? Rest assured, I am aware that you are unworthy of what I feel for you, I am acquainted with all your bad qualities. However (if all I have done for you may earn me some small consideration on your part for the favour I ask), I beg you not to write to me any more, and to help me forget you completely. Were you to give me even the slightest hint that reading this letter caused you some sorrow, I might believe you; and it could be that your avowal and your consent might irritate and anger me, and this could stir me up. So do not interfere with my behaviour, you would undoubtedly upset all my plans whichever way you handled the matter. I have no wish to know the outcome of this letter; do not disturb the state of mind I am adopting; it seems to me you can rest content with the harm you are already causing me, whatever plan you may have made to assure my unhappiness. Do not deliver me from my uncertainty; my hope is that with time I shall make something peaceable out of it. I promise not to hate you, I am too mistrustful of violent feelings to venture into hatred. I am sure that I may find here in this country a more faithful and a worthier lover. Alas, though, who could give me love? Would another's passion possess me? Did mine have any effect on you? Should I not feel that a heart that has been touched never forgets the one who introduced it to emotions hitherto unknown to it, but of which it was capable? That all its emotions remain attached to the idol it has created? That its first promptings, its first wounds can be neither cured nor effaced? That all the emotions brought to its aid, which attempt to satisfy it and requite it, do nothing more than bear empty promises of an inner sensitivity now beyond all recall? That all the pleasures it seeks, but does not wish to find, serve only to acquaint it with the fact that there is nothing it cherishes more than the memory of its sufferings? Why have you introduced me to the inadequacy, the mortification of an attachment that is not to last forever, and the pains attendant upon a passionate love, when it is not reciprocated? And why is it that a blind attachment and a cruel destiny generally insist on setting our hearts on those who are responsive to a different person?

Even if I could hope for some diversion out of a new affair, even if I were to find a person of good faith, I so deplore my own situation I should be very hesitant to place the last man on earth in the condition to which you have reduced me. And although I am not obliged to show you any consideration, I could not bring myself to wreak on you so cruel a vengeance, if it depended on me, by a change that I do not foresee. At this moment what I am trying to do is make excuses for you, and I realise that as a rule a nun is hardly a person to love. Still, it seems that if one were capable of finding reasons for the choices one makes, one might form an attachment to them in preference of other women. Nothing prevents them from devoting unremitting thought to their passion, they are not disturbed by the thousand things that in the world occasion distraction and preoccupation. I imagine it is not all that agreeable to see those one loves endlessly preoccupied with a thousand trivial concerns, and one must be rather lacking in delicacy to endure, without being driven to despair, their constant talk of social gatherings, dressmakers' fittings, and outings. One is constantly exposed to fresh jealousies; they are required to show courtesy, complaisance, to make conversation: who can rest assured that they derive no pleasure from all these social occasions, that they always endure their husbands with an extreme distaste and an absence of good will? Those women ought to be wary of a lover who does not hold them to a rigorous account on that score, who accepts readily and happily whatever they tell him, and who remains easy in his mind and entirely trusting as he sees them submit to all these duties! But I do not propose to prove to you by good reasoning that you ought to love me; these are very shabby methods, and I have made use of far better ones with no greater success. I am too familiar with my destiny to try to overcome it; I shall be unhappy all my life: I was so, after all, when I was seeing you every day. I was frightened to death that you were being unfaithful to me, I wanted to see you the whole time, and that was not possible. I was anxious about the dangers you ran when you entered this convent. I was more dead than alive when you were on active service. I was in despair for not being more beautiful, more worthy of you, I grumbled at the mediocrity of my condition, I often thought that the feelings you seemed to have for me could be detrimental to you. I felt I did not love you enough, I feared for you as I thought of my parents' anger, in fact I was in as pitiable a condition as the one I suffer at present. Had you accorded me some token of your passion since you left Portugal, I would have made every effort to leave the country, I would have disguised myself to come and join you. Oh, but what would have become of me if you had taken no further interest in me after I arrived in France? What a convulsion! What bewilderment! What a peak of shame for my family, whom I dote upon now that I no longer love you. As you see, I am clear-sighted enough to realise that I might have been in an even more pitiable condition than the one I am in; and at least I am for once in my life addressing you in moderate terms. How my very moderation will please you, how gratified I shall make you! Well, I do not want to know, I have already asked you not to write to me any more, this I beg of you.

Have you never paused to reflect on the way you have treated me? Does it never occur to you that you have a greater obligation to me than to any person alive? I loved you to the point of madness; all I have received is disdain! Your conduct has not been that of a gentleman; you must have had an instinctive aversion for me as you did not lose your heart to me. I allowed myself to be seduced by some very mediocre qualities: whatever did you do that was supposed to captivate me? What sacrifice did you ever make for me? Did you not go in pursuit of a thousand other gratifications? Did you give up gaming and hunting? Were you not the first to report for active duty? Were you not the last to return from the army? At the front you took mad risks, even though I begged you to take good care of yourself for love of me; you never looked to find a way to settle in Portugal, where you were well regarded; one letter from your brother and away you went without a moment's hesitation; and I am not unaware that during the voyage you were in a thoroughly good mood. It must be confessed, I have to hate you like a poison. Ah, but all my sorrows are of my own making: first I accustomed you to a grand passion too naïvely, while [it] takes guile to excite love; some measure of address is needed to light upon the means to generate passion, and love on its own does not call forth love. You wanted me to love you, and in forming this objective, you would have taken no steps to achieve it; you would even have persuaded yourself to love me had this proved necessary, but you were aware that you could succeed in your enterprise without passion, and that you had no need of any. What bad faith! Do you think you could deceive me with impunity? Should some chance bring you back to this country, I promise you I shall turn you over to the vengeance of my parents. I have long lived in a state of unreserved idolization that horrifies me, and I am persecuted with intolerable severity by my remorse. I am all too sensitive to the shame of the crimes you made me commit, and, alas, I no am longer possessed by the passion that prevented me from appreciating their enormity. When will my heart stop being torn? When shall I be delivered from this cruel embarrassment? I believe, nonetheless, that I do not wish you ill, and that I could bring myself to consent to your being happy; and yet how could you be happy if you have a heart? I want to write you a further letter to show you that I shall perhaps be more at peace in a while. What a pleasure it will be for me to be able to tax you for the injustice you have done me once I am no longer so sensitive to it, and when I make plain to you how I despise you, to be able to say this in total indifference to your betrayal, with all my pleasures and pains forgotten, and in complete forgetfulness of you except when I choose to call you to mind! I concede that you have a considerable advantage over me, and that you induced in me a passion which drove me to insanity; but this should afford you scant self-satisfaction: I was young, I was naïve, I had been shut up in this convent since I was a child, I had seen only disagreeable people, I had never heard the praises you were constantly lavishing on me; it seemed to me that I owed to you the graces and beauty you found in me and which you brought to my notice. I heard good reports of you, everyone spoke in your favour, you did all that was necessary to give me love. But I have finally awoken from this spell, you were of considerable help, and I admit that I stood in urgent need of it. As I sent back your letters I shall carefully keep the last two you have written to me, and I shall re-read them even more often than I read the first ones, so as not to relapse into my weakness. Oh but how dearly they have cost me, and how happy I should have been had you been willing to suffer me to love you forever! I realise well enough that I am still a little too much taken up with my reproaches and your infidelity, but bear in mind that I have promised myself a more tranquil state and that I shall achieve it, or else that I shall take some extreme resolution against myself that you will learn of with no great regret. But I want nothing more from you. I am mad to keep saying the same things over again. I must leave you and spare you not another thought. In fact I think I shall not write to you again; do I have to give you an exact account of all the various things I am feeling?

———

From Olinda to Cloridon in Catharine Trotter's <u>Olinda's Adventures: Or the Amours of a Young Lady</u>, an epistolary novella that first appeared in volume 1 of <u>Familiar Letters of Love and Gallantry and Several Other Subjects. All Written by Ladies</u> (1693). Trotter (1679–1749), a dramatist and writer, wrote this work in her early teens and published it anonymously. The work is made up of eight letters: seven to a platonic male friend, Cleander, and one to an older, but married suitor, Cloridon, whom Olinda rails against. The story concerns Olinda's attempts to defend her honor against the advances of Cloridon and to let her mother arrange a marriage for her. However, Cloridon plans the kidnapping of Olinda's intended groom, Orontes, and the novel ends with the letter from Olinda to Cloridon.

Letter VIII
Olinda to Cloridon

In answer to a letter which he sent her with the copy of verses in the sixth of the foregoing ones.

'tis not an Hour ago since I believ'd I hated you: I thought I could have rail'd at you, have call'd you base, seducer of my Honour, Traytor, that under a pretence of Love, design'd my Ruin; but Ah! Those tender Excuses which you sent me, soon discover'd the mistake, and show'd me it was only Angry Love, that so Transported me: And now 'tis turn'd to as violent a Grief, which wou'd fain ease it self in Complaints: But I am so wretched, that even that poor Comfort is deny'd me; for who can I complain to, when in lamenting my Misfortune I must expose our Crime: For yours my Lord, has involv'd me in the guilt; and all those thoughts and Actions, which were innocent before, must be condemn'd as the Causes of such ill Effects: For if I had never lov'd you, or if I had never own'd it, nor consented to see you, you had not desir'd any thing of me that could shock my Virtue: Now, I can't think of 'em without Shame and Anger. That Love which shin'd before so Pure and Bright, appears now the Blackest thing in Nature; and I hate my self for not hating you; for I own (tho' I blush in owning) that I love you still; Nay, I believe that I forgive you too; but I must never, never see you more: No, though you swear you Repent, and that you would not repeat your Crime, if you were certain of success. Would not you believe I should as easily Pardon your breach of this Vow, as I did the last, which you made me as solemnly? Yes, you would, my Lord, and I should be betray'd to things I never thought of yet: For all is solid, convincing Reason that you speak; and I should soon believe any thing you would have me. Curse on that fond Credulity that first deceiv'd me into a belief, that 'twas no Sin to love you. Yet sure it could not be an unpardonable Fault, to value one that so infinitely deserves it: To Love, to See, and Talk with one whole Conversation is so Charming as yours; and that was all I wish'd. All that know you do the same; Why then am I more guilty? Ah! If your Fame had been as pure as mine, we had both been Happy and Innocent; so innocent, that she, that happy she, who claims all your love as her due, (even she, I think, if she had known our Hearts) could not have been offended at it: But who is there, the most uninterested, that would not now condemn us; Nay, the most Partial could not excuse us; even we should blame our selves. Why will you then importune me still to see you; ask me no more, what I dare never grant; and believe—but you know, 'tis not unkindness makes me Refuse you: You know I must be Wretched in your Absence; yet think me easie and satisfied, if it will contribute any thing to your quiet; or rather don't think of me at all. Let us make our selves as happy as we can; I will endeavour to forget you; don't Write to me, if you love me well enough to forbear it: And if you can cease to love me, without hating me; for I don't find I have force enough to bear so great a misfortune, which is the only one can add to the weight of those which have already almost sunk

The Poor
Olinda.

———

From <u>The Female Critick: Or, Letters in Drollery from Ladies to Their Humble Servants,</u> published anonymously in 1701. The work consists of over forty letters written by women to men they find unacceptable as suitors. According to William Graves, who wrote the introduction to the 1972 Garland reprinting, <u>The Female Critick</u> "is notable for its intrinsic interest as a witty, smoothly written collection of letters and as one of the vehicles that carried the traditions of seventeenth-century genres to the novel of the next century." In addition to the following letter—written to a serial flirt—<u>The Female Critick</u> includes letters to "a Poet," "a Gentleman that had a red Nose," "a Gentleman lamentably in Love," "an Old Batchelor," "a big fat Gentleman," "a great Drinker," and "a Gentleman that had a great Opinion of himself."

LETTER XVI.
To a Gentleman that courted all he came near.

Had I been left out of your Catalogue of Saints, I had fancy'd my self thrown by like the common Rubbish of the World: but now take not a little Pride to shine in the Firmament of Stars. But you tell me a Paradox, That you will now be constant; which is impossible; for shou'd you be constant to One, you wou'd be inconstant to your own nature, which is always given to change. Besides, it wou'd be a great disadvantage to you; for now the same Complement [*sic*] serves our whole Sex, whereas shou'd you fix to one, Variety wou'd be expected: and doubtless the reason why you make but one Address to the same Person, is because you know not what to say a second time. Methinks it were a more fit use, than to make a Husband of you, to drive a Spike through your Sconce, and fix it on a Spire for a Weather-cock, where it might turn to court every fresh Blast of Wind. Nor would there be danger of hurting your Brains: for had you any, you cou'd not be of this fickle Humour; since it shews want of Judgment in your Choice, or of Reason in your Desisting. Or if ever you had any Brains, doubtless that Windmill in your Head hath ground them to Mustard by this time; which yet are not wholly lost to you, that being, you know, proper Sawce for a Goose. But I admite, since you still cover a change of good Faces you can bear with the repetition of your own in a Glass! except it be, that when you are just come from an handsome one, you view your own for variety. Yet, after all, (to confess the truth) I really believe that you are wrong'd in your Character; and that your continually changing ariseth not from an Inconstancy in your own Nature, but from the Unkindness of our Sex; whilst You, finding the Wind begin to veer about, sail off with a Side-wind, before it blow full in your Face, as it will speedily do, if you fly no with speed, and for ever after desist from farther attempts upon,

Sir, &c.

From <u>Letters from the Marchioness de M*** to the Count de R***</u> (1735) by Claude Prosper Joylot de Crebillon (1707-1777). In this epistolary novel, the married Marchioness writes to her indifferent and unfaithful lover, the Count, alternately expressing her love for him and reproaching him for his inconstancy. After her husband is promoted to a post abroad, the Marchioness dies of grief, anguished over the prospect of being forced apart from the Count.

LETTER LX

It would really be very singular, should I still continue to love you; and I agree with you, that my Conduct, in that Particular, would be extremely pleasant. But I can assure you, my poor Count, that my Mirth is much abated, and I had reason to acquaint you, that you would not find the Conclusion of the Comedy so agreeable as you might imagine. Were you truly sensible what a ridiculous Part you act at present, you would not have any Power to personate it much longer. You are extremely languid and disengaged, I confess; Lady*** had rejected your Assiduities, and I am diverted at your Surprize. What a number of Mortifications must you needs sustain! Comfort yourself, however, for most Men have experienced the fame Fate: But how could it possibly happen to you; and that, as amiable as you are, you should be repulsed from two different Quarters? But you have one Resource, after all; for it seems you once have loved me, and have been so successful as to deceive me; have Recourse then to your fruitful Imagination for some new Method of deluding me. I am perfectly acquainted with your disconsolate Air, on those Occasions; but neither that, nor the affected Sighs you breathe from the bottom of your Heart; the little Flows of Language you express with so much Delicacy; the Letters you pen with so much Elegance; the weeping Languor of your Eyes; your dejected Mien, nor all the Arts you have already assumed, will ever touch me for the future; and I believe these are the only Dexterities you can practise, to regain me. Even your Wit is all effectual, since it will be unobserved by me: You therefore judge very properly, that all these polite Attractions will be unavailing. What still contributes to your Misfortune is, that you pass for a Deceiver, and that few Women of tolerable Understanding ever credit your Protestations: And, as you are not fond of Conquests that are too easy, I doubt your Sighs will not be so soon rewarded as you may wish. You see how unhappy you are! Your Passion for me began to disgust you; I was no longer capable of inspiring you with Tenderness; and you forgot that you ever thought me amiable. You treated me in a perfidious manner, and endeavoured to render yourself happy with other Objects; but when you had the Mortification to be disappointed, you grew desirous of returning to me. I received you with some Severity, and you are now more amorous than ever. What a charming Heart is yours, and how delightful it must be, to have the Disposal of all its Emotions! You, however, have ranged the Circumstances of this Adventure, with great Judgment: According to your Plan I must needs continue to love you; and you think that Passion would be natural to me, were it not a little disconcerted by Caprice: But you thought yourself confident that my Sentiments, in your favour, could not long be discontinued, and I cannot blame you, if you are surprized to find me so different from what you expected. You are not able to comprehend this Incident, tho' it proves more important than any other. But it is time for me to finish this little Pleasantry, and answer your Letter. I owe you some good Advice, as well as a free Confession of the Sentiments I entertain on your account. I must therefore acquaint you, that my Passion is entirely extinguished: I could have told you the same, in the Height of my Resentment, but not with so much Sincerity as at present. When our Minds are agitated to an extreme Degree, we may easily impose upon ourselves; but a soon as the first Emotion is over, we consider Things with Calmness, and are not so liable to be deceived. You may therefore receive it, from me, as an infallible Truth, that I neither love you at this time, nor ever shall for the future. Your Repentance may possibly be sincere, but it will never affect me. We seldom grant our Pardon, but when it affords us some Pleasure to offer it, and when the Injuries we have sustain'd have not been so considerable as to extinguish our Affection. You are sensible of the Injustice I have suffer'd from you, and I shall not condescend to repeat the Particulars. Let your Heart be its own Judge; may it over-whelm you with all the Reproaches you merit, and place your Conduct before you, in such an odious Light, as may prevent you from afflicting any other with the Injuries you have offer'd me. I once lov'd you to Adoration, and my Passion was incapable of a Moment's Insincerity; but you have, at last, caus'd it to expire. You assure me, at present, that I am the only Object of your Tenderness; but you will be too unhappy, if you entertain any Sentiments, with which my Heart is unable to correspond. But were even this pos-sible, you ought to be cautious of indulging any flattering Thoughts. Render Justice to yourself, and renounce all Hope: Per-haps you may not have Discretion enough to discontinue your Visits to me, and therefore I shall make it my part to prevent them. Absence is our only Cure on such Occasions, and when we suffer by unfortunate Passions, the Sight of the Object that created them, gives us the severest Torments. However, if your Departure is to be so sudden as you inform me, I grant you my Permission to visit me, in order to take your final Leave. I neither am, nor ever intend to be your Enemy; and it is equally certain, that I shall never be your Lover. Let not my Goodness betray you into any false Expectations; were it less than it really is, you might entertain what Hopes you pleas'd; but you ought to regard my Consent to see you, as an infal-lible Proof of my Indifference.

———·———

From __Letters from a Peruvian Woman__ (1747) by Françoise de Graf-figny (1695–1758). In the book, Zilia, a Peruvian princess, has fallen into French hands after being captured by the Spanish. At first Zilia writes to Aza, the Inca prince she was to have married, and then to the Chevalier Deterville, a young French nobleman who is in love with

her. In this letter, Zilia outlines her reasons for refusing his proposal of
marriage.

XLI
To the Chevalier Deterville
IN PARIS

I have received at practically the same time, Monsieur, news of your departure from Malta and of your arrival in Paris. Whatever pleasure I may feel at the idea of seeing you again cannot overcome the sorrow caused by the note you wrote me on arriving.

Oh Deterville! After having take it upon yourself to conceal your sentiments in all your letters, after having given me reason to hope that I would no longer have to combat a passion that grieves me, you abandon yourself more than ever to its violence!

What is the use of affecting a deference that you can contradict at the same moment? You ask permission to see me, you assure me of your blind submission to my wishes, and yet you endeavor to convince me of the sincerity of sentiments that could not be more opposed to those wishes and that offend me, wishes of which I will never approve in any event.

But since you are seduced by a false hope and abuse my trust and my state of mind, I must tell you of the resolutions I have adopted, resolutions more steadfast than yours.

It is in vain that you would flatter yourself to think that you can make my heart take on new chains. The betrayal of my trust does not undo my oaths. Please heaven it should make me forget that ingrate! But if I do, I will remain true to myself and not be unfaithful to my own feelings. Cruel Aza has abandoned a possession that was once dear to him, but his rights over me are no less sacred for having done so. I may recover from my passion, but I will never have passion for anyone but him. All the sentiments that friendship inspires are yours, and you will never share them with anyone else, for I owe them to you. I pledge them to you and will be faithful to that promise. You will enjoy my trust and sincerity to the same degree, which is to say that you will enjoy both without limit. All manner of vivid, delicate feelings that love has produced in my heart will turn to the advantage of friendship. I will allow you to see with equal frankness my regret at not being born in France and my insuperable penchant for Aza, the desire I would have to owe you the advantage of being able to think and my eternal gratitude to the person who obtained it for me. We shall read from each other's souls. Trust is as capable of making time pass quickly as love. There are a thousand ways of making friendship interesting and of driving boredom from it.

You will give me some acquaintance with your sciences and your arts; you will savor the pleasure of superiority. I will regain the upper hand by developing virtues in your heart with which you are not acquainted. You will adorn my mind with that which can make it amusing and will take pleasure from your work; I will endeavor to make agreeable to you the childlike charms of simple friendship and will find happiness in succeeding at this.

By sharing her tenderness with us, Celine will infuse our conversations with the merriment they might otherwise lack. What more will be left for us to desire?

You fear needlessly that solitude might damage my health. Believe me, Deterville, solitude never becomes dangerous save on account of idleness. Always occupied, I will know how to fashion new pleasures from all that habit renders insipid.

Without gaining deeper understanding of nature's secrets is not the mere examination of nature's marvels enough to bring constant variety and renewal to ever pleasant occupations? Does one lifetime suffice to gain a superficial yet interesting acquaintance with the universe, my surroundings, my own existence?

The pleasure of being—a forgotten pleasure not even known to so many blind humans—that thought so sweet, that happiness so pure, "I am, I live, I exist," could bring happiness all by itself if one remembered it, if one enjoyed it, if one treasured it as befits its worth.

Come, Deterville, come learn from me to economize the resources of our souls and the benefits of nature. Renounce tumultuous feelings, those imperceptible destroyers of our being. Come learn to know pleasures innocent and lasting, come enjoy them with me.

You will find in my heart, in my friendship, in my feelings, all that can compensate you for the ravages of love.

From the epistolary novel <u>Clarissa</u> (1747) by Samuel Richardson (1689–1761). Clarissa Harlowe writes to Mr. Roger Solmes, "a man of sordid manners, disagreeable in his person and address, [and] immensely rich," whose offer of marriage Clarissa rejects. (Her family wishes for her to marry Solmes to improve their economic and social standing.) After her rejection of Solmes, Clarissa abandons her home and takes up with a Mr. Robert Lovelace, whom she trusts to protect her but, who, in the end, lures her to a London brothel and drugs and rapes her. She later dies. Before the publication of his <u>Clarissa</u>—the longest novel in the English language—Richardson was best known as a printer. In 1739 he was asked by two acquaintances in the book business to compose a letter-writing manual, but he temporarily abandoned the project to write the epistolary novel <u>Pamela; or, Virtue Rewarded</u> (1740). Richardson returned to his letter-manuals as he worked on other epistolary novels, publishing the manual <u>Familiar Letters on Important Occasions</u> (see p. 262). <u>Clarissa</u> can be considered one of the most important eighteenth-century works, influencing the use of epistolarity in fiction by such writers as Goethe and Rousseau (see p. 247).

[Letter 33.1: Clarissa Harlowe] to Roger Solmes, Esq.

Wednesday, Mar. 15

Sir,

You will wonder to receive a letter from me, and more still at the uncommon subject of it. But the necessity of the case will justify me, at least in my own apprehension, and I shall therefore make no other apology for it.

When you first came acquainted with my father's family, you found the writer of this one of the happiest creatures in the word [*sic*], beloved by the best and most indulgent of parents, and rejoicing in the kind favour of two affectionate uncles, and in the esteem of every one.

But how is this happy scene now changed!—You was [*sic*] pleased to cast a favourable eye upon me. You addressed yourself to my friends. Your proposals were approved of by them; approved of without consulting me, as if my choice and happiness were of the least signification. Those who had a right to all reasonable obedience from me, insisted upon it without reserve. I had not the felicity to think as they did, almost the first time my sentiments differed from theirs. I besought them to indulge me in a point so important to my future happiness: but, alas, in vain! And then (for I thought it was but honest) I told you my mind; and even that my affections were engaged. But, to my mortification and surprise, you persisted, and still persist.

The consequence of all is too grievous for me to repeat: you, who have such free access to the rest of the family, know it too well: too well you know it, either for the credit of your own generosity, or for my reputation. I am used, on your account, as I never before was used, and never before was thought to deserve to be used; and this was the hard, the impossible condition of their returning favour, that I must prefer a man to all others, that of all others I cannot prefer.

Thus distressed and made unhappy, and all for your sake, and through your cruel perseverance, I write, sir, to demand of you the peace of mind you have robbed me of: to demand of you the love of so many dear friends, of which you have deprived me; and, if you have the generosity that should distinguish a man, and a gentleman, to adjure you not to continue an address that has been attended with such cruel effects to the creature you profess to esteem.

If you really value me, as my friends would make me believe, and as you have declared you do, must it not be a mean and selfish value? A value that can have no merit with the unhappy object of it, because it is attended with effects so grievous to her? It must be for *your own sake* only, not for *mine*. And, even in this point, you *must* be mistaken; for would a prudent man wish to marry one who has not a heart to give? Who cannot esteem him? Who therefore must prove a bad wife?—And how cruel would it be to make a poor creature a bad wife, whose pride it would be to make a good one?

If I am capable of judging, our tempers and inclinations are vastly different. Any other of my sex will make you happier than I can. The treatment I meet with, and the obstinacy, as it is called, with which I support myself under it, ought to convince you of this; were I not able to give so good a reason for this my supposed perverseness, as that I cannot consent to marry a man whom I cannot value.

But if, sir, you have not so much generosity in your value for me, as to desist for my own sake, let me conjure you, by the regard due to yourself, and to your own future happiness, to discontinue your suit, and place your affections on a worthier object: for why should you make me miserable, and yourself not happy? By this means you will do all that is now in your power to restore me to the affection of my friends; and if that can be, it will leave me in as happy a state as you found me. You need only to say that you see there are no HOPES, as you will perhaps complaisantly call it, of succeeding with me (and indeed, sir, there cannot be a greater truth than this) and that you will therefore no more think of me; but turn your thoughts another way.

Your compliance with this request will lay me under the highest obligation to your generosity, and make me ever

Your well-wisher, and humble servant,
Clarissa Harlowe

———

From the two-volume Epistles for the Ladies *(T. Gardner, 1749) by novelist/playwright Eliza (Fowler) Haywood (1693–1756). Haywood, the wife of a clergyman, was one of the most prolific and widely read writers of the eighteenth century, and edited* The Female Spectator, *the first English periodical written by and for women. In* The Life and Romances of Mrs. Eliza Haywood *(Columbia University Press, 1915),*

George Frisbie Whicher called <u>Epistles for the Ladies</u> a work of Haywood's maturity "most renowned for [its] pious intent." The letters were apparently not meant as models but, "to convey moral precepts in an agreeably alleviated form."

EPISTLE XLVII.

From Astrea to a Gentleman, who being under some Misfortunes, and relieved by her, had mistook her Good-Nature for the Effects of a secret Liking of his Person, and on that Supposition presumed to send her a Love-Letter.

Sir,

I am extremely sorry that what I thought a Virtue in me should be construed into a Vice, and that my Hospitality and Readiness to do you any little Service on the Account of your Misfortunes, instead of exciting in you a grateful esteem, has drawn on me the greatest Affront that, in my Opinion, was in your Power to offer. I am not, however, so much concerned for your own Sake, who I perceive have Vanity enough to buoy you up under any Disappointment, as I am for that of many others, who, through the Calamities of the Times, may stand in need of Assistance from those to whom Fortune has been less averse; because it will make me for the future fearful of conferring the least Obligation on any Person of a different Sex, as I cannot be assured he will not return it in the Manner you have done.—I send you back your Letter, and with it this Advice,—to be more wary for the future how a too good an Opinion of yourself tempts you to mistake *Pity* for *Love,* lest you convert the *one* into *Contempt,* instead of inspiring the least Share of the other.—I am pretty confident your Observation of this Rule will be of singular Use to a Man of your Way of thinking, and is the last Act of Charity you must ever expect from

Astrea.

From <u>Lettres de Mistriss Fanni Butlerd</u> *(1757), by French actress and writer Marie-Jeanne Riccoboni (1713–1792). Riccoboni's first novel, Fanni Butlerd was based on the writer's relationship with the Comte de Maillebois, a nobleman who abandoned her for another woman in 1745. The book, made up of 116 letters, deals with the love affair and subsequent breakup between Fanni, a young Frenchwoman, and the British nobleman Lord Alfred.*

Mistriss Fanni, to a Single Reader:

What is natural and true gives these letters all their merit. If they gain the public's favor and chance causes you to read them, if you recognize the expressions of a heart you possessed and some feature reminds you of a feeling you reciprocated with the basest ingratitude, may the vanity of having been the object of so tender and delicate a love never cause you to name the woman who had so much confidence in you. At least show her, by keeping her secret, that you are not totally unworthy of the sincere affection she had for you. It is not the desire to gain admiration for her wit that impels her to publish these letters. Rather, that of immortalizing, if possible, a passion which was her happiness, whose initial pleasures still occupy her mind, and whose memory she will always cherish. No, it is not this passion which made her tears flow, which filled her soul with pain and bitterness. She accuses only you of the pain she has suffered; she recognizes only you as the cause of her troubles. Her love was the source of everything good. You cruelly poisoned it! She doesn't hate love, she only hates you.

From <u>Persian Letters</u> *(published posthumously in 1761) by Charles de Secondat Montesquieu (1689–1755). The narrative is made up of letters between two Persian travelers—Usbek and Rica—and the people they have left back home. The following letter to Usbek is from Roxana, one of the wives in his harem, who, like the other women, is being closely watched over by a group of eunuchs. In this letter Roxana tells*

Usbek of her infidelity with a young man and her decision to poison herself because she cannot tolerate life in his harem.

Letter 161
Roxana to Usbek, at Paris

Yes, I deceived you. I suborned your eunuchs, outwitted your jealousy, and managed to turn your terrible seraglio into a place of delightful pleasures.

I am going to die; poison will flow through my veins. What is there for me to do here, since the only man who kept me alive breathes no more? I am dying, but my spirit will depart properly escorted: I have just despatched in advance the sacrilegious guards who shed the most precious blood on earth.

How could you have thought me credulous enough to imagine that I was in the world only in order to worship your caprices? that while you allowed yourself everything, you had the right to thwart all my desires? No: I may have lived in servitude, but I have always been free. I have amended your laws according to the laws of nature, and my mind has always remained independent.

You should even be grateful to me for the sacrifice that I made on your account, for having demeaned myself so far as to seem faithful to you, for having had the cowardice to guard in my heart something that I ought to have revealed to the whole earth, and finally for having profaned the name of virtue by permitting it to be applied to my acceptance of your whims.

You were surprised not to find me carried away by the ecstasy of love; if you had known me properly you would have found in me all the violence of hate.

But you had for a long time the benefit of thinking that a heart like mine was subject to you. We were both happy: you thought that I had been deceived, while I was deceiving you.

Such language is new to you, no doubt. Is it possible that after having overwhelmed you with grief I could force you to admire my courage? But it is all over, the poison is destroying me. I am losing my strength, the pen is falling from my hands, I can feel even my hatred growing weaker; I am dying.

From the seraglio at Isaphan, the 8th of the first moon of Rabia, 1720

———

From Julie, or the New Heloise: Letters of Two Lovers Who Live in a Small Town at the Foot of the Alps *(1761), by Romantic philosopher Jean-Jacques Rousseau (1712–1778). The story concerns a young woman, Julie d'Étange, and her tutor, St. Preux, who fall in love with one another but must keep their romance a secret (Julie's father, the stern Baron d'Étange, has promised her hand to a Monsieur de Wolmar, and St. Preux, unlike the d'Étanges, is not of the nobility). Fearful of the wrath of Baron d'Étange, Julie and St. Preux conduct their romance in secret (primarily through letters delivered via discreet intermediaries) but Julie's mother soon learns of the affair and dies from the stress, prompting Julie to write a final farewell letter to St. Preux and marry Monsieur de Wolmar. After her wedding, Julie receives a letter from St. Preux asking if she is happy in her newly married state; this is her answer.*

LETTER XX.
From Julie.

You ask me whether I am happy. This question touches me, and by raising it you help me to answer it; for far from seeking to forget, as you suggest, I confess I could never be happy if you ceased to love me: but I am happy in every respect, and my happiness wants nothing but yours. If I avoided speaking of Monsieur de Wolmar in my previous letter, I did so out of consideration for you. I was too aware of your sensibility not to fear embittering your sufferings: but since your uneasiness about my fate compels me to tell you about the man on whom it depends, I can do so only in a manner worthy of him, as it behooves his spouse and a friend of truth.

Monsieur de Wolmar is nearly fifty; his steady, measured life and tranquil passions have preserved in him such a sound constitution and hearty air that he looks scarcely forty, and nothing about him betokens advancing age save experience and wisdom. His physiognomy is noble and prepossessing, his bearing simple and open, his manners are civil rather than profuse, he says little and with much sense, but without affecting either concision or sententiousness. He is the same for everyone, neither seeks out nor flees anyone, and never has other priorities than those of reason.

Despite the natural coldness of his disposition, his heart abetting my father's intentions thought it sensed that I was well-suited to him, and for the first time in his life he contracted an attachment. This moderate but durable inclination has been so well governed by decorum, and has been maintained so evenly, that he has had no need to change his tone in changing his status, and without offending conjugal gravity he has retained with me since his marriage the same manners he had before. I have never seen him either gay or sad, but always content; never does he speak to me of himself, rarely of me; he does not seek me out, but does not dislike my seeking him, and is reluctant to leave my side. He does not laugh; he is grave without disposing others to be; on the contrary, his serene bearing seems to invite me to merriment, and as the pleasures I enjoy are the only ones he seems to appreciate, one of the attentions I owe him is to try to keep myself entertained. In a word, he wants me to be happy; he does not say this, but I see it; and is desiring the happiness of one's wife not to have achieved it?

However carefully I may have observed him, I have been able to discover no passion of any kind in him except the one he has for me. Moreover this passion is so even and so temperate that one would say he loves only as much as he means to and means to only as much as reason allows. He is genuinely what Milord Edward believes himself to be, in which respect I find him quite superior to all us people of sentiment who admire ourselves so; for the heart deceives us in a thousand ways and acts only on a principle that is always suspect; but reason has not end save what is good; its rules are sure, clear, easy in the conduct of life, and never does it go astray but in futile speculations that are not right for it.

Monsieur de Wolmar's greatest predilection is for observation. He likes to make judgments on men's characters and on the actions he observes. He makes them with profound wisdom and the most perfect impartiality. If an enemy did him harm, he would discuss his motives and means as calmly as if it were a matter of complete indifference. I do not know how he has heard about you, but has spoken to me of you several times with high regard, and I know him to be incapable of pretending. Sometimes I have thought I noticed him observing me during these conversations, but there is good reason for believing that this so-called noticing is merely the secret reproach of a conscience on alert. However that may be, I have done my duty in this matter; neither fear nor shame have led me to be unjustly reserved, and I have done you justice when speaking to him, as I do him when speaking to you.

I almost forgot to tell you about our income and its management. The remains of Monsieur de Wolmar's estate combined with that of my father, who set aside only an annuity for himself, comprise a respectable and moderate fortune for him, of which he makes noble and wise use, by affording in his house, not the inconvenient and vain display of luxury, but plenty, the true comforts of life, [footnote deleted] and the necessities of needy neighbors. The order he has brought into his house is the image of the one that prevails in his heart, and seems to imitate in a small household the order established in the governance of the earth. One finds here neither that inflexible regularity that is more annoying than advantageous, and is bearable only to the one who imposes it, nor that misguided disorder that for possessing too much renders the use of anything impossible. The master's hand can always be recognized and is never felt; he has so well ordained the original arrangement of things that now it runs all by itself, and discipline and freedom are enjoyed at the same time.

That, my good friend, is an abbreviated but faithful notion of Monsieur de Wolmar's character, as far as I have come to know it since I have been living with him. As he appeared to me the first day, so he appears to me the most recent without the slightest alteration; which makes me hope I have observed him accurately, and that there is nothing more for me to discover; for this I cannot imagine he could have turned out otherwise without some loss.

From this tableau you can answer yourself in advance, and you would have to greatly look down on me not to think me happy with so much cause for being so. [footnote deleted] The thing that long deluded me and perhaps still deludes you is the idea that love is essential to a happy marriage. My friend, this is an error; honesty, virtue, certain conformities, less of status and age than of character and humor, suffice between husband and wife; that does not prevent a very tender attachment from emerging from this union which, without exactly being love, is nonetheless sweet and for that only the more lasting. Love is accompanied by a continual anxiety of jealousy or deprivation, ill suited to marriage, which is a state of delectation and peace. One does not marry in order to think solely about each other, but in order to fulfill conjointly the duties of civil life, govern the household prudently, raise one's children well. Lovers never see anyone but themselves, are endlessly occupied with each other alone, and the only thing they can do is love each other. That is not enough for Spouses who have so many other duties to attend to. There is no passion that gives us so strong an illusion as love: its violence is taken for a sign of its durability; the heart, replete with so sweet a sentiment, extends it, so to speak, into the future, and as long as that love lasts one believes it will never end. But on the contrary, its very ardor consumes it; it wears with youth, fades with beauty, burns out under the snows of age, and since the world began a pair of white-haired lovers sighing for each other has never been seen. Lovers must therefore assume that sooner or later they will cease to worship each other; then the idol they served being destroyed, they see each other as they are. They search with astonishment for the one they loved; not finding that person any more they take out their spite on the one who remains, who instead of being embellished by the imagination is now disfigured to the same degree; there are few people, says La Rochefoucauld, who are not ashamed of having loved each other, once they cease to do so. [footnote deleted] How much is it then to be feared lest tedium follow upon sentiments that were too intense, lest their decline without pausing at indifference turn directly into disgust, lest the two ultimately become utterly sated with each other, and for having loved each other too much as lovers come to hate each other as husband and wife! My dear friend, you have always seemed to me very attractive, much too much so for my innocence and peace of mind; but I have seen you only as a lover, how could I know what you would have become once you ceased being in love? Spent love would still have left you your virtue, I allow; but is that enough for happiness within a bond the heart must confirm, and how many virtuous men are nevertheless insufferable husbands? With respect to all this you can apply the same things to me.

As for Monsieur de Wolmar, no illusion prepossesses us for each other; we see each other such as we are; the sentiment that joins us is not the blind transport of passionate hearts, but the immutable and constant attachment of two honest and reasonable persons who, destined to spend the rest of their lives together, are content with their lot and try to make it pleasurable for each other. It seems that if we had been created expressly to be joined together it could have not been done more satisfactorily. If his heart were as tender as mine, it would be impossible to prevent so much sensibility on both sides from clashing occasionally, and nothing but quarrels ensuing. If I were as tranquil as he, there would be too much coldness between us, and it would make company less agreeable and pleasing. If he had not loved me, we would get along badly; if he had loved me too much, I would have found him importunate. Each of us is precisely what the other requires; he enlightens me and I enliven him; we are enhanced by being together, and it seems we are destined to constitute but a single soul between us, of which he is the intellect and I the will. Even his somewhat advancing age turns to our common advantage: for given the passion by which I was tormented, it is certain that, had he been younger, I would have married him even more reluctantly, and this excessive repugnance would perhaps have prevented the felicitous revolution that has taken place in me.

My friend: Heaven enlightens the good intentions of fathers, and rewards the docility of children. God forbid I should mean to make light of your distress. Solely the desire to reassure you completely about my fate leads me to add what I am about to say. Were I, with the sentiments I formerly had for you and the knowledge I now possess, still free, and mistress to choose a husband, I call as witness of my sincerity the God who is good enough to enlighten me and who reads the depths of my heart, it is not you I would choose, it is Monsieur de Wolmar.

It may matter to your complete recovery that I finish telling you what is still on my heart. Monsieur de Wolmar is older than I. If as punishment for my faults, Heaven took from me the worthy spouse I have so little deserved, it is my firm intention never to take another. If he was not fortunate enough to find a chaste maiden, at least he will leave behind a chaste widow. You know me too well to believe that, having once made you this declaration, I am the kind of woman who could ever retract it.

What I have said in order to end your doubts can also serve to answer in part your objections to the confession I believe I must make to my husband. He is too wise to punish me for a humiliating act that repentance alone can wrest from me, and I am not more incapable of employing the ruse of the Ladies you mention than he is of entertaining such a suspicion. As for the reason for which you contend this confession is not required, it is surely a sophism. For although a woman is bound to nothing in respect to a spouse she does not yet have, that does not authorize her to represent herself to him as other than she is. I had sensed this, even before my marriage, and if the vow extorted by my father prevented me from doing my duty in this regard, I was only the guiltier for it, since it is a crime to take an unjust vow, and yet a second to keep it. But I had another reason which my heart dared not admit to itself, and which made me much guiltier still. Thank Heaven it no longer subsists.

A more legitimate and weightier consideration is the danger of needlessly troubling the peace of an honorable man who owes his happiness to the esteem in which he holds his wife. It is certain that he no longer has the power to sever the bond that unites us, nor I the power to have better deserved him. Thus by confiding indiscreetly in him I run the risk of causing him utterly needless affliction, without gaining any other advantage by my sincerity than to unburden my heart of a baneful secret that weighs cruelly upon it. I can tell I will be the more tranquil for it after declaring it to him; but he perhaps will be less so, and it would be a poor reparation indeed of my wrongs to prefer my own peace of mind to his.

What shall I do then in my present state of doubt? While waiting for Heaven better to enlighten me about my duties, I will follow the counsel of your friendship; I will remain silent; I will conceal my faults from my husband, and try to expunge them through a conduct that might some day merit their forgiveness.

To begin so necessary a reform, kindly consent, my friend, that we cease henceforth all relationship between us. If Monsieur de Wolmar had received my confession, he would decide to what extent we may maintain the sentiments of friendship that join us and afford each other innocent tokens of it; but since I dare not consult him on that, I have too well learned at my expense how far the most apparently legitimate habits can lead us astray. It is time to become prudent. Despite the security of my heart, I no longer wish to be judge of my own cause, nor as wife succumb to the same over-confidence that was my undoing as maiden. This is the last letter you shall receive from me. I beg you also to write me no more. Yet as I shall never cease to take the tenderest interest in you and since this sentiment is as pure as the light of day, I will be most pleased to have news of you be-times, and see you achieve the happiness you deserve. You may write from time to time to Madame d'Orbe on those occasions when something interesting happens for you to tell us about. I hope the honesty of your soul will always be manifest in your letters. Moreover my Cousin is virtuous and discreet enough to communicate to me only what is fit for me to see, and suppress this correspondence if you were capable of abusing it.

Farewell, my dear and good friend; if I believed fortune could make you happy, I would say to you: pursue fortune; but perhaps you are right to disdain it, possessing treasures enough of your own. I prefer to say to you: pursue felicity, it is the wise man's fortune; we have always felt that there could be no felicity without virtue; but take care lest that word virtue, too abstract, be more glittering than solid, and an ostentatious name that serves more to dazzle others than content ourselves. I shudder when I think that people who carried adultery in the depths of their hearts dared speak of virtue! Do you quite realize what a term so respectable and so profaned meant to us, at the same time we were involved in a criminal relationship? Beneath that sacred enthusiasm the frantic love that so inflamed us both disguised its transports to make them still dearer to us and prolong our delusion. We were made, I dare believe, to follow and cherish genuine virtue, but we deceived ourselves in our pursuit of it and were following nothing but a vain phantom. It is time for the illusion to cease; it is time for those who have been too long astray to come home. My friend, for you this return will not be difficult. You bear your guide within you, you may have neglected it, but you have never rejected it. Your soul is sound, it clings to all that is good, and if it sometimes loses its grasp, that is for failing to use all its strength holding on. Search deep in your conscience, and see if you might not find there some forgotten principle that would help better to organize all your acts, connect them more firmly, and with a common purpose. It is not enough, believe me, for virtue to be the base of your conduct, if you do not establish that base itself on an unshakable bedrock. Remember those Indians who think the world is borne by a huge elephant, and then the elephant by a tortoise, and when they are asked what bears the tortoise they do not know what to say.

I implore you to pay some attention to this friend's words, and choose a surer route to happiness than the one that so long led us astray. I shall not cease to ask Heaven to grant both you and me this pure felicity and will not rest easy until I have obtained it for us both. Ah! If ever our hearts in spite of us recall the errors of our youth, let it be at least in such a way that the redirection they have produced justifies the remembrance, and that we may be able to say with the ancient: alas we would perish had we not perished!

Here end the lady preacher's sermons. From now on she will have enough on her hands with preaching to herself. Farewell, my gentle friend, farewell forever; so decrees inflexible duty. But do believe that Julie's heart cannot forget what she has cherished . . . oh God! what am I doing? . . . you will see too well from the condition of this paper. Ah! has one not the right to wax tender when extending to one's friend a final farewell?

———

From Les Liaisons Dangereuses *(1782) by Choderlos de Laclos (1741–1803). The book, an epistolary novel based on the romantic intrigues of a libertine pair, the Marquise de Merteuil and the Vicomte de Valmont, was received with shock and criticism when it was first published. Marie-Jeanne Riccoboni, author of* Lettres de Mistriss Fanni Butlerd *(see p. 245), wrote to Laclos, outraged by the work's negative portrayal of women; the book itself was condemned and burned publicly in 1823.*

As the story explains, Valmont seduces the prudish Madame de Tourvel, only to fall in love with her in spite of himself. Jealous, the marquise demands that Valmont break off the romance, which he does, much to Madame de Tourvel's enormous grief.

In this letter, Madame de Tourvel begins to write to Valmont of her anguish and rage after she becomes aware that she was merely a pawn in a sick game, but soon she yields to the disorder of her emotions. As Armine Kotin Mortimer, a professor of French literature and Laclos scholar at University of Illinois at Urbana-Champaign explains, "Madame de Tourvel seems first to speak to Valmont, but then to no one because to so many." (Mortimer has supplied brackets to illustrate the various persons Tourvel is addressing.) Three days after this letter is written, Madame de Tourvel dies of a broken heart. Her letter is never sent. Valmont later dies in a duel.

LETTER CLXI (161)
(Dictated by her and written by her waiting-woman)

[Valmont. But also possibly 'the devil']
 Cruel and malevolent being, will you never grow weary of persecuting me? Is it not enough for you that you have tormented me, degraded me, debased me, that you wish to ravish from me even the peace of the grave? What! In this dwelling-place of darkness in which I have been forced by ignominy to bury myself, is pain without cessation, is hope unknown? I do not implore a mercy I do not deserve; I will suffer without complaint if my sufferings do not exceed my strength. But do not make my tortures unendurable. Leave me my grief, but take from me the cruel memory of the treasures I have lost. When it is you who ravished them from me, do not again draw their agonising image before my eyes. I was innocent and at peace; it is because I saw you that I have lost my peace of mind; it is by listening to you that I became criminal. You are the author of my sins; what right have you to punish them?

 [Others]
 Where are the friends who cherished me, where are they? My misfortune terrifies them. None dares to approach me. I am crushed and they leave me without aid! I am dying and none weeps for me. All consolation is refused me. Pity stays on the brink of the gulf into which the criminal plunges. He is torn by remorse and his cries are not heard!

 [Her husband]
 And you, whom I have outraged; you, whose esteem adds to my torture; you, who alone have the right to avenge yourself, what are you doing so far from me? Come, punish a faithless wife. Let me

suffer deserved torments at last. Already I should have submitted to your vengeance, but courage failed me to confess my shame to you. It was not dissimulation, it was shame. At least may this letter tell you my repentance. Heaven took up your cause and avenges you for an injury you did not know. It is Heaven which bound my tongue and restrained my words; it feared you might have pardoned a fault it wished to punish. It has removed me from your indulgence which would have wounded its justice.

[No one]
Pitiless in its vengeance, it has delivered me up to him who ruined me. It is at once through him and by him that I suffer. I try to fly him, in vain, he follows me; he is there; he besets me continually. But how different he is from himself! His eyes only express hatred and scorn. His mouth only utters insult and blame. His arms embrace me only to rend me. Who will save me from his barbarous fury?

[First Valmont, and then her female friends, Mme de Volanges and Mme de Rosemonde]
But what! It is he . . . I am not deceived; I see him again. O! My charming love! Receive me into your arms; hide me in your bosom; yes, it is you, it is indeed you! What disastrous illusion made me mistake you? How have I suffered in your absence! Let us not separate again, let us never be separated. Let me breathe. Feel my heart, feel how it beats! Ah! It is no longer fear, it is the sweet emotion of love. Why do you refuse my tender caresses? Turn that soft gaze upon me! What are those bonds you try to break? Why do you prepare that equipment to death? What can have so altered those features? What are you doing? Leave me; I shudder! God! It is that monster again! My friends, do not abandon me. You [Mme de Volanges] who called upon me to fly, help me to combat him; and you [Mme de Rosemonde], more indulgent, you who promised to lessen my pain, come nearer to me. Where are you both? If I am not allowed to see you again, at least answer this letter; let me know that you still love me.

Hell Hath No Fury

[Valmont, but it is not clear]

Leave me, cruel one! What new frenzy animates you? Are you afraid some gentle sentiment might pierce to my soul? You redouble my tortures; you force me to hate you. Oh! how painful hate is! How it corrodes the heart which distills it! Why do you persecute me? What more can you have to say to me? Have you not made it impossible for me to listen to you, impossible to reply to you? Expect nothing more of me.

Farewell, Monsieur.

The
Prescriptive
Letter

Pre•script•tive (prĭ-skrĭp´tĭv) *adj.* Sanctioned or authorized by long-standing custom or usage; making or giving injunctions, directions, laws, or rules.

The Prescriptive Letter *n.* A breakup letter in a letter-writing manual that purports to instruct its readers how to deal with various romantic, personal, and business situations.

LETTER-WRITING MANUALS BLOSSOMED in the eighteenth and particularly nineteenth centuries, both in France and in England, where many students made letter writing part of their grammar-school studies. Although these manuals ostensibly served a practical or educational purpose, they also played to readers' aspirations and delight in drama. In his *Correspondence* (Polity Press, 1997), Roger Chartier says that such manuals—known as *secretaries* in France—served as windows into the world of upper-class society; they helped readers learn about the ordering of the social world or penetrate "a remote and 'exotic' universe, that of aristocratic ways." Letter-manuals also mimicked the methods of fiction, using dramatic and narrative techniques to the point that the line between such instructive letter-volumes and letters meant for entertainment was often blurred. (The letters created for these manuals were often in pairs, the second letter answering a question or referring to a problem presented in the first). According to Robert Adams Day, the well-known manual *Familiar Letters on Important Occasions,* (1741) by Samuel Richardson (also the author of *Clarissa,* see p. 241), was a prime example of how a manual meant to be of practical use might subconsciously adopt story-telling elements that led "inevitably toward fiction."

The publication of letter-manuals dropped off sharply in the twentieth century, mostly due to the spread of public education and literacy, and most of the existing titles from this period make no attempt to instruct readers on how to end affairs. Even etiquette books, such as Emily Post's *Etiquette; the blue book of social usage* (Funk & Wagnalls, 1955) or Amy Vanderbilt's *Complete Book of Etiquette* (Doubleday, 1995) do not refer specifically to "breakup letters" but address the issue in a roundabout manner: Post's advice to "young girls who feel impelled to pour out their emotions in letters to men" is simply *"don't!"* To my knowledge, the only modern manual to address the breakup letter—and address it exclusively—is *Kiss Off Letters to Men* (see p. 281). As with many older manuals, it is as entertaining as it is instructive—perhaps more so.

† † †

*From <u>Familiar Letters on Important Occasions</u> by Samuel Richardson,
George Routlege and Sons, Ltd. First edition 1741, reprinted 1928.*

LETTER CXXXI
From a young Maiden, abandoned by her Lover for the sake of a
greater Fortune.

Mr. John,

I must take up my pen and write, tho' perhaps you will only scoff
at me for so doing; but when I have said what I have to say, then I
shall have eased my mind, and will endeavor to forget you for ever. I
have had so many cautions given me against the false hearts of men,
and was so often told how they will vow and forswear themselves, that
I ought to have been on my guard, that's true: And indeed, so I *was* a
great while: You know it well. But you courted me so long, vowed so
earnestly, and seem'd so much in love with me, that it was first *pity* in
me, that made me listen to you; and, oh! this nasty *pity,* how soon did
it bring—But I won't say *love* neither [*sic*]. I thought, if all the young
men in the world besides proved false, yet it was impossible *you*
should. Ah! poor silly creature that I was, to think, tho' every body
flatter'd me with being sightly enough, I could hold a heart so sor-
didly bent on *interest,* as I always saw *yours* to be! But that, thought I,
tho' 'tis a meanness *I don't like,* yet it will be a security of his making
a frugal husband in an age so fruitful of *spendthrifts.*

But at length it has proved, that you can prefer Polly Bambridge,
and leave *poor me,* only because she has a greater portion than I have.

I say nothing against Polly. I wish *her well.* Indeed I do. And I
wish *you* no harm neither. But as you knew Polly *before,* why could
you not have made to yourself a merit with *her,* without going so
far with *me?* What need you have so often begg'd and pray'd, sigh'd
and vow'd (never leaving me, day nor night), till you had got me
foolishly to *believe* and *pity* you? And so, after your courtship to

me was made a *town talk,* then you could leave me to be laugh'd at by every one I *slighted for you!* Was this just, was this well done, think you?

Here I cannot go out of doors but I have some one or other *simpering* and *sneering* at me; and I have had two *willow-garlands* sent me; so I have—but what poor stuff, in some of my *own sex* too, is this, to laugh at and deride *me* for *your* baseness? I can call my heart to witness my virtue in thought, in word, and in deed; and must I be ridiculed for a *false one,* who gives himself airs at *my* expence, and at the expence of his own truth and honour? Indeed, you cannot say the least ill of me, that's my comfort. I defy the world to say any thing to blast my character: Why then should I suffer, in the *world's eye,* for *your* baseness?

I seek not to move you to return to the fidelity you have vow'd; for by this time, mayhap, you'd be as base as Polly as you have been to *me,* if you did; and I wish *her* no *willow-garlands,* I'll assure you. But yet, let me desire to speak of me with decency. That is no more than I deserve, well you know. Don't (to brave thro' the perfidy you have been guilty of) mention me with such fleers [mocking comments], as, I hear, you have done to several; and pray call me none of *your poor dear girls!* And, *I hope she won't take it to heart, poor thing!*—with that insolence that so little becomes you, and I have so little deserved. I thought to have appeal'd to your *conscience,* on what has passed between us when I began. I thought to have put the matter *home* to you! But I have run out into this length, and now don't think it *worth while* to write much more: For what is *conscience* to a man who could *vow* as you have done, and *act* as you have done?

Go then, Mr. John, naughty man as you are! I will try to forget you for ever. Rejoice in the smiles of your Polly Bambridge, and glad your heart with the possession of an hundred or two of pounds more than I have; and see what you'll be the *richer* or *happier a few years* hence. I wish no harm to you. Your *conscience* will be a greater trouble to you than I wish it to be, if you are capable of *reflecting.* And for *your sake,* I will henceforth set myself up to be an adviser to all my sex, never to give an ear to a *man*, unless they can be sure that his *interest* will be a *security* for his *pretended affection* to them. I am, tho' greatly *injured* and *deceived*, naughty Mr. John,

Your Well wisher.

———

The following letters were published in <u>The Lovers' Letter-Writer</u>, publisher and publication date unknown.

Reply to a letter sent by a Stranger who saw a Woman at Church. Reply No. 1

Sir,—I am very reluctant to reply at all to your most improper and unjustifiable letter. I only do so in order that you may not have the least pretext for mistaking my feeling on the subject. Under any circumstances I should not think of permitting an acquaintance to be commenced by such an introduction as you appear to consider sufficient. The accident of your attending the same place of worship as myself, and that you have somehow learned my name, are matters over which I have no control. Of that fact you take an unworthy advantage. More than this, you show disrespect towards your professed religion, and a contempt for its observances, when your attendance thereon is made but the occasion of affront to a lady—for an affront I must consider your letter to be.

Amanda

Angry Reply to a Letter from a Jealous Man

Sir,—You ask too much in demanding that I should decline to receive civility from my friends. I have not yet promised to seclude myself entirely from those friends, nor do I consider that you have a right to expect that I should. Your letter is so uncomplimentary that no better answer can be given, and if your engagement is a burden to you, I for one shall wish it ended. Jealousy is worthy of no return but aversion and scorn.

Maria M—

Reply to a letter from a Gentleman in Moderate Circumstances to a Rich Lady.

Sir,—If ever a woman had no other good reason for rejecting the addresses of one who seeks her hand, she would find it in the apology which he makes for being poor, and his fear that the world will deem him a fortune-hunter. Such a confession and fear prove in my estimation that his proffered love is but spurious, and that he is the very thing which he affects to despise. The next time that you fall in love, I would advise you to spare your correspondent the imputation that she could rate her pecuniary advantages above the dictates of her heart and her common sense. Whether I might have ever been disposed to place my future in your hands or not is now of no consequence. You have coupled with your declaration thoughts very repugnant to me, and which render it impossible that you can be more than one of my distant acquaintances.

Lavinia

Unfavorable Reply to a letter regarding a Reverse of Fortune and the Duty arising therefrom.

Dear Mr. H—,

I am much pained by the receipt of your note, although I

anticipated such a one, from my knowledge of your honorable character. You may be sure that I am much grieved by your misfortune, and hope that it will be but temporary.

I thank you for the frank manner in which you allude to our engagement, and the new aspect in which, under existing circumstances, it must be viewed. I cannot but agree with you that our relations to each other are materially, I may say entirely, changed, by the unfortunate occurrence you describe, and if with equal frankness with your own I accept your proposal to separate, you will, I trust, think me not unkind, nor unjust. I shall be glad to hear of your prosperity, and watch for it with the anxiety which all your friends must feel. I hope you will continue to include me among those friends, although we mutually agree to close our engagement, and wishing you every success, I remain,

Yours truly,
Kate N—

Unfavorable Reply to a letter from an ardent young Man, avowing a passion he had entertained for a length of time, fearful of disclosing it.

Sir,—I do not know whether your epistle was intended in a jest, in which case its absurdity might have been excused on the grounds of its plagiarisms. But if you can really write *in earnest* to any woman whom you profess to esteem I must express my humble opinion that such is not the proper course by which to excite a reciprocal feeling.

Regretting that you should have adopted a tone of writing which neither modern usage, nor common sense at any time could sanction.

I remain, Sir,
Your obedient Servant,
Mary——

Reply to a letter from a Gentleman desirous of discontinuing his addresses.

Sir—I acknowledge the receipt of your last letter, which now lies before me, and in which you convey the intimation that the position in which, for some time past we have regarded each other must from henceforth be abandoned. Until the receipt of this letter, I had regarded you in the light of my future husband; you were, therefore, as you have reason to know, so completely the possessor of my affections, that I looked with indifference upon every other suitor. The remembrance of you had never failed to enhance the pleasures of daily life, and you were in my thoughts at the very moment in which I received this most unkind and unexpected letter. But deem me not so devoid of proper pride as to wish you to revoke your determination, from which I will not attempt to dissuade you, whether it may have been made in cool deliberation, or in precipitate haste. Sir, I shall endeavor to banish you from my affections as readily and completely as you appear to have banished me from yours; and all that I now require is, that you will return to me whatever letters you may have of mine, and which I may have written under a mistaken confidence in your attachment and when you were accredited as the future husband of

Sir. Yours, etc.
Eliza—

———

The following letter was published in <u>The new universal letter-writer, or, Complete art of polite correspondence: containing a course of interesting letters on the most important, instructive, and entertaining subjects; to which are prefixed, an essay on letter-writing, and a set of complimental cards, suited to occasions on which an extraordinary degree of politeness should be observed.</u> (Philadelphia: Hogan & Thompson, ca.1834)

LETTER XLII.—From a Young Lady, to a Gentleman that courted her, whom she could not like, but was forced by her parents to receive his visits, and think of none else for a husband.

Sir,

It is a very bad return which I make for the respect you have for me, when I acknowledge to you, that though the day of our marriage is appointed, I am incapable of loving you. You may have observed in the long conversations we have had at those times we were left together, that some secret hung upon my mind. I was obliged to an ambiguous behavior, and durst not reveal myself further, because my mother, from a closet near the place where we sat, could conveniently hear our conversation. I have strict commands from both my parents to receive you, and am undone for ever, except you will be so kind and generous as to refuse me. Consider, Sir, the misery of bestowing yourself upon one who can have no prospect of happiness but from your death. This is a confession made perhaps with an offensive sincerity; but that conduct is much to be preferred to a secret dislike, which could not but pall all the sweets of life, by imposing on you a companion that doats [*sic*] and languishes for another. I will not go so far as to say, my passion for the gentleman whose wife I am by promise, would lead me to any thing criminal against your honor. But I know it is dreadful to a man of your sense to expect nothing but forced civilities in return for tender endearments, and cold esteem for unreserved love. If you will on this occasion let reason take place of passion, I doubt not but fate has in store for you some worthier object of your affection, in recompense for your goodness to the only woman that could be insensible to your merit.

I am, Sir,
Your most humble servant.

———

This letter was published in <u>The American lady's and gentleman's</u>
<u>modern letter writer: relative to business, duty, love, and marriage</u>
(Philadelphia: Henry F. Anners, 1847)

A Lady Refusing Proposals

Sir,

There must surely have been something in my behavior toward
you upon which must have set a misconstruction. Of what it con-
sisted I am wholly unconscious; but that such has been the case, I
feel convinced by an attentive perusal of your letter, which I have
just received. I assure you that I feel much flattered by your preference of me, as well as by your proffer of our becoming mutually
better acquainted; but, with every feeling of regard toward you, I
beg respectfully to decline your addresses. What my reasons may be
for so doing, you will not, I trust, inflict upon me the pain of
declaring; suffice it to say, that I can not admit them, and I confidently hope that henceforward you will feel the propriety of not
recurring to this subject. If, from any motives, you should still urge
your suit by making an appeal to my parents, I may venture to
declare that such an appeal would be unavailing. I am satisfied that
they would never thwart my wishes in an affair of this delicacy, and
in which my happiness is so much involved. With my best wishes
for your future welfare, allow me to subscribe myself,

Yours, most respectfully,
"—."

The following letters were published in Samuel Orchart Beeton's
<u>Beeton's Complete Letter-Writer for Ladies and Gentlemen, A Useful</u>
<u>Compendium of Epistolary Materials Gathered From the Best Sources,</u>
<u>and Adapted to Suit an Indefinite Number of Cases,</u> New and Revised
Edition, (London: Ward, Lock & Co., Limited, 1873). Beeton

(1831–1877) and his wife Isabella (1836–1865) were the authors and publishers of a number of domestic how-to books, including The Book of Household Management (1861).

No. 85.
Answer to a Missionary's Proposal negatively.

Vermont, Southwold,

(Date in full—)

MY DEAR SIR,

Were I free to consult my own wishes, my answer to your kind and generous letter would be "Yes," as since you first became a visitor at my father's house I saw much in your character to admire. But my parents, to whom I showed your letter, consider that I am constitutionally unfitted to reside in a climate so trying as Africa, and wish me to remain still with them. They are, with myself, grateful for all that you say; and, were it not that you go abroad, their consent would have been willingly given. I feel myself, too, that I would be only an encumbrance even were I spared; and at a missionary station there should be no encumbrances.

You will allow me to call myself your sincere well-wisher, if nothing more, and hope that your efforts in Africa will be crowned with success.

Believe me,
My dear Sir,
Yours sincerely,
MARY BURTON.
(Name and Address).

No 92.
Maid Servant answering a cool Letter from her Lover:

Whitelands, Dorking,

(Date in full—)

WILLIAM,

I can hardly believe you wrote the letter which I received this morning. It is so different from any of the others I have in my box, that you must have either deceived me greatly, or your character has strangely altered for the worse during the last two months: Do you remember telling me over and over again that nothing would change your feelings towards me? And yet you write as coldly as though we were mere acquaintances. I will not again ask you the reason of the change, because, if you have not, I have some little self respect. You wish, I think, to be free to marry another girl, and, instead of telling me in a manly way that such is the case, you try to shake me coolly off. Your letter hardly deserved an answer, and I don't think I would have answered it were it not my wish to tell you that you are no longer anything to me and need never write to me again.

CLARA MANNING.

———

The following letters were published in <u>The Practical Letter-Writer,</u> <u>showing plainly How to Write and Direct a Letter, so that Persons Who</u> <u>Can Write a Letter Well Can Learn to Do So Better, and Those Who</u> <u>Never Wrote May Now Learn to Write Well and Easily</u> . . . *(New York: Hurst & Co, 19—])*

Letter 113, an answer to a letter from a Young Man just out of his Apprenticeship, to his Sweetheart in the neighborhood

Dear Jack,

I received your very kind letter, but I do not know what to say in answer. Although I would be glad to marry, yet you men are so deceiving, that there is no such thing as trusting you. There is Tom Timber the carpenter, and Jack Hammer the smith, who have not been married above six months, and every night come home drunk and beat their wives. What a miserable life is that, Jack, and how do I know but you may be as bad to me? How do I know but you like them may get drunk every night, and beat me black and blue before morning! I do assure you, Jack, if I thought that would be the case, I would scrub floors and scour saucepans as long as I live. But possibly you may not be so bad; for there is Will Cooper the braiser, and Oliver Smith the painter, who are both very happy with their wives; they are both home bringing husbands, and have every day a hot joint of meat. I know not yet what I shall do, but as I like to walk to Vauxhall I will meet you at the Battery on Sunday after dinner, and then we will talk more of the matter.

I am, dear Jack, your most humble servant

Letter 125, From a Lady to a Gentleman, complaining of indifference

Sir,

However light you may make of promises, yet I am foolish enough to consider them something more than trifles; and am likewise induced to believe that the man who voluntary breaks a promise will not pay much regard to an oath; and if so, in what light must I consider your conduct? Did I not give you my promise to be yours, and had you no other reason for soliciting than merely to gratify your vanity? A brutal gratification, indeed, to triumph over the weakness of a woman whose greatest fault was that she loved you. I say loved you, for it was in consequence of that passion

I first consented to become yours. Had your conduct, sir, been consistent with my submissions, or your own solemn profession? Is it consistent with the character of a gentleman first to obtain a woman's consent, and afterwards boast that he had discarded her, and found one more agreeable to his wishes? Do not equivocate; I have too convincing proofs of your insincerity; I saw you yesterday walking with Miss Benson, and am informed that you have proposed marriage to her. Whatever you may think, sir, I have a spirit of disdain, and even of resentment, equal to your ingratitude, and can treat the wretch with a proper indifference, who can make so slight a matter of the most solemn promises. Miss Benson may become your wife, but she will receive into her arms a perjured husband; nor can ever the superstructure be lasting which is built on such a slight foundation. I leave you to the stings of your own conscience. I am the injured.

The following letters were published in <u>The Love letter writer,</u> *Third Edition, by Uncle Wamek. (Tema, Ghana: Otighe Book Agency, 19—).*

Letter 42, From a young woman to her lover notifying him of her breaking away

Dear Mr.

I am extremely sorry to inform you that for some time ago, I have been sensing a cooling off of love, for what I imagined to be a deep affection of my love for you, was nothing more than personal admiration.

As you are aware I had been very happy with you for sometime, but now I feel that my feelings towards you was [*sic*] no love and equally so, was [*sic*] yours for me.

You have not made any attempt to marry me, but rather you have been feeding your physical lust on me in the sense of a husband and his wife, whilst there is nothing like that. You have thus killed the thrills, hope, joys and happiness of love in me. To be frank, I do not believe your words any more. You are using me as means to an end.

I am informing you by this letter that I have now broken away from you, and from now onwards you have no claim on me as your sweetheart, and I have none on you as my lover.

I do hope that this will not cause you too much pain. Goodbye.

Yours sincerely,

Letter 54, A reply to "a letter of courtship from an elderly man to a girl of nineteen".

Dear Sir,

Your letter with its contents of surprises has been received with thanks. I would have gladly become your own but the principle of unity with an elderly man is against my will.

Do you not realize sir, that if you take me to the alter [*sic*] the priest would surprisingly ask you "what sir, have you led this child to be baptized? "And what a shame! Would you sir in that case reply that you have brought me to be married? What a fun [*sic*] would it be?

It would be an empty marriage if I force myself to accept your offer for wealth [*sic*] sake. I know a widow who by your permission I shall mention you to her to night[.] She is young about 28 years old, plumpy [*sic*]and charming with romantic and magnetic air about her; she is pleasant in manners, winning in speech, beamy in appearance, precious in character and healthy. I shall mention the affair to her and do advise you to write to her.

Good luck.

Yours respectfully

———

From <u>Love Letters: containing the etiquette of introduction, courtship and proposals: also a large number of new and original letters to be</u>

used as models for any style of love letter. *(Philadelphia: Penn Pub. Co., 1925)*

A reply "from one who has experienced a change of feeling, but wishes to express herself in as kind a manner as possible".

My Dear Ernest,

It is with much shame and regret that I send this letter to you—shame at my own fickle heart, and regret lest I cause you pain, which, if possible, I would avoid. Ernest, when we made our promises to each other, I truly thought that my love was yours; but, indeed, I find that it does not belong to anyone but my own selfish self. It must have been a fascination that caused me to mistake my feelings, and for weeks, Ernest, I have been trying to blind myself to the real state of affairs, and force my ardor in your direction, and you see what I have made of it.

My esteem for you remains unshaken. I respect you thoroughly, and shall always hope to call you a true friend, but, Ernest, I cannot make myself love you as you should be, nor can I think of marriage with anything but aversion. If you only knew how I have tried and how I have wept over it all, for I feel like a culprit—one disgraced.

Please forgive me for causing you, perhaps, bitter disappointment. I can never forgive myself, and I know that swift retribution is deserved. I will return all your letters and gifts, and, of course, it will not be necessary to ask you to do the same. Believe me, Dear Ernest,

Your real friend,
Janet

———

From The Applying The Break Dept., which appeared in the October 1979 issue of Mad magazine (issue No. 210) and was written by Frank Jacobs.

APPLYING THE BREAK DEPT.
For every woman there comes a day when she must write a letter ending a relationship with the guy who no longer is the man of her dreams. Such a missive is called a "Dear John" letter, and MAD would like to assist all women who have the unpleasant job of writing one. Here it is: Simply fill in the numbered blanks from the corresponding numbered lists . . . and you'll have . . .

MAD'S ALL INCLUSIVE DO-IT-YOURSELF "DEAR JOHN LETTER"

Dear John:

I don't know quite how to tell you this, but 1)_____. I think I first knew it 2) _____, 3)_____, and I saw you 4) _____ 5)_____. I'm sure you're 6) _____ enough to see 7) _____.

I'm returning 8) _____, but I'm holding on to 9) _____ as a keepsake. I want you to know that I'll 10) _____ your 11) _____.

12) _____.

Wilma

1) our romance is over
   our affair is dead
   I'm entering a convent
   I loathe you
   our horoscopes clash
   you are a sickie
   you need to bathe more
   I'm a street walker
   your nostrils offend me
   there's a contract out for you

you're a schmuck
I'm in love with your sister

2) that night
last year
skinny-dipping
tripping on tangerine seeds
last Arbor day
when you shackled me
when I threw up
when I saw that shrunken head
when your dwarf bit me
reciting "Gunga Din"
swapping tennis shoes
when your sheepdog went berserk

3) in your pad
in your camper
outside Poughkeepsie
under the bus
in your closet
while eating enchilladas
with Reverend Moon
in drag
at the Hare Krishna prom
on the funny farm
in a trance
with the Mondales

4) make a pass at
insult
ignore
punch out
pour syrup over
carve your initials on

277

tear the clothes off
apply leeches to
render impotent
yank the toupee off
sit on
exercise

5) my best friend
my father
E. F. Hutton
my whoopee cushion
my spinach souffle
Bert and Ernie
my avocado plant
my penpal in Ghana
my Franklin Mint Collection
the Oakland front four
my Billy Carter statue
that crazed monk

6) man
sensitive
open-minded
ashamed
stoned
gutless
scarred
Mongol
masochistic
perverted
senile
Republican
frostbitten

7) how miserable I've been

what a bore you are
your Datsun sucks
your acne is terminal
I've had a sex change
there is no Mid-East solution
we're first cousins
there is no Santa Claus
I'm allergic to your hamster
I dig sanitation men
that I'm bionic
that "The Gong Show" stinks

8) your ring
your love letters
your Darth Vader poster
your pet rock
to the commune
those slides of Altoona
your dentures
to sleeping around
our matching Snoopy bibs
your Bicentennial truss
to Saturn
your bag of immies

9) your photo
those oil stocks
my virginity
your neighbor Ralph
the results of the blood test
your left ear
your suicide note
your mother
my sanity
your ant colony

   your police record
   Murray's leotards

10) always treasure
    never forget
    try to blot out
    inform the I.R.S. about
    always feel unclean about
    never scoff openly at
    make a movie based on
    tell the "Enquirer" about
    inform the asylum about
    get nauseous thinking of
    tell my priest about
    be a lot better off without

11) friendship
    senility
    new life as a clone
    Eskimo incarnation
    capo Angelo
    cocaine habit
    passion for fieldmice
    Jackie Mason imitations
    embarrassing rash
    eggplant fetish
    screwing up World War II
    hatred of Tampa

12) Fondly
    Sincerely
    Painfully
    Eat your heart out
    with disgust

with great relief
Up yours
Your undying enemy
Best to your frog Leonard
Now bug off
Good luck on your parole
Regards to your creepy family

———

From the book <u>*Kiss-Off Letters to Men*</u> *(Crown, 2001), a slim paper-back volume of prescriptive breakup letters written by Erica Dankoff and Muara Johnston. The following letter appeared in the chapter titled "Hate . . . all is fair," which the authors describe as letters for those times you need to let "him know just how loathsome and despi-cable he is."*

Dear,

I know you think you're "all that," and you are . . . but not where it counts. I used to find your self-confidence inspiring, but there's a fine line between confidence and narcissism and baby, you're walking a tightrope.

We all know that good self-esteem is important, but I'm tired of hearing you go on and on about what a great catch you are, how talented you are, how special you are, how successful you are. I guess if you say anything authoritatively and often enough you'll start to believe it. Did your mother tell you you were the Second Coming? Guess what? She lied!

I would hardly say living with your mother, working for your uncle, driving a used Ford, and wearing Old Spice makes you a woman's dream come true. It seems to me you're a washed-up, middle-aged lackey who needs to get a reality check.

Could you give me directions to that little world you live in?

———

Hell Hath No Fury

The following is a "Dear Jerk Sample Letter" letter from "The Original Dump Kit," a novelty-in-a-box created by Patti Watkins, forty-eight, a film consultant in Kansas City, Missouri. Watkins came up with the idea after a night out with girlfriends, some of whom were going through breakups and relationship problems. The kit—which debuted in 2001—consists of a voodoo doll, target with dart, soap, button of affirmation, wristband, and the following letter (with envelope). It retails for $15.00.

Dear:

    __ Butt Head,
    __ Slime Sucker,
    __ Jerk Face,

I'm so
    __ glad to be rid of you.
    __ sorry you stuck around as long as you did.
    __ thrilled to hear about your recent kidney stone.

If only I had
    __ realized what a weasley wimp you were sooner.
    __ known that you were irritating as hell.
    __ left YOU and the horse you rode in on.

I'd always suspected that
    __ you'd come out of the closet someday.
    __ you'd learned your table manners from a chimp.
    __ someday you'd realize that size does matter.

I never want to
    __ see your skanky face again.
    __ admit I ever even dated you.
    __ hear your Pee Wee Herman–like voice again.

__ Kindly drop dead,
__ Please eat soap and froth,
__ May you pee in your shoe daily,

(Sign here) _____

P.S. I was only pretending. I never liked your
__ dog.
__ mother.
__ cologne.

The
Fictional
Letter

Fic•tion•al (fĭk´shə-nə-l) *adj*. Pertaining to, or characterized by, fiction; fictitious; formed or conceived by the imagination.

The Fictional Letter, *n*. A breakup letter that appears in a work of fiction—usually narrative fiction—published after the year 1800.

From Corinne, or Italy (1807) by writer and French Revolutionary activist Germaine de Staël (1766–1817). In the novel, Corinne, a mysterious, beautiful Italian poetess, falls in love with the Scottish Lord Nevil, who then abandons her for the woman he was obligated to marry: Lucile, a mute English girl who is also Corinne's half-sister. This letter is written to Nevil in response to one of his letters, in which he explains why he had to choose Lucile over her and asks to see her once more to obtain her forgiveness. Corinne later dies of grief.

Corinne's reply

'If, to forgive you, I needed only to see you, I would not have refused for a moment. I do not know why I have no resentment against you, though the sorrow you have caused me makes me shudder with terror. I must still love you since I do not have any feeling of hatred against you. Religion alone would not suffice to disarm me in this way. I have had moments when my mind was deranged. At other times and these were the most soothing, the pain burdening my heart made me think I would die before the day was done; at others I doubted everything, even virtue. For me, you were its image here below. To my thoughts, as to my feelings, I no longer had a guide, since the same blow struck my admiration and my love.

'What would have become of me without divine help? There is nothing in this world that was not poisoned by the memory of you. At the bottom of my heart, one single refuge remained; God received me into it. My physical strength goes on declining, but that is not the case with the passion which sustains me. To make oneself worthy of immortality is the only purpose of life; happiness, suffering, everything, is a means towards that end; this is what I am happy in believing. You have been chosen to uproot my life from this earth; I was clinging to it by too strong a bond.

'When, I heard of your arrival in Italy, when I saw your writing again, when I knew you were on the other side of the river, I felt a terrible perturbation in my heart. I had to keep on reminding myself that my sister is your wife, so that I could struggle against what I was feeling. I will not conceal from you that to see you again would be a happiness, an indefinable emotion that my heart, again impassioned, preferred to centuries of calm. But Providence did not desert me in that peril. Are you not the husband of another woman? What then could I have to say to you? Was it permissible for me to die in your arms? And what would be left for my conscience if I made no sacrifice, if I still wanted one last day, one last hour? Perhaps now I shall appear before God more confidently, since I have been able to give up seeing you. This great resolution will calm my heart. Happiness, as I experienced it when you loved me, is not in accord with our nature: it excites, it disturbs, it passes so quickly! But a regular prayer, a religious meditation aiming at self-perfection, at deciding everything by a feeling of duty, is a pleasant state, and I cannot know what ravages the mere sound of your voice might produce in the calm life to which I have attained. You grieved me very much by telling me your health was affected. Oh, it is not I who look after it, but it is still I who suffer with you. May God bless your days, my Lord. Be happy, be happy out of pity. A secret communication with the divine seems to place within ourselves the being who confides and the voice which replies; out of two friends it makes one soul. Would you still seek what is called happiness? Oh, will you find anything better than my affection? Do you know that in the deserts of the New World I would have blessed my lot if you had allowed me to follow you? Do you know that I would have served you like a slave? Do you know that I would have prostrated myself before you as before an emissary from heaven if you had loved me faithfully? But what have you done with so much love? What have you done with that affection which is unique in this world, with an unhappiness equally unique? So lay no further claim to happiness. Do not hurt me by believing you can still achieve it. Pray as I do, pray, and may our thoughts come together in heaven!

'When I feel, however, that I am quite at the end of my days, perhaps I will put myself in some place to see you pass by. Why should I not? When my sight becomes dim, when I can see nothing of the outside world, your image will appear. If I had recently seen you again, would this illusion not he more vivid? In the ancient world, the gods were never present at the time of death. I shall keep you away from mine. But I should like to be able to recall a recent memory of your features in my expiring soul. Oswald, Oswald, what have I said? You see what I am like when I lose myself in remembering you.

'Why did not Lucile want to see me? She is your wife, but she is also my sister. I have kind, even generous, words to say to her. And our daughter, why has she not been brought to see me? I ought not to see you, but those around you are my family; am I rejected by it? Are you afraid that poor little Juliet will be saddened at the sight of me? It is true that I look like a ghost, but I would know how to smile for your child. Farewell, my Lord, farewell. Realize that I could call you my brother, because you are my sister's husband. Oh, at least you will wear mourning when I die; as a relative you will be present at my funeral. It is to Rome that my ashes will first be conveyed. Have my coffin carried by the route traversed in the past by my triumphal chariot, and take a rest in the exact place where you gave me back my laurel crown. No, Oswald, no, I am wrong. I do not want anything which would grieve you. I want only a tear and some glances towards heaven, where I shall await you.'

———

From <u>Sense and Sensibility</u> *(1811) by Jane Austen (1775–1817). The manipulative Lucy Ferrars, formerly Lucy Steel, writes to her ex-beau, Edward Ferrars, to tell him that she has married his brother Robert. This turn of events allows Edward the freedom to propose to the woman he really loves, Elinor Dashwood, who has fallen in love with him, and waited patiently for events to work themselves out, one way or another. She represents the "sense" in the book's title.*

"Dear Sir,
    Being very sure I have long lost your affections, I have thought myself at liberty to bestow my own on another, and have no doubt of being as happy with him as I once used to think I might be with

you; but I scorn to accept a hand while the heart was another's. Sincerely wish you happy in your choice, and it shall not be my fault if we are not always good friends, as our near relationship now makes proper. I can safely say I owe you no ill-will, and am sure you will be too generous to do us any ill offices. Your brother has gained my affections entirely, and as we could not live without one another, we are just returned from the altar, and are now on our way to Dawlish for a few weeks, which place your dear brother has great curiosity to see, but thought I would first trouble you with these few lines, and shall always remain,

Your sincere well-wisher, friend, and sister,
Lucy Ferrars

I have burnt all your letters, and will return your picture the first opportunity. Please to destroy my scrawls—but the ring with my hair you are very welcome to keep."

———

From The Seducer's Diary *(1843) by Danish existentialist philosopher Søren Kierkegaard. (1813–1855). Written under the pseudonym Victor Eremita,* The Seducer's Diary *appeared in Kierkegaard's book* Either/Or *(1843), a text made up of the "writings" of a Judge William and "Mr. A,". In Kierkegaard's construction, "Mr. A"—who claims to have found the letters that make up* The Seducer's Diary—*represented the aesthetic approach to living, which posits that one lives in immediacy, with a impulsiveness, a desire for immediate gratification, a detachment, and an irony towards life that leads to an underlying despair. "Judge William" represented the ethical approach, wherein life is not simply a matter of satisfying one's inclinations, because there are duties and tasks towards the good that will bring one closer to living a genuinely human life.*

In the story, a young man named Johannes, attempts to seduce

Cordelia, a young woman, with a "poetic" approach: enjoying the process and enjoying reflecting on it, but with a detachment that protects him from real involvement with another human being. Kierkegaard argued that the aesthetic position is our immediate nature, but could/should be overcome, with a focus on the ethical and the religious.

After the publication of The Seducer's Diary, Kierkegaard's brother Peter became angry with him for writing it, feeling that, taken alone and not in the context of all of Either/Or, it would be read superficially and for titillation. From Howard V. and Edna H. Hong's translation, 1987.

Johannes,

There was a rich man; he had great flocks and herds of livestock large and small. There was a poor little maiden; she possessed but a single lamb; it ate from her hand and drank from her cup. You were the rich man, rich in all the glories of the world; I was the poor one who possessed only my love. You took it, you delighted in it. Then desire beckoned you, and you sacrificed the little that I possessed— you could sacrifice nothing of your own. There was a rich man; he possessed great flocks and herds. There was a poor little maiden, she possessed only her love.

Your Cordelia

———

From The Way We Live Now (1875) by Anthony Trollope (1815–1882). In this satire of upper-class Victorian England, an indictment on the corrosive effect of greed, Winifred Hurtle, an American divorcee in her mid-thirties, is writing to Paul Montague, a young businessman who is torn between his concern and sense of obligation to Hurtle and his love for Henrietta Carbury, a young virgin.

Hurtle, variously described by other characters as a "wretched, bad, bold American intriguing woman" and a "horrid" "American wild cat," had engaged in a liaison with Montague while he was visiting

America, and is in England to win him back. Hurtle sends the following letter in response to Montague's rejection of her. (Carbury and Montague eventually marry.)

Trollope was prolific in the use of letters in his fiction and there are breakup letters from women to men in his stories Ayala's Angel, Dr. Thorne, and Phineas Redux, among others. As George Mason University English professor Ellen Moody put it in her essay "Partly Told In Letters: Trollope's Story-telling Art," ". . . epistolarity is a basic important concept of Trollope's story-telling art . . . with lightning speed characters who were close friends or lovers can become wholly alienated from one another . . . badgering, spiteful, revengeful, and brutal letters occur frequently in or dominate The Way We Live Now, The Prime Minister, Is He Popenjoy . . . and Mr. Scarborough's Family."

Dear Paul,

You are right and I am wrong. Our marriage would not have been fitting. I do not blame you. I attracted you when we were together; but you have learned and have learned truly that you should not give up your life for such attractions. If I have been violent with you, forgive me. You will acknowledge that I have suffered.

Always know that there is one woman who will love you better than any one else. I think too that you will love me even when some other woman is by your side, God bless you, and make you happy. Write me the shortest, shortest word of adieu. Not to do so would make you think yourself heartless. But do not come to me.

For ever,
W.H.

Paul Montague,

I have suffered many injuries, but of all injuries this is the worst and most unpardonable,—and the most unmanly. Surely there never was such a coward, never so false a liar. The poor wretch that I destroyed was mad with liquor and was only acting after his kind.

Even Caradoc Hurtle never premeditated such wrong as this. What;—you are to bind yourself to me by the most solemn obligation that can join a man and a woman together, and then tell me,— when they have affected my whole life,—that they are to go for nothing, because they do not suit your view of things? On thinking over it, you find that an American wife would not make you so comfortable as some English girl;—and therefore it is all to go for nothing! I have no brother, no man near me;—or you would not dare do this. You can not but be a coward.

You talk of compensation! Do you mean money? You do not dare to say so, but you must mean it. It is an insult the more. But as to retribution; yes. You shall suffer retribution. I desire you to come to me,—according to your promise,—and you will find me with a horsewhip in my hand. I will whip you till I have not a breath in my body. And then I will see what you will dare to do;—whether you will drag me into a court of law for the assault.

Yes; come. You shall come. And now you know the welcome you shall find. I will buy the whip while this is reaching you, and you shall find that I know how to choose such a weapon. I call upon you to come. But you should be afraid and break your promise, I will come to you. I will make London too hot to hold you;—and if I do not find you I will go with my story to every friend you have.

I have now told you exactly as I can the condition of my mind.

Winifred Hurtle

Having written this she again read the short note, and again gave way to violent tears. But on that day she sent no letter. On the following morning she wrote a third, and sent that. This was the third letter;—

Yes. Come.

W.H.

From the short story "Falso in scrittura" (A Lie in Writing) by Italian writer Matilde Serao (1856–1927), which appeared in her book <u>Fior di Passione</u> (1899). The short story is made up of three letters. In the two letters that precede this, a man has propositioned the narrator, and she has told him she cannot be unfaithful to her husband. But in the second letter she asks him to come see her when her husband is away so they can have four days of passion together.

December 4

My friend. I have, without a doubt, reached the most painful hour of my life. I cannot tell you what I am suffering in this moment; I cannot describe it. It is a torment without a name. I feel as if a fingernail were ripping up my heart: drop-by-drop, I'm losing the richest blood of my life. I cannot cry, cannot scream, cannot sob: but I'm suffocating. My dear friend, the tragic week of our love has arrived. I must unite all of my courage to tell you that this love must end. The light of our existence, the jocundity of our youth, must end, die. Fate wills it. These days have seen me crying, praying, asking God for the strength to make this sacrifice. Today I am in agony, but I'm resolute. The noble voice of duty speaks to my heart. We sinned too much. We deceived a trusting and peaceful man, a man who believes in my honor and my love, in your honor and your friendship. By silencing our conscience, we erred, sweetly but gravely. We wore the mask of virtue while we were guilty. I held my melancholy wife's head high, while my lips burned with the heat of our kisses. We should repent together. I didn't want this, remember. Remember my first letter. I was surprised, stupefied. I lost my head: but you were a man, why were you not the wise one, the cold one? I didn't want this. Maybe I didn't love you. I loved you after. Cesare, I still love you, but I'm leaving you. I can't continue this life of shame and dishonor: I turn scarlet in front of my husband, the servants. I yearn for the final shame, the discovery of my betrayal. Oh Cesare, such desperation!

This takes so much courage. Help me. Stay calm. Don't become desolate in my presence, don't write me, don't come by the house. Leave me to my nighttime tears, to my ardent prayers. Don't wish me to die from dishonor and from pain. I have to live for this man whom I've betrayed, for whom I am a consolation. I am an undeserving, but repentant wife. I still love you, I'll love you yet longer, and I'll never forget you. You've been my joy, my only love. But everything is past now. I'll keep living, mechanically, like a watch, without affections, without comfort, in the singular, dry satisfaction of duty done. Goodbye, Cesare; be happy. Love another, if you can. But perhaps you cannot. Goodbye, Cesare—Adriana.

How many years have passed? I don't know, I don't remember. Many, surely. But as much time has passed, as much as I've studied, I've never been able to ascertain in which of the three letters that woman was lying.

From Love Letters *of an Irishwoman (The Mutual Book Company, 1901) by F. C. (Frank Corey) Voorhies (1877–?). The preface to the book, titled "APOLOGY", says that the letters were*

> *"found by Riley the junk dealer in the dump that is situated just back of the canning factory across the street from McCarthy's lot. These dainty epistles were, no doubt, meant only for the eyes of 'Mike,' but as the love-letters of kings, queens, jacks, and English women have been cast upon the public, we feel sure that Nora will forgive us for handing her 'billets-doux' down to posterity in cold, black type."*

LETTER 10

Oh, Mike—

Now I know, Mike, Mike, why it is that your love for me is getting the chills. Ellen O'Brien told me and Mrs. Grundy told her.

Hell Hath No Fury

Now I don't know who this Mrs. Grundy is but Ellen says that the woman knows for a fact that you are in love with and paying attention to Maggie Finnegan. The Grundy woman said you were with her three nights last week and them was the three nights you did not come to see me. I'm on, Mike, I'm on. Oh, what shall I do. I am not so sore to think that you are not for me any more as I am to think that a frozen face like the Finnegan girl could snatch my pray from me. That's what puts my tender heart through the wringer. And such a looking piece of calico as she is to. Now I'll admit I'm not stunning Back Bay beauty myself but *Miss* Finnegan—Oh my, oh my,—she never could get close enough to a prize in a beauty show to know that there was one. She might draw a prize at a food fair as a heavy weight lobster—but oh that face. And figure—tie a rope around a sack of potatoes and you have her just as she is. She looks like a number 8 with a cheap dress on. I don't see how you could fall out of love with me and into love with her so quick unless it is because she wears red silk shoe laces. Is it that Mike? If that's all you should have loved me two days longer because as soon as Mrs. Smith pays me the money she owes me for a wash I am going to get *lavender* laces and put them in my boots with the bows at the toes. Then no girl at the Hod Carriers Picnic would be better dressed than me. But no you are impashunt and you let your love grow froze a few days to soon. And such a voice as that Finnegan thing uses when she tries to talk. She sounds like the canning factory whistle when the factory opens up after a three months shut down. She talks so horse that when you hear her at a distance you think she is coughfin. And how did she get her larux in such a condition that her bronkal tubes won't work right—why you know, Mike. You know. She was a cheap waiter in a cheap sandwich depo on a cheap street down town and she lost her voice yelling "Ham" and "Draw one" and "boil two meedyum." That's how she did it so she did and still you love her and let her take you away from me after I had worked so hard evenings to show you that I needed you for my Lord and master. Never mind Mike, take your chop house has been and fairy chambermaid, take her and be happy. Whatever you may do there will always be a kozy corner in my young heart for you. I will forget my grief by doing as all romantic maidens do after a "affair de cur" that turns out to be on the bum. I will enlist in a comic opry chorus so fare the well and so long, sweetheart that was.

Yours—onst
Nora.

———

From the novel The Vagabond *(1910), by the French novelist Colette (1873-1954). In the story, Renée Néré, a thirty-something woman, has just left her cruel and demanding marriage and become a performer and mime. During this journey of self-discovery, Renée falls in with a man named Maxime (Max), an independently wealthy but intellectually inferior bachelor, a relationship that underscores her struggle to remain independent while enjoying the comforts of a loving partner and a home. Renée eventually makes up her mind to leave him, which she does in the following letter.*

Goodbye, my darling. I am going away, to a village not very far from here; after that I shall no doubt leave for America, with Brague. I shall not see you again, my darling. When you read this you will not think it is a cruel game, since the day before yesterday you wrote to me; "My Renée, do you no longer love me?"

I am going away, it is the least hurt I can do you. I am not cruel, Max, but I feel myself quite worn out, as though unable to resume the habit of loving and afraid lest I should have to suffer again because of it.

You did not think I was so cowardly, my darling? What a small heart mine is! Yet once upon a time it could have been worthy of yours, which offers itself so simply. But now . . . what could I give you, oh my darling? In a few years' time the best of myself would be that frustrated maternity that a childless woman transfers to her husband. You do not accept that and neither do I. It is a pity. There are days when I, who watch myself growing older with a resigned terror, think of old age as a recompense.

My darling, one day you will understand all this. You will understand that I must not belong to you or to anyone, and that in spite of a first marriage and a second love, I have remained a kind of old maid, like some among them who are so in love with Love that no lover appears to them beautiful enough, and so they refuse themselves without condescending to explain; who repel every sentimental misalliance and return to sit for life before a window, bent over their needle, in solitary communion with their incomparable vision. Like them, I wanted everything; a lamentable mistake punished me.

I no longer dare, my darling, that is the whole trouble, I no longer dare. Don't be cross if I have hidden so long from you my efforts to resuscitate myself the enthusiasm, the adventurous fatalism, the blind hope, the whole cheerful escort of love. The only delirium I feel is that of my senses. And alas, there is none whose intervals are more lucid. You would have consumed me to no purpose, you whose gaze, whose lips, whose long caresses, whose moving silence cured, for a little while, a distress which is not your fault.

Goodbye, my darling. Seek far from me that youth, that fresh, unspoilt beauty, that faith in the future and in yourself, in a word, the love that you deserve, the love that once upon a time I could have given you. Don't seek me out. I have just enough strength to flee from you. If you were to walk in here, before me, while I am writing to you . . . but you will not walk in.

Goodbye, my darling. You are the one being in the world whom I call my darling, and after you I have no one to whom to give that name. For the last time, embrace me as if I were cold, hold me very close, very close, very close . . .

Renée

From The Dangerous Age: Letters and Fragments from a Woman's Diary *(1910) by Danish writer Karin Michaëlis (1872–1950). In the novel, Elsie Lindtner, a thirty-two year old woman going through a midlife crisis, divorces her husband, abandons her young lover, and retreats to an island. This letter is to her ex-husband.* The Dangerous Age *became a controversial novel at the time of its publication for its critique of the politics of aging among women—particularly menopause—and its uncompromising voice. The book's sequel—titled* Elsie Lindtner*—was published in 1912.*

MY DEAR, KIND FRIEND, AND FORMER HUSBAND,
Is there not a good deal of style about that form of address? Were you not deeply touched at receiving, in a strange town, flowers sent by a lady? If only the people understood my German and sent them to you in time!

For an instant a beautiful thought flashed through my mind: to welcome you in this way in every town where you have to stay. But since I only know the addresses of one or two florists in the capitals, and I am too lazy to find out the others, I have given up this splendid folly, and simply note it to my account as a "might-have-been."

Shall I be quite frank, Richard? I am rather ashamed when I think of you, and I can honestly say that I never respected you more than to-day. But it could not have been otherwise. I want you to concentrate all your will-power to convince yourself of this. If I had let myself be persuaded to remain with you, after this great need for solitude had laid hold upon me, I should have worried and tormented you every hour of the day.

Dearest and best friend, there is some truth in these words, spoken by I know not whom: "Either a woman is made for marriage, and then it practically does not matter to whom she is married, she will soon understand how to fulfil [*sic*] her destiny; or she is unsuited to matrimony, in which case she commits a crime against her own personality when she binds herself to any man."

Apparently, I was not meant for married life. Otherwise I should have lived happily for ever and a day with you—and you know that was not the case. But you are not to blame. I wish in my heart of hearts that I had something to reproach you with—but I have nothing against you of any sort or kind.

It was a great mistake-a cowardly act-to promise you yesterday that I would return if I regretted my decision. I know I shall never regret it. But in making such a promise I am directly hindering you. . . .Forgive me, dear friend . . . but it is not impossible that you may some day meet a woman who could become something to you. Will you let me take back my promise? I shall be grateful to you. Then only can I feel myself really free.

When you return home, stand firm if your friends overwhelm you with questions and sympathy. I should be deeply humiliated if anyone—no matter who—were to pry into the good and bad times we have shared together. Bygones are bygones, and no one can actually realise what takes place between two human beings, even when they have been onlookers.

Think of me when you sit down to dinner. Henceforward eight o'clock will probably be my bedtime. On the other hand I shall rise with the sun, or perhaps earlier. Think of me, but do not write too often. I must first settle down tranquilly to my new life. Later on, I shall enjoy writing you a condensed account of all the follies which can be committed by a woman who suddenly finds herself at a mature age complete mistress of her actions.

Follow my advice, offered for the twentieth time: go on seeing your friends; you cannot do without them. Really there is no need for you to mourn for a year with crape on the chandeliers and immortelles [funeral flowers] around my portrait.

You have been a kind, faithful, and delicate-minded friend to me, and I am not so lacking in delicacy myself that I do not appreciate this in my inmost heart. But I cannot accept your generous offer to give me money. I now tell you this for the first time, because, had I said so before, you would have done your best to over-persuade me. My small income is, and will be, sufficient for my needs.

The train leaves in an hour. Richard, you have your business and your friends—more friends than anyone I know. If you wish me well, wish that I may never regret the step I have taken. I look down at my hands that you loved—I wish I could stretch them out to you . . .

A man must not let himself be crushed. It would hurt me to feel that people pitied you. You are much too good to be pitied.

Certainly it would have been better if, as you said, one of us had died. But in that case you would have had to take the plunge into eternity, for I am looking forward with joy to life on my island.

For twenty years I have lived under the shadow of your wing in the Old Market Place. May I live another twenty under the great forest trees, wedded to solitude.

How the gossips will gossip! But we two, clever people, will laugh at their gossip.

Forgive me, Richard, to-day and always, the trouble I have brought upon you. I would have stayed with you if I could. Thank you for all. . . .

ELSIE.

That my feeling for you should have died, is quite as incomprehensible to me as to you. No other man has ever claimed a corner of my heart. In a word, having considered the question all round, I am suffering simply from a nervous malady—alas! it is incurable!

———

From the book Love Letters of a Divorced Couple *(Doubleday Page & Company, 1915) by writer/publisher and onetime* Vogue *managing editor William Farquhar Payson (1876-1939). The book consists of a series of letters between Kenneth, a newly divorced architect, and Sybil, his young wife, after the two are granted a divorce in Reno, Nevada. The* New York Times Book Review *of March 28, 1915 called* Love Letters of a Divorced Couple *"quite an exciting and romantic little idyl" and claimed that it would make "wholesome reading for mutually irritated couples" because it not only makes fun of the troubles between men and women but "indicates . . . what medicaments are pretty sure to cure them."*

Hell Hath No Fury

1687 K Street, Washington, D.C.,

April 16, 19—.

Good-bye then, Kenneth, for the last time. But I can't say it without suggesting a few "Don'ts" for your club life.

Don't sit up too late playing auction [bridge]. You always need at least eight hours' sleep.

Don't smoke too many cigarettes. You have a nice speaking voice, and they spoil it.

Don't drink too many cocktails. They are fattening, and there's a tendency to fatness on both sides of your family. It would be very unbecoming to you, and besides there's danger of apoplexy.

Don't sit in draughts. That's the one way you catch cold.

Don't sit in the club window with a lot of old-timers and gaze regretfully at young girls passing on the avenue. There's something so pathetic in that—when it's not merely senile.

Don't gossip about divorced women; I'm one.

Don't discuss actress'[s]good looks. You never discuss things without talking like a connoisseur—and that might give a wrong impression.

Don't be led into going out to suppers to meet them. You're such a funny combination of man of the world and infant in arms that there's no telling what might happen to you.

Don't let the fact that we made an awful botch of our marriage make a botch of your life.

In short, be a good boy, Kenneth, and, above all,

Don't utterly forget

Your recent companion,
Sybil

———

From Summer *(1917), a novel by Edith Wharton (1862–1937). The book's heroine, Charity, a young orphan living as the ward of the lawyer Mr. Royall, falls in love with Lucius Harney, an architect, after meeting him in the library in which she works. Although Mr. Royall asks Charity repeatedly to marry him, she declines and begins a clandestine affair with Harney. When Mr. Royall catches them together and questions Harney's intentions, Harney claims he will marry Charity after he returns from a trip. But soon after Harney's departure, Charity hears that he is actually engaged to another woman, Annabel, and writes him the following letter.*

She took a sheet of letter paper from Mr. Royall's office, and sitting by the kitchen lamp, once night after Verena had gone to bed, began her first letter to Harney. It was very short:

I want you should marry Annabel Balch if you promised to. I think maybe you were afraid I'd feel too bad about it. I feel I'd rather you acted right.

Your loving
Charity

From "A Very Short Story" (1925) by Ernest Hemingway (1899–1961). This passage was based on Hemingway's actual experience of receiving a Dear John letter, from Agnes von Kurowsky (see p. 170).

He went to America on a boat from Genoa. Luz went back to Pordenone to open a hospital. It was lonely and rainy there, and there was a battalion of *arditi* [shock troops] quartered in the town. Living in the muddy, rainy town in the winter, the major of the battalion made love to Luz, and she had never known Italians before, and finally wrote to the States that theirs had been only a boy and girl affair. She was sorry, and she knew he would probably not be able to understand, but might some day forgive her, and be grateful to her, and she expected, absolutely unexpectedly, to be married in the spring. She loved him as always, but she realized now it was only a boy and girl love. She hoped he would have a great career, and believed in him absolutely. She knew it was for the best.

The major did not marry her in the spring, or any other time. Luz never got an answer to the letter to Chicago about it. A short time after he contracted gonorrhea from a sales girl in a loop department store while riding in a taxicab through Lincoln Park.

———

From Mary ("Mashekna") by Vladimir Nabokov (1899–1977). Published in 1926, Mary is the story of Lev Ganin, a young Russian émigré, who discovers that his neighbor Alfyorov is married to his first love, Mary. Mary is not in Berlin—where Ganin and Alfyorov reside—but in Russia, and she is on her way by train to the German capital. The following fragment of a letter was written by Mary to Ganin at the time of their breakup, and Ganin's memories of his relationship with Mary make up bulk of the novel. Nabokov also used the breakup letter to good effect in Lolita (1995), in the form of Charlotte Haze's letter to her boarder (and future husband) Humbert Humbert.

Floorbrush in hand, Ganin returned to his own room. On the table lay a mauve rectangle. By a rapid association of thought, evoked by that envelope and by the reflection of the desk in the mirror, he remembered those very old letters which he kept in a black wallet at the bottom of his suitcase, alongside the automatic pistol that he had brought with him from the Crimea.

He scooped up the long envelope from the table, pushed the window open wider with his elbow and with his strong fingers tore the letter crosswise, then tore up each portion and threw the scraps to the wind. Gleaming, the paper snowflakes flew into the sunlit abyss. One fragment fluttered onto the windowsill, and on it Ganin read a few mangled lines:

ourse, I can forg
ove. I only pra
hat you be hap

He flicked in off the windowsill into the yard smelling of coal and spring and wide-open spaces. Shrugging with relief, he started to tidy his room.

———

From <u>New Portuguese Letters</u> (1972) by "The Three Marias" (Maria Isabel Barreno, Maria Teresa Horta, Maria Velho da Costa) a trio of Portuguese feminists and writers who decided to meet to discuss their lives as women and as writers. Eventually they put together <u>New Portuguese Letters,</u> which was partially inspired by <u>The Love Letters of a Portuguese Nun.</u> The three women were arrested upon its publication on charges of "abuse of the freedom of the press" and "outrage to public decency." In 1974 the charges were dropped.

Sixth and Final Letter from Dona Mariana Alcoforado, a Nun in Beja, to the Chevalier de Chamilly, Written on Christmas Day of the Year of Grace 1671

Senhor,

It is not my intention ever to send you these lines to read, for their sole purpose is to be committed to paper. When I sent you words set down in the heat of passion and without restraint, I did not know that by putting them down in writing I was holding the reins of suffering in my hands, with the result that merely by grasping them my grief appeared to grow more intense, but in reality it was becoming more and more divorced in hand. But today I know that the love or the talents that lead one to pick up a pen and thus allay one's pain are of great value, for they put an end to what is merely transitory and enhance the real and enduring goods that are the only ones that merit being put into words.

Hell Hath No Fury

I wrote you letters full of great love and great torment, Senhor, and after having had no commerce with you for so long, I began to love them and the act of writing about them more than I loved your image or the memory of you. I have penned many more missives than I have cared to send you, for this was a way of taking pleasure in the act of writing and hearing how my words sounded and of impressing my companions here in this house with my talents at composing elegant love letters. As others did embroidery, worked in the garden, or prepared sweetmeats for us to enjoy, or delighted us with their voices raised in song, so my task here, among those assigned each of us, was to set down in writing all the unusual hours that troubled this house or made it a happy place: I wrote of feast days and of sorrows that afflicted none of the others save myself, and composed letters for our Reverend Mother or for young novices to send on with their own signatures—thus taking hold of my life by letting myself go. I also read a great deal, as had always been my habit, though I now did so in order to learn from excellent teachers how best to tune my delightful instrument. And as for my grievous laments for you, Senhor, two years after I no longer even remembered them, having found such pleasure in fulfilling these new duties assigned me, willingly performing a task that I had originally embarked upon for reasons quite contrary to my will. When one is puffed up with pride, one finds many sources of pleasure, and perhaps realizes only on his or her deathbed how vain such pleasures were, and hence only death takes away the joy of writing elegant or witty love letters—or of performing pious and charitable deeds.

And so it was that by writing and by reading works by our writers of old and even many Frenchmen (for I am allowed to read whatever I choose since my family and my superiors are so pleased to see how reasonable and well-behaved I've become) I came to understand, Senhor, that I had composed nothing that had not already been expressed, in other ways and in other times, in works that had touched the hearts of their authors' contemporaries and the hearts of many succeeding generations. And it was then that I began to smile at my sorrows, since what was really mine, really genuine about them I had never contrived to set down in words, and it now seems to me that for what is really true there are no words, only outcries as writhings in one's vitals, and two torments will have nothing in common save what is least important about them. Hence I am beginning to ask myself whether I ever really loved you, whether I ever really cared to discover who you really were, above and beyond your outward appearance, and to ask myself what attracted you to me. And the truth demands that I confess that I for my part found in you only the attraction of rebellion and gay abandon, in those days of mine as a young novice who had been deprived of everything and was by nature so given to both these feelings myself. You were adventure, novelty, the unpredictable life to which I had seemed forever fated. I thus did not love you truly, just as I did not truly love myself, and the only good and lasting thing that has remained in my memories of you are your silences and the seriousness with which you looked at me, as though you were waiting for something. That has been your legacy to me, a hope for after the love that I professed for you, for after the writings that I took such pleasure in, a hope for afterwards. It was as though in our love affair I had been the cavalier who gallops astride his cleverness and gracious manners and taste for adventure and you the lady entirely at peace with herself who is no longer offended or amazed at anything because she is so full of wisdom and virtue. Hence our commerce with each other was profound, Senhor, since everything that everyone expected of each of us became completely reversed. You ceased to be possessed and sought after, and I, with my calculated coldness of heart and my inflamed senses, was content merely to possess you and keep you at my mercy, thus behaving towards you as men customarily behave towards their women. You wanted only to die or to depart, and the one thing left for me to do was to continue to enhance my power and freedom in the same domains and in the same ways that I had once been so cruelly deprived of. You should see how respectfully my family and the clergy behave towards me today, how many people come to kiss my hand and to seek my advice, since they are impressed both by my fine style and my subtle wisdom, and I seem to them to be both someone who is acquainted with many authors' writings and ways of expressing suffering that others never speak of, and someone whose behaviour serves as an example of the seemly manner in which one's duties ought to be fulfilled.

I therefore write to you, Senhor, in order to humble myself by remembering your troubled smile, though I am certain that, however genuine my sentiment may be, I am again merely indulging in a vain exercise. The only real pain that I perhaps feel in my heart today is not knowing who I might have been had I not been born enslaved, had I been born a male. And even with my propensity for enmeshing myself in intricate lies, for allowing my vivid imagination to run away with me, and for indulging in flights of fancy that have served to make me feel sure of myself, I do not know whether, had I chanced to have been born a man, I could ever have displayed towards someone whom I had at my mercy, someone far more humble than myself, and a woman and a nun in the bargain, the same high-handed and heedless love as you displayed towards me.

I cannot praise God for the paths He has traced for my life to take, since I have never become resigned to them. Nonetheless I praise Him for my having found you along them, since if this had not come to pass, how would I ever have experienced such feelings as shame and deceitfulness on being extravagantly complimented for charms and talents that were worth nothing? How would I have discovered myself to be—though cloistered and a liar despite myself—someone who in the end was well-loved and lovable, the possessor of something worthwhile that you who were free did not possess?

I know that you have wedded a lady with few charms, though she is a cultured gentlewoman with exquisite manners, who is devoted to you and whose behaviour is most modest and circumspect. I have also heard tell of your sense of justice and your rigorous devotion to God and the pious works and reading of edifying texts that occupy you at present. Pray pardon me, Senhor, if I find it laughable that those whom great sufferings neither kill nor free find their lives slowly draining away in such a mediocre way.

Your servant, then, and your sister in the grace of Our Lord.

Mariana
26.7.71

———

From the epistolary novel <u>A Woman of Independent Means</u> *(1978) by Elizabeth Forsythe Hailey (b.1938). Hailey's first novel—which she originally wanted to title "Letters from a Runaway Wife"—was based loosely on the life of her own grandmother, Bess Kendall Jones. In the novel, readers follow heroine Bess Steed Gardner's life through youth to old age, and her experiences with business, marriage, child rearing, widowhood, and friendship. The following letter is from Bess to a suitor, Arthur Fineman, a friend and financial advisor from Texas who has proposed marriage to her.*

August 25, 1920

Dear Arthur,

I have not written sooner because I was not sure what tone my letter should take. I can no longer write as I did before, as a friend seeking advice and recounting anecdotes. Since Boston, an intimacy exists between us even in our silence—an intimacy I treasure and trust I have not betrayed by rejecting its marital translation. Please do not think it vain of me to want to continue just as I am now, like one of the maidens on the Greek urn so admired by Keats, suspended for eternity in the moment of pursuit . . . By the way I see in the *Wall Street Journal* that a new company has been formed in Texas to explore the market for natural gas. I foresee an unlimited future for any product that is a source of energy. Can I afford to be part of this venture? Please give careful scrutiny to my portfolio in terms of growth potential. I own nothing I could not be persuaded to sell.

Love always,
Bess

———

From the novel <u>Great Expectations</u> (1982) by Kathy Acker (1948–1997), a novelist, screenwriter, critic, porn star, and professor, who was called "the best of the punk writers" by Elizabeth Benedict in Esquire magazine. <u>Great Expectations</u> is a "plagiarism" of Charles Dickens's novel of the same name (1861) and Pauline Réage's <u>The Story of O</u> (1954), interspersed with documentary material (letters, diaries) from Acker's own life. According to writer and Acker intimate Chris Kraus (see p. 323), "The letters, and other diaristic sections of the book ground the extrapolated fantasy of these pirated classics where they belong, in Acker's own life."

Dear Peter,

I think your new girlfriend stinks. She is a liar all the way around because her skin is yellow from jaundice, not from being Chinese like she pretends. She's only pretty because she's wearing a mask. You're hooked on her tight little cunt: it's only a sexual attraction I know you're very attracted to sex 'cause when you were young you were fat and no girl wanted to fuck you. What you don't know is that this cunt contains lots of poison—not just jaundice—a thousand times more powerful than the coke she is feeding you to keep you with her—especially one lethal poison developed by the notorious Fu Manchu that takes cocks, turns their upper halves purple, their lower parts bright red, the eyes go blind so they can no longer see what's happening, the person dies. Your new girlfriend is insane and she's poisoning you.

Love,
Rosa

P.S. I'm only telling you this for your own good.

From <u>A Love Letter Never Sent</u> by Taiwanese writer Li Ang (Shih Shu-tuan) (1952–). The story first appeared in the collection <u>The Butcher's Wife and Other Stories</u> (1995) and is written in the form of a letter from a woman to a man she had fallen in love with long ago.

Dear G. L.:

It is now three o'clock in the morning, and I'm lying in bed as the rain falls outside my window. We've had a wet spring this year, starting way back in January, when the weather was still cold, and not only did the rains continue through February, but they didn't even let up in March, when the days should be getting warm. Everywhere you look there's a layer of damp moss. It's like tears of sadness, which can give the same feeling of pervading dampness if they flow long enough.

It's the weather and the lateness of the hour that compel me to write this letter. You probably don't even know who I am. I'm just someone who touched your life for a fleeting moment, without leaving a trace. Some might describe it as a "hands-off love affair." And that's what it was. I'm not going to sign this letter, and if you can't recall who I am when you've finished reading it, then I'll just have to deal with an unspeakable sadness. If what I want to say to you doesn't come through clearly, then what good is language? Besides, you and I are separated by the vast Pacific Ocean and more than ten years in time, so even if I wanted to tell you what's in my heart, I wouldn't know where to begin . . .

When I met you I wasn't yet twenty years old, an age when most girls are in the bloom of their youth. They fancy pretty clothes, look forward to going out on dates, secretly read love letters at home or wait eagerly for telephone calls as they stare in their mirrors at their radiant faces and dazzling eyes, or sit there brushing their hair and dreamily recalling all the lovely things that have happened to them.

When most other girls were dating, I could only look on, eventually losing myself in one novel after another. That's right, I read novels, all kinds of them, from the so-called classics by women novelists to best-sellers available in bookstalls. One type of book still moves me; funny as it sounds, it always leads to cheap tears and pleasures. I'm talking about popular romances, both Chinese and Western. . . .

G. L., can you possibly understand the heart of a young girl who has been so polluted by love? You see, I used the word "polluted." But it's true. I, and many girls like me of my generation, have been polluted, not just by popular romances, but by all sorts of things that have promoted romantic love. The reason is simple: as we were growing up, everything we knew about love we learned from our reading, things that we'd try out later when it was time to fall in love. Instead of spending time with boys, and letting nature take its course in matters of love, our notions of love came from the pages of books, and these were the foundation upon which our later loves were to be built.

That's how it was when I met you. What a glorious year that was! When I recall that year, I see a beautiful, clear autumn day, with you standing on a Taipei street, bright golden sunlight covering your back like a screen and lighting up your face. You had just returned from America, a talented student who had completed a Ph.D. in comparative literature at the age of thirty, a man with the airs of someone who had made great sacrifices for his country, and who now announced that he was returning to Taiwan to live in his home-town in the south . . .

Then I saw you, someone who had returned from the States, a progressive country where people had the courage to try new things and seek new adventures, and when I gazed up at you as you stood behind the podium at the USIS office on Nan Hai Road in Taipei, Taiwan, dressed in a casual Western herringbone suit, a blue dress shirt and a maroon tie, I was enchanted. . . .

How I loved and respected you! You were the center of my uni-verse, the foundation of my frame of mind. And so I followed you: from autumn through winter, all the way to the beginning of spring; from the USIS offices to one college and university after another, even to high-school lecture halls. I was always there in the audience, gazing up at you from a distance as you stood behind the podium, always so close and yet so far. . . .

G. L., back then my heart was filled with the need to preserve my girlish virtue, and when I learned that you had a wife, my first reaction was that it would be impossible for you to ever love me (I won't deny that I had stayed close to you in the vague hope that someday you would learn of my love for you and return that love). The news that you were married convinced me that the loving relationship I had hoped for was only a dream . . .

For the first time in my life I experienced the pain that love was capable of producing, and I knew that my love was doomed. And yet that love was as strong as ever. For several days I was unable and unwilling to get out of bed, and not a second went by that my heart wasn't stabbed by the pangs of a love that could never be. I wanted to die. I didn't get out of bed until my family grew frantic, thinking I had some mysterious and serious disease, and were about to take me to the hospital.

At the moment I spotted your wife sitting at your desk I understood that my love for you had ceased to exist. Only she, your lawfully wedded wife, could sit in your chair when your whereabouts were unknown and straighten up the manuscripts on your desk, one page at a time. And in the future, no matter what happened to you, only your lawfully wedded wife could stand up in court and speak on your behalf; even if you were convicted and put away, only she, your wife, could visit you and bring you food and clothing.

For the first time in my life I understood that the institution of marriage was greater than everything else, that it embraced a love that was irreplaceable, especially during times of difficulty. That knowledge was just what I needed to free myself from the intense emotions that had entangled me for more than a year.

But, G. L., that doesn't mean I stopped loving you, you must believe that. For it was then that I knew just how deep my love for you really was. As time passed, the depressing emptiness in my heart gradually disappeared, while my understanding of my love for you increased. The love I felt then, was greater than any hopes of being with you, purged of that chaotic, confining infatuation; my love was transformed into a profound emotion that painlessly filled my heart, with no more waves of agitation . . .

My husband is a decent man, progressive and possessed of many husbandly virtues. And I have been the best wife I could possibly be, except for my wedding night, when all I could see as I accepted the first man in my life was your melancholic face and the ever-changing expression in your eyes . . .

So now you know why I've written you this letter, G. L. Finally, after all these years, I'm able to deal with my past, and I find no need to keep you ignorant of the path I've taken. I'm confident you'll understand and treasure the enormous impact, which time itself cannot erase, that you've had on my life. I'm also writing to let you know that even though my love for you back then brought me pain and ridicule, I can state unequivocally that I have no regrets . . . And yet, G. L., no matter what choice I make, as I walk the road ahead I'll never regret in the slightest the love I once felt for you. Of that I'm sure.

I hope you can recall who I am,

C.T.

The
Unsent
Letter

Un•sent (ŭn-sĕnt) *adj.* not dispatched or transmitted; "the letter remained unwritten and unsent."

The Unsent Letter *n.* A breakup letter written but not sent to its intended recipient, usually because it was written in a diary or journal, or because it was meant to expel, rather than communicate, emotion.

MANY WOMEN WHO HEARD about *Hell Hath No Fury* explained that they had written breakup letters but never sent them, often because of some oft-heard maternal edict not to put anything in writing (or at least not to send it). The more I thought about unsent letters, the more I suspected that it would be necessary to reserve a section in the book just for them. My suspicions were confirmed in the fall of 2001 when I stumbled across SoThere.com, a Web site devoted solely to posting people's unsent letters. As I scoured the site's voluminous archives—(SoThere has published a letter a day for the past five years)—I was struck by the enormous number of letters that were not only written by women but written by women to men with whom they'd broken up. Almost every subgenre was represented in full force—the Autopsy, the Tell Off, the Other Woman/Other Man, the Just Friends—but they were all unsent. Clearly, there was something to this "unsent" business: I had over a thousand examples on one Web site alone. What's more, I soon recognized that including an Unsent chapter would be a great opportunity to include the contributions of some of the best young female writers around, many of whom graciously and excitedly pulled out *their* old notebooks and sketch pads or agreed to sit down and write the letters they "wish they'd written."

From artist Alma Schindler (later Mahler-Werfel) (1879–1964), the future wife of composer Gustav Mahler, Walter Gropius, and author Franz Werfel, to painter Gustav Klimt (1862–1918), when she was around twenty years old. At first Klimt was an acquaintance in Alma's circle of friends, but Alma became increasingly fond of the young artist and obsessed and anguished over his intent towards her. The two became mildly involved in early 1899, but that May, Alma's disapproving stepfather Carl Moll demanded that she not speak with Klimt

alone again; according to Suzanne Keegan's biography The Bride of the Wind *(Secker and Warburg, 2001), Moll also "extracted a promise from Klimt that he would have no further amorous dealings with Alma." Klimt responded with a letter denying any romantic intent, and Alma, upon hearing this, branded him a traitor. The letter appeared in Mahler-Werfel's journal—she never sent it.*

Friday, 9 June [1899]

Since yesterday evening I've been wondering: what if I were at death's door and were to write to KL? I don't know why, but I can't take my mind off the idea. If for a moment I stop talking, my thoughts promptly turn to that letter. It would start like this:

Klimt,
    You are unworthy of me! Before I die, I want to tell you so openly and honestly. I am just as much an artist as you are, I have no need to look up to you as if to a god. And I have the great advantage of having truly loved you, while you merely played with me. I know perfectly well that there was a time when I appealed to you. But the fact that you fell back into the arms of your sister-in-law proves you weren't serious about me for a moment. And already on the way to Florence you had the nerve to accost a young lady, who felt so intimidated that she got off the train at Udine. That alone serves as proof that for you the whole thing was just a joke.
    I was foolish enough to believe it to be more than a joke, and for that I have been amply punished.
    In reward for my boundless affection, you surrendered without a struggle, betrayed me. All I can bequeath to you now are beautiful memories, for which you have me to thank, and my diaries. Read them, and you will know me better.
    Farewell—farewell for eternity!

Yours, yours, yours
Alma

If I were dying *now,* that's roughly what I'd write. For the future, namely, I can guarantee nothing.—

Is my love genuine? Let me cast it out. It's nothing but unnecessary ballast, time-consuming and nerve-racking. It's time to put paid to such folly. I've already suffered enough on that account. I have no desire to go on with it. Take courage, Alma. You must find the energy, self-confidence and pride to tell yourself: 'I shall wash this fatal passion out of my hair, shall forget the most wonderful hours of my life or simply look back on them as something experienced by strangers.' I want to forget *everything*—and prove that I can survive perfectly well without him. . . .

From Henrietta Szold (1860–1945) to Dr. Louis Ginzberg, (1873–1953), when Szold was forty-five years old and Ginzberg, thirty-two. Szold, the founder of the women's Zionist organization Hadassah, met Ginzberg, a Talmudic scholar, in 1903 at The Clara de Hirsch Home, a trade school for working and immigrant women in New York. She wrote the following letter—which was never sent—in July 1905, around the time her passion for him first bloomed, and as a reply to an imaginary letter of his.

Over the next few years, Szold's feelings for Ginzberg intensified and she engaged in a form self-torture that, although horrific and heartbreaking, is painfully familiar to any person on the "wrong" end of an ambiguous relationship or serious crush. Szold's diary entries paint a picture of a sensitive, accomplished woman very much in love, yet so terrified and unsure of her feelings that rather than admit to them, she picks them apart and analyzes the potential romantic subtext of her love's every word and gesture. It was only in 1909, after Ginzberg informed her of his engagement to a young German woman, that Szold finally broke down and confessed her feelings. According to Baila Round Shargel's book Lost Love: The Untold Story of Henrietta Szold *(Jewish Publication Society, 1997), "Ginzberg claimed shock and surprise, and cavalierly assured her that the infatuation would soon pass."*

Hell Hath No Fury

Szold fell into a deep depression, and Ginzberg "communicated with her only in writing and snubbed her when they met by chance."

July, 1905

Dear Friend,

I have been sitting with your precious letter in my hand all day long. I cannot delay longer—I must make the reply that is my own death warrant. Heaven help me! I feel I am going to be un-Jewish, unwomanly. Perhaps before I reach the point of returning the treasure of love your letter gives me, my unreserved will have forfeited it. But I cannot otherwise—I cannot be prudent and restrained. I must once before I renounce pour my heart out to you. And, indeed, what harm can there be? You must know all. In these hard months of my solitary struggle with myself, I must have betrayed myself to your clear vision over and over again by my very efforts to exercise self-control. You must have divined it, that I was tranquil only when I was near you, one of the slight services my powers can accomplish; only when you permitted me to do something for you, that at all other times I was restless, disturbed, unable to do the tasks I set myself, and which never before had found me distracted. Why, then, should I refrain from telling you in explicit words that my whole happiness lies with you—that you are the first to give my soul its woman's heritage, a soul that up to the time it was awakened by you—Oh! So many wearily happy months ago—had known only filial passion. You guess all the rest, all I have suffered to pretend indifference to you, all I would suffer to win you and hold you forever. You remember my definition of a woman's love—the opportunity for self-effacement. Your favorite Zarathustra [quotation] expresses what I mean: *"Das Glück des Mannes heisst, Ich will; das Glueck des Weibes heisst, Er will"* [A man's luck is his own desire; a woman's, her husband's desire].

Yet there remains a good deal to be said; and it is hard, bitter to say it, but it is better I send it across the waste of waters. Then when you come back, I shall be fortified to look you in the eyes without flinching.

Somebody has sinned, or I should not have been exposed to the temptation of loving you—loving?—of adoring you—and you would have been spared the disharmony of being loved by me. Either I sinned against myself, or others sinned against me. Certainly it is not in nature that my spring-time should come when the lines in my face are hard and set, when my hair is whitening—it has grown much whiter since you went away, from my intense sorrowful thinking of you. But whoever sinned, one sin is not expiated by another. And I should be committing a grave sin against you, your young manhood, your high scholarship and ideals and gifts and prospects, were I to hang myself as a millstone about your neck. When you went away I wept and wept and prayed that this one time yet you might come back to me heart-free, so that I might have a space to grow accustomed to the idea that you would belong to some other woman. And then I grew bolder—I prayed for what has happened—I prayed that you would learn to love me. Happened, do I say? How we delight in deceiving ourselves! It has happened only because you guessed at the tumult in my soul and because you are chivalrous. For how can one like you spontaneously love one like me?

But whatever wild idea came into my disordered head and heart, I never lost sight of this one—that in the end I should have to practice renunciation, a more absolute self-effacement that given my definition of a woman's love calls for. I dare exercise no claim upon you. You belong to a happy, sprightly young creature, one that has not known the heat and burden of life, who will not so much give you intellectual sympathy—you do not need it, your penetrating, sane, unclouded mind suffices unto itself—as she will give you warmth and color to glorify your life. With me you would walk in the gray shadow of sorrows.

Only one thing I ask of you, my dear friend. Do not think it easy for me to give you up. If you could see what I see before me now: my own future dark as night, cold as death. I can never go back to the ignorance of my passionless days. You have made me to eat the fruit of the tree of knowledge, and my eyes have been opened—only to behold my own misery, only to pity my past self which was so stupid, to pity my future self which is doomed to unhappiness. And yet I kiss your hand for the fruit it gave me to taste of, for I still may love you, worship you, only I may not purchase my happiness with yours. And so I hug my misery; it is at least a pale similitude of the happiness I know exists for another.

I give you back then what you offer me, I shall bear my lot bravely. You will see how I shall control myself through my heart break. And if my strength gives out, I shall go away from where you are, and shall thank you evermore for the moment's glimpse of genuine living which you in the richness of your ample nature granted me—shall thank you for the happy "might have been." God bless you and that other one!

———

From novelist Jennifer Belle, thirty-four, author of Going Down *(River-head, 1996) and* High Maintenance *(Riverhead, 2001) to a man she dated for nine months, then broke up with, then dated again for nine months six years later. "It was written in my diary, not meant to be sent," says Belle. "I learned in elementary school never to send notes to boys. Girls who wrote notes always regretted it. As tempted as I might be, I would never send a letter to a man. I know I would want to try to get it back in some sort of Lucille Ball–esque maneuver, dress up as a postman and break into the post office or something like that. It always seemed a lot smarter to pick up the phone and leave a message, making it sound spontaneous no matter how well rehearsed. As mortifying as this letter is, I like it because it somehow manages to tell the entire story of a relationship I had with a man for nine months and then again for nine months six years later."*

Diary entry 11/7/94

Dear Richard,

I am very surprised and hurt by your breaking up with me so

suddenly like that. I knew you were losing interest in me when you wouldn't go to that wedding with me. I can't believe you wouldn't talk to me and tell me how you felt. I wonder how many weeks or months passed with you not wanting to be with me anymore. I wonder if you felt that way the whole time I was visiting you at the hospital and taking care of you at your house. It wasn't until today that it finally sunk in that you were really ending it. If you're seeing someone else I wish you would just tell me. Now I am sitting in your warm lobby just as I did 6 years ago. I was twenty. I have changed a little despite the fact that I am sitting on this bench. (Sitting on a different side.) For all I know you're at home. If I don't get the Jane Austen from you my mother will kill me. Emma.

I've been here for almost thirty minutes. I'm not going to Vanya I guess. I'll go tomorrow. I feel very sad. I will never be able to trust or depend on a man. I will never be in love or get married. I can't even imagine going on a date, having sex. I am doomed.

———

The following excerpt is taken from the epistolary novel, <u>I Love Dick</u> (Semiotext(e), 1997) by Chris Kaus (1959–). On the verge of turning forty, Kraus, then an experimental filmmaker, responds to the flirtatious advances of "Dick," a noted cultural critic and friend of her husband's. She "falls in love" with him and begins, with her husband's encouragement, writing letters to Dick. Dick neither responds nor asks her to stop. Kraus sees the book as an act of "performative philosophy," and the letters become a means of writing her way out of her present life. She leaves her husband and moves to the country, where her letters become essays. In the process of defining her relation to Dick, Kraus redefines such issues as the uses of "privacy," the fate of feminist artwork, the cultural politics of reputation and fame. Dick's only response was a "Cease and Desist" letter, attempting to bar Kraus from publishing her own letters to him. Semiotext(e) published the book anyway. It has since become a new feminist classic.

Eagle Rock, Los Angeles,

July 6, 95

Dear Dick . . .

26. On Saturday, April 8 we spent a perfect afternoon together. You arrived at the motel around noon and I was kind of shaky. Instead of going to the gym that morning I'd stayed home writing about Jennifer Harbury. She was in the news that month after almost single-handedly bringing down the military government of Guatemala. Jennifer, an American leftist lawyer, had spent the last three years demanding that the Guatemalan army exhume the body of her husband, a disappeared Indian rebel leader. Jennifer's story was so inspiring . . . and I was glad to've discovered it, even though my only motivation to write about her story was to take the heat off you. I'd cut back and forth between Jennifer and Efraim, me and "Derek Rafferty." You'd been so horrified to see your name in the last two stories and I thought if I could write about how love can change the world then I wouldn't have to write about you personally.

Fuck her once, she'll write a book about it, you or anybody else might say.

I was becoming you. When I pushed you from my thoughts you came back into my dreams. But now I had to prove my love for you was real by holding back and considering what you wanted. I had to act responsively, responsibly . . . I was spewing words and syntaxes I remembered reading in your book, *The Ministry of Fear.* . .

28. We talked awhile and drank some fruit juice. You liked the way I'd rearranged things in the motel room. (It was crammed with talismans and artworks that my LA friends had given me, thinking rightly that I needed some protection.) We looked at Sabina Ott's scratched-up yellow drawing, Daniel Marlos' photo of people with banana-dildos in the desert. You were intrigued by this, by images of sex that weren't heterosexual, a bit disturbed that dicks could be the butt of jokes. The photos of Keith

Richards and Jennifer Harbury—motifs for this bogus story about my fictional cowboy love for "Derek Rafferty"—scotch-taped to the wall didn't go unnoticed. We talked some more and you explained how you'd ignored me at the opening last night because everything was getting too referential. I understood. Then both of us were hungry. We ate lunch at a soul-food restaurant up on Washington and I told you all about the failure of my movie. Then you confessed how, over the past two years, you'd stopped reading. This broke my heart. Outside the store-front restaurant the East Pasadena Saturday afternoon was clanging. You paid the bill, then we drove my rental car up to the wilderness preserve above Lake Avenue.

"Let's go to But-ter-fly Creek!"

Walking up the dirt track along the still-green mountain, every-thing between us flattened out. You seemed so open. You told me all about yourself at 12 years old, a young boy sitting at the edge of a playing field somewhere in the English midlands, reading stories of great emperors and wars in Latin. You'd read your way into the world just like my husband. You told me other things about your life and what you'd left behind. You were so unhappy. Emotional seduction. The sun was very warm. When you took your shirt off you seemed to be inviting me to touch you but I refrained. To yearn responsibly. You had the softest palest skin, an alien's. "The Pacific starts here," I said. The landscape on the hill reminded me of New Zealand. . . .

There weren't any butterflies on the hill in Pasadena. But you come out to a clearing, and there's a waterfall, and then I told you how I admired you, and you said or you implied that what I'd done had helped you burn through some things in your life. And every-thing seemed as pliant as a macrocarpa branch, fragile as an egg.

29. In the blinding sunlight of the Vagabond Motel parking lot you asked me if I'd call again before I left LA. Perhaps we could have dinner. We embraced, and I was first to break away.

30. Sunday, April 9: Writing in my notebook after visiting Ray Johannson in Elysian Park: Bliss.

31. And so I called you up on Monday night. I was booked to leave at 10 pm on Tuesday. "The schizophrenic reacts violently when

any attempt is made to influence him. This is so because a lack of ego boundaries make it impossible for him to set limits of identification." (Roheim) The schizophrenic is a sexy Cyborg. When I reached you you were cold, ironic, wondering why I'd called. I hung up sweating. But I couldn't leave like this, I had to try and make it better.

I called you back, apologized, "I—I just felt like I had to ask you why you sounded so distant and defensive."

"Oh," you said. "I don't know. Was I defensive? I was just looking for something in my room."

I threw up twice before getting on the plane.

32. Dear Dick,

No woman is an island-ess. We fall in love in hope of anchoring ourselves to someone else, to keep from falling,

Love,
Chris

———

From Rhiannon, forty-four, an administration officer and resident of Sheffield, South Yorkshire, England. Rhiannon wrote the following letter to her ex, Simon* in 1998 after a relationship of four years came to an end via a note pinned to the front door, telling her it was over. Says Rhiannon, "It's not exactly a letter but a direct swipe at an ex-partner who spent four years trying to control me, often behaving more like a critical parent than a lover. For those four years I endured constant criticism about everything: the way I signed my name, the way I walked across the room, my clothes, my hair . . . everything. I could not even eat oranges because of the resulting mess. I never sent it, but wrote it for myself, as an affirmation of my control over my life, although I was not conscious of that at the time. It really was a vital part of the healing process."

Now you're gone I shall eat oranges and grow my hair long—even though you said it doesn't suit me. I'll deliberately forget to wash the bath after me and I won't call your mother on her birthday. Now that you're gone I shall get a cat—you always disliked cats, that should've warned me about *you* from the start. And I shall talk to it as if it understands me. And it probably will—better than you did, anyway. You won't be around to cringe with embarrassment when I do. Now that you're gone I shall play Elvis at 2 am and fry my bacon instead of grilling it. I shall eat an unhealthy diet—lots of sugar and junk food—and I won't cut my toe nails for a month, But when I do I shall do it in bed *and* leave the clippings there afterwards. On your side! I'm claiming my life back. I don't live by your rules anymore. I am a single entity. I'm one. I'm me. And I'm going to start by eating oranges.

———

From Trece, twenty-one, a medical records assistant in Maryland. The letter written when she was eighteen to her ex-boyfriend Quentin,* then twenty-one. Fourteen months before this letter was written, Latrece became pregnant, and, after the baby's birth, discovered that Quentin had been seeing a sixteen-year-old girl who, as it turns out, was also carrying his child. She never sent the letter.

[1999]

Dear ex,

I haven't told you the real reason why i can't forgive you but if i gave you a little insight as to why maybe just maybe you'd understand but then again maybe not. When I met you I didnt like you, you helped change that as we saw the different seasons change i noticed a change in the both of us a life forming inside me and you starting your life with someone else i have to admit you did cover your tracks pretty well when the baby came i saw alot of things in you i never imagined i thought it was me but it was clear the problem was not the times you ran yourself ragged around the house to keep me from finding out she slept over when you begged me to stay that same night yeah you remember that was the same night i almost ran you over what about when you got her pregnant and our baby wasn't even 3 mths whats funny is that you say you love both of us and don't want to chose well i chose for the both of us and even though i didnt break up with you you said i'd never find anyone who want me a single mother, someone did and it's been 2yrs and now you want me back maybe you should read this letter again if you still don't understand why there won't be a you and me anymore

p.s. These are the reasons its hard to forgive and forget you at the same time

trece

———·———

From Kim W., twenty-seven, a college student in California, to Tobey,* a man she met on match.com. She wrote the following two letters to him in April 2001 but sent only the second. "I sent the one I did out of anger but I think the other one, the longer, more thoughtful one is more powerful," she says. "Oh well, hindsight is 20/20."

Hi Tobey,

Well, you've made it obvious that you have no desire to talk to me. I'll leave you alone after I write this letter. I feel the need to explain myself a bit since I don't usually behave the way I did with you. Not that you care, you probably won't even read it. I need to write it for myself though.

You've hurt me. I know, that it is silly to let yourself be hurt by someone you've only met twice, but I'm a trusting person. I assume people aren't playing games and when you replied to my ad which makes it very clear that I am not just looking for a fling, I assumed that you were interested in connecting. That you wanted more than quick physical satisfaction.

Yes, I regret what happened that last night. I wouldn't have if you had called on Monday or even sometime early this week, but now, over a week later, having been stood up for the plans we made and never having heard from you, I do. That's not something I do easily (that night was an exception for me). I can count the number of men that's happened with on one hand. Lucky you. I guess that is all you wanted and I played right into your little game. I am innocent and naive sometimes. I wish I wasn't but I just don't understand that world. Why do people only want to connect on that physical level? Why in the world would anyone not want to get to know a person. Sex can be so much better with someone you know and trust. You get to know what the other person likes, you perfect the art of turning them on, you can do all the crazy stuff while feeling safe, laughing occasionally, and getting truly blown away by the pleasure of it all. Maybe it's different for men. Maybe you're more interested in the thrill of the newness, or the chase, or whatever. I don't know.

I truly am interested in connecting with someone and I felt like that was what was happening with us. Apparently I was wrong. Why would you respond to my ad? There are plenty of ads out there of women who are looking for a physical relationship. Why would you choose to hurt me? I just don't understand. Maybe I was too demanding, asking you to call me the next day. I like a little reassurance once I've been physical with someone. Maybe you thought I was the kind of woman who was going to demand time from you every day, or that I was looking for marriage or something. Who knows? I'm way too busy for that, and I believe that people need their space. I realize that I didn't do a good job of giving you space this week. I was so bewildered by your not calling. I honestly thought something must have happened to you. You had seemed so interested in me, and then you stood me up. You seemed so sincere when you were telling me all about your childhood and the issues around your father's death. You should go into acting.

Please don't prey on other women like this. You're hurting people. Maybe it's all a game to you, but it's not to us. There are women who will play the game with you, but make sure you're both on the same page before you begin. I know you were hurt growing up, that much was obvious. Perhaps that has led you to want to hurt others now. I don't know. I don't understand. If you ever want to explain it to me, I'd love to hear. Maybe it was something I did, or maybe it's something in you. Call me or write if you're interested.

Goodbye Tobey,

Good luck finding something that will soothe your soul.

Here is the letter Kim W. actually sent.

You are the spineless little prick of a maggot, eating it's [sic] way through the shit of a diseased camel which is laying on the dirty, cracked cement floor of a small, poorly run zoo somewhere in small town america.

At first I was confused, then I was hurt. I don't do what I did with you very often. Now I remember why. Now, I'm angry. You are a weak, spineless, poor excuse for a man. Thanks so much for replying to my ad, it's obvious that you were truly looking to connect with someone.

Kim

———

From writer Elizabeth Hayt, forty, to Anthony Joseph Costagliola,* a man she dated briefly in the late summer and fall of 2001. The two met when Costagliola came to Hayt's Upper East Side apartment to install some drapery she had ordered. "He was gorgeous," Hayt says, "so of course I had to ask him out." The two made a plan to visit the Whitney Museum of American Art, but Costagliola canceled at the last minute, saying he was sick.

Hayt's next attempt was more successful: The two had a successful dinner date and soon began seeing one another on a regular basis. "I fell in love with him, as girls are wont to do with guys who have a high emotional IQ and are good in bed," laughs Hayt. But a few weeks into the relationship, Costagliola announced he was moving to Europe to find himself; and, while there, ignored Hayt's repeated E-mails requesting that he return a few possessions she had lent him.

This note was in response to a particularly patronizing E-mail he eventually sent. "Last thing I heard he was moving to South Africa with a woman he met in London who quit her job for him," says Hayt. "It just goes to show the power of the prick."

August 2001

Dear Anthony,

if you didn't have a goatee and thumb ring, I might have paid attention when you told me you were born in a heroin clinic and had been arrested for dealing drugs in your 20's.

if you didn't laugh at everything i said and told me i was beautiful and sexy, i might have paid attention when you said you were a born-again christian.

if you weren't both handy around the house and carried a well-worn copy of Anna Karenina, i might have paid attention that you smoked two-packs a day and drank two bottles of wine by yourself every night.

if you didn't invite me to go to italy with you, i might have paid attention when you told me about the ex-girlfriend who took a baseball bat to all your stuff after you went out with another woman.

if you didn't have such a great body, i might have paid attention that you didn't have a job.

if i wasn't blinded by my own hormones and romantic hopes, i might have paid attention that being a good fuck doesn't change the fact that you're a total loser.

---·---

From "Rebecca" to "Randy," as posted on SoThere.com, a Web site that publishes a different unsent letter every day. The site, begun in late

1997, describes itself as "your chance to get it off your chest. To say what should have been said a long time ago. Or yesterday. It's a chance to take it back, or to finally say it out loud . . . It's about getting it out and letting it go. It's about closure." The majority of the letters on the Web site were written by women to men with whom they had once been romantically involved.

October 18, 2001

Randy,

For three and a half years you have been my life. All I've been able to see is you and all I've been able to think about is the way things were going to be when you finally got yourself together and realized that you and I are perfect when we're together. I've never blamed you for keeping me waiting, because you could do nothing wrong in my eyes. We've circled each other for so long, sometimes coming together and sometimes drifting apart. Either way, you've always been in the front of my mind and I've always been in the back of yours. That all has to stop.

I want you to know that you no longer have me to fall back on. You can no longer pick me up and drop me down whenever it's convenient for you to care about me. I never noticed that you did that until now. The person I've been for the past three years has had everything to do with you. The person I am about to become at the close of this letter will have everything to do with me. It's about time I learn who I am in relation to myself instead of in relation to you. You've had so long to do something about us and you've now missed your chance. In doing so, you've missed me and I hope you realize that you miss a lot in effect. There are so many things I want to say to you, but the only one that I think you'll really hear is simply, "goodbye". I still love you as a person, but I've realized that I finally love myself more.

Love,
Rebecca

———

From writer/comedian Lynn Harris, thirty-three, author of <u>Breakup</u>
<u>*Girl to the Rescue! A Superhero's Guide to Love, and Lack Thereof*</u>
(2000), to Daniel,* thirty-two, her ex-boyfriend of eight months. The
two started dating in April 2000, explains Lynn, and the relationship
became serious very quickly: "I was sure he was the one," she says. "We
talked about kids, their names, where to raise them. I even went to Paris
with him and his family after only six weeks."

Three months into the relationship Daniel "started drifting" and
a few months later Lynn confronted him. "I finally did the you-
don't-bring-me-flowers thing," she says, "and he had no response
other than to vanish." They broke up that December. "This hap-
pened four days before I got laid off from my dream job, and shortly
after my dog had died," says Lynn. "Cue country song." She wrote
the letter on the one-year anniversary of their breakup. She was
tempted to send it, she says, but is now glad that her mom convinced
her otherwise.

[December 2001]

Dear Daniel,

I heard that you and Mattie were moving to Duluth.

I wish I were in a position to wish you the best.

On the one hand, I'm totally over you. You are a non-issue for
me—a non-entity, even.

On the other, well, do you remember saying that when you told
me you loved me, you meant it at the time?

Well, when I told you I forgave you, I meant it at the time.

There are some things I need to say—and for you to hear—even
now, months later, even now that I have moved on. Back then, for
the sake of my own dignity and closure—I let you off far, far too
easily. It's not THAT things ended, it's HOW things ended—HOW
you treated me—that is and will remain unforgivable. You had the

opportunity to handle a painful and tricky situation with dignity and respect, and you blew it.

After eight months, Paris, talk of sapphires vs. emeralds, combined-income math . . . just disappearing—literally LEAVING THE STATE for work—without telling me, when, though things were weird between us, I was still your girlfriend? Telling me later you honestly "didn't even have a moment" to call? Same week, not calling me when I went home to my parents to PUT MY DOG TO SLEEP? Even if we HAD been fighting, Daniel. As long as she is your girlfriend, she goes home to put her beloved dog to sleep, you call her. It is the law.

By the way, I broke up with you that weekend, the dog weekend. By myself. I just didn't get around to telling you until you, you know, had a moment.

All that because you didn't have the decency, or the balls, to look me in the eye and say "I'm so sorry, but I've just got to go."

"Self-absorbed," "selfish," "childish," even "cruel" doesn't begin to cover it. It's not that I think you're a bad person, it's that I think you're not a whole person. It's as if you're missing the part of oneself that understands that others—friends, lovers, whoever—also have not only flaws, but, more important, feelings. The part of oneself that allows one to have a true, giving, loving, lasting relationship with anyone. I hope, for Mattie's sake, that you've changed.

Lynn

———

A letter she wishes she'd written from Molly Jong-Fast, twenty-four, author of Normal Girl *(Villard, 2000), to the first boy she ever loved. "I was sixteen and too young to know better; he was in his twenties, married, a compusive gambler, and a neurotic mess," says Jong-Fast. "And he dropped me like a hot potato for a girl who worked in a video store." If he is reading this, she adds, "I thank him for all the CDs he left at my house. It was the least he could do."*

Married Fashion Designer
4 Married Man Way
Designertown, Manland.

Dear Almost-Famous-Married-Fashion-Designer,
    It's over.
    Here's what's no longer working for me:
    The wife, the kids, the drugs, the hookers, the escorts (I know
they're almost the same thing), the vomiting in my car, the gam-
bling, the modelizing, the 3am booty calls, the Hilton sisters (you
know what I'm referring to), the 4am trips to Atlantic City, the
drinking my little brother's Codeine cough syrup to see if you can
get a buzz on, the chair throwing, the unanswered phone calls, the
nights at Fox Woods making me pay for every meal, your diva fits
and jealous rages about Michael Kors and Marc Jacobs, the 5am
trips to see the dealer, that darn Robert Downey Jr. (doesn't he
have somewhere else he needs to be), the nights at Wax, the nights
at the new (new-old as opposed to new-new) Spy Bar, the nights
at The Tenth Street Lounge, the After Hours Clubs (Save The
Robots and Brownies are the worst offenders), the little unmarked
clubs on the Lower East Side, the cheating, the screaming, the
dish throwing, the late night door banging, the bloody noses, the
endless cigarettes, the numb gums, the nights that end at 10am,
the walks home when my body feels beyond dead, these are the
things that no longer work for me. Here are the things I will do
now that you are no longer in my life: I will make my bed, learn
to dance the waltz, swim every morning at the Y, do my own
laundry, visit my parents, remember to feed the dog, remember to
call my dying grandpa every day just to tell him 'I love him', walk
the dog, go for long bike rides in the country, make Christmas
cookies in the summer and press flowers. I will not drink, not
smoke, not snort everything I can find, not drive drunk, not crash
my car into my parents garage door, not practice death, not hope
the plane crashes, not want to die because you haven't called. I will

not call your house and hang up. I will go back to school and graduate college. I will not drive by your house and hang-up on your lovely wife as she breathes lightly into the phone. I will do the crossword every day. I will read the paper cover to cover. I will fold everything including the dog. I will read all the great books including *Middlemarch,* which I will read twice. I will mop the floors until they bleed. I will be the kind of person who owns only beautiful furniture and knick-knacks. I will only eat organic things. I will brush my hair a hundred times a-day. I will give up flour. I will do Power Yoga. I will eat less salt. I will stop with the potato chips. I will lose those last ten pounds. I will not think about you all the time. I will read only Fay Weldon novels. I will become the girl you dumped me for and then dump you again and again and again and again and again and again and again and again. You get the point. It's over. Self-destruction and nihilism are so passe, so '90s.

So good-bye
moll.

———

From novelist Lucinda Rosenfeld, now thirty-two, then nineteen, to an ex-boyfriend ("X"). Rosenfeld says that she honestly can't remember much about him other than the fact that she was in love with the guy. Her first novel, What She Saw . . . *(Random House, 2000), chronicles fifteen years of a girl's life (from age eleven to twenty-five), as told through her encounters with fifteen different members of the male species, most of them old boyfriends, but some of them pen pals and con men. None of the characters in* What She Saw . . . *bear any resemblance to any one Rosenfeld has ever met, including the guy to whom this letter is addressed. She is currently working on a still-untitled second novel; a sequel, of sorts, to* What She Saw . . . *It is due out from HarperCollins in the fall of 2003.*

"Embarrassing and Pretentious College-Era Love Letter I'm Glad I Never Sent"

Dear X:

"Oh no," you say. "Another letter."

Well, I have decided that life is one long greeting card—a string of clichés. Language never does justice to the truth; words seem so inadequate right now. Maybe this is because my life is no more than a cliché. And yet, I would prefer to think it was more complex than everyone else's.

I have heard no word from you in recent weeks. All of my better judgment tells me that I must let you go. But I can't stand the idea that I can't have what I want. It all seems so unfair! Why am I the one left feeling abandoned by you (and not vice versa)? Yes, I must let you go and disappear into your world, of which I have no part. We are really of no use to each other except as lovers. . . .

The problem is that I couldn't give a shit about better judgment.

A year ago at this time I had so many more illusions—or maybe I should say, delusions.

This year, I have decided to reject everything I ever believed in, including superstition, feminism, manners, wisdom, truth, beauty, astrology, science, psychoanalysis, love, romance, diligence, marriage, families, the work ethic, culture, classical music, liberalism, manipulating men (it always back-fires), good and evil, tennis, and washing your hair every day.

Now I have nothing to believe in; whether or not you believe it, this is partly your fault/influence. Now I am a wandering soul in search of a new identity. You, on the other hand, are more secure than ever. . . .

Oh, X, how can you be so cold and indifferent to me?! I am so angry at you for making me feel useless and ridiculous. Why did you bother to make me fall in love with you when it was all so meaningless to you? I will never understand what kind of kicks you got from watching me grow jealous, unhappy, and demoralized.

You have no idea what it has been like for me. I guess you never bothered to think about it. Does it not bother you that you have hurt me like this?

And why does everything seem so tragic?! (Am I just adolescent, or is this the nature of existence?) Maybe I should just find someone in life to blame. (You are certainly one possibility.)

I have always told you that the only way I could get you out of my system was to hate you. Well, I have almost reached that point.

Except when I wake up in the morning, sometimes, I have these terrible longings; I try to recreate what it was like waking up with you. I miss you so much. All I have ever wanted to know is that you care.

Good-bye, X. (I am saying it out loud with a cigarette in the left hand and a glass of wine in the right.)

I chain-smoke thinking about what I have lost.

With many sighs attached,

L.

———

The following is a series of letters Leigh L., a writer and filmmaker living in Los Angeles wishes she'd written. Addressed to ex-boyfriends, the letters offer to the years of Leigh's life between 1991 and 2001.

Dear Brian,

Thanks for taking my virginity and then telling everyone in high school that I was tight. It was really romantic doing it for the first time on your bunk bed. Oh, and thanks for telling all of your friends that I thought a gold coin condom was actually hannukah gelt. I guess that comes with being a good Jewish girl in bed with a Mexican.

Dear Josh,

Thanks for telling me my kisses taste like a 40 ounce of Old English. You're the only one to ever tell me that I taste like cheap beer. Can I also thank you for something disturbing, yet memorable? I'm talking about the time I didn't listen to you when you told me never to come over to your house without calling first. You see, when your 500 pound agoraphobic mother answered the door and screamed at the top of her emphysema-plagued lungs "Blonde girl at the door, HELP! Call the cops," well, that was priceless.

Dear Sam,

Thanks for picking me up in your yellow hippie van and for introducing me to Pink Floyd. I really liked it when I told you how nice you smelled and then you suddenly reached in your flannel pocket and introduced me to Patchouli oil. Thank you for bringing your twisted psycho friend Neal to my best friend's birthday party so he could use his car club to beat the shit out of my best friend's sister's boyfriend. He's now deaf in one ear. Then again, you know this because you were wrongly arrested that night and ended up having your lawyer show up at my doorstep with a subpoena. Thanks for dumping me flat on my young ass. Maybe that's why I hear you're a born-again Christian these days. Though it's not always instant, I guess karma gets ya.

Dear Paul,

Thanks for force-feeding me marijuana whilst bumping and grinding me on your full-sized water bed. Thanks for taking me to my first Grateful Dead show and then leaving me in the parking lot without my ticket. It wouldn't have been so scary if you hadn't slipped me a tab of acid. I thought you were joking when you wanted to put a little piece of paper with a happy face on the top of my tongue. Thanks for cheating on me and getting her pregnant. At least it wasn't me. Thanks for stealing my parent's sacred collection of vinyl records. I stole them back one night when you passed out on your own front lawn.

Dear Christian,

Thanks for letting me take your Panamanian virginity away. Thanks for never calling me. Thanks for pretending you didn't know me when I ran into you at the college student center. Thanks for coming out of the closet as a grade-A homosexual. Now I don't feel so bad.

Dear Will,

Thanks for giving me a peck on the cheek under the mistletoe hanging in the doorway of your dorm room. Thanks for introducing me to Kung-Fu by absolute default. At the time, I was only pretending I loved martial arts in hopes that you would one day love me. I hear you joined the army after college and ended up marrying some British chick. But that one meaningless peck got me through a semester of longing. I really have a thing for Kung-Fu these days.

Dear Johnny,

Thanks for turning down my offer for sex after a 4 hour make-out session. Thanks for puking on my bathroom floor and passing out in my bathtub. Now I know how to clean up someone else's vomit. Thanks for all the times you made me pay for dinner and coffee and movies and everything else. Thanks for the time we were in the editing room and you decided it was the perfect time for sex. Thanks for manipulating me with foreplay to the point where I stripped down completely only to be humiliated when our professor opened the door and saw my tits. Rumor has it that you can't really get it up anyway. But I'll never know, will I?

Dear David,

Thanks for being 9 years older and introducing me to the hair on your back. Did I mention that all of your hair was red? Thanks for telling me that I was immature when in reality I was just WAY YOUNGER than your so-called "mature" self. Thanks to your mother for moving to LA at the climax of our relationship. Thanks for inviting her to join us on all of our evening outings. I really enjoyed dating the both of you. Thanks for letting me break your heart. I realized it was actually possible for me to crumble someone else's heart. I hear you're engaged now. That really pisses me off. The only thing I'm engaged in is my own self-serving analysis. L'Chaim!

Dear Zack,

Thank you for turning me on with your graffiti. Thanks for letting me fuck my friend over by sleeping with you, the guy she was cheating on her boyfriend with. Thanks for being a drug addict and a manic-depressive and thanks for stealing close to ten thousand dollars. Thanks for the crabs. Thanks for the hip-hop. Thanks for your drug-dealings. Thanks for the trip to Arkansas and thanks for letting me experience my one and only redneck Christmas. Thanks for leaving my heart swollen and heavy. Thanks for leaving me poor and alone. I have one of your paintings hanging on my wall. I wish I could throw it away but who knows, maybe it will be worth something one day . . . that is . . . when you quit your job at the Little Rock Budget Rent-a-Car and take up your art.

Dear Rapper,

Thanks for letting me add a newly-signed rap artist to my sexual collection. Thanks for introducing me at Brother's BBQ to DMX and Eve and other Ruff Riders. These are the one-night stands that stick like a one-hit wonder. I felt like a homie for one hapless night. Thanks for never calling me again. Had you called me, I might have had a more juicy story. I'll never forget you, thanks to your weekly appearances on the music charts and TRL. I'm sure I'm not the only one.

Dear Max,

Thanks for nothing but the smallest penis ever—probably worthy of Guinness Book status. Thanks for taking me out for my birthday on your parent's credit card. Thanks for telling me that you and your father had a long talk about our sex life. Thanks for telling me what your therapist really thinks of me. Thanks for buying me a shitty book of poetry for my birthday. Thanks for telling me your email password and not thinking that I'd eventually check it out. Thanks for the completely traumatic things I read when I did the evil deed of checking your email. Thank you for breaking up with me. My mother said you were the ugliest guy I've ever gone out with. Thank you for sucking the energy out of eight months of my precious life. Thank you for nothing at all.

Dear Ethan,

Thanks for telling me that you've had a change of heart—that you've switched from Christ being your lord savior to cocaine being your lord savior. I was so very turned on by that idiotic comment. Thanks for a few months of good sex and bad dialogue. Thanks for getting back together with your ex-girlfriend the very second I went on a one month vacation to Spain. Thanks for calling me a few months later and sharing your distaste for your current girlfriend and asking if I would be into having an affair with you. I said no. I set boundaries. I was STRONG! Adios to you! And thank you for nothing but good sex and a sudden surprise of victory.

————

From Chandra,* a Yale University student, to a boyfriend/best-friend ("now vehemently ex- in both respects") after attending his twenty-third *birthday party. She was going to send it, "but at the burn-no-bridges advice of friends I refrained from doing so, and decided simply never to speak to him again." Of her ex, she says: "Basically, [he's] one of those people whom everyone loves and makes them believe he loves them in return, then abdicates all emotional responsibility and even interpersonal decency (e.g., returning a phone call) when they need him most. He is a wealthy, well-educated yet thoroughly bourgeois faux bohemian who drinks, smokes, takes drugs, sleeps with random girls, all in the name of exploring the limits of pleasurable human experience. I was much younger when I developed for him an affinity, the stupidity of which baffles me now."*

[2002]

Ellis,*

One imagines a birthday to be an index of incremental maturity. Yet you remain the natural liar, emotional coward, thoughtless hypocrite I always thought you'd outgrow.

Endear, equivocate, reconcile; be, in O'Hara's words, "specific and disloyal." Iterate and you have a winning strategy. Others in their own neediness will eagerly forgive, in their stupidity overlook. You can believe you intentions are honorable. Your friends, loving the parts of you they know and misinferring the parts they do not, will rush to your defense. Deny all you wish, cite charisma as victim. As usual, it will only confirm your fraudulent obliviousness and your self-alienation.

I am uninterested in uni-directionality. Intellectual conversations with you have been embarrassingly remedial, personal interactions cavalierly Elliscentric, social situations consistently shallow. From beginning to end, knowing you has been a protracted and painful waste.

Lest you mismap my motives, recall that you have never known me.

cd

The
Goodbye
Letter

Good•bye (good-bī´) ´*n.* an expression of farewell.

The Goodbye Letter *n.* A breakup letter in which the writer bids a final adieu to a husband, boyfriend, or suitor, often discouraging further contact.

From Julie de Lespinasse (1732–1776) to Jacques Antoine Hippolyte, Comte de Guibert (1743–1790). Lespinasse, the celebrated French hostess of an influential salon, was plucked from a her life as a governess in her teens by the reigning Parisian hostess, Madame du Deffand, who remade her into a companion and assistant. In 1764 Deffand, increasingly jealous of Lespinasse's popularity and vigor, dismissed her from the salon, and Lespinasse soon set up one of her own. In 1773 Lespinasse met and became infatuated with Guibert, a French military thinker and writer (Essai generale de tactique, 1772) whose theories of tactical maneuvering influenced Napoleon and Frederick the Great. Guibert, however, did not reciprocate her passion and eventually married another woman, Mademoiselle de Courcelles. Lespinasse, now three years into her torment over Guibert, is said to have died of an overdose of opium or a broken heart the same month this letter was written.

Letter 238

Saturday, 4 o'clock, May, 1776

You are too good, too kind, my friend. You would like to revive and sustain a mind which is at last sinking beneath the weight of a long-continued grief. I feel all the value of what you offer me, but I no longer deserve it.

There was a time when to be loved by you would have left me nothing to desire; alas! Perhaps it would have smothered my regrets, or at least softened their bitterness. I should have wanted to live; today I want nothing but to die. There can be no amends, no consolation for the loss I have suffered; I ought not to have survived it. That, my friend, is the only trace of bitterness towards you which I can find in my heart. But, Heavens, how much the fatal impulse which attracted you to me at that moment has cost me in tears and pain, and in the end my life is sinking under it.

I should much like to know your destiny; I should like you to be happy in your circumstances, for your character and your emotions will never make you very unhappy. I received your letter at one o'clock; I had a burning fever. I cannot tell you how much time and labour it cost me to read it; I did not want to put it off until to-day, and that almost made me delirious.

I hope to have news of you this evening.

Good-bye, my friend; if ever I come back to life, I should like to spend it again in loving you, but there is no time left.

———

From <u>Vindication of the Rights of Women</u> *(1792) author Mary Woll-stonecraft (1759–1797) to Gilbert Imlay (1754–1828) a writer (<u>The Emigrants</u>, 1794) and former officer during the American Revolution. Wollstonecraft met Imlay in Paris in 1793 and, although they never married, Imlay registered Wollstonecraft as his wife at the American embassy in France. The two had a daughter, Fanny, in May 1794— but the relationship soon turned sour, with Imlay traveling extensively, behaving icily, and conducting affairs with other women. Deeply hurt, Wollstonecraft attempted suicide in October 1795 by flinging herself into the Thames. She later married English political writer and novelist William Godwin (1756–1836). Their daughter was Mary Wollstone-craft Shelley, author of <u>Frankenstein.</u>*

[London, ca. March 1796]

You must do as you please with respect to the child.—I could wish that it might be done soon, that my name may be no more mentioned to you. It is now finished.—Convinced that you have neither regard nor friendship, I disdain to utter a reproach, though I have had reason to think, that the "forbearance" talked of, has not been very delicate.—It is however of no consequence.—I am glad you are satisfied with your own conduct.

I now solemnly assure you, that this is an eternal farewell.—Yet I flinch not from the duties which tie me to life.

That there is "sophistry" on one side or other, is certain; but now it matters not on which. On my part it has not been a question of

words. Yet your understanding or mine must be strangely warped—
for what you term "delicacy," appears to me to be exactly the contrary. I have no criterion for morality, and have thought in vain, if
the sensations which lead you to follow an ancle or step, be the
sacred foundation of principle and affection. Mine has been of a
very different nature, or it would not have stood the brunt of your
sarcasms.

The sentiment in me is still sacred. If there be any part of me that
will survive the sense of my misfortunes, it is the purity of my affections. The impetuosity of your senses, may have led you to term
mere animal desire, the source of principle; and it may give zest to
some years to come.—Whether you will always think so, I shall
never know.

It is strange that, in spite of all you do, something like conviction
forces me to believe, that you are not what you appear to be.

I part with you in peace.

[Unsigned]

---

*From poet and novelist Charlotte (Turner) Smith (1749–1806),
author of such novels as Emmeline (1788) and The Old Manor House
(1793), to her husband Benjamin Smith (1742–1806). In 1765, at
the age of fifteen, she married Smith, the twenty-three-year-old son of a
West Indian merchant. He soon proved to be violent, selfish, and financially irresponsible, at one point fleeing to France to escape creditors.
Charlotte regretted the marriage, describing herself to her friend Sarah
Rose as "sold a legal prostitute" and, shortly after her wedding, even
writing to her sister about it:*

> *"No disadvantage could equal those I sustained; the more my
> mind expanded, the more I became sensible of personal slavery;
> the more I improved and cultivated my understanding, the far-
> ther I was removed from those with whom I was condemned to*

pass my life; and the more clearly I saw by these newly-aquainted lights the horror of the abyss into which I unconsciously plunged."

In 1874, at age thirty-seven and the mother of twelve children, Charlotte left her husband.
This letter was written to him sixteen years after their separation.

Frant 1st March 1803

Sir,

I have only to repeat in answer to your second lunatic Letter re[ceive]d to day, that if you will have the £400 & know how to get it, there is no occasion for me to enter with you into any treaty about it. It is Lord Egremont to whom you must apply, & if his Lordship chuses to let you have it, it is nothing to me. I never said, Mr Benjn Smith, that I would pay you the 400[pounds] on such & such conditions, for it is not and never could be mine to pay, nor have I the least power over it. I said that if you would suffer the business to go on to a conclusion under the direction of *two* friends of your own, without tormenting Lord Egremont any more, I would then exert myself to get in the rest of the Debts due in Barbadoes, & take that trouble for want of which they will be lost, & I said that these two friends should be put in possession of the residue on your account, of course I could not well starve you as you now do me and my poor unhappy children. Your cause must indeed be a wretched one that you dare not leave to two friends of your own. But I shall canvass nothing with you, wretched compound of folly and wickedness—The Curse of your whole family—a being who disgraces the name of Man and the object at once of abhorrence and contempt.

There are means to *make* you do your Duty, and to those, they who depend on you must be compelled to have recourse.

For my own part, I will answer no more of your Letters nor trouble myself any more about you. The very sight of your sprawling hand is hateful to my Eyes, and the evident proof you give of your insanity, which is of a species not to excite pity but horror, humbles me so much that I sicken to think I have given birth to creatures who may partake and I fear will of your diabolical disposition. Unnatural, barbarous, selfish, hateful in the sight of Heaven and a Burthen to the Earth.

Do what you will with your nonsense & your *ultimatum*. Go to Law; get into Chancery. Take Rope enough & hang yourself. I shall not cut you down. I have written to Lord Egremont & desired him to go directly to Chancery. I really do not care one farthing what you do.

I leave this place this Evening with your unhappy Harriett, dearer to you than "the ruddy drops that visit your *bad* heart", but you should have written bilious and poisonous for ruddy, for not one drop of human blood have you in that piece of putrid flesh which you wear quasi heart. Not one sensation that belongs to a Man or a Gentleman.

Eight and thirty years have you now been my tormentor. Here it ends—for you shall not have the *power* of worrying me any more.

If Lord Egremont chuses it, he may pay you the £400, but I cannot advise it as I know it is his own wish.

I cannot sign a name I detest.

I shall certainly advise Miss Smith and the Legatees, & *all* your Children who are all interested, not to consent to giving you 400 [pounds]. If you are in Debt, you ought not to be, and you have robbed them too much already.

But what need this *if* you can get the money by force.

I shall leave Orders with the Postmaster here to return any Letters that may come after I am gone with the Hamilton Postmark.

From "The Yellow WallPaper" (1892) author and feminist Charlotte Perkins Gilman (1860–1935) to her husband, the painter Charles Walter Stetson (1858–1911). The letter from Gilman was recorded in

Stetson's diary, dated June 15, 1888, while the two were living apart. The two met in 1882 and, after repeated proposals on Stetson's part, Gilman married him in 1884, though not without her own internal conflicts about marriage and her role as a wife. These conflicts— which may or may not have contributed to Gilman's struggle with depression—doomed the marriage and, in 1888, a little over four years after their wedding, Gilman left him. In her autobiography, The Living of Charlotte Perkins Gilman *(1935), Gilman says that her ex-husband was "quite the greatest man, near my own age, that I had ever known" and that Stetson was bitter with grief and loss after the divorce. In his diary, Stetson wrote that Gilman's letter "seems to have laid a heavy hand on my heart, half suffocating me, and making a lump in my throat" and that he could never love again and "should never trust love again." The two divorced in 1894, and Gilman remarried in 1900.*

[June 1888]

I'm not homesick a bit, don't think of missing you and am getting well so fast. I am astonished at myself. I haven't felt *unhappy* once since I left. The fogs and mists are rolling away; I begin to feel alive and self-respecting. Oh the difference! You are very dear to me my love; but there is no disguising the fact that my health and work lie not with you but away from you.

———

From Paula Modersohn-Becker (1876–1907) a German painter, to her husband, the painter Otto Modersohn (1865–1943), with whom she battled emotionally and artistically (he was also an artist). She eventually returned to Otto after this letter was written, but died a little over a year later of an embolism after the birth of a daughter. In two letters previous to this one, dated March and April 1906, Paula asked Otto to try to get used to the idea of their going separate ways, and told him that it hurt her to cause him pain and suffering.

Paris, 15, avenue de Maine

September 3, 1906

Dear Otto,

The time is getting closer for you to be coming. Now I must ask you for your sake and mine, please spare both of us this time of trial. Let me go, Otto. I do not want you as my husband. I do not want it. Accept this fact. Don't torture yourself any longer. Try to let go of the past—I ask you to arrange all other things according to your wishes and desires. If you still enjoy having my paintings, then pick out those you wish to keep. Please do not take any further steps to bring us back together. It would only prolong the torment.

I must still ask you to send money, one final time. I ask now for the sum of five hundred marks. I am going to the country for a while now, so please send it to B. Hoetger, 108, rue Vaugirard. During this time I intend to take steps to secure my livelihood.

I thank you for all the goodness that I have had from you. There is nothing else I can do.

Your Paula Modersohn

The following letter was written by Dora Carrington (1893–1932) to her lover Gerald Brenan (1894–1987), an army man, and the best friend of her husband Ralph Partridge (1894–1960). In June 1922 Partridge found out about the two through his own jealous mistress and demanded a meeting with Brenan, in which he grilled him about the particulars of the relationship. Partridge then forbade Carrington to write to Brenan, and the two spent a number of months out of contact with one another, until the prohibition was repealed, that December. Even when they began corresponding again, however, things did not improve: Not only was Partridge jealous of Brenan, but Brenan was jealous of Partridge, and felt neglected. The letter was written after

Carrington had received a letter from Brenan in which he asked her not to write (they were back together the next month). Throughout Carrington's life, and despite her marriage—which was often less than fulfilling—she shared a deep and abiding love for writer Lytton Strachey. Despondent over Strachey's death from cancer in January 1932, Carrington fatally shot herself that next March.

Friday morning, 10:30 [November 7th, 1924]
Ham Spray House, Hungerford

Amigo, I have written you two long letters—one last night immediately after you telephoned and another this morning. I thought about our relation and you continuously all night. I feel rather tired in consequence this morning. Nothing has really altered I see since last Thursday evening. Your telephone message last night confirmed that it was madness to believe the calmness of your letter in the morning. I get on your nerves you yourself admit, and you are constantly filled with suspicions. I can't help feeling our relation is in a bad state. I care, passionately, for a better relation. If it's impossible I would rather have no relation than these agitations, and unhappinesses. *You* can't be unhappy without affecting *me*. I have come to the conclusion after thinking very hard that it is best to keep to the conclusion we came to last Thursday. Not to see, or write to each [other] for some months until we both feel quite tranquil and altered and that you are working again without nervous agitations.

Forgive the incoherence of this letter, but I am as tired of writing as I am of thinking about it. I have written two long letters already. The real truth is I know I can't make you happy in the way you want, and I can't bear to be the person who makes you unhappy, so I want to go away from everything for a time.

I won't see you again, and I rely on you to promise to tell me when you want to see me again later. I shall never stop caring for you. I hate myself for making you a single hour unhappy.

Let us remember last Thursday evening and write no more—That was a perfect momentary parting.

It mattered, and still matters that you care for me.

You will always wire for me, if you are ill.

I cannot say any more because I am too gloomy, I am glad to have that last letter from you because it matters so much to me that you care. But please believe I have come to this decision after a great deal of thinking and through caring for you. My fondest love my dear one.

Yr Cirod

PS Please don't write back I feel I can't bear any more thinking, or decisions.

From Laurel Stalla, thirty-nine, to Josh, her ex-boyfriend, with whom she lived for six years. After Josh took a job in Hong Kong and moved, Stalla packed up their house, found new homes for their pets, and prepared to meet him in Hawaii where they would get married, then continue on with him to Hong Kong. "He kept putting me off for months," says Stalla. "He finally broke up over the phone with me a year ago New Year's Day."

Stalla later found out that he met someone else while he was abroad, and wrote this letter—following many angry ones—after she accepted the fact that she needed to move on. "It's been a year now and it has been very hard and slow but I have moved on," she says. "I know now that we weren't meant to be a match but we were both comfortable and lazy in our relationship . . . and that he is a blistering boil on a goat's ass!"

June 13, 2001

Josh,

I parked across from our old house on Knollwood. For some reason I had the urge to walk the dog over there.

The first thing I did was stand in front of the house and stare. I saw MY old whiskey barrel right where I left it. This time there were no pansies in it.

I let Woo sniff around. I thought maybe she would remember. She may have. I took our old route. God, that street was beautiful. I remember every thought I ever had during those walks. The deer were still in the same yards. The ceramic duck was still front of that lady's house. I saw the exact spot where Woo collapsed the first time that we took her for a walk when she was a pup.

The smell of the blooming magnolias were in the air. I used to love that scent on those hot humid nights. I used to imagine what it would be like to live in one of those huge houses. I wondered how I would landscape each yard. What it would be like to play football on the big grassy front lawns on Thanksgiving Day. What it would be like to live there with my family for years and years. That seemed to be the ultimate sense of security.

I remembered the fights that we had. I couldn't even recall what one subject was. I just remember feeling pain and crying. Even through that, I still had the illusion that everything would work it's [sic] self out and that the disagreements were a normal part of a relationship.

It seemed as if the hills were so much easier for me to walk up this time. I realized that was the only place I ever lived that made me feel at home. I felt I was a part of a great neighborhood. I felt that if I surrounded myself with things that I want to strive for, that I would eventually achieve it. I felt like I belonged there. Was it because of you?

Years ago that was the beginning of our life together. Today I went to say goodbye to that life. I have a new life now. I didn't want one, but I have one. I am pleased with what I have created out of the rubble that you left for me. I may never understand why you left, but you did. I am doing the best that I can now. My heart died with you but will be revived with someone else, some other day. You took away what we had but you haven't stolen away the dream of it. If home is where the heart is, I guess I am homeless.

Laurel

———

From Alex Kuczynski, thirty-two, a reporter for the <u>New York Times</u>, to her ex-boyfriend, M., forty, a venture capitalist. After dating for six months, Kuczynski called off the relationship because of M's erratic behavior and frequent disappearances. Seeking a second chance, M suggested that he and Kuczynski see a couples therapist; she agreed. "A few days later I called a former girlfriend of M's who lived in another city," recalls Kuczynski. "Her number had been appearing with increasing regularity on M's Caller ID." During the course of the conversation the woman revealed to Kuczynski that she was no former girlfriend of M's, but a current one, meaning that M had been lying to the two women on what Kuczynski calls "a sociopathological scale." More disturbingly, he'd taken the other woman to a couples therapist the very same week of his appointment with Kuczynski. When confronted with the deceit, M swore he would never see the other woman again, asked Kuczynski to marry him and proposed going to City Hall the very next day. She declined. "In the months that followed, he sent dozens of roses and gifts of expensive jewelry," remembers Kuczynski. "He sent eight dozen roses on what would have been the eight-month anniversary of our first meeting. He sent volumes of poetry and pictures of himself. He had friends call and and attest to his otherwise sterling character. And on the one-year anniversary of our meeting, he sent a love poem he had scripted by a calligrapher." Many months later, after Sept. 11, he called again, tearful, begging for Kuczynski to come back and, failing that, for her forgiveness. She refused. Instead, she threw away his letters, books, cards, photographs and poetry, and sold the jewelry to a dealer, who gave her a very good price for the lot. Kuczynski was married in the fall of 2002 to a man who is nothing like M.

September 21 2001

Dearest M.:

It is Friday the end of two long weeks and I have thought long and hard about whether I can see you and talk to you.

Do you know the Whitman poem "Of the Terrible doubt of

Appearances"? A section from *Leaves of Grass.* It is one of my favorites. First, because I understood it so well for so long—that love is a chimera, and that we must always mistrust the shadows—and then when we started dating, it again became a favorite, because for a brief time I really believed that I no longer, in fact never would, have to doubt those appearances. And now, it is so bitterly sad: I see that all is illusion.

I enclose a copy.

In rereading it, my heart broke again and again, all over again. And I realized that it would just be too painful for me to see you. I can't. What happened to us cleaved my heart in two. I am a changed person because of it, an older person and a sadder person.

I know you want forgiveness, but I cannot give it to you. You hurt me too much. And I can't have any sort of fun, casual friendship with you, with its implications of forgiveness. I am sorry for that, and sorry for everything.

Please respect my wish not to see you, M., as much as it breaks my heart as I write that—and in some measure it will break every day for the rest of my life, for what we lost—but I cannot.

Alexandra

———

An E-mail from Lisa G., twenty-five, a marketing director in Manhattan, to a suitor named Lee, after the two began an E-mail correspondence through the help of a mutual friend. "At first it was fun, because it was something to take my mind off of the breakup with my long-term boyfriend," says Lisa. But Lisa soon realized that she and Lee were very different from one another, and that a relationship wouldn't work out. "He would call me a lot but I didn't return his calls, hoping he'd get the hint," she says. "But I drew the line when he called me at 12:30 A.M." The E-mail was written and sent on October 29, 2001. Lee responded to it by telling Lisa that God didn't look down on her habits, and that she was a nice girl.

[October 29, 2001]

Lee,

    I am sorry if I was rude on Saturday night, I just don't feel it necessary for people to call so late. I am also sorry if I have led you on in any way, you and I are very different people. I don't go to church, probably never will, I smoke pot and party hard. You are a nice guy and I am sure the right girl will come along.

Take Care, Lisa

Afterword

People have been curious to know what I think of *Hell Hath No Fury* now that almost a year has passed since its publication. As I flip through the book, a number of things come to mind. First, I've attained a much better sense of what constitutes a good breakup letter, the inclusions or exclusions that make such letters effective (take a look at the letter written by novelist Kate Christensen to see what I mean by "effective"). Second, although I had the last-minute jitters as to whether *Hell Hath No Fury* would resonate with readers, I now feel confident that the book successfully addresses and illuminates the long, rich tradition of women using writing to work through their woes (romantic woes in particular). Finally, I've also come to believe that breakup letters not only make for good reading but for good listening as well: In the past year I've been involved in or witnessed no fewer than three readings from the book, and each one was a rousing success, engendering laughter, tears, sentiment—and yes, even shock. In fact, by the time you read this, there may actually be a *Hell Hath No Fury* stage show making the rounds (a writer friend of mine jokingly suggested I title such a show "The Vagina Epilogues").

However, there's one subject with regard to *Hell Hath No Fury* that continues to gnaw at me (and somewhat self-centeredly, I might add): the realization that my own breakup letter—written to my ex, Arthur, and included in the book's Introduction—sucks. Although I didn't incorporate it into the body of the book because I didn't believe it merited comparison with the other letters, I did place it in the Introduction to provide a jumping-off point for how the book was conceived. Maybe I've grown and matured a lot in the three years since I wrote it, but the letter seems to have been written by a different me. A much, much younger me. A more dramatic me. Why? Well, its whiny, for starters. And self-righteous. And condescending. And peppered with psychobabble (the fact that I used the word "toxic" is unconscionable). Hindsight is 20/20, I guess.

Many friends, colleagues, and readers have inquired as to whether Arthur ever found out he'd inspired this book. The answer is yes, but not immediately. Although I did run into Arthur while conducting research for the book (read the Introduction for the details of that strange enounter), I never informed him of my doings, nor did we have friends in common who could or would have passed on that information. However, in late January 2003, about four months after *Hell Hath No Fury* had been published, I received an e-mail from Arthur in which he announced that he'd just come across the book in a New York City Barnes & Noble and wanted to congratulate me on it. He also made a halfhearted attempt at an apology, claiming that he had continued to "regret for some time," although what exactly he regretted he didn't explain. If he was flattered, he didn't say, but I wrote him back and thanked him, saying that I appreciated his compliments and hoped he was well. And that was that.

It was nice to get Arthur's congratulatory e-mail, but of course the best part about publishing *Hell Hath No Fury* was—and continues to be—the enthusiastic response from complete strangers. In the year since the book came out I've received a rash of e-mails from women telling me how much they've enjoyed it, some confessing that they've been inspired to write their own letters and, in some cases, generously sharing those letters with me. Even the negative commentary the book has received has been helpful, if only because it means that some felt strongly enough about it that they just had to share their opinions (like the one man on slate.com who claimed that the book was "the work of the devil").

Devil or no devil, I was lucky to get a lot of fantastic press upon the book's publication. *Marie Claire, Elle, O: The Oprah Magazine,* and *Glamour* all covered its release, as did numerous daily newspapers, online magazines, and radio stations around the country. I went on NPR. I was invited onto *The Today Show.* The *New York Times* even covered my book party. Often, interviewers would ask me for my thoughts on what makes a good breakup letter, so I concocted some "rules and regulations" with regard to writing breakup letters. One of them, which I outlined to *The Today Show*'s Ann Curry, was that a breakup letter should be one page for every year of a relationship, and no more. Another, as explained to a young woman writing for a Web magazine, was that one shouldn't resort to name calling or insults and should just stick to facts ("You cheated on/abandoned/devastated me") and feelings ("I'm really hurt/angry/sad"). Interviewers loved my quips, and I, in turn, loved giving them. I was thoroughly enjoying my new role as expert in writing breakup letters.

All that changed in February 2003, when I discovered that my professional opinions on breakup letters had no bearing on the raw realities of my personal life. I had been dating a guy, William (not his real name), for about six months, and when the relationship came to a screeching halt a few days after Valentine's Day (no coincidence, I might add), I felt compelled to write him a letter. Although I'd been with William less than a year, my letter was close to six pages long, which means that I'd written one page for each *month* of our relationship. I also called William names, but in a somewhat sneaky, roundabout way (when I told him that he had "no close or lasting bond" with any other human being I might as well have scrawled, "You're a loser!").

Part of me was humbled that I couldn't practice what I'd preached. Part of me was embarrassed that I'd written William a letter in the first place (Of course I'm writing him a breakup letter, I thought to myself. It is simply "what I do"). Yet another part of me wondered whether William would take any of what I wrote to heart or whether he would simply consider my letter to be a performance of sorts (I don't know what he thought of it, because he never responded to me, which was pretty much our relationship in a nutshell). But letter or no letter, response or no response, what the experience taught me, thankfully, is that in the heat of a breakup, *there are no hard-and-fast rules.* And the ones that do exist are simply made to be broken.

Anna Holmes
September 2003

Acknowledgments

The process of finding the letters in *Hell Hath No Fury* was time-consuming and at times very, very random. I didn't so much have a comprehensive plan of attack as a scattered, always-evolving, and admittedly hare-brained series of new ideas (some of which actually worked). I started my search the obvious way: by E-mailing friends and acquaintances and asking them to pass on my query. I got responses, but many of them were from women I knew, and I did not want the book to be a collection of breakup letters from the same demographic in which I revolve. I decided that the best way to get the email addresses of a more diverse group of women was to find them through what they liked: the books and CDs that they buy. So I went online and copied the email addresses from the customer review pages for hundreds of women-friendly books and CDs—from Helen Fielding to Terry MacMillan to Fiona Apple and the Dixie Chicks. I wanted men stationed overseas to give me their letters, so I E-mailed public information officers on aircraft carriers and battleships as well as the staff of British and American Antarctic research crews. I wanted college students, so I emailed the English and Women's Studies departments of every university I could think of and asked them to post a Call for Submissions. I posted author's queries in newsletters, on online discussion boards, and on history, women's studies, and archival listservs. I faxed the letters-to-the-editor pages of every major American newspaper and posted signs in bars and restaurants in the New York area. Here I'd like to thank all those who helped, responded, suggested, advised, and even rebuffed me in my efforts; without your input and knowledge this book could never have been done.

Acknowledgments

Many thanks go to the archivists and librarians at research centers throughout the country, including Becky Cape of the Lilly Library at Indiana University; Jim A. Davis at the North Dakota Historical Society; Ellen Doon at Yale University's Beinecke Rare Book and Manuscript Library; June Edwards at the State Library of South Australia; Anne Engelhart at the Schlesinger Library, Harvard University; Christina Favretto, formerly of Duke University; Andrew George at the West Yorkshire Archive Service, Bradford; Lisa Hazirjian at the Sallie Bingham Center for Women's History and Culture at Duke University; James Henley at the Sacramento History Center; Larry Hibpshman at the Alaska Historical Society; David Huddlestone at the Public Record Office of Northern Ireland; Pat Johnson at the Sacramento Archives; Caroline Knight; Karen Koka of the Nebraska Historical Society; Karen Kukil of the Neilson Library at Smith College; Nancy Noble at the Maine Historical Society; Rachel Onuf at the Historical Society of Pennsylvania; Aideen Ireland at the National Archives of Ireland; Liz Rees at the Society of Archivists, United Kingdom; Jeff Rollinson at the Chester County Archives in West Chester, Pennsylvania; Craig Wright at the Minnesota Historical Society.

Were it not for the help of some very talented undergraduate and graduate level students, much of the material in this book would not have been found or identified. To Deborah Friedell, Kara Loewentheil, Nicole Wallace, Lindsay Nordell, Molly Haupt, Jess Matthews, Megan Refice, Natalia Truszkowska, Brandy King, Jess Eldridge, Rebecca Lewis, Daniel Park, Jason Assir, Amanda Merchant, Kirsten Flagg, Esther Lee, Christopher Murphy, Katherine Marino—thank you, thank you, thank you for taking the time out of your hectic and demanding schedules to help look for letters, and for your enthusiasm for the subject. Thanks also go to Mimi Halpern, Anita Angelone, Sharon Bowman, and Karen Myers, who translated many letters into English for me, and to Michelle Mahealani Morgan, who scoured the archives at the Wisconsin Historical Society and came up with the gem of a letter by Clara Bewick Colby.

Acknowledgments

Despite all my frenzied electronic busywork trying to send my message out to the world, I found the bulk of the letters for the book in an oasis in my own backyard: the New York Public Library. This book could not have been done without the resources of a major research library like the NYPL and, most importantly, its staff, who were generous, patient, pleasant, informative, and kind. Thank you all: I'll miss my afternoons on the third floor with you.

I knew nothing about the history of women's letters before beginning this project, and I want to thank those scholars, writers, professors, historians, biographers. and academics who took the time to respond to my wordy, wide-eyed emails and to suggest material I might otherwise have missed. When I began working on the book, I knew that I would come across material I didn't know existed, but I had no idea exactly how much I would find and how wonderful that material would be. I owe perhaps my greatest thanks to these individuals, as it was through their generosity of knowledge that this book—which originated purely on a whim—became, for me, a fascinating and rewarding research project. Thank you to Marianna Archambault of Bucknell University; Paul Archambault of Syracuse University; Nancy Armstrong of Brown University; Roger Bagnall of Columbia; Joanne Banks; Elizabeth Barron of Wake Forest University; Virginia Beauchamp of the University of Maryland; Linda Hunt Beckman of Temple University; Betty T. Bennett of American University; Anne Bower of Ohio State University; Clare Brant of Kings College, London; Niels Buch of Cornell University; Julie Buckler of Harvard University; Edward Burns of William Paterson University; Dr. Christine Carpenter of the University of Cambridge; Odile Cazenave of MIT; Kang-i Sun Chang of Yale University; Roger Chartier of L'Ecole des Hautes Etudes en Sciences Sociales; Patricia Clarke; Moira Collins; Kris Comment of the University of Maryland; Elizabeth Heckendorn Cook of UC Santa Barbara; James Daybell of the University of Reading; Patricia De Meo of Dalhousie University; Julia De Pree of Agnes Scott College; William M. Decker of Oklahoma State; Joan DeJean of the University of Pennsylvania; John Desmond of Whitman College; Carlos L. Dews of the University of West Florida; Konstantin Dierks of Indiana University; Millicent Dillon; Marjorie Housepian Dobkin; Francine du Plessix Gray; Thomas Dublin of SUNY Binghamton; A.C. Elias, Jr.; Jane Eskridge; Barbara C. Ewell of Loyola University; Margaret Ferguson of UC Davis; Lynn Festa of Harvard; Anne M. Fields of Ohio State; Kristen M. Figg of Kent State University; Amanda Foreman; Stephanie Forward of the University of Warwick; Roslyn Reso Foy of the University of New Orleans; Elizabeth Frank of Bard College; Ginger Frost of Samford University; Jane Fletcher Geniesse; Luc Gilleman of Smith College; Rose Gladney of the University of Alabama; Elizabeth Goldsmith of Boston University; Joyce Goodfriend of the University of Denver; Dena Goodman of the University of Michigan; Susan Goodman of the University of Delaware; Roger Grant of Clemson University; Richard Greene of the University of Toronto; Germaine Greer; Jonathan Gross of DePaul University; Charles Hamm of Dartmouth College; Jim Hammerton; Janice H. Harris of the University of Wyoming; Sharon Harris of Texas Christian University; Antony H. Harrison of North Carolina State University; Melanie Hawthorne of Texas A&M University; Peter Hays of UC Davis; Ann Heilmann; James Hepokoski of Yale University; Paul Herron of Sky Blue Press; Mary A. Hill of Bucknell University; Quintin Hoare; Barbara Holland; John Hollander of Yale University; Kenneth L. Holmes; Glenn Hooper of the University of Aberdeen; Helen L. Horowitz of Smith College; Robert Hudspeth of the University of Redlands; Belinda Jack of Christ Church, Oxford; Philip K. Jason; Judy Johnston of the University of Western Australia; Thomas Jenkins of Trinity University; Margaretta Jolly of the University of Exeter; John Kaminski of the University of Wisconsin; Carla Kaplan of the University of Southern California; Christopher Kelly of Boston College; Gillian Kersley; Kimball King of the University of North Carolina; Thomas King of Georgetown University; William Davies King of UC Santa Barbara; Alice H. Kinman of the University of Georgia; Sally Kitch of Ohio State University; John Klassen of Trinity Western University; Anna Klobucka of the University of Massachusetts, Dartmouth; Donna Landry of Wayne State University; Ann J. Lane of the University of Virginia; Zachary Leader of Roehampton University of Surrey; Vicki Leon; Kai-ling Lieu of the National Cheng Kung University in Taiwan; the late Ruth Limmer; Gerald MacLean of Wayne State University; Deirdre Mahoney of Northwestern Michigan College; Regina Marler; Joanna Martin; Ralph Maud; Georges May of Yale University; Kevin McCarthy of the University of Florida; Susan McClary of UCLA; Juliet McMaster of the University of Alberta; Marion Meade; Nancy Milford; Nancy K. Miller of the City University of New York; Ellen Moody of the Trollope Society; Armine Kotin Mortimer of the University of Illinois at Urbana-Champaign; Carolyn Moss of Southern Illinois University; Barbara Mujica of Georgetown University; Erika Murr; Elisa F. New of Harvard University; Barbara Newman of Northwestern University; Kathleen Nigro; Donna Orwin at the University of Toronto; Beverly Palmer of Pomona College; Ruth Panofsky of Ryerson University; Makarand Paranjape of Jawaharlal Nehru University; Katherine Patterson of the University of British Columbia; Kathy Peiss of University of Pennsylvania; Dale Peterson; Mark Pottle of Wolfson College; David A. Powell of Hofstra University; Leah Price of Harvard University; Annabelle Rea of Occidental College; Diane Richard-Allerdyce; Diana Robin; Suzie Rodriguez; Camille Roman of Washington State University; Augusta Rohrbach of Harvard University; Gabriella Romani of Princeton University; Kari Ronning of the Cather Scholarly Edition at the University of Nebraska, Lincoln; Franklin Rosemont; Ruth Rosen of UC Davis; Ellen Rothman of the Massachusetts Foundation for the Humanities; Evelyn Salz of Western New England College; David A. Sand of Hofstra; Stephanie Sandler of Harvard University; Max Saunders of King's College, London; Haun Saussy of Stanford University; Gail Savage of St. Mary's College of Maryland; Nancy Schoenberger; Bonnie Kime Scott of San Diego State University; Rebecca Sexton of Morehead State University; Barbara Seaman; Anne Sienkewicz; Nancy Simmons of Virginia Tech; Sunka Simon of Swarthmore College; Judith B. Slagle at East Tennessee State University; Antoinette Sol of

Acknowledgments

the University of Texas at Arlington; Helen Southworth of the University of Oregon; Margaret Smith; Merrill Smith; Karen Smythe of Algoma University College; David Sorensen of Saint Joseph's University; Judith Stanton; Joan Stewart of the University of South Carolina; Phillip Stewart of Duke University; Janis P. Stout of Texas A&M; Simon Stow of UC Berkeley; Felicia Sturzer of the University of Tennessee; Suzanne Stutman of Penn State; Gunther Stuhlmann; Rodger Tarr of Illinois State University; Tim Taylor of Columbia; Janet Todd of Glasgow University; Lara Delage-Toriel; Emily Toth; Jacqueline Vansant of the University of Michigan; Martha Vinicus of the University of Michigan; Henry Vivian-Neal; Ann Waldron; Beth Kowaleski Wallace of Boston College; Altina Walker of the University of Connecticut; Robert Walser of UCLA; Janet Wallach; Jill Watts of California State, San Marcos; Aurora Wolfgang of California State, Santa Barbara.

For their help in my search to locate the radio program "Dear John," which was broadcast on Armed Forces Radio, thank you to Don Aston, Ray Barfield, Marvin R. Bensman, Ed Carr, Don Corey, Jack French, Danny Goodwin, Michele Hilmes, Michael C. Keith, Steven Kelez, William Kenny, Richard King, John M. Kittross, Patrick Morley, Christopher Sterling, Bob Stoffel, Larry Weide, S.A. Wells, Gerry Wright, John K. Yim, and especially Harry Mackenzie.

For responding to my emails about the prevalence of Dear John letters sent to personnel stationed at the South Pole, thanks to Linda Capper of the British Antarctic Survey and Peter Milner, Eric Sandberg, Ryan Emond, R. Allan Baker, Robert DeValentino, and Meghan Prentiss, all researchers and support staff stationed at that most remote place on earth.

For their thoughts, recollections, opinions, and help with placing queries to veterans and active military personnel, thank you to Albert A. Acena of the College of San Mateo; John Aldecoa; LTJG Erica M. Anderson of the USS *Bonhomme Richard;* Louise Arnold-Friend of the Military History Institute; Brian Bowers of *The Stars and Stripes;* Donna Braun of White Sands Missile Range; Dave Brickson; James

Brindy; Donovan Brooks of *The Stars and Stripes;* Patricia Brown of *VFW* magazine; Lisa Burgess of *The Stars and Stripes;* Anthony Burgos of *The Stars and Stripes;* John Clark; Kevin Clark; Cara Day; Olivia Feher of *The Crusader;* Pat Dickson at *The Stars and Stripes;* Bob Doughty; Kent Draper; Jim Ehrman; SSG Jeff Ege of the U.S. Army War College; John Farquhar, Lt. Col., USAF; W.G. Ford of *Leatherneck* magazine; "Gene in Toronto"; Joshua Geren of the USS *Abraham Lincoln;* Joe Giordono at *The Stars and Stripes;* JO1 Todd Hack of the USS *Nimitz;* Ken W. Hart; Guy Hunter; Paul M. Johnson; Jeremy Kirk of *The Stars and Stripes;* Randy Knight of the (Utah) American Legion; Edward Kruska at the *Coast Guard Reservist;* Henry E Kwiatkowski; Michael Lee Lanning; Jim Lea of *The Stars and Stripes;* Steve Liewer of *The Stars and Stripes;* Gordon Angus Mackinlay; Patricia Marschand of the *American Legion* magazine; Ray Merriam; Ralph Moore; Gene Moser; Jill Mueller of *The Citizen;* Kevin Murphy in West Point's Department of History; Ensign Stephanie Odell on the USS *Cleveland;* Lt. Matt O'Neal of the USS *Carl Vinson;* Dan Ortiz of the California chapter of Veterans of Foreign Wars; Raymond J. Pard, Sr.; AO3 Dallas Perrin of the USS *Abraham Lincoln;* Beth Reece at *Soldiers* magazine; Tonya L. Riley of *The Canoneer;* Ron Roizen; Calvin D. Rose; Veronica Roth of *Coast Guard* magazine; Julie Rust; Ron Sailor; Paul Scott; Bridget Ruiz on the USS *Duluth;* Andy Savoie of *The Stars and Stripes;* James Sawyer; Ann-Marie Sedor at AMVETS; Mike Shaw; Capt, Dave "Sammy" Small of the 1st Fighter Wing, Langley Air Force Base; David Smith of the University of Wales; Jerome Steigmann; Jerry Stringer of *Airman* magazine; John E. Suttle of *Soldiers* magazine; Yvonne Voll; Robert D. Weiss; Lester White on the USS *Abraham Lincoln;* Ted Wilson of the University of Kansas; SFC Warren Wingard; Mike Wiswell; Jack Witter; John Zachodny, Jr. and to the members of the American Armed Forces and Veterans Organizations who agreed to publish my rather strange query in their newsletters and magazines.

Special thanks to Deirdre Bair for her help on the letters and relationships of Anaïs Nin; Kristin Mapel Bloomberg for her help on the life of Clara Bewick Colby; Andrew Carroll of the Legacy

Acknowledgments

Project for his advice on war letters and permissions; Isobel Grundy of the University of Alberta for her help with the work of Lady Mary Wortley Montagu; Howard V. Hong for his scholarship on the writings of Kierkegaard; Jen Jourdanne of SoThere.com for thoughts on unsent letters; Peter Kurth for sharing his scholarship on Isadora Duncan and Dorothy Thompson with me; Michelle Lovric for her thoughts on love letters and love-letter anthologies; Heather McMaster at the Feminist Press for her support and help; Miwa Messer for her general wit and advice on the book business; Karen Myers of Brandeis for her work on Vera Kommissarsheva; Chris Kraus for her help with Kathy Acker's letters and for answering my initial fawning E-mail; Sari Locker for her help on putting together a proposal; Judith H. McQuown, a meticulous and intelligent copyeditor whose outstanding work made a world of difference to the finished manuscript; Kate Millett for responding to my letter and talking alpacas with me; Richard Nash for sharing his knowledge about permissions; Susan Orlean for suggesting the wonderful chapter The Autopsy and for her generosity of conversation and opinion; Dannye Powell at the *Charlotte Observer* for her interest-generating article; Francine Prose for responding to my initial query letter with her generous offer to write the foreword; Paul Sahre for his creativity, generosity, and patience; James Salter for his reminiscences of his time in the Pacific; Mary Siegel at the Alexander Street Press for her help with the wonderful American Women's Letters and Diaries project; Sharon Thesen for her thoughts and knowledge of the life and letters of Frances Boldereff; and Paul Tough for his advice regarding letters posted online.

To Elizabeth Sheinkman, who listened to my initial pitch way back in early 2001: thank you for your immediate enthusiasm, your belief, your tenacity, your wealth of knowledge, experience, and opinion, and, of course, your friendship.

To Tina Pohlman, my editor and dear friend: your belief in this book exhibited itself in so many wonderful and meaningful ways. Thank you for your excitement, for your consideration of every crazy idea I came up with, for taking my many calls with patience and enthusiasm, for humoring my tendency to write too long, for allowing me to express my particular and very strong opinions of what this book should be, inside and out. Your taste, humor, and professionalism are unparalleled, and this book was made all the more enjoyable because of your personal and professional involvement.

I'd also like to thank all those friends who kept me sane and motivated as I disappeared to immerse myself in researching and editing the material, and most of all, my family for inquiring how I was doing, asking what they could do to help, and expressing their love for me, even when I interrupted their phone calls with "Can't talk!" or left their E-mails unanswered. I love you Mom, Dad and Mere. Your going along for the ride—even from three thousand miles away—has meant a lot to me.

Lastly, I'd like to thank all of the amazing women and men who shared their written and received letters with me, trusted me with intimate and at times ugly emotions, responded with enthusiasm to my queries, and had the foresight to save the letters in the first place. Your courage and generosity is much appreciated, for without you there would be no book.

Bibliography

General Bibliography

Bower, Anne. *Epistolary Responses: The Letter in 20th-Century American Fiction and Criticism.* Tuscaloosa: University of Alabama Press, 1997.

Buck, Claire, ed. *The Bloomsbury Guide to Women's Literature.* London: Bloomsbury, 1992.

Carroll, Andrew, ed. *Letters of a Nation: A Collection of Extraordinary American Letters.* New York: Broadway, 1999.

Chartier, Roger, Alain Boreau, and Cécile Dauphin. *Correspondence: Models of Letter-Writing from the Middle Ages to the Nineteenth Century.* Cambridge, U.K.: Polity Press, 1997.

Cook, Elizabeth Heckendorn. *Epistolary Bodies: Gender and Genre in the Eighteenth- Century Republic of Letters.* Stanford, Calif.: Stanford University Press, 1996.

Davidson, Cathy N., ed. *The Book of Love: Writers and Their Love Letters.* New York: Plume/Penguin, 1992.

Davis, Gwenn, and Beverly A. Joyce, eds. *Personal Writings by Women to 1900: A Bibliography of American and British Writers.* Norman: University of Oklahoma Press, 1989.

Dawson, Jill. *The Virago Book of Love Letters.* London: Virago, 1994.

Day, Robert Adams. *Told in Letters: Epistolary Fiction Before Richardson.* Ann Arbor: University of Michigan Press, 1966.

Decker, William Merrill. *Epistolary Practices: Letter Writing in America Before Telecommunications.* Chapel Hill: University of North Carolina Press, 1998.

DeJean, Joan. *Tender Geographies: Women and the Origins of the Novel in France.* New York: Columbia University Press, 1991.

Earle, Rebecca, ed. *Epistolary Selves: Letters and Letter-Writers, 1600-1945.* Brookfield, Vt.: Ashgate, 1999.

Bibliography

Fraser, Antonia, ed. *Love Letters: An Anthology.* London: Weidenfeld & Nicolson, 1976.

Goldsmith, Elizabeth C. *Writing the Female Voice: Essays on Epistolary Literature.* Boston: Northeastern University Press, 1989.

Goodman, Dena. *The Republic of Letters: A Cultural History of the French Enlightenment.* Ithaca, N.Y.: Cornell University Press, 1994.

Hamilton, Robin, and Nicholas Soames, eds. *Intimate Letters.* London: Marginalia, 1994.

Hoffmann, Leonore, and Margo Culley, eds. *Women's Personal Narratives: Essays in Criticism and Pedagogy.* New York: Modern Language Association of America, 1985.

Jensen, Katharine Ann. *Writing Love: Letters, Women, and the Novel in France, 1605-1776.* Carbondale: Southern Illinois University Press, 1995.

Kauffman, Linda S. *Discourses of Desire: Gender, Genre, and Epistolary Fictions.* Ithaca, N.Y.: Cornell University Press, 1986.

Kenyon, Olga, ed. *The Inmost Heart: 800 Years of Women's Letters.* New York: Konecky & Konecky, 1992.

———. *Women's Voices: Their Lives and Loves Through Two Thousand Years of Letters.* London: Constable, 1995.

Kermode, Frank, and Anita Kermode, eds. *The Oxford Book of Letters.* Oxford, England: Oxford University Press, 1995.

Lewis, Jon E., ed. *The Mammoth Book of Private Lives.* New York: Carroll & Graf. 2000.

Lovric, Michelle, ed. *Love Letters: An Anthology of Passion, with Facsimiles of Real Letters and Quotations from Lovers' Correspondence Throughout the Ages.* London: G. Weidenfeld & Nicolson, 1994.

———. *Passionate Love Letters: An Anthology of Desire, with Facsimiles of Real Letters and Quotations from Lovers' Correspondence throughout the Ages.* New York: Shooting Star Press, 1996.

Lystra, Karen. *Searching the Heart: Women, Men, and Romantic Love in Nineteenth-Century America.* New York: Oxford University Press, 1989.

MacArthur, Elizabeth J. *Extravagant Narratives:* Closure and Dynamics in the Epistolary Form. Princeton, N.J.: Princeton University Press, 1990.

Perry, Ruth. *Women, Letters, and the Novel.* New York: AMS Press 1980.

Bibliography By Chapter

1. The Tell Off

Andrews, Wayne. *Germaine: A Portrait of Madame de Staël*. New York: Atheneum, 1963.

Bair, Deirdre. *Anaïs Nin: A Biography*. New York: Putnam, 1995.

Baldwin, C. L. *Nine Desperate Men, with Three Pen and Ink Drawings by Dicki*. New York: Gemor Press, 1946.

———. *Quinquivara*. New York: Gemor Press, 1944.

D'Auvergne, Edmund B. *The Dear Emma: The Story of Emma, Lady Hamilton, Her Husband & Her Lovers*. London: G. G. Harrap & Co., Ltd., 1936.

Fitch, Noël Riley. *Anaïs: The Erotic Life of Anaïs Nin*. Boston: Little, Brown, 1993.

Foot, Michael. *H. G.: The History of Mr. Wells*. Washington, D.C.: Counterpoint, 1995.

Franklin, Benjamin V. *"Anaïs Nin"*, in *Dictionary of Literary Biography, Volume 2: American Novelists Since World War II*. Edited by Jeffrey Helterman and Richard Layman. Detroit, Mich: Gale Research, 1978.

Fraser, Flora. *Emma, Lady Hamilton*. New York: Knopf, 1987.

Gribble, Francis. *Madame de Staël and Her Lovers*. London: E. Nash, 1907.

Gutwirth, Madelyn. *"Germaine de Staël"*, in *Dictionary of Literary Biography, Volume 119: Nineteenth-Century French Fiction Writers: Romanticism and Realism, 1800-1860*. Edited by Catharine Savage Brosman. Detroit, Mich.: Gale Research, 1992.

Herold, J. Christopher. *Mistress to an Age: A Life of Madame de Staël*. Indianapolis: Bobbs-Merrill, 1958.

Hoare, Philip. *Noël Coward: A Biography*. London: Sinclair-Stevenson, 1995.

Lesley, Cole. *Remembered Laughter: The Life of Noël Coward*. New York: Knopf, 1976.

Middlebrook, Diane Wood. *Anne Sexton: A Biography*. Boston: Houghton Mifflin, 1991.

Rollyson, Carl E. *Rebecca West: A Saga of the Century*. London: Hodder & Stoughton, 1995.

Sexton, Anne. *Anne Sexton: A Self-Portrait in Letters*. Edited by Linda Gray Sexton and Lois Ames. Boston: Houghton Mifflin, 1977.

Bibliography

Simpson, Colin. *Emma: The Life of Lady Hamilton.* London: Bodley Head, 1983.

Tours, Hugh. *The Life and Letters of Emma Hamilton.* London: V. Gollancz, Ltd., 1963.

West, Rebecca. *Selected Letters of Rebecca West.* Edited by Bonnie Kime Scott. New Haven, Conn.: Yale University Press, 2000.

Wilson, R. McNair. *Madame de Staël, High Priestess of Love.* New York: R. M. McBride, 1931.

2. The Silent Treatment

Barry, Joseph. *Infamous Woman: The Life of George Sand.* Garden City, N.Y.: Doubleday, 1976.

Benstock, Shari. *No Gifts from Chance: A Biography of Edith Wharton.* New York: Scribner, 1994.

Bernstein, Aline, and Thomas Wolfe. *My Other Loneliness: Letters of Thomas Wolfe and Aline Bernstein.* Edited by Suzanne Stutman. Chapel Hill: University of North Carolina Press, 1983.

Brady, Frank, and Frederick A. Pottle. *Boswell on the Grand Tour: Italy, Corsica, and France, 1765–1766.* New York: McGraw-Hill, 1955.

Brooks, A. Russell. *James Boswell.* New York: Twayne, 1971.

Cate, Curtis. *George Sand: A Biography.* Boston: Houghton Mifflin, 1975.

Daiches, David. *James Boswell and His World.* New York: Scribner, 1976.

Finlayson, Iain. *The Moth and the Candle: A Life of James Boswell.* New York: St. Martin's, 1984.

Grebanier, Bernard D. N. *The Uninhibited Byron: An Account of His Sexual Confusion.* New York: Crown, 1970.

Halsband, Robert. *The Life of Lady Mary Wortley Montagu.* New York: Oxford University Press, 1960.

Hutchinson, Roger. *All the Sweets of Being: A Life of James Boswell.* Edinburgh, Scotland: Mainstream Pub., 1995.

Jack, Belinda Elizabeth. *George Sand: A Woman's Life Writ Large.* London: Chatto & Windus, 1999.

Jordan, Ruth. *George Sand: A Biography.* London: Constable, 1976.

———. *Sophie Dorothea.* London: Constable, 1971.

Lewis, Jon E. *The Mammoth Book of Private Lives.* New York: Carroll & Graf. 2000.

Martin, Peter. *A Life of James Boswell.* London: Weidenfeld & Nicolson, 1999.

Montagu, Lady Mary Wortley. *Lady Mary Wortley Montagu, Selected Letters.* Edited and translated by Isobel Grundy. New York: Penguin, 1997.

Morand, Paul. *The Captive Princess: Sophia Dorothea of Celle.* Translated from the French by Anne-Marie Geoghegan. New York: American Heritage Press, 1972.

Paston, George, and Peter Quennell, eds. *"To Lord Byron": Feminine Profiles Based upon Unpublished Letters, 1807-1824.* London: J. Murray, 1939.

Pottle, Frederick A. *James Boswell: The Earlier Years, 1740-1769.* New York: McGraw-Hill, 1966.

Sand, George. *Correspondance [de] George Sand.* Edited by Georges Lubin. Paris: Garnier Freres, 1964.

Strickland, Margot. *The Byron Women.* London: P. Owen, 1974.

Wharton, Edith. *The Letters of Edith Wharton.* R. W. B. Lewis and Nancy Lewis, eds. New York: Scribner, 1988.

Wilkins, W. H., ed. *The Love of an Uncrowned Queen. Sophie Dorothea, Consort of George I., and Her Correspondence with Philip Christopher Count Königsmarck* (now first published from the originals). London: Hutchinson & Co., 1900.

3. The Autopsy

Field, Kate. *Kate Field: Selected Letters.* Edited by Carolyn J. Moss. Carbondale: Southern Illinois University Press, 1996.

Fitzgerald, F. Scott. *Correspondence of F. Scott Fitzgerald.* Edited by Matthew J. Bruccoli and Margaret M. Duggan. New York: Random House, 1980.

Fitzgerald, F. Scott, and Zelda Fitzgerald. *Dear Scott, Dearest Zelda: The Love Letters of F. Scott and Zelda Fitzgerald.* Edited by Jackson R. Bryer and Cathy W. Barks. New York: St. Martin's, 2002.

Milford, Nancy. *Zelda: A Biography.* New York: Harper & Row, 1970.

Sayers, Dorothy L. *The Letters of Dorothy L. Sayers, 1899 to 1936: The Making of a Detective Novelist.* Edited by Barbara Reynolds. New York: St. Martin's, 1996.

Whiting, Lilian. *Kate Field: A Record.* Boston: Little, Brown, 1900.

Bibliography

4. The "Just Friends?"

Alexander, Paul. *Rough Magic: A Biography of Sylvia Plath*. New York: Viking, 1991.

Allentuch, Harriet Ray, ed. *Madame de Sévigné: A Portrait in Letters*. Baltimore: Johns Hopkins Press, 1963.

Appignanesi, Lisa. *Simone de Beauvoir*. New York: Penguin Books, 1988.

Arthur, Sir George. *Sarah Bernhardt*. London: Heinemann, 1923.

Ascher, Carol. *Simone de Beauvoir: A Life of Freedom*. Boston: Beacon Press, 1981.

Austin, Cecil. *The Immortal Ninon: A Character-Study of Ninon de L'Enclos*. London: Routledge, 1927.

Baring, Maurice. *Sarah Bernhardt*. London: P. Davies, 1933.

Bernhardt, Sarah. *My Double Life: The Memoirs of Sarah Bernhardt, Translated from the French*. London: P. Owen, 1977.

Beauvoir, Simone de. *Force of Circumstance. Translated from the French by Richard Howard*. New York: Putnam, 1965.

——. *A Transatlantic Love Affair: Letters to Nelson Algren*. New York: New Press, 1998.

Bieber, Konrad. *Simone de Beauvoir*. New York: Twayne, 1979.

Botham, Noel. *Margaret: The Untold Story*. London: Blake, 1995.

Brandon, Ruth. *Being Divine: A Biography of Sarah Bernhardt*. London: Secker & Warburg, 1991.

Bret, M. *Ninon de Lenclos*. London: Humphreys, 1904.

Butscher, Edward, ed. *Sylvia Plath: The Woman and the Work*. New York: Dodd, Mead, 1977.

Carrington, Dora de Houghton. *Carrington: Letters and Extracts from Her Diaries. Chosen and with an introduction by David Garnett*. London: J. Cape, 1970.

Cohen, Edgar H. *Mademoiselle Libertine: A Portrait of Ninon de Lanclos*. Boston: Houghton Mifflin, 1970.

Cottrell, Robert D. *Simone de Beauvoir*. New York: F. Ungar Pub. Co., 1975.

Crosland, Margaret. *Simone de Beauvoir: The Woman and Her Work*. London: Heinemann, 1992.

Evans, Mary. *Simone de Beauvoir*. London: Sage, 1996.

Farrell, Michèle Longino. *Performing Motherhood: The Sévigné Correspondence.* Hanover, N.H.: University Press of New England, 1991.

Ford, Ford Madox, and Stella Bowen. *The Correspondence of Ford Madox Ford and Stella Bowen.* Edited by Sondra J. Stang and Karen Cochran. Bloomington: Indiana University Press, 1993.

Francis, Claude, and Fernande Gontier. *Simone de Beauvoir: A Life, A Love Story.* Translated from the French by Lisa Nesselson. New York: St. Martin's, 1987.

Geniesse, Jane Fletcher. *Passionate Nomad: The Life of Freya Stark.* New York: Random House, 1999.

Gold, Arthur, and Robert Fizdale. *The Divine Sarah: A Life of Sarah Bernhardt.* New York: Knopf, 1991.

Gerzina, Gretchen. *Carrington: A Life of Dora Carrington, 1893-1932.* London: J. Murray, 1989.

Hawthorne, Melanie C. *Contingent Loves: Simone de Beauvoir and Sexuality.* Charlottesville: University Press of Virginia, 2000.

Hayman, Ronald. *The Death and Life of Sylvia Plath.* London: Heinemann, 1991.

Izzard, Molly. *Freya Stark: A Biography.* London: Hodder & Stoughton, 1993.

Judd, Alan. *Ford Madox Ford.* London: Collins, 1990.

Lenclos, Ninon de. *Ninon de l'Enclos, the Celebrated Aspasia of France; with her Remarkable Letters on Love, Courtship, and Marriage, and the Mysteries of Marriage.e* Philadelphia: T. B. Peterson and Bros. [pref. 1849].

MacShane, Frank. *The Life and Work of Ford Madox Ford.* London: Routledge & K. Paul, 1965.

Magne, Émile. *Ninon de Lanclos.* Edited and translated by Gertrude Scott Stevenson. New York: Henry Holt & Co., 1926.

Middlebrook, Diane Wood. *Anne Sexton: A Biography.* Boston: Houghton Mifflin, 1991.

Mizener, Arthur. *The Saddest Story: A Biography of Ford Madox Ford.* New York: World Pub. Co., 1971.

Ojala, Jeanne A., and William T. Ojala. *Madame de Sévigné: A Seventeenth-Century Life.* New York: St. Martin's, 1990.

Osborne, Dorothy. *The Love Letters of Dorothy Osborne to Sir William Temple.* New York: E.P. Dulton, 1914.

Bibliography

Osborne, Dorothy. *The Love Letters of Dorothy Osborne to Sir William Temple, 1652-54*. Edited by Edward Abbott Parry. New York: Dodd, Mead, 1901.

Richardson, Joanna. *Sarah Bernhardt and Her World*. London: Weidenfeld & Nicolson, 1977.

Sexton, Anne. *Anne Sexton: A Self-Portrait in Letters*. Edited by Linda Gray Sexton and Lois Ames. Boston: Houghton Mifflin, 1977.

Stanley, Arthur [A. S. Megaw]. *Madame de Sévigné: Her Letters and Her World*. Norwood, Pa.: Norwood Editions, 1978.

Stark, Freya. *Over the Rim of the World: Selected Letters of Freya Stark*. Edited by Caroline Moorehead. London: John Murray (Publishers) Ltd., in association with Michael Russell, 1988.

Stevenson, Anne. *Bitter Fame: A Life of Sylvia Plath; with additional material by Lucas Myers, Dido Merwin, and Richard Murphy*. New York: Viking, 1989.

Wagner-Martin, Linda. *Sylvia Plath: A Biography*. New York: Simon and Schuster, 1987.

Waugh, Elizabeth. *The Princess with the Golden Hair: Letters of Elizabeth Waugh to Edmund Wilson, 1933-1942*. Edited by John B. Friedman and Kristen M. Figg. Madison, N.J.: Fairleigh Dickinson University Press, 2000.

Williams, Charles G. S. *Madame de Sévigné*. Boston: Twayne, 1981.

5. The Other Woman/Other Man (Real and Virtual)

Agar, Eileen (in collaboration with Andrew Lambirth). *A Look at My Life*. London: Methuen, 1988.

Arthur, Sir George. *Sarah Bernhardt*. London: Heinemann, 1923.

Baring, Maurice. *Sarah Bernhardt*. London: P. Davies, 1933.

Bernhardt, Sarah. *My Double Life: The Memoirs of Sarah Bernhardt, translated from the French*. London: P. Owen, 1977.

Black, Stephen A. *Eugene O'Neill: Beyond Mourning and Tragedy*. New Haven, Conn.: Yale University Press, 1999.

Blair, Fredrika. *Isadora: Portrait of the Artist as a Woman*. New York: McGraw-Hill, 1986.

Boulton, Agnes. *Part of a Long Story*. Garden City, N.Y.: Doubleday, 1958.

Boulton, Agnes, and Eugene O'Neill. *A Wind is Rising: The Correspondence of Agnes*

Boulton and Eugene O'Neill. Edited by William Davies King. Madison, N.J.: Fairleigh Dickinson University Press, 2000.

Brandon, Ruth. *Being Divine: A Biography of Sarah Bernhardt.* London: Secker & Warburg, 1991.

Crawford, Anne, ed. *The Letters of the Queens of England, 1100-1547.* Dover, N.H.: A. Sutton, 1994.

Givner, Joan. *Katherine Anne Porter: A Life.* Athens: University of Georgia Press, 1991.

Gold, Arthur, and Robert Fizdale. *The Divine Sarah: A Life of Sarah Bernhardt.* New York: Knopf, 1991.

Hamburger, Lotte, and Joseph Hamburger. *Contemplating Adultery: The Secret Life of a Victorian Woman.* New York: Fawcett Columbine, 1991.

————. *Troubled Lives: John and Sarah Austin.* Toronto: University of Toronto Press, 1985.

Jenkins, Elizabeth. *Ten Fascinating Women.* London: Macdonald & Co., 1968.

Kurth, Peter. *Isadora: A Sensational Life.* Boston: Little, Brown, 2001.

————. *American Cassandra: The Life of Dorothy Thompson.* Boston: Little, Brown,. 1990.

O'Connor, Barbara. *Barefoot Dancer: The Story of Isadora Duncan.* Minneapolis: Carolrhoda Books, 1994.

Olson, Charles. *Charles Olson and Frances Boldereff: A Modern Correspondence.* Edited by Ralph Maud and Sharon Thesen. Hanover, N.H.: University Press of New England, 1999.

Porter, Katharine Anne. *Letters of Katherine Anne Porter.* Selected and edited by Isabel Bayley. New York: Atlantic Monthly Press, 1990.

Richardson, Joanna. *Sarah Bernhardt and her World.* London: Weidenfeld and Nicolson, 1977.

Sanders, Marion K. *Dorothy Thompson: A Legend in Her Time.* Boston: Houghton Mifflin, 1973.

Texier, Catherine. *Breakup: The End of a Love Story.* New York: Doubleday, 1998.

Thirkell, Angela Mackail. *The Fortunes of Harriett: The Surprising Career of Harriette Wilson.* London: H. Hamilton, 1936.

Bibliography

6. The Divorce Letter

Benson, Brian Joseph, and Mabel Mayle Dillard. *Jean Toomer.* Boston: Twayne, 1980.

Benstock, Shari. *No Gifts from Chance: A Biography of Edith Wharton.* New York: Scribner, 1994.

Crawford, Anne. *The Letters of the Queens of England, 1100-1547.* Dover, N.H.: A. Sutton, 1994.

Gallagher, Christine. *The Woman's Book of Divorce: 101 Ways to Make Him Suffer Forever and Ever.* New York: Citadel, 2000.

Hahn, Emily. *Mabel: A Biography of Mabel Dodge Luhan.* Boston: Houghton Mifflin, 1977.

Kurth, Peter. *American Cassandra: The Life of Dorothy Thompson.* Boston: Little, Brown, 1990.

Luhan, Mabel Dodge. *Intimate Memories: The Autobiography of Mabel Dodge Luhan.* Edited by Lois Palken Rudnick. Albuquerque: University of New Mexico Press, 1999.

McKay, Nellie Y. *Jean Toomer, Artist: A Study of His Literary Life and Work, 1894-1936.* Chapel Hill: University of North Carolina Press, 1984.

Rothman, Ellen K. *Hands and Hearts: A History of Courtship in America.* New York: Basic Books, 1984.

Saaler, Mary. *Anne of Cleves: Fourth Wife of Henry VIII.* London: Rubicon Press, 1995.

Sanders, Marion K. *Dorothy Thompson: A Legend in Her Time.* Boston: Houghton Mifflin, 1973.

Sheean, Vincent. *Dorothy and Red.* Boston: Houghton Mifflin, 1963.

Wharton, Edith. *The Letters of Edith Wharton.* Edited by R. W. B. Lewis and Nancy Lewis. New York: Collier Books, 1988.

7. The "Dear John"

The American Heritage Dictionary of the English Language, 4th Edition. Boston: Houghton Mifflin, 2000.

Carroll, Andrew, ed. *War Letters: Extraordinary Correspondence from American Wars.* New York: Scribner, 2001.

Hemingway, Ernest. *The Complete Short Stories of Ernest Hemingway: The Finca Vigía Edition.* New York: Scribner, 1987.

Kurowsky, Agnes von. *Hemingway in Love and War: The Lost Diary of Agnes von Kurowsky, Her Letters, and Correspondence of Ernest Hemingway.* Edited by Henry Serrano Villard and James Nagel. Boston: Northeastern University Press, 1989.

Lighter, J. E., ed. *Random House Historical Dictionary of American Slang.* New York: Random House, 1994.

Litoff, Judy Barrett, and David C. Smith, eds. *Since You Went Away: World War II Letters from American Women on the Home Front.* New York: Oxford University Press, 1991.

Mellow, James R. *Hemingway: A Life without Consequences.* Boston: Houghton Mifflin, 1992.

Meyers, Jeffrey. *Hemingway: a Biography.* New York: Harper & Row, 1985.

Reeder, G. A. *Letter-Writing in Wartime: "How and What to Write About."* New York: Books, Inc., 1943.

Salter, James. "Dear John and Other Epistles." In *Civilization,* December 1998/ January 1999.

Seaman, Barbara. *Lovely Me: The Life of Jacqueline Susann.* New York: Seven Stories Press, 1996.

Sledge, E. B. *With the Old Breed, at Peleliu and Okinawa.* Novato, Calif.: Presidio Press, 1981.

8. The Marriage Refusal

Bassnett, Susan. *Elizabeth I: A Feminist Perspective.* New York: St. Martin's, 1988.

Bell, Quentin. *Virginia Woolf: A Biography.* London: Hogarth Press, 1972.

Brimacombe, Peter. *All the Queen's Men: The World of Elizabeth I.* Stroud, Gloucestershire, U.K.: Sutton, 2000.

Brontë, Charlotte. *The Letters of Charlotte Brontë: With a Selection of Letters by Family and Friends, Volume One.* Edited by Margaret Smith. Oxford: Oxford University Press, 1995.

Burney, Fanny. *The Early Journals and Letters of Fanny Burney.* Edited by Lars. E. Troide. Oxford: Clarendon Press, 1988.

Bibliography

Campbell, Ian. "Jane Baille Welsh." In *Dictionary of Literary Biography, Volume 55: Victorian Prose Writers Before 1867*. Edited by William B. Thesing. Detroit, Mich.: Gale Research, 1987.

Cecil, David, Lord. *A Portrait of Charles Lamb*. London: Constable, 1983.

Chisholm, Kate. *Fanny Burney: Her Life, 1752-1840*. London: Chatto & Windus, 1998.

Conover, Anne, and Mollie Bidwell. *Love Letters Written by Anna Conover and Mollie Bidwell to José Maria Eça de Queiroz*. Edited by A. Campos Matos. Lisbon, Portugal: Assírio & Alvim, 1998.

Courtney, Winifred F. *Young Charles Lamb, 1775-1802*. London: MacMillan, 1982

Crawford, Anne. *The Letters of the Queens of England, 1100-1547*. Dover, N.H.: A. Sutton, 1994.

Doody, Margaret Anne. "Fanny Burney." In *Dictionary of Literary Biography, Volume 39: British Novelists, 1660-1800*. Edited by Martin C. Battestin. Detroit, Mich.: Gale Research, 1985.

Dunn, Jane. *A Very Close Conspiracy: Vanessa Bell and Virginia Woolf*. London: J. Cape, 1990.

Ellis, Henry, ed. *Original letters, illustrative of English history; including numerous royal letters*. London: Harding, Triphook & Lepard,. 1824.

Gaskell, Elizabeth Cleghorn. *The Life of Charlotte Brontë*. London: Folio Society, 1971.

Haigh, Christopher. *Elizabeth I*. New York: Longman, 1998.

Harman, Claire. *Fanny Burney: A Biography*. London: HarperCollins, 2000.

Hume, Martin Andrew Sharp. *The Courtships of Queen Elizabeth: A History of the Various Negotiations for Her Marriage*. London: E. Nash & Grayson, 1926.

Kilpatrick, Sarah. *Fanny Burney*. Newtown Abbot: David & Charles, 1980.

Montagu, Lady Mary Wortley. *Selected Letters: Lady Mary Wortley Montagu*. Edited and translated by Isobel Grundy. New York: Penguin, 1997.

Reid, Panthea. *Art and Affection: A Life of Virginia Woolf*. New York: Oxford University Press, 1996.

Simons, Judy. *Fanny Burney*. Houndmills, Basingstoke, Hampshire, U.K.: Macmillan, 1987.

Somerset, Anne. *Elizabeth I*. London: Weidenfeld & Nicolson, 1991.

Spater, George, and Ian Parsons. *A Marriage of True Minds: An Intimate Portrait of Leonard and Virginia Woolf.* London: J. Cape, 1977.

Stone, Lucy, and Henry B. Blackwell. *Loving Warriors: Selected Letters of Lucy Stone and Henry B. Blackwell, 1853 to 1893.* Edited and introduced by Leslie Wheeler. New York: Dial Press, 1981.

Weir, Alison. *Elizabeth the Queen.* London: J. Cape, 1998.

Williams, Neville. *The Life and Times of Elizabeth I.* London: Weidenfeld &Nicolson, 1972.

Woolf, Virginia. *The Letters of Virginia Woolf.* Edited by Nigel Nicolson and Joanne Trautmann. New York: Harcourt Brace Jovanovich, 1975.

9. The Classic

Abelard, Peter. *The Letters of Abelard and Heloise.* Edited and translated by Betty Radice. New York; London: Penguin, 1974.

Anonymous. *The Female Critick; or, Letters in Drollery from Ladies to Their Humble Servants.* New York: Garland Pub., 1972.

Anonymous. *The Letters of an Italian Nun and an English Gentleman.* Translated from the French of J. J. Rousseau. Philadelphia: James Carey, 1796.

Beasley, Jerry C. "Aphra Behn." In *Dictionary of Literary Biography, Volume 39: British Novelists, 1660-1800.* Edited by Martin C. Battestin. Detroit, Mich.: Gale research, 1985.

Crébillon, Claude-Prosper Jolyot de. *Letters from the Marchioness de M*** to the Count de R***.* [Translated from the original French by Mr. Humphreys]. With a new introduction for the Garland edition by Josephine Grieder. New York: Garland Pub., 1972.

Crenne, Hélisenne de. *A Renaissance Woman: Helisenne's Personal and Invective Letters.* Edited and translated by Marianna M. Mustacchi and Paul J. Archambault. Syracuse, N.Y.: Syracuse University Press, 1986.

Day, Robert Adams. *Told in Letters: Epistolary Fiction before Richardson.* Ann Arbor: University of Michigan Press, 1966.

Doody, Margaret Anne. "Samuel Richardson." In *Dictionary of Literary Biography, Volume 39: British Novelists, 1660-1800.* Edited by Martin C. Battestin. Detroit, Mich.: Gale Research, 1985.

Eaves, T. C. Duncan, and Ben D. Kimpel. *Samuel Richardson: A Biography.* Oxford: Clarendon Press, 1971.

Bibliography

Ericson, Donald E. *Abelard and Heloise: Their Lives, Their Love, Their Letters.* New York: Bennett-Edwards, 1990.

Graffigny, Françoise de. *Letters from a Peruvian Woman.* Translated by David Kornacker. New York: Modern Language Association of America, 1993.

Guilleragues, Gabriel de Lavergne, Vicomte de. *The Love Letters of a Portuguese Nun.* London: Harvill Press, 1996.

Harris, Jocelyn. *Samuel Richardson.* New York: Cambridge University Press, 1987.

Haywood, Eliza. *Epistles for the Ladies: 1749-50.* London: H. Gardner, 1776.

——. *Selected Fiction and Drama of Eliza Haywood.* Edited by Paula R. Backscheider. New York: Oxford University Press, 1999.

Laclos, Choderlos de. *Les Liaisons Dangereuses.* New York: Knopf Everyman's Library, 1992.

Montesquieu, Charles de Secondat, Baron de. *Persian Letters.* Translated with an introduction and notes by C. J. Betts. New York: Penguin Books, 1973.

Ovid. *Heroides.* Edited and translated by Harold Isbell. New York: Penguin Classics, 1990.

Richardson, Samuel. *Clarissa, or, The History of a Young lady . . .* Edited with an introduction and notes by Angus Ross. London: Folio Society, 1991.

——. *The Novels of Samuel Richardson, Volumes 1-2.* New York: AMS Press, 1970.

Rousseau, Jean-Jacques. *The Collected Writings of Rousseau.* Edited by Roger D. Masters and Christopher Kelly. Hanover, N.H.: University Press of New England, 1990.

Saxton, Kirsten T., and Rebecca P. Bocchicchio. *The Passionate Fictions of Eliza Haywood: Essays on Her Life and Work.* Lexington: University Press of Kentucky, 2000.

Sturzer, Felicia, and Ruth P. Thomas. "Marie-Jeanne Riccoboni: Lettres de Mistriss Fanni Butlerd (1757), The Bee (1761)." In *Writings by Pre-Revolutionary French Women,* edited by Anne R. Larsen and Colette H. Winn. New York: Garland Pub., 2000.

Thelander, Dorothy R. *Laclos and the Epistolary Novel.* Geneva, Switzerland: Librarie Droz, 1963.

Trotter, Catharine. *Olinda's Adventures; or, The Amours of a Young Lady* (1718). Introduction by Robert Adams Day. Los Angeles: Augustan Reprint Society, 1969.

Whicher, George Frisbie. *The Life and Romances of Mrs. Eliza Haywood, by George Frisbie Whicher.* New York: Columbia University Press, 1915.

Wood, Diane S. *Hélisenne de Crenne: At the Crossroads of Renaissance Humanism and Feminism*. Madison, N.J.: Fairleigh Dickinson University Press, 2000.

10. The Prescriptive Letter

The American Lady's and Gentleman's Modern Letter-Writer: Relative to Business, Duty, Love and Marriage. Philadelphia: Henry F. Anners, 1847.

Beeton's Complete Letter-Writer for Ladies and Gentlemen: A Useful Compendium of Epistolary Materials Gathered from the Best Sources, and Adapted to Suit an Indefinite Number of Cases, New and Revised Edition. London: Ward, Lock & Co., Ltd., 1873.

Dankoff, Erica M., and Muara C. Johnston. *Kiss-Off Letters to Men: Over 70 Zingers You Can Use to Send Him Packing, Mess with His Head, or Just Plain Dump Him*. New York: Three Rivers Press, 2001.

Ingram, Isabelle, *Love Letters: Containing the Etiquette of Introductions, Courtship and Proposals*. Philadelphia: Penn Pub. Co., 1925.

Jacobs, Frank. "Applying the Break Department: Mad's All Inclusive Do-It-Yourself 'Dear John Letter.'" *Mad Magazine*. October 1979. New York: E. C. Pub.

The Lovers' Letter-Writer. N.p., n.d.

The New Universal Letter-Writer, or, Complete Art of Polite Correspondence: Containing a Course of Interesting Letters on the Most Important,Instructive, and Entertaining Subjects; to Which Are Prefixed, an Essay on Letter-Writing, and a Set of Complimental Cards, Suited to Occasions on Which an Extraordinary Degree of Politeness Should Be Observed. Philadelphia: Hogan & Thompson, 1834.

Post, Emily. *Etiquette: The Blue Book of Social Usage*. New York: Funk & Wagnalls, 1955.

The Practical Letter-Writer, Showing Plainly How to Write and Direct a Letter, So That Persons Who Can Write a Letter Well Can Learn to Do So Better, and Those Who Never Wrote May Now Learn to Write Well and Easily. New York: Hurst & Co., [19—]

Richardson, Samuel. *Familiar Letters on Important Occasions*. London: Routledge, 1928.

Vanderbilt, Amy. *New Complete Book of Etiquette: The Guide to Gracious Living*. Garden City, N.Y.: Doubleday, 1963.

Wamek, Uncle. *The Love Letter Writer*. Tema, Ghana: Otighe Book Agency, [19--].

Bibliography

11. The Fictional Letter

Who Was Who in Literature, 1906-1934. Detroit, Mich.: Gale Research, 1979.

Acker, Kathy. *Blood and Guts in High School, Plus Two.* London: Pan Books, 1987

Ang, Li. *The Butcher's Wife and Other Stories.* Edited and translated by Howard Goldblatt. Boston: Cheng & Tsui Co., 1995.

Austen, Jane. *Sense and Sensibility.* Edited and with and introduction by Claire Lamont. London: Oxford University Press, 1970.

Barreno, Maria Isabel, Maria Teresa Horta, and Maria Velho da Costa. *New Portuguese Letters.* Translated with a preface by Helen R. Lane. Columbia, La.: Readers International, 1994.

Colette. *My Mother's House, and The Vagabond.* Garden City, N.Y.: Doubleday, 1955.

Contemporary Authors, "Nabokov." Detroit, Mich.: Gale Research, 1963, 1969.

Davies, Margaret. "Colette." In *Dictionary of Literary Biography, Volume 65: French Novelists, 1900-1930.* Edited by Catharine Savage Brosman. Detroit, Mich.: Gale Rsearch, 1988.

Gisolfi, Anthony M. *The Essential Matilde Serao.* New York: Las Americas Pub. Co., 1968.

Hailey, Elizabeth Forsythe. *A Woman of Independent Means.* New York: Viking, 1978.

Hemingway, Ernest. *The Complete Short Stories of Ernest Hemingway: The Finca Vigía Edition.* New York: Scribner, 1987.

Kierkegaard, Søren. *Either/Or.* Edited and translated by Howard V. Hong and Edna H. Hong. Princeton, N.J.: Princeton University Press, 1987.

——. *The Essential Kierkegaard.* Edited by Howard V. Hong and Edna H. Hong. Princeton, N.J.: Princeton University Press, 2000.

Lassner, Phyllis. "Karin Michaelis." In the *Dictionary of Literary Biography, Volume 214: Twentieth-Century Danish Writers.* Edited by Marianne Stecher-Hansen. Detroit, Mich.: Gale Research, 1999.

Michaëlis, Karin. *The Dangerous Age: Letters and Fragments from a Woman's Diary.* Translated from the Danish. New York: Macaulay, 1913.

Moody, Ellen. "Partly Told in Letters: Trollope's Story-telling Art, 1999." *Trollopiana: A Journal of the Trollope Society,* February 2000.

Nabokov, Vladimir. *Mary: A Novel.* Translated by Michael Glenny. New York: Vintage, 1989.

Hagopian, John V. "Vladimir (Vladimirovich) Nabokov." In *Dictionary of Literary Biography, Volume 2: American Novelists Since World War II.* Edited by Jeffrey Helterman, and Richard Layman. Detroit, Mich.: Gale Research, 1978.

Payson, William Farquhar. *Love Letters of a Divorced Couple.* Garden City, N.Y.: Doubleday, Page & Company, 1915.

Serao, Matilde. "Falso in scrittura." In *Fior de Passione: nouvelle.* Firenze, Italy: Adriano Salani, 1913.

Smith, Paul. *A Reader's Guide to the Short Stories of Ernest Hemingway.* Boston: G. K. Hall, 1989.

Staël, Madame de. *Corinne, or, Italy.* Edited and translated by Sylvia Raphael. New York: Oxford University Press, 1998.

Trollope, Anthony. *The Way We Live Now.* New York: Knopf, 1950.

Voorhies, Frank C. *Love Letters of an Irishwoman.* Boston: Mutual Book Company, 1901.

Wharton, Edith. *Summer: A Novel.* New York: D. Appleton and Co., 1917.

12. The Unsent Letter

Keegan, Susanne. *The Bride of the Wind: The Life and Times of Alma Mahler-Werfel.* London: Secker & Warburg, 1991.

Kraus, Chris. *I Love Dick.* New York: Semiotext(e), 1997.

Szold, Henrietta. *Lost Love: The Untold Story of Henrietta Szold: Unpublished Diary and Letters.* Edited by Baila Round Shargel. Philadelphia: Jewish Publication Society, 1997.

Werfel, Alma Mahler. *Diaries, 1898-1902, Alma Mahler-Werfel.* Edited and translated by Antony Beaumont and Susanne Rode-Breymann. Ithaca, N.Y.: Cornell University Press, 1999.

13. The Goodbye Letter

Barry, Joseph. *Infamous Woman: The Life of George Sand.* Garden City, N.Y.: Doubleday, 1976.

Becker, Paula Modersohn. *Paula Modersohn-Becker, the Letters and Journals.* Edited and translated by Arthur S. Wensinger and Carole Clew Hoey. Evanston, Ill.: Northwestern University Press, 1990.

Bibliography

Carrington, Dora de Houghton. *Carrington: Letters and Extracts from her Diaries* Chosen and with an introduction by David Garnett, with a biographical note by Noel Carrington. London: J. Cape, 1970.

Cate, Curtis. *George Sand: A Biography.* Boston: Houghton Mifflin, 1975.

Duckworth, Alistair M. "Mary Wollstonecraft." In the *Dictionary of Literary Biography, Volume 39: British Novelists, 1660-1800.* Edited by Martin C. Battestin. Detroit, Mich.: Gale Research, 1985.

Fletcher, Loraine. *Charlotte Smith: A Critical Biography.* New York: St. Martin's Press, 1998.

Gerzina, Gretchen. *Carrington: A Life of Dora Carrington, 1893-1932.* London: J. Murray, 1989.

Gilman, Charlotte Perkins. *The Living of Charlotte Perkins Gilman, an Autobiography* by Charlotte Perkins Gilman. New York: D. Appleton-Century, 1935.

———. *The Diaries of Charlotte Perkins Gilman.* Edited by Denise D. Knight. Charlottesvile: University Press of Virginia, 1994.

Goodman, Dena. "Julie de Lespinasse: A Mirror for the Enlightenment." From *Eighteenth-Century Women and the Arts,* edited by Frederick M. Keener and Susan E. Lorsch. New York: Greenwood Press, 1988.

Hill, Mary Armfield. *Charlotte Perkins Gilman: The Making of a Radical Feminist, 1860-1896.* Philadelphia: Temple University Press, 1980.

Jack, Belinda Elizabeth. *George Sand: A Woman's Life Writ Large.* London: Chatto & Windus, 1999.

Jordan, Ruth. *George Sand: A Biography.* London: Constable, 1976.

Lespinasse, Julie de. *Letters of Mlle. de Lespinasse, with Notes on Her Life and Character by d'Alembert, Marmontel, de Guibert, etc. and an Introduction by C. A. Sainte-Beuve;* tr. by Katharine Prescott Wormeley. Boston: Hardy, Pratt & co., 1901.

Napier, Elizabeth R. "Charlotte Smith." In *Dictionary of Literary Biography, Volume 39: British Novelists, 1660-1800.* Edited by Martin C. Battestin. Detroit, Mich.: Gale Research, 1985.

Royde-Smith, Naomi. *The Double Heart: A Study of Julie de Lespinasse.* New York: Harper [1931].

Sand, George. *Correspondance [de] George Sand.* Edited by Georges Lubin. Paris: Garnier Freres, 1964.

Segur, Marquis de. *Julie de Lespinasse.* New York: E. P. Dutton & Co., 1927.

Smith, Charlotte. *The Collected Letters of Charlotte Smith.* Edited by Judith Stanton. Bloomington: Indiana University Press, 2002.

Stetson, Charles Walter. *Endure: The Diaries of Charles Walter Stetson.* Edited by Mary Armfield Hill. Philadelphia: Temple University Press, 1985.

Wollstonecraft, Mary. *Collected Letters of Mary Wollstonecraft.* Edited by Ralph M. Wardle. Ithaca, N.Y.: Cornell University Press, 1979.

———. *Letters to Imlay;* with a prefatory memoir, by C. Kegan Paul. London: C. Kegan Paul & Co., 1879.

Permissions
Acknowledgments

Excerpt from "A Love Letter Never Sent" was previously published in *The Butcher's Wife and Other Stories*, by Li Ang. Translation © copyright 1995 Howard Goldblatt. Used with permission of Cheng & Tsui Company, Inc.

Annette to Sylvan "Sol" Summers letter from *War Letters: Extraordinary Correspondence from American Wars*, edited by Andrew Carroll (Scribner, 2001). Used with permission of Andrew Carroll.

Sarah Austin to Prince Hermann von Puckler-Muskau letter from *Contemplating Adultery* by Lotte Hamburger and Joseph Hamburger, copyright © 1991 by Lotte Hamburger and Joseph Hamburger. Used by permission of Ballantine Books, a division of Random House Inc.

Excerpt from *Great Expectations* © copyright 1982 Kathy Acker. Used with permission of Matias Viegener, executor for the Estate of Kathy Acker.

Simone de Beauvoir to Nelson Algren letter © 1997 from *A Transatlantic Love Affair: Letters to Nelson Algren* (New Press, 1998). Reprinted by permission of The New Press and Sylvie Le Bon de Beauvoir.

Jennifer Belle to Richard letter © copyright 1994/2002 Jennifer Belle. Printed with permission of Jennifer Belle.

Sarah Bernhardt to Jean Mounet-Sully and Jean Richepin letters from *The Divine Sarah: A Life of Sarah Bernhardt* by Arthur Gold and Robert Fizdale, copyright © 1991 by Robert Fizdale. Used by permission of Alfred A. Knopf, a division of Random House, Inc.

Aline Bernstein to Thomas Wolfe letters from *My Other Loneliness: Letters of Thomas Wolfe and Aline Bernstein* edited by Suzanne Stutman, with a foreword by Richard S. Kennedy. Copyright © 1983 by the University of North Carolina Press. Used with permission of the publisher and Houghton Library, Harvard University (bMS Am1883.1 (60)).

Betsy to Ben letter © copyright 2001/2002 Betsy. Printed with permission of Betsy.

Mollie Bidwell to José Maria Eça de Queiroz letter from *Love Letters written by Anna Conover and Mollie Bidwell to José Maria Eça de Queiroz* copyright © 1998 Assírio & Alvim. Reprinted by permission of Assírio & Alvim.

Frances Boldereff to Charles Olson letter from *Charles Olson and Frances Boldereff: A Modern Correspondence* (University Press of New England, 1999), © copyright 1950 Frances Boldereff Phipps. Used with permission of the University of Connecticut Libraries and Lucinda Wilner.

Permissions Acknowledgments

Agnes Boulton to Eugene O'Neill letters from *A Wind is Rising: The Correspondence of Agnes Boulton and Eugene O'Neill* (Fairleigh Dickinson University Press, 2000). Reprinted with permission of Maura O'Neill Jones.

Stella Bowen to Ford Madox Ford letter from *The Correspondence of Ford Madox Ford and Stella Bowen,* edited by Sondra J. Stand and Karen Cochran (Indiana University Press, 1993). Reprinted by permission of Indiana University Press and David Higham Associates, London, executors of the Estate of Stella Bowen.

Charlotte Brontë to Henry Nussey letter © Margaret Smith 1995. Reprinted from *The Letters of Charlotte Brontë, With a Selection of Letters by Family and Friends, Volume I: 1829-1847,* edited by Margaret Smith (1995) by permission of Oxford University Press.

Fanny Burney to Thomas Barlow letter from *The Early Journals and Letters of Fanny Burney,* edited by Lars E. Troide (McGill-Queens University Press, 1991). Used with permission of McGill-Queens University Press.

Carol to Michael Hansen letter courtesy of Michael B. Hansen.

Dora Carrington to Gerald Brenan letter from *Carrington: Letters and Extracts from her Diaries* (Jonathan Cape, 1970); copyright as provided by Jonathan Cape. Reproduced by permission of the Estate of Dora Carrington c/o Rogers, Coleridge & White Ltd., 20 Powis Mews, London, W11 1JN.

Chandra to Ellis letter © copyright 2002 Chandra. Printed with permission of Chandra.

Kate Christensen to John letter © 1987/2002 Kate Christensen. Printed with permission of Kate Christensen.

Cindy Chupack to Rick letter © 2001/2002 Cindy Chupack. Printed with permission of Cindy Chupack.

Natasha Carrie Cohen to Peter letter © 2001/2002 Natasha Carrie Cohen. Printed with permission of Natasha Carrie Cohen.

Letter from *The Vagabond* by Colette, translated by Enid McLeod. Translation copyright © 1954, renewed 1982 by FSG, Inc. Reprinted by permission of Farrar, Straus and Giroux, LLC.

Violet Coward to Arthur Coward letter from *Remembered Laughter: The Life of Noël Coward,* by Cole Lesley, copyright © 1976 by Cole Lesley. Used by permission of Alfred A. Knopf, a division of Random House, Inc.

Clara Bewick Colby to Leonard Wright Colby letter from *Clara Bewick Colby Papers,* Wisconsin Historical Society.

Danielle to Adam letter © copyright 2001/2002, Danielle. Printed with permission of Danielle.

Letter from *Kiss-Off Letters to Men,* by Erica Dankoff and Muara Johnston, copyright © 1999, 2001 by Erica Dankoff and Muara Johnston. Used by permission of Three Rivers Press, a division of Random House, Inc.

Isadora Duncan to Paris Singer letter from *Donald Oenslager Collection of Edward Gordon Craig,* General Collection, Beinecke Rare Book and Manuscript Library, Yale University.

Kate Field to Albert Baldwin letter from *Kate Field: Selected Letters,* edited by Carolyn J. Moss, © 1996 by the Board of Trustees, Southern Illinois University. Reprinted by permission of Southern Illinois University.

Kathy Fitzgerald Sherman to M letter © copyright 2000/2002, Kathy Fitzgerald Sherman. Printed with permission of Kathy Fitzgerald Sherman.

Zelda Fitzgerald to F. Scott Fitzgerald letter reprinted with permission of Scribner, an imprint of Simon & Schuster Adult Publishing Group, from *Zelda Fitzgerald: The Collected Writings,* edited by Matthew J. Bruccoli. Copyright © 1991 by The Trustees under Agreement dated July 3, 1975, Created by Frances Scott Fitzgerald Smith.

Lola Fondue to Ira letter, © copyright 2001/2002, Lola Fondue. Printed with permission of Lola Fondue.

Beatrice Forbes-Robertson to Swinburne Hale letter from *Swinburne Hale Papers,* Manuscripts and Archives Division, The New York Public Library, Astor, Lenox and Tilden Foundation. Used with permission of The New York Public Library.

Lisa G. to Lee letter, © copyright 2001/2002, Lisa G. Printed with permission of Lisa G.

Jean Gelatt to Jack letter © copyright 2001/2002 Jean Gelatt. Printed with permission of Jean Gelatt.

Charlotte Perkins Gilman to Charles Stetson letter from *Endure: The Diaries of Charles Walter Stetson* (Temple University Press, 1985). Reprinted by permission of Mary Armfield Hill.

Excerpt from *Letters from a Peruvian Woman* by Francoise de Graffigny. Translation © copyright 1993 David Kornacker. Reprinted by permission of the Modern Language Association of America.

Ellen Coile Graves to Henry Graves letter from *Chester County Archives and Records Services,* West Chester, PA. Used with permission of Chester County Archives and Records Services.

Excerpt from *The Love Letters of a Portuguese Nun* by Gabriel de Lavernge, Vicomte de Guillerages, published by Harvill Press. Reprinted by permission of The Random House Group Ltd.

"Letter: August 25, 1920", from *A Woman of Independent Means by Elizabeth Forsythe Hailey,* copyright © 1978 by Elizabeth Forsythe Hailey. Used by permission of Viking Penguin, a division of Penguin Putnam.

Lynn Harris to Daniel letter © copyright 2001/2002, Lynn Harris. Printed with permission of Lynn Harris.

Elizabeth Hayt to Anthony Joseph Costagliola letter © copyright 2001/2002 Elizabeth Hayt. Printed with permission of Elizabeth Hayt.

Helisenne's Third Invective Letter, from *A Renaissance Woman: Helisenne's Personal and Invective Letters* (Syracuse University Press, 1986). Translation © copyright Marianna M. Mustacchi and Paul J. Archambault, 1986. Reprinted by permission of Marianna Archambault, Paul Archambault and Syracuse University Press.

Heloise to Abelard Letter from *The Letters of Abelard and Heloise.* Translated by Betty

Permissions Acknowledgments

Jean-Jacques Rousseau, Letter XX, pp.304-310 from Julie from Julie or the New Heloise: Letters of Two Lovers Who Live in a Small Town at the Foot of the Alps from *The Collected Writings of Rousseau*, Vol. 5 © 1997 by the Trustees of Dartmouth College, reprinted by permission of University Press of New England.

George Sand to Michel de Bourges letter from *Correspondance [de] George Sand (Garnier Freres*, 1964). Translation © Copyright 2002, Sharon Bowman.

Dorothy L. Sayers to John Cournos letters from *The Letters of Dorothy L. Sayers, 1899 to 1936*, edited by Barbara Reynolds. Reprinted by permission of David Higham Associates, London, executors of the Estate of Dorothy L. Sayers.

Excerpt from Matilde Serao's "A Lie in Writing" from *Fior de Passione: Nouvelle* (Adriano Salani, 1913). Translation © copyright 2002 Anita Angelone.

Anne Sexton to Torgie letter and Anne Sexton to Philip Legler letter from *Anne Sexton: A Self-Portrait in Letters*, edited by Linda Gray Sexton and Lois Ames (Houghton Mifflin, 1977). Reprinted by permission of Sterling Lord Literistic, Inc. © Copyright 1977 by Anne Sexton.

Rosemarie Keller Skaine to letter © copyright Rosemarie Keller Skaine, 1954/2002. Printed with permission of Rosemarie Keller Skaine.

Charlotte Smith to Benjamin Smith letter from *The Collected Letters of Charlotte Smith*, edited by Judith Stanton (Indiana University Press, 2002). Used with permission of Lord Egremont, owner of the Petworth House Archives.

Corinne to Lord Nevil letter, translations copyright © the executor of Sylvia Raphael, 1998. Reprinted from *Madame de Staël: Corinne, or Italy*, translated and edited by Sylvia Raphael (Oxford World's Classics, 1998) by permission of Oxford University Press.

Laurel Stalla to Josh letter © copyright 2001/2001, Laurel Stalla. Printed with permission of Laurel Stalla.

Freya Stark to Stewart Perowne letter from *Over the Rim of the World: Selected Letters*, edited by Caroline Moorehead (Murray in association with Michael Russell, 1988). Reprinted with permission from John Murray (Publishers) Ltd.

Jacqueline Susann to Irving Mansfield letter from *Lovely Me: The Life of Jacqueline Susann*, © copyright 1987, 1996 Barbara Rosner Seaman. Used by permission of Seven Stories Press.

Henrietta Szold to Louis Ginzberg letter from *Lost Love: The Untold Story of Henrietta Szold*, © copyright 1997, Jewish Publication Society. Reprinted by permission of Jewish Publication Society.

Tanya to Ryan letter, copyright © 2000/2002. Printed with permission of Tanya.

Catherine Texier to Joel Rose letter from *Breakup: The End of a Love Story*, by Catherine Texier, copyright © 1998 Catherine Texier. Used by permission of Doubleday, a division of Random House, Inc.

Dorothy Thompson to Josef Bard and Sinclair Lewis letters from *Dorothy Thompson Papers, Syracuse University Library Department of Special Collections*. Portions of the letter dated January 25, 1927 first appeared in Peter Kurth's *American Cassandra* (Little,

Brown, 1990); reprinted by permission of McIntosh and Otis. Letters dated December 29, 1926 and January 27, 1927 © Copyright 2002 by the Estate of Dorothy Thompson. Printed by permission of McIntosh and Otis. Letter dated 1938 reprinted by permission of McIntosh and Otis.

Nina Toomer to Nathan Toomer letter from *Jean Toomer Papers,* Beinecke Rare Book and Manuscript Library, Yale University. Printed with permission of Margot Toomer Latimer.

Trece to Quentin letter © copyright 1999/2002 Trece. Printed with permission of Trece.

Helene Verin to Luke letter © copyright 1997/2002, Helene Verin. Printed with permission of Helene Verin.

Virginia to Leonard M. Owczarzak letter courtesy of Leonard M. Owczarzak.

Kim W. to Tobey letter © copyright 2001/2002 Kim W. Printed with permission of Kim W.

Original Dump Kit letter from *The Original Dump Kit,* © 2001 Patti Watkins, www.dumpkit.com. Used with permission of Patti Watkins.

Elizabeth Waugh to Edmund Wilson letter from *The Princess with the Golden Hair: Letters of Elizabeth Waugh to Edmund Wilson, 1933-1942* (Fairleigh University Press, 2000). Reprinted by permission of Kristen Figg and John Friedman.

Letter to H. G. Wells from Rebecca West of March 1913 from *Selected Letters of Rebecca West* (Yale University Press, 2000), Copyright © Rebecca West 1913 and reproduced by permission of Peters, Fraser and Dunlop on behalf of the Estate of Rebecca West.

Edith Wharton to W. Morton Fullerton letters from *The Letters of Edith Wharton,* edited by R.W.B. Lewis and Nancy Lewis (Scribner, 1988). Reprinted with permission of Watkins/Loomis Agency, agents of the Estate of Edith Wharton.

Charity Royall to Lucius Harney letter from *Summer: A Novel,* by Edith Wharton (D. Appleton & Co., 1917). Reprinted with permission of Watkins/Loomis Agency, agents of the Estate of Edith Wharton.

Etta May White to George H. White letter courtesy of the *Sacramento Archives and Museum Collection Center,* Sacramento County Superior Court, Civil Cases.

Excerpts from *The Letters of Virginia Woolf, Volume I: 1888-1919:* copyright © 1975 by Quentin Bell and Angelica Garnett, reprinted by permission of Harcourt, Inc.

Elisa Zuritsky to Zach letter © 2001/2002 Elisa Zuritsky. Printed with permission of Elisa Zuritsky.

The editor has taken all possible care to trace the ownership of letters under copyright and to acknowledge their use. If there are any errors, please contact the publisher so that they can be corrected in future editions.

Index

Index

Index

Index

suicide, 7, 90, 94, 122, 199, 211,
    246, 347, 348, 354
Summer (Wharton, 1917), 303
Summers, Sylvan (Sol) (1945), 174-75
Susann, Jacqueline (1943), 171-72
Susie Q. (1970), 177-82
Szold, Henrietta (1905), 319-22

Tanya (2000), 20-26
tape/radio broadcast, Vietnam War
    ("Dear John" letter), 177-82
Tatischev, Sergei (1896), 196-97
tell-off letters, 1-28, xxiii-xxiv
Temple, Sir William (Archbishop of
    Canterbury) (1653), 77-80
Texier, Catherine (1997), 126-36
thank you, 16-17, 27-28, 330, 338-42
themes
    abortion, 13, 20-26, 54-57
    desertion. *See* divorce letters
    divorce, 58, 88, 95, 107, 109,
        110-13, 115-16, 120-21.
        See also divorce letters
    drugs, 18, 95-97, 310, 331, 335,
        339, 341, 342, 343, 347, 359,
        xxii
    eunuchs, 212, 245-47
    forgiveness, 31, 38, 333, 357-58,
        xxi
    friendship
        See also "Dear John" letters
        1600-1800, 5, 6, 32, 34-35,
            78-80
        1800's, 38-40, 52, 81, 106-
            107, 191-92, 192-93,
            194-95, 290
        1900's, 11, 43-44, 45-46,
            83-84, 88, 89, 93-94,
            108, 114-15, 118-19,
            198, 275
        2000's, 27, 100, 358

homosexuality, 32-33, 88-89,
    137, 338-42
indifference, male, 4, 32-33, 98,
    227, 272. *See also* silent treat-
    ment letters
Internet, 17, 18, 20-21, 26-27,
    65, 318, 328, 331-32
married man
    1700-1900, 3, 105, 106, 287-89
    1900's, 7, 10-11, 14, 48, 82,
        107, 109, 122, 125, 198, 313
    2000's, 137-38, 334-36
married woman
    1600-1900, 5, 31, 36, 37, 40,
        294-95
    1900's, 45, 84, 94, 95, 107,
        125, 137, 299, 353
mental states, 351
    1900's, 7-8, 15, 57-59, 60,
        90, 95-97, 117, 301, 310,
        320, 352
    2000's, 18-19, 64, 161-63,
        341, 357
other man, 289, 303, 353.
    See also Dear John letters; other
    woman/other man letters
other woman. *See also* married
    man; other woman/other man
    letters
    1600-1900, 5, 37, 143, 262-
        63, 287-89, 318, 355
    1900's, 10, 43, 82-83, 113-
        16, 151, 273, 295-97,
        303, 310, 320-22, 327-28
    2000's, 26-27, 98-99, 99-100,
        331, 333-34
pleading, 4, 6, 41, 48
refusal to work, 9-10
sin, 211-20, 294-95, 321
submission, 4, 6, 32, 35, 38-39,
    41, 320

Index

© Hobermann Studio

About the Author

ANNA HOLMES is a writer and journalist whose work has appeared in such publications as *Glamour, O: The Oprah Magazine, The New York Times, Entertainment Weekly, Sports Illustrated, Harper's, People,* and Salon.com. Holmes has written on topics ranging from women's issues, relationships, and style to sports, politics, and pop culture. She has appeared on *The Today Show, CBS This Morning,* MTV, and National Public Radio. Anna is currently working on adapting material from *Hell Hath No Fury* into a theater performance. She lives in New York City.